BEARS ON BEARS

BEARS ON BEARS

Interviews and Discussions

BY RON JACKSON SURESHA

alyson books
los angeles | new york

MANUFACTURED IN THE UNITED STATES OF AMERICA.

THIS TRADE PAPERBACK ORIGINAL IS PUBLISHED BY ALYSON PUBLICATIONS,
P.O. BOX 4371, LOS ANGELES, CALIFORNIA 90078-4371.
DISTRIBUTION IN THE UNITED KINGDOM BY TURNAROUND PUBLISHER SERVICES LTD.,
UNIT 3, OLYMPIA TRADING ESTATE, COBURG ROAD, WOOD GREEN,
LONDON N22 6TZ ENGLAND.

FIRST EDITION: FEBRUARY 2002

02 03 04 05 06 **a** 10 9 8 7 6 5 4 3 2

ISBN 1-55583-578-3

LIBRARY OF CONGRESS CATALOGING-IN-PUBLICATION DATA
  SURESHA, RON JACKSON.
    BEARS ON BEARS : INTERVIEWS AND DISCUSSIONS / RON JACKSON SURESHA. — 1ST ED.
    INCLUDES BIBLIOGRAPHICAL REFERENCES.
      ISBN 1-55583-578-3
      1. GAYS—IDENTITY. 2. GAY MEN—PSYCHOLOGY. 3. BODY IMAGE IN MEN. 4. GENDER
  IDENTITY. 5. GROUP IDENTITY. 6. MASCULINITY. I. TITLE.
  HQ76.25.S87 2002
  305.38'9664—DC21   2001053411

CREDITS
•"AN INTERVIEW WITH JACK FRITSCHER" © 2000 BY WWW.JACKFRITSCHER.COM.
•COVER DESIGN BY MATT SAMS.
•COVER PHOTOGRAPHY BY PHOTODISC.

Contents

Acknowledgments **xi**
Introduction **xv**

PART ONE: BEAR PHILOSOPHY AND IDENTITY

1   BEARS AS SUBCULTURAL SUBVERSIVES
     An Interview With Eric Rofes **3**
2   BIG B BEARS AND LITTLE B BEARS
     *A Discussion With Wayne Hoffman, Chris Wittke, and
     Rex Wockner* **18**
3   YOU CAN LEAD A BEAR TO CULTURE BUT...
     *A Discussion With David Bergman and
     Michael Bronski* **30**
4   BEAR ESSENTIALS: BEAR SPIRIT IN COMMUNITY
     *A Discussion With Al Cotton, Alex Damman, and Jim
     Mitulski* **50**

PART TWO: BEAR HISTORY AND EVOLUTION

5   THE BIRTH OF GIRTH & MIRTH
     An Interview With Reed Wilgoren **63**
6   BEARNESS'S BIG BLANK: TRACING THE GENOME OF
     URSOMASCULINITY
     An Interview With Jack Fritscher **77**
7   THE RAINBOW MC AND THE OLD LONE STAR
     A Discussion With Pete Vafiades **97**
8   FROM CULT TO SUBCULTURE TO COUTURE: EVOLVING BEAR
     COMMUNITY
     A Discussion With Les Wright **114**

PART THREE: BEAR ICONS AND CELEB-BEAR-TIES

9   WHAT MAKES A BEAR PORN LEGEND?
     An Interview With Jack Radcliffe **125**
10   LET THE LAUGHING BEAR LEAD
     An Interview With Rick Trombly **137**
11   SURVIVING AS A FAT NAKED FAG
     An Interview With Rich Hatch **143**

12   PORTRAIT OF THE CARTOONIST AS A MIDDLE-AGED BEAR
     An Interview With Tim Barela **153**
13   HOPING FOR SOMETHING BIGGER
     An Interview With Bruce Vilanch **163**

PART FOUR: BEAR SEX AND STYLES
14   WEIGHT AND FAT AS MASCULINE DRAG
     A Discussion With Dr. Lawrence Mass **175**
15   BEAR BEAUTY AND THE AFFIRMATION OF BEAR CONTESTS
     *A Discussion With Craig Byrnes, Gene Landry, and
     Michael Patterson* **189**
16   BEAROTICA AND THE SELLING OF BEAR SEX
     A Discussion With Richard Labonté and Tim Martin **199**
17   CIRCUIT BEARS AND THE BEAR CIRCUS
     *A Discussion With Lou Dattilo, Frank Perricone, Adam
     Steg, and Danny Williams* **211**

PART FIVE: BEAR AGES AND STAGES
18   BEAR MATURITY, BEAR MASCULINITY
     *A Discussion With Arnie Kantrowitz and Mark
     Thompson* **223**
19   TOURISTS IN BEARLAND: NONBEARISH BEAR LOVERS
     A Discussion With Manny Lim and Kirk Read **242**
20   ETHNIC BEARS AND BEARS OF COLOR
     *A Discussion With David Gerard, Ali Lopez, and George
     Varas* **255**
21   FROM BOOMER BEARS TO GEN-X BEARS TO BEAR YOUTH
     *A Discussion With Terry Jamro, Brian Kearns, and
     Heath McKay* **270**

PART SIX: BEARS AND BEYOND
22   LESBEARS AND TRANSBEARS: DYKES AND FTMS AS BEARS
     *A Discussion With Sharon Jill Bear Bergman, Drew
     Campbell, Michael "Mike" Hernandez, and Matt Rice* **283**
23   TECHNOBEARS AND CYBEARSPACE
     *A Discussion With Steve Dyer, Jeff Glover, Mike Ramsey,
     and Alex Schell* **297**
24   A SPACE BEYOND BEARDOM: POSTBEARS AND EX-BEARS
     *A Discussion With Van Buckley, Steven Evans, and Tim
     Morrison* **306**

25   INTERNATIONAL BEAR BROTHERHOOD
A Discussion With Eduardo Chavez, Seumas Hyslop,
Xavier Navarro, Marcelo Perales, Glen Purdon, Mali
Sahin, Woody Shimko, and Justin Spooner **318**

CHRONOLOGY OF INTERVIEWS AND LISTING OF EXCERPTS **341**
GLOSSARY **345**
SELECTED BIBLIOGRAPHY, REFERENCES, AND RESOURCES **347**
ABOUT THE AUTHOR **351**

To Kitten, from Tiger;
to Bunky, from Spunk;
and
in loving memory of my father, Jack,
from Jackson

ACKNOWLEDGMENTS

As this book attempts to describe a community from the inside out, this work owes its existence to a great many folks who gave so generously of their time, knowledge, and other resources.

I offer my deepest devotion and respect to my beloved late father, Jack, who made me proud to be a bookseller's son; to my beloved late mother, Naomi, who would've *kvelled* to see this book; and to my spiritual father, Baba Muktananda, who initiated me into the path of transcendent love shining within. My gratitude also goes to Claudia Day, who has been a loving combination of mom and friend.

Scott Brassart at Alyson believed in the project from its nascent promise and brought to its nurturance tremendous skill, creativity, tact, and genuine friendship. I also thank the rest of the Alyson staff, who ably assisted in bringing the book to fruition.

Mike Frisch, Michael Smith, and Martha Stone read early drafts of the book and offered insight, criticism, and support. David Keepnews also read portions of the book and answered countless substantial and trivial questions. To them, especially Martha, I offer spirited recognition.

Tim Martin first agreed to publish the interviews in *American Bear* and offered a sturdy soapbox on which these voices could project themselves. Les Wright, of Bear History Project, offered many helpful contacts and insights invaluable to this book.

I am greatly indebted also to writerly Bearish friends David Bergman, Michael Bronski, Jack Fritscher, Dan Jaffe, Larry Mass, Franco Mormando, Eric Rofes, and to the other participants in this collection, all of whom taught me a great many things about community. Paws held high in salute to Bear-pals Steve Evans, Brian Kaufman, John Maiscott, Pax McCarthy, Dee Michel, Paul Sproul, and Bill Wise for their support.

The following persons graciously spoke or corresponded with me in preparation for other published interviews: Alison Bechdel, Eric Orner, and Dave Brousseau (for Tim Barela); Pat Hoff, Aaron Aharonian, and Charlie Brown (for Reed Wilgoren); John Caldera (for Bear Contests); J.P. Kucera (for Gen-X Bears); Peter Millar (for Bearotica); Forrest from

BearPress, Neil Miller, and Howard Watson (for International Bears). In addition, Craig Anderson, Sharon Bergman, Jeff Glover, Andy Mangels, and Adam Steg helped locate contacts in far-flung places.

I also owe a wealth of appreciation to Mark Hemry of Palm Drive Publishing, for generously underwriting the cost of transcription of the interview with Jack Fritscher; shutterbear Lynn Ludwig, for his outstanding photographic contributions; Tony Nicosia, for his International Bear Rendezvous camaraderie and invaluable transcription services; Bucky Chappell, for his photography and, along with Jim Fauntleroy, several champagne technical interventions of the highest order; Steve Dyer and Eric Mulder, for additional cyber support beyond the call of duty; Jeff Shaumeyer, bearoticist and Web designer of www.bearsonbears.com; Meir Amiel, friend and legal advisor par excellence; beloved honorary Bears Joel Kleinman, Ann Robins, and Bob Publicover; Stephen Harrington, for his caring counsel; Prof. Barry Sanders, coauthor of *The Sacred Paw*, for his kind interest and support; Richard Schneider, Martha Stone, and the rest of *The Gay & Lesbian Review* ensemble; the dear and talented folks at my former employers, Shambhala Publications, who allowed me boxes of recycled paper for printing drafts and more importantly taught me well about trade bookmaking; the men (and others) of Bears Mailing List, New England Bears, Rhode Island Grizzlies, Motor City Bears, and Lavender Country & Folk Dancers; and friends Don Abare, Terry Galbraith, Kevin Kelly, Jim Kuzlotsky, Jim Palmer, Ted Ramsey, and Denis Reidy, for offering refuge and friendship at crucial moments.

I owe particular recognition to Prof. Warren Hecht of the University of Michigan's Residential College, my writing mentor during my tumultuous college years. Warren embodied the physical, emotional, and intellectual attributes I desired in such a mentor, and very much was a warm-hearted Bear, albeit a straight one. In my convoluted attempts to describe in writing my attraction to him, I was able to articulate to myself that my affectional preference was for Bears, although I hadn't quite hit upon that particular word.

Finally, I offer heartfelt thanks to my former lover, *Überbehr,* Chris Nelson, for his continued friendship and support. And to Michael Paul Smith, a Beary guy with a heart of gold, my bedrock during the entire process of this book: Thanks and thanks and thanks again always.

I kindly ask forgiveness of anyone in whose debt I remain yet unacknowledged.

A portion of the author's proceeds from sales of this book will be given to Brown Bear Resources, based in northwest Montana. Since 1989, BBR has worked proactively to give humans an understanding and a respect for grizzlies as an indicator of the health of other species, as well as the ecosystem in which we all live. BBR is a resource and research nonprofit corporation endorsed by federal, state, and tribal agencies. BBR uses a variety of educational and resource mediums, including educational trunks, "Be Bear Aware" presentations, a nonprofit gift store, a quarterly newsletter, Adopt-A-Grizzly program, and a Web site. Readers are encouraged to contribute further. More information is available at www.brownbear.org.

INTRODUCTION

I am not a bear.

I am *Homo sapiens,* of course—a thickly hairy-chested, usually full-bearded, increasingly middle-age-paunched, and balding gay man.

Does that make me a Bear, a capital B Bear, one who identifies with the gay male subculture that was birthed in mid 20th-century gay masculine culture, came of age in 1980s San Francisco, and is flourishing in its young adulthood worldwide as we turn the corner into the 21st century?

Good question.

We (meaning you, the reader, and the participants in this book, and I, too) will spend our time in this book dancing around that question.

Les Wright, author of *The Bear Book: Readings in the History and Evolution of a Gay Male Subculture,* commented to me in a 1999 personal note: "The discussion seems to have shifted from 'What is a Bear?' to 'Who is a Bear?'"

Bears on Bears attempts to answer the "Who is a Bear?" question by presenting candid interviews of and discussions with Bears in an accessible format. From a rich variety of perspectives and backgrounds, this book allows Bears, as well as some non-Bearish Bear lovers, to describe, in their own words, themselves, their lives and loves, their sense of masculinity, and their flourishing community-cum-culture.

One self-identified Bear, Seumas Hyslop from Sydney, says, in chapter 25, "To me, the notion of Bear is incredibly empowering. To others, they see the stars [Bear pinup icons] as an impossible standard, from which the next step is [to conclude] that they're not big enough, not hairy enough, and so on—at which point it becomes limiting."

Oddly, although most self-identified Bears seem aware of the limitations of Bear identity, few actually seem to want to truly expand the notion of what "Bear" could actually be. As David Bergman states in chapter 3, Bears could be "a force of resistance against the fashion industry, the style industry, and other types of classist ways of separating people."

In a June 1999 Suck.com column, writer Jonathan Van Decimeter smartly observed, "These days, the only real boundary- (and belt-buckle-) busting gay subculture is the riot grrrs of the Bear movement, whose chief distinction is their rough embrace of beer-bellied, hairy masculinity. Really, though, Bears are just part and parcel of the relentless supersizing of America."

Unfortunately, most Bearfolk seem content to lurk within the limitations of a gender-based sexual identity. Personally, if all that being gay and Bear signifies is what I call my body, that's an identity I can do without. Increasingly, though, Bear subculture seems less about any sort of political, spiritual, or even social aspect than about how I package my body—having the right masculine Bear look. A not uncommon complaint about Bear subculture in this book—coming from Bears and non-Bears alike—is that "it seems less about me as an individual and more about me as a big, furry-assed doppelgänger."

Bear culture tends to emphasize a homogenous masculine identity—the "Bear uniform" barely a step forward from "clones"—at the same time it expresses diversity in gay images. In this manner, I think that "Bear" exemplifies the American tendency toward monoculture: Bears = gays as straight-acting, or at least straight-appearing, men.

Bears have made exciting cultural inroads where other gay men have dared not set their paws. Consider that in a period of less than six months:

- Bearish gay corporate trainer Richard Hatch successfully won not only the reality-based TV game show *Survivor* but also highly lucrative product endorsements;
- Actor John Goodman portrayed a big gay man in the TV network sitcom *Normal, Ohio,* and later spoke about Bears with Bruce Vilanch in the December 19, 2000, issue of *The Advocate*; and
- Reuters news wire service broke the story of the Bears of Turkey controversy with the wrestling match at Kirkpinar and brought the idea of Bears to international gay and mainstream news.

This activity represents a level of acceptance and integration of the gay Bear body type and psyche into the fabric of straight culture.

As Judith Halberstam writes about another emerging contemporary (yet far more marginalized) queer masculinity in *The Drag King Book*, "Obviously the stakes are highest in all identity skirmishes when people feel that their lives and their proclamations about their lives are in danger of being trivialized by the claims others make about them." This statement reflects not only my own life but also the lives of thousands of Bear-identified men. Such trivializing messages received from both the mainstream and the gaystream (to use Jack Fritscher's term) have affected the way many Bears view their bodies and selves.

Yet there must be more to Bearness than rejection of the rejectors.

There have been moments in the process of preparing for and conducting these interviews and discussions when I have glimpsed something greater than the sum of the many limited parts of Bear life, as it were. My desire to root out the meaning buried underneath the shrubbery of the subculture is what compelled me to compile this collection of voices and views in the first place.

Come closer, my furry friends.

Now, don't tell anyone, but I suspect that our connection with Bears touches something inside us even deeper than sex. I think it speaks to our need to connect with the natural world, to the lost ancient myths, to the rhythms of the sacrificial hunt and the renewal of hibernation, to the protective nurturing of the Bear (Earth) Mother, and the heroic activity of the Bear-son warrior.

Somewhere amidst all the cybear chatting and Bear circuit event-hopping, we have forged a new primal community, one that affirms and celebrates our uncommodified selves.

For the most part, however, my Bear brothers have no idea how cutting-edge and beautiful they are. These men in the Bear tradition, are foregrounding a new generation of gay men whose mature, masculine sexuality is strongly held, despite the onslaught of AIDS in the gay community, and a lot of cultural fluff obscuring the face of the beast.

Right now Bearness seems to be about celebrating ourselves on the outside, but truly there's a profound shift taking place in the lives of these men that reflects, I believe, a paradigm shift in masculinity. Here's a population of men learning to feel handsome, wanted, attractive, erotic, and valued.

This is why Bears matter. This is what makes the Bear subculture vital to contemporary emergent masculinities. This is why it is worth identifying as a Bear, despite the ever-encroaching T-shirtization. Bears may be a subculture, but our lives are far from trivial, and we should resist all efforts from anyone who tries to invalidate our looks, our sexuality, our social identity, our affectional preferences.

But are Bears merely a subculture, a splinter group of homosexuals, a narrow slice of thin-filled pie? By conservative estimates, there may be half a million self-identified Bears around the world (this estimate from the combined Bear-themed magazine minimum circulation and worldwide Bear-club membership figures). That number may be arguable, but what's indisputable is that we're not a cult anymore.

It may be hard to imagine how this community can be both cutting-edge and mainstream, but Bear-men must be assumed able to live with ambiguity of sex, gender, and political identity. Bearness is perhaps not more ambiguous, however, than any other postmodern self-identity.

I hope this book lets each of its 57 contributors speak his (or her) mind about the topics at hand. I've tried to create panels and ask challenging questions that would elicit thoughtful responses, but often it has been enough to kick back and listen to others tell their stories. Where practicable, participants were offered the chance to review and revise their words. Although I've corrected factually inaccurate statements, several participants made comments I found disagreeable, even repugnant. I have allowed certain remarks to go unchallenged in the interest of offering here the greatest range of views about Bear masculinity and presenting interviewees' voices as they most likely would speak them to the reader's face.

One aspect of these conversations not easily translatable to the written page is the lighthearted playfulness of the contributors. For space considerations, much of the incidental laughter and joking that peppers these dialogues has been omitted. I hope to find a means (perhaps online) of presenting to interested readers some of the excellent material—comic and otherwise—excised from the final manuscript.

I've resisted the impulse to contribute analytical or conclusive summaries to each chapter for two reasons. The obvious reason is length constraints—what is printed in these pages is a fraction of the total amount of raw material that was generated. The more significant reason I've avoided in-depth analysis, however, is because I hope that readers will do that work themselves.

Rather than providing my own facile conclusions, I suggest that individuals and local Bearclubs start their own *Bears on Bears* reading groups, taking a chapter or two every week or so and discussing the issues at hand: What self-esteem issues do we have in common as Bears? Why are there so few Bears of color? What kind of masculinity do I mean when I say, "I am a Bear"? What exclusionary tendencies does our club have? What can Bears do to educate others about acceptance? Readers interested in further exploration and discussion can find out more at www.bearsonbears.com.

I wish to note here that *Bears on Bears* is, to my knowledge, the first interview book (gay-themed or otherwise) to be compiled primarily from online interactions. A handful of pieces were conducted via traditional methods such as face-to-face and telephone, but most were conducted using online chat technology. This innovative journalistic method seems uniquely appropriate for a subculture that has grown up alongside the Internet. Using various Internet chat services created access to people otherwise unavailable; indeed, conducting a discussion of Bears around the world, spanning 14 time zones, would otherwise have been unthinkable.

The disadvantages were relatively small, by comparison, but peculiar. The chat technology, still in its adolescence, constrained participants to type only a few lines at a time, yet allowed several people to write at once, often leading to confusing sequences of dialogue. Sometimes conversational nuance, inflection, and spontaneity suffered at the expense of having to use pat typewritten conventions, such as *G* (grin) and the ubiquitous emoticons (for which a glossary is provided).

As I began pawing around in Bears' lairs, the scope of this book expanded exponentially. Somehow a dozen pieces became twice as many, as one "must-do" topic after another was suggested, or suggested itself. I wish this work could include far more voices, data, photos, and resources. But this is an interview book—another jumping-off point in the lineage of Bear-themed books—based on Les Wright's work and hopefully serving as the basis of books and information systems yet to come.

Although there are a few theory-intensive sections in the book, I've tried to maintain a Bear-on-the-street tone throughout the work. I ask readers to remember to keep a light mental touch while reading— enjoy yourselves, enjoy the pictures of the contributors (OK, I'll say it first: "Woof!") and watch out for grisly Bear puns! The advantage of presenting so many voices here is that some of them will speak to all readers, scholars and lay Bears alike. I hope this book is a large enough stream from which all furry woodland creatures—Bears of every stripe, grizzlies, cubs, otters, wolves, foxes, and the rest—will be able to drink their fill.

Taken as a whole, the many voices assembled should provide a complete, composite photograph of who Bears are at the millennium. May you find this collection of voices gathered from in and around the edge of the subculture to be both entertaining and enlightening.

Ron Suresha
Boston/Detroit
January 2001

Eric "Bucky" Chappelle

PART ONE

BEAR PHILOSOPHY AND IDENTITY

CHAPTER 1
BEARS AS SUBCULTURAL SUBVERSIVES
~ AN INTERVIEW WITH ERIC ROFES ~

ERIC ROFES is an impassioned longtime activist and the author of nine books, including *Socrates, Plato, and Guys Like Me: Confessions of a Gay Schoolteacher* and *Reviving the Tribe: Regenerating Gay Men's Sexuality and Culture in the Ongoing Epidemic*. His most recent book is *Dry Bones Breathe: Gay Men Creating Post-AIDS Identities and Cultures*, which *The Nation* called "perhaps the most important book about gay communities and cultures of the past decade." He also contributed a seminal essay, "Thoughts on Middle-Class Eroticization of Workingmen's Bodies," to *The Bear Book*. Although Eric has called San Francisco home for the past decade, he travels widely. In August 1999, Eric began teaching as a professor of education at Humboldt State University in the Redwoods, 300 miles north of San Francisco.

In May 1999, while commuting between his home in San Francisco and his interim teaching job at Bowdoin College in Maine, Eric met with me in Boston to discuss Bear subculture. Eric's unique perspective as a self-identified Bear as well as a longtime gay community activist intrigued me. The insights into the multivaried cultural influences of the Bear subculture that he brought to this interview greatly broadened my own perspectives, and served as a groundspring for several lines of critical thinking crucial to the development of this book's topics.

RON: What was your introduction to Bears, Eric?

ERIC: I arrived in San Francisco in 1989, luckily for me, right at the same time the old Lone Star opened, which to me was one of the premier events of the Bear phenomenon. I also remember the earthquake that destroyed the old bar, the opening of the new one, the Bear groups starting to form all over the country, and the first issues of *Bear* magazine.

When I first walked into the Lone Star, it felt like everyone was looking at me. For the first time it wasn't just one single guy in the bar who's into guys like me. This was a place where people went to look for men who look like me. That experience was mind-blowing!

RON: How did that initial experience affect your sense of yourself sexually? Did it alter your self-image at all?

ERIC: I think that the early Lone Star affected different types of guys who look like or identify as Bears in different ways. There are the Bears who are attracted to other Bears, and then there are the Bears who aren't, who don't so narrowly fetishize that. It was a different kind of experience for some of my friends, who are Bear icons yet not attracted primarily to Bears, than for myself, who has always been a Bear primarily attracted to Bears. All of my lovers and a good 80 percent of my tricks have been the kind of guys who would go to the Lone Star or who look like they would be pictured in one of the Bear magazines.

RON: Was this mutual attraction among similar-bodied men what initially formed a sense of community?

ERIC: A sense of community, but not yet subculture, is how I would say it. We knew each other, we were friends, your ex-lovers became your friends, your ex-tricks became your ex-lovers' best friends—that whole complicated mix. That emerged long before the subculture emerged.

I call what developed then, and what we have now, a subculture because then we began to have bars, clubs, T-shirts, magazines, and conferences. That second emergence was an exciting kick to me because it felt like it wasn't just the 20 of us who had slept together for the last 10 years. I knew then that this hairy group of guys must be large enough to warrant producing a magazine, or to pack a bar. It was fun, as well as affirming and exciting, to realize that we had achieved a critical mass.

RON: It seems the initial affirmation by Bear spaces was followed rather quickly by commodification of Bears, such as magazines and other Bearaphernalia.

ERIC: I think there's always been commodification of Bears. I don't think we form identity and community in the contemporary world without commodification occurring. I'd call it commodification because I used to buy certain kinds of porn magazines and then draw the hair on men's bodies, which was certainly not a mass-market commodification, but it was my own commodification, my own creation of that. The success of '70s porn stars such as Paul Barresi and Bruno and...

RON: Richard Locke.

ERIC: Yes. The fact that these guys were niche-marketed was another kind of commodification happening then. My discomfort with commodification isn't with commodification itself; it's with the perceived seriousness of it all. It's a problem we have when we become unable to laugh at ourselves, or to understand that each of us is really quite different from other Bears, even if we do have some things in common. When a nationalism emerges, however—such as the Bear flag—that's something different that I'm not so comfortable with.

RON: What makes it different?

ERIC: The use of a flag, or other kinds of narrow symbols and signs, often brings with it pressure to be like everyone else within that same group. And if it were simply that we all had to be bearded or hairy guys, that would be one thing. But then come the debates on "What's a Bear/What's not a Bear?"—very narrow, picky arguments. Now, we can all have fun with these questions, but a lot of people take it seriously, and feelings get hurt, and it gets ugly.

RON: Would you associate that quality with Bearclubs?

ERIC: Certainly some Bearclubs are like that. I associate that quality with America, how America organizes society, and I think the Bear subculture just copies that. Some Bearclubs become very contentious, and in a little teeny state you end up having two or three Bearclubs, and then this Bearclub doesn't talk to that one. To me, that's not about Bears, that's simply about Americans' dangerous tendency to organize around cultures without specific values or politics at its forefront.

RON: Would you characterize the Bear subculture as apolitical?

ERIC: Most of Bear subculture, again like most of American culture, is very narrow, very apolitical. This is not a good time for people to overtly attempt political organizing. I hope it will be, soon, but it distresses me to watch gay subcultures change, over the last 15 years, from being highly politicized and highly aware politically to becoming very self-centered, individualized, and then depoliticized.

RON: Daniel Harris, in his book *The Rise and Fall of Gay Culture*, characterizes Bear subculture as "one of the most violent assaults that gay men have made to date against the overgroomed bodies of urban homosexuals." Is such a criticism valid? Is there really such a war under way?

ERIC: I think a lot of critics who look at Bears misread us because they see only the superficial. Harris may be having fun by making statements like these, but in so doing he also does considerable damage. Although Harris is really smart and talented, in his writing he puts forward only pieces of the analysis. It's superficial and doesn't consider the multiple sources that are contributing to something.

For example, in his so-called analysis of an erotic fiction piece from *Bear* magazine, Harris describes "[t]he contradiction implicit in the Bear aesthetic between the ghetthoized mindset and the urban homosexual in his bucolic fantasies, which hark back to the bygone era of the Hatfields and the McCoys..."

Now, I don't think there's a contradiction. Of course, you can read Bears as contradictory—or you can read us as complicated people who are hybrids, who are combining pieces of different things.

RON: That's a greater vision of who we are—not unlike Walt Whitman's saying, "I am large.... I contain multitudes."

ERIC: Harris then continues his discussion of this Daddy Bear story in terms of pedophilia. First of all, this kind of conflating of Bear fantasy life with pedophilia is extremely misguided and to me shows no understanding of what's going on with either Bears or pedophilia. I'm not particularly phobic around pedophilia but I think that's an example of him pushing together random aspects of Bear life that don't really belong pushed together. He makes statements like these because he knows it'll incite people and push some buttons. He knows it's kind of a hot thing to say.

RON: Pedophilia is definitely a hot topic these days. However, it seems far more sensible to characterize the Bear fetish, even among Gen-X Bears, as focused on older men, not children.

ERIC: Harris also talks about the "Bear look" as "unnatural," as if we created this consciously. First of all, is any look "natural"? What exactly is a "natural look"? Is there any human being in America today—particularly anyone younger than 30 who's grown up with MTV—who doesn't create images that could be called "unnatural"? My guess is that probably ever since mirrors were invented, people have been conscious of their own self-images, and have altered them in some way.

RON: Harris largely confines himself to criticism of what is evident in a couple of *Bear* and *American Bear* magazines without any seeming personal contact with a single self-identified Bear.

ERIC: The truth is that his understanding of Bears—as well as the other subcultures he snipes at—is severely limited.

RON: It's similar to the more positive but also empirical characterization of Bears made by [*Sexual Personae* author] Camille Paglia on Salon.com, which I'd like to quote here:

"In their defiant hirsutism, gay Bears are more virile than the generic bubble-butt junior stud, since body hair is stimulated by testosterone. But the Bears' fatness resembles not the warlike Viking mass of a Hell's Angel but the capacious bosom of the primal earth mother. The gay Bear is simultaneously animalistic and nurturing, a romp in the wild followed by nap time on a comfy cushion."

ERIC: I think Paglia is on to something. Bears defy traditional gender norms even as they affirm aspects of traditional masculinities. We are nurturing and macho at the same time. This is what I find to be the radical potential of the Bear movement.

RON: She continues: "The Greek-style pretty ephebe is a cold visual icon, tauntingly remote and ultimately ungraspable. The Bear, however, offers warm, soothing regression to what Freud calls the polymorphous perverse, the whole-body tactility of early childhood. My working theory is that the gay Bear as a sexual persona is a mythic father-mother, a parental fusion like the androgynous Egyptian river god Hapi or the Roman Father Tiber, bearded and jovially recumbent amid his swarm of rollicking cherubs."

ERIC: The historical use of the Bear image suggests that Paglia has the right general idea here, but I caution against a simplistic and singular reading of "Bear."

This is the risk of cultural studies work, when people read texts and magazines and stories and then judge communities based on those stories. They don't have data on real people and real bodies and what's really going on among gay men. Instead they just read the texts. To me it's like Jerry Falwell reading our magazines and making assumptions about us and putting that forward. It's not effective.

RON: Some critics of Bear culture, such as Harris, regard the genesis of the Bear phenomenon largely as a reaction to AIDS.

ERIC: Again in this case Harris demonstrates a total lack of understanding for nuance and complexity and consistently defaults to really simpleminded and smug conclusions. One reason I don't like the critiques of Bear subculture by Daniel Harris, and other writers trying to be trendy, is that they attribute it too narrowly to too few sources. They see it only as a response to AIDS and the wasting away of bodies, for example. Subcultures are multifaceted realities. Lots of things feed into them, and I'd like to point out here a few sources that I think have gone unnoticed.

First of all, Bear culture emerged from the same phenomenon that gave us the Log Cabin Republicans. In the '70s there was a very small community of people who identified as gay men, but slowly through the '80s and certainly by the '90s, the community had gotten exponentially bigger. As communities in America get bigger and bigger, they splinter and segment. And one result of that splintering is gay Republicans. And gay anti-abortionists and gay stamp collectors and Bears. So the development of this subculture was part, I think, of a broader fragmenting of the gay community once it reached a certain critical mass.

Bears had to happen because gender is a critical issue for gay men— as more men flooded into gay venues, more kinds of masculinities needed to become available and gayified, if you will.

RON: That's a fascinating idea—that a gay masculine special-interest group like Bears *had* to happen. What else do you attribute Bear culture to?

ERIC: Bear culture also draws from some interesting dynamics occurring in heterosexual masculinities like the macho wrestler culture— namely, the Hulk Hogan/WWF [World Wrestling Federation] phenomenon. These images and their popularity boomed in straight culture at the same time that the Bears came forward in gay male culture. True, not all those men have body hair—but many shave it, many have beards, many are big, hairy, even fat guys. There is definitely a strong correspondence there between the advent of these heteromasculine images—which of course straight men don't analyze—and the Bear image.

RON: So it's not coincidental that professional wrestling, which is now a huge entertainment industry with millionaire superstars, attracts a lot of Bears.

ERIC: Not at all a coincidence. I am not a great fan of professional wrestling, though I turn on to many of the images that the wrestlers have embraced. I'm a greater fan of boxing and the *Fight Club* movie images and cultural politics.

One last but very important aspect I want to emphasize here is that the Bear subculture reflects a kind of reaction or backlash of men who look different from the cultural "ideal." When one specific Anglo-Nordic, Waspy look dominates cultural images, what happens to other white ethnics who look different? Those other men—particularly Italian, Latino, and Eastern Europeans, who are not perceived as being as attractive as that blond, pretty-boy, good-looking type—seek to affirm themselves by creating alternatives to the mainstream culture.

RON: Do Bears really help subvert the dominant paradigm of ethnic bigotry? Since Bears are primarily white themselves, it would seem that to some extent they reinforce it by creating divisions by which they can marginalize others.

ERIC: Ethnic bigotry is different from racial bigotry, just as ethnicity is not the same as race. Within white ethnic populations, the Anglo-Saxon and Nordic/Aryan ethnicities have long been associated with privilege and beauty in ways that Mediterranean, Eastern European, and Arabic/Semitic looks have not. All I am saying is that the Bear aesthetic is a site where a range of ethnicities—especially those with body hair—can exist and be seen as hot and viable sexualized forms of gay masculinity.

Sure, I've seen hostility from some Bears to "pretty boys," and this is unfortunate, but part of the letting off of steam accumulated through years of aesthetic ranking that has derided bulk, body hair, facial hair, and swarthiness.

RON: Do you feel that these different-looking men, who were alienated from Waspish images, helped to galvanize the Bear emergence to some extent?

ERIC: Yes, but I wouldn't term it that way. I don't think it was people who were alienated. I think it was more the return of the repressed—that anything you put down, anything you vanish, anything you remove from the scene, will all of a sudden become desirable. It's the same thing that I think is feeding the current barebacking trend as a kind of eroticized thrill for some people. After more than 15 years of telling people to "use a condom every time," you're certainly going to increase desire for people to fuck without condoms. And I believe it's the same kind of thing in symbolic images, like masculinities.

RON: The more underground that particular phenomenon is pushed, the greater the backlash.

ERIC: Yes. So, I think that these are some of the other strains that people don't often bring into our discussion of this broader aesthetic.

RON: In your *Bear Book* essay, you ask some hard questions about how Bears image themselves in the form of lower-class cultural trappings. One of the most striking questions in that piece: "What kinds of symbolic violence are visited upon authentically poor and working class men through these [Bears'] attempts at impersonation and ventriloquism?" How do you respond to your own question here, given the vantage point of the four years since you wrote that?

ERIC: That statement is about economic and political violence, not performed violence. It's not about hurting people's feelings. It's about the following scenario and what it means.

What happens when men, from different classes and with different privileges, come together in the same space and all put on the look of working-class or poor men, yet don't discuss the economic differences between themselves? What does it mean that these men don't deal with the underlying assumptions that some people are doctors and lawyers not because they worked hard in school but because they come from middle-class backgrounds? And that you're not a doctor and a lawyer, not because you're a bad person or because you're a fuckup or because you didn't work hard enough, but because the opportunity system doesn't favor people from poor and working-class backgrounds?

I feel that there's a certain kind of symbolic violence enacted because we play with these issues, sexually and physically and culturally, but not politically and analytically. Because we don't have a broader analysis of things. I think that takes its toll.

RON: So, instead of discussing these matters, which should be of concern to us, in relationship to our friends and tricks and buddies, it's acted out some other way?

ERIC: Well, it's acted out in any case. The question is whether or not it's *also* analyzed. In America we love to do things without discussing the political implications or the ramifications or the complexities, so certain things go unstated that go on hurting people in very real, material ways.

RON: What's your opinion of the notion that working-class men don't feel comfortable in Bearclubs and conventions? They find themselves surrounded by software developers in flannel shirts—sheep in

Bear's clothing, so to speak—and feel somewhat displaced.

ERIC: There's another side to that, which is the way that people believe we perform our looks. First of all, I think a lot of people believe we perform our body hair. Many people believe we perform our fatness, for those of us who are fat. They think that we decide to be this way.

Now, there definitely is a certain element of choice in how people look. I also believe, however, that there are certain white ethnic identities that don't usually get represented in the sexual arena and that some of us who are in Bear subculture embody those ethnicities and those looks. I view only an aspect of Bear subculture as performance.

Of course, as a middle-class guy, when I affect working-class looks, I'm aware that I'm doing that, but I'm also aware that as a lower-middle-class Jew in America I have a pretty twisted class identity. And I know I am traditionally comfortable in working-class sites—even before Bear culture this was always true for me—so for me there is that aspect of class performance there.

But I disagree with people—including yourself, I think—who argue that working-class men do not feel comfortable in this subculture. Working-class men have been part of this subculture—in fact, have been part of building this subculture—for a while. For a lot of my friends who are lower-middle class, or working class who were raised poor, Bear spaces are the only sites where they feel comfortable.

Now, I'm sure there are some working-class guys who respond to all these middle-class guys, all these doctors and lawyers pretending to be stevedores and dock workers and stuff. But truly speaking, I think the working-class people are more comfortable because those sites look more like the places they came from. And I think this is particularly true for rural men. In my year living in Maine, I found there were a lot of Bears living there, many of whom don't even know they're Bears. It's just the way Maine men look.

RON: There are some with-it straight men I know who, when I asked them about Bears, don't necessarily see them as gay. To a large extent I think Bears are invisible to straights, and are only partially visible to gay and lesbian culture.

ERIC: Certainly that's true for heterosexuals, because they don't organize masculinities in the way we do. They don't have any of the narrow fetishes around masculine identity. They do have that for women. They have "bimbos," for example. They have different looks and categories for women, but they don't organize them for men because men, in the heterosexual world, aren't considered as the ones gazed upon. They're considered as the ones who do the gazing.

In lesbian and gay worlds, though, there's been a shift. I certainly think many, many gay men are aware of the Bear phenomenon, and increasingly more lesbians. I think we're marginalized, though. Even in a city like San Francisco, we're certainly not at the center of the community.

RON: Is this because Bears are misunderstood?

ERIC: Yes, but I don't know if it can all be accounted to that—everyone's kind of misunderstood. It's that there really isn't a sophisticated sense of subcultures among gay people these days. I do a lot of work studying and analyzing subcultures of gay men, and whether we're talking about "circuit boyz" or the leather scene or Bears, the analysis that's put out in journals and magazines and then picked up and discussed by men in bars and gyms and around dinner tables is extremely superficial.

RON: At Bear weekend conferences and other events, there seems to be a studied avoidance of scheduling any kind of activity other than general fraternizing.

ERIC: I don't go to Bear conferences very often, but I do go to gay and lesbian health conferences, gay political conferences, and gay academic conferences. Gay academic conferences, frankly, are the best in terms of resisting the tendency that occurs in those other places to see any population of gay men as sick, diseased, and a problem, in the way that homophobia controls our understanding of ourselves. It's true of other minority groups as well, but part of the position of being in the margins is that people start buying into societal phobias about themselves.

So then gay folks start to see gay men as an at-risk population; we see gay youth as a depressed, suicidal population; we see Bears or leather queens as people who are abusing masculinities, who have unresolved feeling from their childhoods. It's actually much more complicated than that in all those cases, yet what we choose to see is not even just one side of the discussion, but a narrow piece of one side of the discussion.

I argue that these subcultures are valuable, that they are in fact life-affirming, that there is more good about them than bad, that people are taking valuable meanings that are often very radical meanings out of those subcultures.

RON: But these critics can't actually subtract the value out of the subculture for those who are in the subculture themselves, can they?

ERIC: When the values, the meanings, are pulled out of the subculture, the subculture stops existing. Subcultures come together because they're meaningful to people. Now, all subcultures have a risky side, an edge side, a dangerous side—and that's certainly there. But they also have hugely valuable meanings.

One of the things very few people think and talk about is this: Many of us were deeply alienated from and very scared of other boys and men. We were brought up as sissies, felt like we didn't conform, picked on or beat up or called names or spat on or forced to eat dirt on the playground. What does it mean for us to have found ways to create spaces where we are in rooms with hundreds of men who seem and look like us? There's something very subversive about that. I was never meant to be in those spaces. I was meant to really be afraid of men. And instead I think we have collectively formed communities and subcultures that have allowed us to find ways to relate to men that are life affirming, and wonderful, and great.

RON: Those spaces indeed become transformative and invested with a sense of the spiritual for many men. I don't think the Lone Star was nicknamed "Bear Mecca" by accident. I know men who saved up for a long time to come from across the country or overseas just to walk into the Lone Star and break into tears, and men who have been filled with an overwhelming sense of awe and belonging at entering a Bear event. For perhaps the first time ever in their lives, they're in a space that affirms their looks, sexuality, and identity.

ERIC: Let me tell a story that illustrates what I'm talking about. I recently went to a hockey game, even though I don't usually go to sports events. I teach college, and some of my students play hockey and one of my students coached, and so I went to one of their games, the state championship.

I didn't particularly care for the action on the ice, so I watched people. I watched the men cheering their kids, and I watched the high school kids cheering each other on. And I watched what they performed. I'm sure that event has meaning for them, but I think it has a meaning that's connected to male supremacy, traditional masculinities, class warfare, and a lot of stuff that feels bad.

I felt so uncomfortable and unsafe that I couldn't stay more than half the game. And it wasn't like I was there with people—no one noticed me. The hockey game just reminded me too much of all that stuff from coaches and gym teachers and my father yelling at me and hitting me. It felt like that same energy.

I don't feel that kind of energy whatsoever any place among Bears. I don't feel that in gay male subcultures. That is the kind of affirmation that I'm talking about.

RON: How, if at all, has your identification as a Bear changed over time?

ERIC: I think there are times when I've felt more a Bear and times when I've felt less a Bear. These days, I feel more like a middle-aged guy than I feel like a Bear. A lot of that has to do with how much I'm focused on spending time in specific subcultural life, and how much time this reverts to being involved with something I like to look at in porn magazines.

Back in college I thought of myself as a college student, but Bears were the images I looked at, although I didn't really think of myself as a Bear at the time. When I met my first lover and lived with a man who also drew hair on body parts in porn magazines, and then later started hanging out more with men who looked this way or who *were* this way, I started thinking of myself more as a Bear.

Over time I also wrestled with my identity in other subcultures: I got involved with the leather scene, with Jewish gay men, and other pieces of my identity. So "Bear" has never been alone there.

Then again, one's identity shifts. I spent an intense period of time—probably during those heightened years of the Lone Star, I'd say '89 through '92—really intensely Bear-focused. And since that time, it has still been a part of my life—certainly the major part of my sex life—but it's less central to my identity in this way.

RON: So to some extent you've backed off from your identification with Bears?

ERIC: No—identity is contextual. It depends on where you place your body, and where you are. To me it has never been just a cerebral kind of thing or a symbolic thing. It's a real thing. So it's not that I've "backed off" that identity. I can feel that identity very heightened the one time a month I go to the Lone Star. But the other 29 days of the month, it's not so central to me, maybe.

RON: How has the shift in your location from the Castro in San

Francisco to the campus outside of Portland, Maine—two very different environments—affected your identification as a Bear?

ERIC: It has influenced my identity far less in Maine, because there I spend most of my time in my identity as a professor, simply because I have a job where I'm working with 19-year-old students. When I go to the gay community events or bars or functions or parties in Maine, I feel like I'm an urban man coming into a different environment, and so it's an urban/rural split.

While I've been in Maine, though, most but not all of the guys I have sex with fit Bear images. For the most part they don't have that identity, primarily since they're married, heterosexually identified men.

RON: Bear subculture seems to be a point of contact between gay men and straight married men. In *Dry Bones Breathe* you speak of the Bears as presenting an alternative to a more mainstream current of gay life. What exactly do you mean?

ERIC: One feature that distinguishes the Bears from some other self-reflective subcultures is that the Bear is a counter-image to the dominant mainstream gay image right now. I like to look at what's *not* being focused on, what's *not* the center of American images. I like it when any group that's at the margins starts to organize and to become, in terms of erotic images, its own fetish. This is hardly different, though, from the ways gays have organized around other looks and fetishes over the last 15 or 20 years.

Another salient feature of Bear subculture—not just the men in it but the magazines and the conferences—is that it does such interesting, subversive things with masculinity. There's a combination of traditional macho images that are subverted to gentleness, kindness, camaraderie, and loving brotherhood. There is that strong strain throughout that to me is countermasculine.

RON: One might say that it takes a big man to incorporate both traditional masculine and feminine qualities.

ERIC: True. It's not traditionally masculine, even if we like to tell ourselves we're only into traditionally masculine men. If we were into only traditionally masculine men, our lives would be as unpleasant and emotionally constipated as most straight men's lives. After all, we're queer! We do homo-gender even when we pretend to do hetero-gender.

Bears as a group are simultaneously both gender-conforming and gender-nonconforming, or gender radicals. At any big gathering of Bears, there are men who are very comfortable looking like big gruff hairy bearded lumberjacks, all the while being total queens—silly and light and fun and warm—characteristics which men are not supposed to share with other men.

My feeling is that a lot of people think of Bears in the same way they think of men on a football team. They perceive that we have this macho, traditionally masculine look and that how we interact with each other is traditionally masculine. And that's not true with my experience of Bears. We may get off on traditional masculinities and play with them in our sex lives, but we create lives for ourselves that are very different from our het comrades.

RON: Some critics look at that sort of feminized masculinity as being a contradiction. Of course, every culture, every human being has some contradictory aspects, but it's the playful aspect of Bears that I appreciate.

ERIC: Precisely. I believe contradiction is subversive, so to me, when I want to imagine politicized masculinities, I would consider Bears one of those, only because we simultaneously affirm and undercut traditional masculinities.

I'm not saying that all Bear-identified men do that. What I am saying is that even in the porn stories that you read in *Bear* magazine or *American Bear*, even in the kind of life at the Lone Star and other places we congregate, there's a powerful subversiveness to traditional masculinities. These places, truly speaking, are not scary places to go. If you just look at the pictures you may think they are scary, yet if you ever actually walk in there and turn up the volume on the conversations, these are wonderful places to go.

RON: The Lone Star always seemed a space where the sublime and the mundane existed side by side. You could discuss philosophy and cosmology with bar patrons in the afternoon, then go home, change into leather and 501s later that night, and come back for heavy cruising.

ERIC: These spaces are friendly, they're warm, they're...silly! I hate using that word but there truly is a silliness, a lightness about it.

The experience of Bear spaces is not like that of leather culture. The leather scene maintains a certain cultural affirmation of traditional masculinities while it sexually undercuts those masculinities.

Bear subculture presents masculinities very differently. We twist gender in new ways, which create men's social worlds that are fulfilling, loving, sexy, and fun—not brutal, abusive, or power-tripping, even if some of our sexual fantasies are that way. I don't see it as a contradiction at all. I see it as a really nice, subversive way of undermining gender.

CHAPTER 2

BIG B BEARS AND LITTLE B BEARS
~ A DISCUSSION WITH WAYNE HOFFMAN,
CHRIS WITTKE, AND REX WOCKNER ~

WAYNE HOFFMAN is a writer living in Greenwich Village. He is coeditor of the award-winning anthology *Policing Public Sex: Queer Politics and the Future of AIDS Activism*. In 1997 he was chosen as one of the country's "Best and Brightest Under 30" by *The Advocate*. As an essayist, his work has appeared in several collections, including *Men Seeking Men*, *Boy Meets Boy*, *Generation Q*, *Mama's Boy*, and *Bar Stories*. As a journalist, his cultural reporting has appeared in *The Advocate*, *Torso*, and dozens of regional newspapers, as well as *The Washington Post*, *The Nation*, and the *Boston Phoenix*. He is the current managing editor of *The New York Blade*.

CHRIS WITTKE writes about hairy-chested, bearded and burly celebrities of stage and screen, television, music, sports, and literature for *Bear* magazine. He was the first paid Features Writer, and later the Features Editor of *Gay Community News*, at the time the nation's oldest gay and lesbian newsweekly. His feature writing has also appeared in *Art Issues*, *Drummer*, *In Touch*, and other publications as well as in the anthologies *Hometowns*, *A Member of the Family*, *Flesh and the Word 2*, *My Life as a Pornographer*, and *Quickies 2*. Currently he works as HIV Prevention Manager for an AIDS service organization.

REX WOCKNER has reported news for the gay press since 1985. His work has appeared in more than 250 gay publications. He has a B.A. in journalism from Drake University, started his career as a radio reporter, and has written extensively for the mainstream press as well. Highlights of his gay news career include going to Denmark the day it first allowed gay marriage, reporting from the first gay-pride events in Moscow and Leningrad, and making early connections with emerging gay movements in the former Eastern Bloc and developing nations. He has also written on Bear bars. Currently he writes the online column "The Wockner Wire" for PlanetOut.com and reports news for a string of 85 gay newspapers, magazines, and Web sites in 18 countries. Wockner lives in San Diego with his partner, Jess.

Wayne, Chris, and Rex are three prominent gay writers, all with extensive experience with the gay press. On different occasions I had the opportunity to talk with them informally about the Bear subculture. I was intrigued that although all three could certainly be described as Bearish, none of them particularly identified as a Bear. As it turned out, they were by far not the only Bearish interviewees for this book who felt that way.

I met with them for an online "roundtable discussion," intending to focus (since all three work in gay media) on how the Bear subculture manifests, particularly in the gay media. What resulted was a fast-moving shooting gallery that revealed their opinions on Bears versus "twinks," male images in the gay press, Bearsex, and the differences between "little B bears" and "big B Bears," which, as we'll see, are two entirely different creatures.

Although the text printed here has been edited for stylistic consistency, in the original online text we were using both caps and lowercase B to describe Bear-identified men, which prompted Rex to make the distinction. (Emoticons, such as ;-), and other online jargon are explained in the glossary on page 345). I should also add, for your information, that an otter is generally considered by the Bear clan to be a thin or trim version of a Bear.

RON: First of all, I'd like each of you to please comment briefly on how you personally relate (or don't relate) to being a Bear.
REX: I can barely relate anymore because it has become too commodified, too commercialized, too fetishized, too contestized. In the beginning it was just supposed to be regular guys who rejected the West

Hollywood look and wanted to fuck regular guys, not twinks.

RON: Rex, when and how did you first hear about Bears?

REX: I have no idea.

RON: Chris?

CHRIS: I've written my *Bear* magazine column since 1991, yet I've always thought that Bearness was in the eye of the beholder. I think I've referred to myself as a Bear approximately three times ever. If other people think I am one, then fine. And I think that the Bearclubs and the Bear bars are really great things for the people who love them. I used to belong to the New England Bears in the early days, but I have never been much of a group person. Kind of a lone wolf, to mix metaphors. Even when I was in 4-H as a kid, I didn't take part in the 4-H clubs; I was what they called a "Lone Member." I am really glad that the clubs exist and that guys really seem to get something out of them.

RON: How did you first connect with *Bear* magazine?

CHRIS: I worked with Frank Strona at *Gay Community News* and he left Boston to be the editor of *Bear* in San Francisco. They were looking for somebody to do a media column, and Frank knew that I had been obsessed with hairy chests since adolescence and suggested me.

RON: Wayne, how did you first connect with Bears?

WAYNE: I must have known about Bears for about 10 years now. I remember interviewing Chris Xefos of [the band] King Missile in 1991 and he said he was a Bear, and I knew what he was talking about, so definitely by then.

RON: How did you first connect with Bears?

WAYNE: For me, it's primarily about fetishizing facial hair, which I started to do in other guys around 1991 when I was 20. Grew my own when I was 22, and it's been a slippery slope ever since. Like Chris, I rarely call myself a Bear but don't mind others pegging me that way. Or sometimes I use it as shorthand. I'm also not much of a joiner and have never been in a Bear group. I don't drink or smoke, so I don't spend much time in bars. When I do go to bars, I'll hit a Bear night, but that's about once a month.

RON: Ty's [a New York City bar]?

WAYNE: Ty's, because it's a block from my house and I like the bartenders. Or the Dugout [another New York City bar] on Sundays if I remember, a few times a year. But my own tastes fall between Bears and clones.... It's just hard to find a clone bar these days! Outside the Castro, that is.

REX: Unfortunately, "Bear" has become just another religion for, as Jesse Ventura would say, those with weak minds. "Bear" was supposed to be about embracing your individuality, not embracing another clone scene. Do I still occasionally go to Bear bars? Sure. On the chance I might meet a regular Bearish guy, instead of a "Bear™."

WAYNE: I agree. It's kind of like guys who like leather, as opposed to guys who like to wear sashes from Mister Leather contests.

CHRIS: I totally agree with these statements, but I want to say again that if other guys get something out of it then more power to them; I am glad they have these venues.

WAYNE: I agree with that too, though sometimes I find it amazing how seriously some of these guys take it all, like a religion instead of a hobby.

REX: Yeah, and if Catholics get something out of Catholicism, it must be a good thing too.

CHRIS: Oh, Rex!

RON: OK, guys, let's turn our attention to the Bear-themed media. Do you see the rise of this "religion" as corresponding with the rise of the media?

CHRIS: Anything that gives people shorthand essentially limits the discourse that people have on a topic.

REX: *Bear* magazine is a great idea—but once something becomes overly self-aware, it's history.

CHRIS: Over my long, long life, I have seen people clamor to have something to belong to: *Rocky Horror* fans when I was a kid, the church, cults...

REX: Bear, Inc. Bear™.

WAYNE: I think some guys' fervor isn't so much connected to Bear media (though media facilitates it) but depends on how rejected or alienated they felt from other gay cultural institutions, bars, groups, media, and the like.

RON: Good point.

WAYNE: I never felt horribly alienated as a 20-year-old clean-shaven twinkie. I gravitated to Bears out of my own sexual fetishes, but not because I felt alienated. Perhaps that's why I don't cling to it so tenaciously. On the other hand, I have some friends who always felt they didn't belong in mainstream gay venues, and they cling to it quite strongly. They "belong" in Bear culture.

CHRIS: Fetishes are great side dishes. I got into writing for the magazine because of my hairy-chest fetish: I'm only there for the hair. In my real life I love a lot of contrast. I don't actually understand "Looks as organizing principle."

WAYNE: I agree, except that looks aren't the organizing principle for how I live my life or identify politically. They are, however, a major organizing principle for my sex life, which is a big part of my life and my identity as a gay man and a human being.

CHRIS: What I meant was that when I walk into a packed Bear gathering, all I have in common with most of the people is how we look.

RON: Well, is that a bad thing, at least as a starting point?

REX: My libido loves a short, fat, bald, hairy, mustached, nubbed, big-dicked, cheese-growin' [uncircumcised], cigar-smokin' cop over 50. Do they have those in Bear bars? Or do I find them just walking down the street minding my own business?

WAYNE: Depends on the street. And the bar.

REX: I tend to find them walking down the street.

CHRIS: Rex, what is "nubbed"?

REX: Unshaven, as in nubs.

CHRIS: Oh, I love the Nub Community! In fact, I've heard about this short, fat, bald, hairy, mustached, nubbed, big-dicked, cheese-growin', cigar-smokin' cop-over-50 bar in Orlando.

RON: So, would you say that Bearness for you is about following your fetishes and not about rejecting ephebic images?

CHRIS: I don't think there is a Bearness for me. I'm a hairy, bearded guy, and like I said before, sometimes I like that in other guys. I think *bear* is a nice metaphor, as in "he's a bear of a man," but my scope is wide-ranging and I am really attracted to difference more than sameness in many instances. A few years ago I thought that the bear metaphor had been stretched to the breaking point—probably around the ten-thousandth time somebody made a "husbear" reference.

WAYNE: *gagging*

REX: These are sheep in Bears' clothing. I find a wide variety of men attractive—hairy or not, fat or not, young or old. If someone has something that clicks with me, it doesn't matter what label or category might fit him. But nonetheless, I probably wouldn't kick a short, fat, bald, hairy, mustached, nubbed, big-dicked, cheese-growin', cigar-smokin' cop over 50 out of my tent.

CHRIS: You have a tent?

REX: Can we distinguish between bears with a small B and Bears with a big B?

RON: I tend to distinguish big B Bears as Bear-type men, and small b bears as the four-legged creatures. Some folks, on the other hand, distinguish Bears as identified with the community and subculture and bears as men who may be Bear types but not identified. But it's messy. Wayne, is there a Bearness for you?

WAYNE: Bearness for me is primarily about taste and fetish. Because Bearness happens to largely line up with my own tastes and fetishes, I happen to like Bears. It's got to be more, however, than rejecting ephebe culture, because there are lots of ways to do that. Years ago I did drag a lot, and that was a different rejection of mainstream gay culture's notions of masculinity, in a different direction.

RON: What do you think is behind this tendency toward twinkaphobia?

WAYNE: Attitude, both ways. Not that it's a level playing field, but it cuts both ways.

RON: Please explain, Wayne.

WAYNE: A lot of bears (and Bears) have taken a lot of shit from twinks for years—attitude, being ignored, put down, written off. And many Bears respond by rejecting twinks from Bear spaces, which doesn't help much either, even though I understand it. Having separate comfortable places for Bears who feel left out of most gay spaces is valuable, but ultimately I'd hope that we'd be trying to make all spaces potentially more comfortable for everyone. New York City has 100 gay bars, and I know I'll get cruised in three or four. But I also know I'll be soundly ignored in 95 of them.

RON: It seems a fundamental principle of sorts, that one goes where one scores, like robbing banks because "that's where the money is." Rex?

REX: I've never been attracted to West Hollywood twinks. I'd rather watch straight porn than see them have sex with each other. So for me, my twinkaphobia is nothing more than saying, "Give me more of what turns me on."

WAYNE: Some of us would rather watch straight porn than any gay porn. Go figure.

REX: Twinks never rejected me; I just am not attracted to them.

WAYNE: Me too, though I see plenty who feel otherwise in Bear spaces—generally those Bears who take all this quite seriously.

REX: Plenty of twinks are looking for a Bearish daddy these days.

WAYNE: Somehow at age 29 I've become a Bearish daddy myself, to 40-year-old twinks!

RON: A daddy already, and at such a tender age!

REX: I get mail from them all the time as a result of my secret AOL Web page.

CHRIS: I guess I am never really in "Bear spaces."

RON: But let's get back to the magazines. Michael Bronski stated in another interview [see chapter 3] that Bears "wouldn't exist except for the magazines." Were the images the magazine's created powerful enough by themselves to launch a subculture of tens (maybe hundreds) of thousands of men? Or is it more complicated than that?

REX: Bronski is correct, I think, in that there would be no Bears, just bears. And bears are much preferable.

RON: Although not as easily found, perhaps. Chris?

CHRIS: In my early twenties, two big burly gay friends of my friend Lynda met me and later told her, "Now, that's a Bear," and I had to ask her if that was a good thing. This was several years before *Bear* magazine. So, well, sure, magazines commodify and unfortunately help people reduce their vocabulary when expanding it would be a better idea. My ex-lover had these friends who were a couple and they each punctuated every statement to each other with "Bear," and I wondered how they knew who was talking.

REX: On the mark, Chris.

CHRIS: Phone-sex lines did it in the early '80s. All of a sudden, guys began repeating bland expressions they had heard a million times before, like "I like a lot of body contact." So instead of really exploring what turns our cranks, we reduce our vocabulary to one word or phrase, or at least some people do. But really, while reading those first few issues of *Bear*—I remember thinking, "*Wow*! Somebody else digs fur, too!"

WAYNE: Rex is right: Without the magazines, there'd still be Bears, although far fewer, I think, who thought about their identity along these lines. They'd still be a subniche inside other groups, like leather, country-western queers. The media helped a lot of these guys put a label on themselves, which is a mixed blessing, if you ask me. But it is a good thing in one important way, I think: for guys just coming out who don't fit what they see as gay culture, as it appears on the cover of *Genre* magazine, they can see a different view on the cover of *Bear* and see another possibility. That's small, but it's something. It has helped some gay pals of mine get a grip on their sexuality.

RON: Right. Sometimes I stop at this suburban adult video store just to check out the action. When I see *Bear* and *American Bear* and *Bulk Male* in their male-to-male section, I can't help but think of a certain kind of non-gay guy who catches a glimpse of a big furry guy on the cover and says to himself, "Wow, there are guys who are into guys who look like me!" And that helps him come out of the closet into what Jack Fritscher called "homomasculinity."

CHRIS: I feel terrible when men don't have a chance to explore their fear of femininity: "Oh, I only like masculine men..." Well, fuck you, homo!

CHRIS: It would be nice if the Bear thing were different from every other niche in gay and mainstream culture, but how can it be?

RON: Some would claim that the Bear movement, as it were—at least to the extent that it has some sort of political or social-change purpose—is all about making visible alternative ways of looking as gay men. Agree? Disagree? Why?

CHRIS: I don't really see Bears: The Movement as political in the way Girth & Mirth once was, or at least the way they were until so much of *that* culture renamed itself "Bear" because it was more palatable or something.

WAYNE: Movement? Where is it moving? Really, let's not get carried away.

CHRIS: It's not a movement.

REX: It's totally apolitical.

RON: Totally? What's it about, then?

REX: It's about sex. Your average Joe Bear is not out to challenge the dominance of the West Hollywood twink porn industry or the *Men* cover models. He likes Real Men™. Real Men™ make his dick hard.

CHRIS: Well, the sexual liberation movement appeals to me as a notion. I hardly see the Bear thing as being all that much about sex.

RON: Not the average Joe Bear, true, but that doesn't mean none of them feel that being a Bear is about subverting the dominant paradigm.

WAYNE: I think the average Bear doesn't read *Men*, or spend much time thinking about those magazines or the dominant paradigm.

REX: A few intellectual eastern Bears may think it's about subverting the dominant paradigm. Here on the West Coast it's about sex.

WAYNE: It's more about ignoring the dominant paradigm than rejecting it actively, in my humble opinion.

REX: It's more about not using words like "dominant paradigm."

CHRIS: Well, sex is good, Rex. I wish it were more about the unbridled joy of sex and not about, say, Bear flags or whatever. I think it's not particularly political. I got involved with the magazine for the fun of it. Any sort of academic scrutiny is going to reveal that it's just a metaphor, for God's sake.

WAYNE: I think a culture that's all about sex is political on some level, though.

CHRIS: Me too—that's why I was lamenting it wasn't more sexual.

WAYNE: I don't think Bears are a movement or consciously political on a group level, but forming a viable alternative gay physicality and foregrounding sex (even a little) is political. It's not a movement, but it's political—consciously or not. It's the same reason I identify at least tangentially with leather, because politically I like a gay subculture that puts sex front and center as opposed to diva worship or fashion.

REX: I agree with Wayne that it is subconsciously political, but I prefer not to dwell on it or I'll lose my hard-on.

WAYNE: Agreed!

CHRIS: I feel like there's a point in the queer community when something happens and things get annualized. I mean, did we really need a National Coming Out Day every year with a nonprofit organization behind it and an executive director?

RON: That annualization phenomenon has been rife in America since the country's bicentennial.

REX: Coming out is as boring as Bear™.

CHRIS: How many Bear titles does the world need?

WAYNE: Zero.

CHRIS: What *is* a Mr. Grizzly title, anyway?

REX: What's an otter?

CHRIS: Someone who otter be rejecting labels.

RON: Let's look a little more closely at Bear images in their own media and elsewhere. How have gay media's representations of Bear images changed over the past 15 years?

CHRIS: I think of how *Bear* magazine went from a small offset printing thing to a magazine with a glossy cover as the big change, and then the other magazines that sprang up in that market as the secondary changes. I don't know about the images. I know that some of the images push my personal buttons and some don't—just like some men in real life—but I don't think I see trends in the images.

RON: Do you think there's been a trend in gay media to integrate Bear images at all? Do we see more Bear-type images around?

CHRIS: Sometimes they let the muscle men in their phone-sex ads have a few weeks' growth of body hair. It's funny when the mainstream smut magazines that generally require shaved bodies put in a picture of somebody with a bush that doesn't look like Hitler's mustache—and they act like it's all wild and exotic.

REX: Gay media have not integrated Bear images. The Bear thing remains separate.

WAYNE: Almost completely.

REX: Therefore, I'd never look to gay media if I wanted to wank to a photo. I'd go online to alt.binaries.pictures.erotica.amateur, or the like.

WAYNE: Ditto.

CHRIS: Egroups.malehiddencam for me. I'm more interested in how the majority gay culture images impact straight culture. Seeing straight professional jocks with their shaved bodies who don't realize that it comes directly from mainstream gay culture is fairly hilarious.

REX: Even the guys in the Bear magazines often are too subcultured-out-looking for me. Instead of just looking like ordinary American males, they look like American urban gay subculture Bears.

CHRIS: Of course, ordinary American maleness is as much in the eye of the beholder as Beardom.

REX: There's a Bear Store™ in San Francisco on Ninth Street. Have you been to it? How did it make you feel?

WAYNE: When I went in, I felt like a poseur Bear—not a "real" Bear. I felt like I wasn't big enough, didn't have a bushy enough beard, didn't have the right belt buckle, and didn't have any clothing with the word *Bear* printed on it.

CHRIS: You know, at some point around Stonewall 25 I had to give up being disappointed by gay culture, with all the tacky tchotchkes for sale and the rejection of marginalized sexuality. Because all forms of U.S. culture are commodified, I find it hard to hold up the Bear thing for particular scorn. I felt more comfortable in the Bear Store than in Don't

Panic!™, a company that puts trademarks on quips!

WAYNE: True.

CHRIS: Isn't there another way to express solidarity than a rainbow sticker in the shape of a cat on your bumper? Is there another way to express what arouses you rather than one word or a canned phrase?

REX: What is an otter? Somebody told me he was an otter the other day and it had something to do with him considering me a Bear.

CHRIS: For me, one of the scariest things on earth was the development of the Bear Code.

REX: The Bear Code looks like some *Star Trek* language from the planet Xenon.

CHRIS: That had nothing to do with *Bear* magazine, but everything to do with the whittling-down instead of the expansion of our sexual vocabularies that is endemic in our culture, not just Bear culture—whatever that is. (I can't believe I just said, "Bear culture.")

WAYNE: Plus it's confusing—you need a decoder ring to figure it out! Hanky codes, even if they were equally limiting and annoying (though sometimes useful), were at least more logical and easy to remember.

CHRIS: Exactly. It's like *1984* and that couple, the friends of my ex-lover's, who called each other "Bear" all the time. In the future, "Bear" will be the only word they say to each other—ever. And they will be happy...

RON: So, what's the verdict? Hopelessly beyond repair?

REX: Very early '90s. Hopelessly retro.

WAYNE: That depends—what were we hoping Bear would accomplish exactly?

REX: Bear never meant to "accomplish" anything. It was about hard-ons. Then it became too self-conscious.

RON: Hard-ons certainly accomplish something.

CHRIS: I think it should just be fun, is all, and that it can't bear the weight of political or academic analysis. (Ha ha, "bear" the weight.)

REX: Bears are just a new set of clones for the early '90s.

CHRIS: I don't think that's fair. Not when the mainstream gay images are still shaved smooth and at this point look like they are wearing corsets.

REX: I meant Bears, big B, not bears, little B.

WAYNE: But Bears are still on the edge of the pond, even if they're in the pond.

REX: Little B bears are what make it worth getting out of bed in the morning.

WAYNE: Or staying in bed in the morning. I'd like to make a last upbeat comment.

RON: Thank you; go ahead.

WAYNE: There are still a few things that seem more apparent in Bear circles than non-Bear gay circles, including physical affection, sexual playfulness, and respect for age. And I think all that stuff is great. The key is to remember not to take it all quite that seriously. Have fun with it and loosen up. And lose the attitude.

REX: Agreed.

CHRIS: I would recommend that people not pin hopes on a Bear movement, because it's just a metaphor! Fun is good, fur is good; expanding our sexual vocabularies is great. I guess that's all.

REX: What's an otter?

RON: We otter wrap up.

CHAPTER 3
YOU CAN LEAD A BEAR TO CULTURE BUT...
~ A DISCUSSION WITH DAVID BERGMAN
AND MICHAEL BRONSKI ~

DAVID BERGMAN is author and editor of a dozen books, including *Cracking the Code*, which won the George Elliston Poetry Prize, *Heroic Measures*, and *Gaiety Transfigured: Gay Self-Representations in American Literature*. His work has also appeared in *The Gay & Lesbian Review*, *The Kenyon Review*, *Men's Style*, *The New Republic*, and *The Paris Review*. He edited the biennial series *Men on Men: Best New Gay Fiction* until its year 2000 edition, when it won a Lambda Literary Award, and with Joan Larkin he edits the book series *Out Lives: Lesbian and Gay Autobiographies*. He teaches at Towson University in Baltimore.

MICHAEL BRONSKI is author of *The Pleasure Principle: Sex, Backlash, and the Struggle for Gay Freedom* and *Culture Clash: The Making of Gay Sensibility* and editor of *Taking Liberties: Gay Men's Essays on Sex, Politics, and Culture* and *Flashpoint: Gay Male Sexual Writing*. His writing has appeared in many publications, including the *Los Angeles Times*, *The Village Voice*, *Z Magazine*, *Out*, and *Gay Community News* as well as in the anthologies *Gay Spirit*, *Friends and Lovers*, *Home Towns: Gay Men Write About Where They Belong*, *Acting on AIDS*, and volumes 2, 3, and 4 of the *Flesh and the Word* series. He has been involved in the gay liberation movement for 30 years.

This discussion on Bear culture was the first I conducted; in fact, it was intended for and eventually saw publication in Les Wright's *The Bear Book II*. At the time it seemed that no "serious" writers were considering the implications of the Bear phenomenon. The piece contains a wealth of insight into so many aspects of Bears, it's not surprising it also saw print as three discrete (but not discreet) excerpts in *Art & Understanding*, *Gay Community News*, and *American Bear* magazine. Its appearance in *Art & Understanding* brought on a slew of responses—including one from Tom Bianchi, who defended his common definition of beauty.

Following separate conversations about Bears with David and Michael, neither of whom, as it turns out, particularly identify as Bears, the three of us came together online for a somewhat hairy but fascinating discussion about Bears in May 1998. In our little cyber den we typed furiously for two hours about the good, the bad, and the grizzly. As Les had requested that we consider the topic of "Literary Bears," I wanted first to discuss what I then considered the only Bear literary tradition I knew—that of the fictional men of the 1960s gay sex pulp series, *Song of the Loon*, written by Richard Amory. The *Loon* books had just been republished online at the time of our cyber chat.

Some of the notions presented here about various features of Bear subculture were dated before they first saw print (such as that of the Bear contests, which had been underway but somewhat undeveloped for several years), as is to be expected of features of an emerging subculture. Nonetheless, this conversation is especially valuable for its initial insights into the underpinnings of Bears and masculine gay men in erotic literature, a topic further developed in the interview with Jack Fritscher (chapter 6) and the discussion with Richard Labonté and Tim Martin (chapter 16). It also lays out some of the general subjects that the rest of this book explores in greater depth, such as "Dykes and FTMs as Bears" (chapter 22) and "Gen-X Bears" (chapter 21).

I have restored here some of Michael's stronger comments as well as a few of the humorous outtakes that never saw print for *The Bear Book II* due to space and other considerations.

RON: Let's start by talking about the *Song of the Loon* pulp sex novel trilogy by Richard Amory (published 1966–8, and now out of print). These books were early representations of Bear types: frontiersmen, cowboys, and Native Americans, most of whom were hairy, bearded, strong, well-endowed, sexually available, and primarily concerned (except for minor plot constraints) with male-to-male love. Are the men of the *Loon* series anything like a Bear archetype?

DAVID: Amory clearly thought he was dealing with an archetype. The *Loon* trilogy is a melding of the cowboy novel of Zane Grey and the classical pastoral romance of Longus—both of which rely more on archetypes than on psychological realism. Gregory Woods, in his book *A History of Gay Literature: The Male Tradition*, has a very fine chapter on the homoerotic element of the pastoral romance, and the Native American has always been associated in the Western mind with male-male sex. The Spanish explorers noted with horror how Native Americans engaged so freely in sodomy. So I think both the *Loon* books and Bear culture are overdetermined by very strong cultural vectors that have shaped it and brought it into being. The myth that developed was of the natural Native releasing the positive aspects of the white man's homosexuality. This mythic sense of the natural powers the appreciation of the hairy, thicker male bodies of Bear culture.

RON: Were the readers of the *Loon* books back in the '60s anything like the readers of *Bear* and *American Bear* today?

MICHAEL: Before the *Loon* books, in the 1950s and '60s, there was very little openly gay material available for gay men to read. There were some quite depressing and even homophobic books that appeared as mainstream novels and then were published as pulps. And they were quite, quite different from the first porn books that appeared in the mid 1960s, which had explicit sexual activity and were not burdened with unhappy endings, but they were not real novels. They were jerk-off books. The *Loon* books were openly gay, sexy, and written as novels. The *Loon* books were read by lots of different people—men looking to read about gay relationships as well as men looking for writing about sex. They were a revelation because they were very positive about gay lives—but I think that their enormous readership was drawn to that, not to the types of men in the books.

RON: Can we discuss the genre of writing—the gay pastoral—that these books represented and its relevant symbolism?

MICHAEL: You have to place the *Loon* books in the larger context of a tradition of U.S. writing that presented the West, the wilderness, the forest—the pastoral in a larger sense—as a symbol of the natural, the healthy, and even the morally right. This tradition is the cornerstone of U.S. writing and includes James Fenimore Cooper's *Leatherstocking Tales*, Melville's *Moby Dick*, and even Mark Twain's *Huckleberry Finn*. In all of these novels men have to leave civilization and go into the wilderness either to find themselves or to find freedom. In the process they also discover deep feelings—and love—with other men: Natty Bumppo and Chingachgook, Ishmael and Queequeg, Huck and Jim. The homoerotic strain in all of this literature is completely self-evident. Leslie Fiedler talks about it at length in *Love and Death in the American Novel*. His famous essay on Huckleberry Finn, "Come Back to the Raft Ag'in, Huck Honey," was published in 1949. This is no secret. And certainly the *Loon* books fit right into this—they are, in essence, a continuation and even, at times, a parody of it.

RON: How does the conspicuous absence of women affect the male characters in these works?

MICHAEL: There are two things to keep in mind with this. The first is that in this tradition, men have to leave civilization because women are preventing them from being full human beings. This situation is predicated on civilization being repressive because men can't act out their inner feelings, and the forest being good because it is natural—no women present. There is a clear understanding in all the work that women make unreasonable, repressive demands upon men to act better—that is, not to be so sexual—and therefore women are to be avoided.

DAVID: I agree with Michael that the absence of women is central to these representations of entering the natural. Of course, this also corresponds to the demographics of the American West, in which the society was dominated by men, and women were scarce.

MICHAEL: It is interesting to look at how people relate to the books now and how they see that context. And I think that this context has to include an observation of all the aspects—historical, social, sexual—that make up the tradition. Why might Bears be attracted to the *Loon* books? Is it just because some of the men have beards—well, lots of men in the Bible have beards and live in the wilderness. Hell—the book of Hosea even describes God as a female bear protecting her cubs.

RON: Earlier in the Old Testament, actually, in Genesis, the character of Esau, Joseph's hairy older brother, might be the first biblical Bear. In order to receive their father's blessing, Joseph impersonates Esau by wearing a pelt. Esau is depicted as a very instinctual and sensual man, and a loving brother, who is in essence Joseph's shadow.

MICHAEL: But to get back to the *Loon* books: Do Bears relate to these books because they are about men getting together away from civilization and being free of social restraints? Some Bears may see these restraints now as getting away from repressive aspects of gay male culture—the gym body, the enforced hairlessness of some porn magazines. But it is also important to think about what it means to indulge in the fantasy of men alone to be sexually free in a broader context as well—can men only be free and sexual without women present? What are the conditions and the fantasies that make all-male—even Bear—groups special, and what does that mean?

DAVID: I think you're falling into the trap of regarding any culture outside of the West as being without constraints, as being without a culture. But the Indians in the *Loon* books have a very elaborate legal and religious system. It just isn't sexually repressive. The *Loon* books and the Bear movement are not escapes from culture but a desire to find a culture that is not repressive of sexual desire and not offended by the realities of the human body, its hairiness, its tendency to sag, its mortality.

MICHAEL: Good point. It is vital not to essentialize non-Western cultures as freer. Certainly Edward Said, in *Orientalism*, has made clear what happens with this process. And certainly nonwhite cultures, in this case Native American cultures, had complex legal, religious, and moral systems. But what I was speaking about was how the white male Eurocentric writer and reader construct this fantasy world. In the Loon books, the freedom—embedded in the complex legal and religious codes (which are, as far as I can tell, pretty much invented by the author)—is predicated on the absence of women, which allows a pervasive homoeroticism.

RON: Turning our attention to more recent times: Some consider the Bears to be one of the first movements following the onset of AIDS to provide gay men with healthy images of sex. It was a way, in part, for some men to reconnect with images of strength and power and virility, and to some extent longevity—qualities connected with masculine Bear body traits: beards, fur, fat, and sexual prowess.

MICHAEL: I wonder what you mean by a movement—as opposed to a bunch of guys that felt good about how they looked, and hung out together, and their good feelings about themselves, all of which helped them to have safe sex. That is great, but is not a movement to feel good about sex. Which is not to say that the Bear thing did not come into being and evolve as a response—directly and indirectly—to AIDS.

RON: Perhaps not a "movement" in a political sense, but in the way it created community, art, and identity that tens of thousands of men around the world can relate to.

MICHAEL: But I'm not sure that I'd call this a movement in a traditional political sense. A movement toward what? It seems to me to be a cultural response or a reaction to social conditions. But as I use the word, a movement is more organized in an, even nascently, political sense. Are bridge clubs a movement? The Junior League? The Boy Scouts—at least as founded by Lord Baden-Powell—was far more of a movement because it did indeed have a political agenda.

I would not personally use the phrase "Bear movement." In fact, when people even begin talking about the oppression of Bears, I view it as being offensive. I see it rather as a phenomenon—a sort of varied, multilevel, mostly grassroots (although increasingly commodified) response to many factors, especially AIDS.

DAVID: I think AIDS is an important part of what brought about the Bear groups, but I think its origins go back further to a desire in certain gay men to find something especially beautiful and sexy in their own masculinity. I think it is also a response to certain cultural images of gay men that gay men produced of themselves which emphasized (perhaps overemphasized) youth, hairlessness, gym bodies, and wealth.

MICHAEL: Of course, that is true. And I think that historically this is an American as opposed to a European image. This is reflected in the *Loon* books and in colonial and post-colonial American Literature and we see it today with the Bears versus the Calvin Klein look. It is natural versus unnatural or manufactured.

DAVID: I was just looking at the Tom Bianchi book of photography, *In Defense of Beauty*—and it represents exactly the problem that the Bear subculture was supposed to respond to. Bianchi can conceive of only one kind of beauty, and that is a sculptural dehumanized beauty in which people look like they are marble rather than flesh.

RON: Bears naturally reacted as outsiders to this dehumanized gay ideal—it was just plain unworkable for Bears to live up to that standard. Nor did they feel they ought to.

MICHAEL: I think it is interesting to call Bianchi's work a problem. For whom? Not for the men who look like they do—wouldn't they like it? There may be a larger social problem, such as social interests prioritizing and promoting one type of body over another. That has been a feminist critique of the media for years. And certainly the Bear thing has been a response to that. Bianchi is not interested in defending beauty—which can mean almost anything—except for a special type of socially approved beauty. Of course, Bianchi—and other photographers, such as Bruce Weber, and so on—dehumanize. That is one way to deal with how scary sexuality is. That is why they are not real or true artists—the purpose of their work is to view the world through a limited, narrow lens, not a broader one that shows its complexity.

RON: As you said earlier, Michael, this enforced hairlessness would seem to point to some exclusion of Bear-type images, as reflected in the types of body images the gay media produces—print, broadcast, photography, advertising, porn.

Has queer media tried to suppress Bear images? Why have Bear images been largely excluded from the gay media, porn in particular?

MICHAEL: I don't think "suppress" is the right word. It isn't like TV refusing to hire African-Americans as newscasters or reporters. Or only covering negative news that happens in minority neighborhoods. The word "suppress" implies a conscious decision not to show something, probably for a clear political or social reason.

Let me clarify this a bit. In the past (and, I am sure, even now) people in the media have said, "Well, we'd use more images of African-Americans, but they don't really help sell the product." This may have been in part true and sounds close to why *Mandate* or *Honcho* may not print more photos of Bears. But it is vital to remember that while the excuse is the same, the social reality is quite different. Black Americans were, and to some degree still are, excluded from a whole range of activities and opportunities because of a pervasive racism. This is simply not true of men who identify as Bears—there is no systematic discrimination against Bears—and because of this, the idea of the suppression of Bear images sounds silly.

RON: I disagree with the idea that Bear types have not been excluded from certain types of activities and opportunities. It's like saying that there has never been a stigma attached to being fat, or hairy, or even bearded. TV stations in fact did not hire men with beards, or big men, for the most part, until the 1990s. And in gay culture, at least as much as in straight culture, this exclusion is reflected in the types of body images that the media produces—print, broadcast, photography, advertising, porn. And if you've ever been the only bearded man cruising in a bar full of clean-shaven guys and clones, you know by experience that particular kind of exclusion, which I call "smoothism."

MICHAEL: This seems to me to be very tricky territory. It is certainly true that certain types of physical types have been excluded from the realm of public presentation, particularly in positions of ostensible authority—newscasters is a good example—and this is true across the board, not just about men with beards. We live in a society in which looks are made to matter and "good" looks have been traditionally defined as thin is better than heavier, white is better than nonwhite, feminine is better than butch for women and the reverse for men. Feminists have been complaining about this for decades and have waged legal fights to stop discriminatory actions like dismissing airline stewardesses (as they were called then) for being too old—at age 35. In this sense Bears—defined, at least in this case, as men with beards—were not hired as newscasters on television. But there is, in my way of thinking, a huge difference between types of men being excluded from being showcased on the media and women or African-Americans being discriminated against being women or black.

RON: It seems to me that those aging stewardesses took legal action not merely because they were women but because they were a type of women.

MICHAEL: There are studies that show that people who are perceived as "overweight" are discriminated against in the workplace, often being passed up for jobs they are qualified for, but even this is not the same thing as Bears—men with beards—being overlooked because there is an accepted "uniform look" that the media or workplace unreasonably enforces. And in fact, in the past 15 years, many of those prohibitions against facial hair or hair length have been changed, in part through legal (or implied legal) challenges but also because of changes in fashion.

I am extraordinarily uncomfortable, in fact outright reject, making any direct correlation between the exclusion that Bears may face and the real discrimination that women, African-Americans, Latinos, or gay people as distinct groups face in the workplace and in many social situations. The paradigms that we use to describe racism, sexism, or anti-Semiticism simply do not apply here in the same way. We have never lived in a world of Bear-only drinking fountains.

RON: Your point is well-taken, but I do feel that we still live in a world of twink-only gay spaces where intense social stigma exists that oppresses Bear men's bodies and way of being. In any case, let's return to the notion of representations of men in porn and gay media.

MICHAEL: The reason why there are few Bear images in some magazines and books is because they are seen as not popular. You know that the minute Bianchi thought he could sell Bears he would; the minute that the fashion world decides that the Bear look is in, the images will be there. The minute Bears become marketable, Bears will be sold as such.

DAVID: Bears are being marketed already, but not as successfully as the buff. However, I think we should be glad that someone isn't marketable and rejoice in that failure.

RON: Amen to that, David. So, the question then becomes—why doesn't it sell?

DAVID: Part of it is technical. It's harder to photograph hairy bodies and get the same sort of physical definition. Light does not come off a hairy body in as photogenic a way as it does a smoothly oiled one. Then there are the class issues of thinness—the rich can afford the diets and exercise one needs to stay thin. But I think there is something else. Hair is a deeply psychological symbol of both sexuality and mortality. Remember, Samson loses his power when he gets his locks shorn—and society in its attempt to control power wants to have us all shorn. But body hair especially is part of the abject—part of the dirty, smelly, detachable parts of the self that are associated with being mortal. And today especially, American society in general, and gay culture in particular, is torn by its feelings about its mortality. So along with the Bianchi models who look like marble statues, we also have the anorexic male models who look like they're on speed or heroin—gaunt figures of the nearly dead.

RON: So what made it possible in the mid 1980s to make Bears marketable?

MICHAEL: First, some men couldn't fit into the youngish, hairless images. Secondly, AIDS became a reality, and somehow that was associated with a gay culture that was too centered on urban life and living. The result was a fantasy flight to the natural and the woods, and the nonurban. Also, there were too many baby boomers who no longer fit a young image. But let's face it: the people marketing *Bear* and *American Bear* would love to have a larger market. That is what happened to

Drummer: it was lost in the dust when every other gay porn mag—*Honcho*, *Mandate*, and the rest—began printing SM images.

DAVID: AIDS left a vacuum in gay image making that allowed a small window for Bears to emerge as a group. Also, the image of thin, willowy models was problematic for gay men because they reminded gay men too much of AIDS. There was a need to see burly, healthy, mature men with hairy bodies to confirm the idea that they had survived. Younger men went to the gym and turned their bodies into stone or metal—body armor to protect them—but other gay men saw protection in fur, as we have always done.

MICHAEL: I like the idea that we have always seen protection in fur, and it's certainly true for some cultures and time periods. But let's not overgeneralize. The invincible gym body is as much a response to AIDS as the Bear body is. If men see themselves at war with a disease, then they want to be fit to fight. This Spartan image is as valid an interpretation as the Bear response. And realistically, not all men can be Bears or choose to appreciate the Bear look. I think it's great that there is now a multiplicity of looks in the gay world, but the slim, boyish look is in as well—look at Leonardo DiCaprio and Matt Damon and Marky Mark [Wahlberg]—all straight-boy icons for some gay men, and certainly for the mainstream media.

DAVID: Michael, I never said the gym body wasn't a response to AIDS. In fact I said just the opposite. But I think during the mid 1980s there was a lot of anxiety about how to regard our bodies and sexuality, and this uncertainty opened a range of possibilities. It has only been in the last few years that I have been receiving, as editor of *Men on Men*, stories that are sexually explicit, and that openness has been fiercely attacked by people such as Larry Kramer. Yes, the willowy, drugged-out body has returned with a vengeance. I think it is also part of the glamorization of the AIDS body. In fact, Bianchi was on the cover of the AIDS arts journal *Art & Understanding* [May 1998]. So AIDS has produced lots of confusion about how gay men regard their bodies.

RON: And the formation of the Bear body helped those types of men achieve a degree of clarity about how they view themselves.

MICHAEL: I think a real question is how much this kind of gay media—as alternative as it is and wants to be seen—actually influences how people see themselves as much as Calvin Klein ads and *XY* magazine do. Do all Bears really want to be Bears? Or is this just another image they have been sold? How much of this influence is natural is as socially constructed as anything else.

DAVID: I don't know about you, Michael, but as for me, I'm never going to have the sleek, hairless, long-legged body of the Calvin Klein ads. I have a Bear body because of genetics. But Bear culture has taught me not to be ashamed of it. And I think that when you have a certain body type, you have trouble imagining yourself ever fitting into a Calvin Klein ad. Certain kinds of gay men for a long time have felt very out of it. Bearness becomes a way of seeing yourself, a discovery of a way to view yourself, that makes it possible to see your body as desirable and gay at the same time.

MICHAEL: Well, actually, I was referring to the proliferation of certain media images of how gay men should look and how that can make people feel that they want to look that way even if it is an impossibility. Certainly, not all women can look like a Cosmo Girl, but many feel that they *should*. The good part is that if Bears now feel that they can resist the temptation to want to look otherwise, we are all better off.

RON: Let's return to this idea of the split in the psyche of Bears between the urban and the wilderness. How does that read into Bear media representations?

MICHAEL: The flight from the urban happened after Stonewall with the gay commune movement, as well as with a back-to-the-wilds impulse in het communities. A strong aspect of gay culture has always been the decadents and a preoccupation with death and decline. The Bianchi and AIDS stuff plays into that. In a sense, the Bears are a rejection of that history. The natural over the unnatural—in drug terms, mushrooms over K and speed. In a sense, urban Bears are an oxymoron—they are displaced people creating a subculture in hostile territory. Gay bars are essentially an urban, decadent phenomenon, and Bears can be in them—meet there—but they're almost antithetical to that impulse to run away from the urban.

DAVID: As Michael is pointing out, Bear culture is paradoxical. Anyone really brought up in the wild knows that it isn't half as romantic as Bear images try to make it. It is an urban fantasy about what a world in the wild would be like. It goes back to the decadents, as Michael says, which was a very urban and urbane movement: what they prized was the artificiality of the so-called natural. I think that is why so many Bears are in love with cyberspace. The Bear idyll has always taken place in a cyberspace, which is nostalgia for something that never was.

MICHAEL: American culture—gay and straight—has always had a love affair with the fantasy of the naturalness of the wild forest or the unexplored. The American Western movie is a prime example. And the conflict in Westerns is: how to tame the West and keep the fantasy. Bear culture grew up in San Francisco—an extraordinarily urbane place—with enough connection to a history of oddness and the West that it allowed the Bear image to grow and become noticed by others. I think we also have to look at the culture of 'zines and that sort of punk counterculture (an anti-Bear one at that) for helping to create publishing networks that allowed *Bear* magazine to really work and grow.

DAVID: The magazines have been a powerful force in gay life, far more a force than for straights. I've often said that the queerest thing about gay people is that they read, and Americans as a rule don't read at all.

MICHAEL: My friend Will Leber has always claimed that if gay people were on TV and in movies, we would not have any gay literature or publishing because it exists only to fill a media void. Gay people are like all Americans—they only read because they have to.

DAVID: But Michael was making another very important point. And that is that Bear culture is an especially American expression (although I can imagine Australians with a similar background having something like a Bear culture). The West of the imagination relies on two opposing forces: the need to conquer nature, and the desire to be absorbed by an alien culture in which one can find oneself. I don't think there will ever be a truly International Mr. Bear.

MICHAEL: My boyfriend Drew lived in Korea for two years and found men there who identified as Bears based on the magazines and media.

RON: There are Bearclubs throughout Western Europe. Australians translate it into Marsupial Bears or Wombats. There's even a Bearclub in Japan. And actually, there is an International Mr. Bear contest, although it primarily features only winners from contests of U.S. clubs.

DAVID: I forget about the hegemony of American culture. Even gay culture is part of the imperialistic spread of America.

MICHAEL: I don't find it surprising to hear that there is an International Mr. Bear because gay culture around the world has historically come from U.S. culture. Is this a good thing or a bad thing? Well,

I think that the more we market looks and trends and fashions as being the way to look—be it disco, hairless gym bodies, or Bears—we have to do some deep thinking and questioning about what is going on. It is all a manifestation of people not wanting to be themselves.

RON: Despite many positive archetypal images of the bear mammal—such as the one in the *Bible* that Michael mentioned, or in the Hindu epic *The Ramayana*, or in Native American lore—contemporary American culture views the creature as negative and fearsome. As the dictionary [*Merriam Webster's Collegiate Dictionary, 10th Edition*] puts it, a bear is a "surly, uncouth, or shambling person." To me this sounds very much like the outlaw biker types among whom the Bear subculture first emerged in San Francisco—but I doubt that is how most self-identified urban Bears now see themselves or would care to see themselves represented.

MICHAEL: Are Bears outlaws or simply refugees from an urban culture they don't feel comfortable in? What does it mean to be an outlaw? It seems to me that Bears may be fashion outlaws because they don't—adamantly refuse—to conform to certain media-produced body types. But real outlaws?—not really. Not socially, or even politically.

Personally, I always saw myself as a renegade motorcycle gang member or a hippie, a political revolutionary or an SM freak. My sense of otherness was far less centered on how I looked than on wanting to be an outlaw. It was a state of mind, not of body.

DAVID: I couldn't imagine myself in a motorcycle gang. Or an outlaw, as much as I was involved in the antiwar movement.

MICHAEL: I can't imagine myself not an outlaw. Unfortunately, the way that outlaw images keep getting enfolded into the mainstream, I am running out of new ways to be on the outside.

DAVID: Yes, that's always the problem. It's hard to maintain a sense of oneself without identifying with some group or other.

RON: How do you feel personally when gay men type you as a Bear?

DAVID: Ironically, I don't even consider myself a Bear. I don't feel bad when people think of me as a Bear. But I'm not comfortable with the instant sort of brotherhood that some people think being a Bear automatically gives you. I find that rather disturbing. It's a false intimacy. But America is the land of false intimacy, so I'm not surprised. I'm just taken a little aback by someone thinking that I was a person who belonged anywhere. I'm not used to that sense of belonging.

MICHAEL: People can think of me any way they like. I am more interested if they will go to bed with me. Not always the case. It is that false intimacy that David mentioned.

DAVID: Michael, I know any number of people who would love to go to bed with you. I hardly think that's your problem.

MICHAEL: Who are they? Who are these people?

DAVID: In any case, I've never gone to Bearclub meetings, or have gotten together with Bears. I've always disliked the clubby kind of mentality that is also so much of American culture. Bearclubs sometimes strike me as Elks clubs for homosexuals.

MICHAEL: America is a country of joiners—from Rotary and Junior League to Girth & Mirth to gay bowling leagues. Why do we think gay people should be different from the rest of the country? People want to be accepted, but that is very tricky. What does acceptance mean? I am far more eager to be accepted because of my wit, or intelligence, or ability to get a job done than by my build, or whiteness, or even my gayness. I generally don't want to be accepted for certain physical aspects, like whiteness, over which I have no control. I am glad to be accepted as a Bear—although I don't identify as such—because that does not set me apart from other people. Being accepted for being white—at least in how our culture is now—is actually predicated on nonwhite people not being accepted. Which is repugnant.

RON: Shouldn't Bear types have their own spaces where they can socialize with other similarly socially identified folks?

DAVID: Bears should have their place as everyone else should be able to claim a space of his own.

MICHAEL: A Bear space seems to be a social space and I think it is interesting to keep thinking about what is going on behind the urge for it.

RON: Bear spaces often become collegial group gropes where practically anybody (thus the egalitarian slant) can participate. But often this is behavior the same men wouldn't think of elsewhere.

DAVID: I don't know how things are in Boston, but in Baltimore where I live, it is clear that I'm not wanted in some of the bars, especially the dance bars. People want to claim a space when they are excluded or made to feel unwanted in other spaces. I don't think there's any mystery to the desire for feeling wanted, for feeling that you belong.

MICHAEL: I am bothered about this idea of claiming space. Is this like restricted country clubs? The very notion that people might want to be with their own kind has, well, a troubled history. There are several things going on here, though, about the nature of difference and the responses to it. Let's say that one does not feel welcomed in a public space like the dance bars David mentioned. Sure, in that case you may want to go to—or create—a space (a Bear bar) in which you would feel comfortable. That is a reaction to a form of social ostracism.

But is the identity of "Bear" simply a reaction to what is experienced as an oppressive gay male culture, or is it something unique in and of itself? This isn't a new question. African-American culture has evolved and flourished in resistance to, and suppressed and harmed by, a dominant culture of white racism. The same is true of gay culture. I don't really see Bear culture as that sort of entity or construction, but it is a question if the Bear identity is proactive or simply reactive. I suspect that the Bear image started out as a reflexive revolt against beauty norms (among other things) but has evolved into a stabilized identity and image that wants to be accepted as mainstream. This, of course, is a contradiction that one sees in the gay movement as well. Are gay people in some way profoundly different, or are we just like everyone else?

RON: This brings up an interesting aspect of Bear representation: How so often urban Bears try to pass as straight, working-class Joes (or Harrys, perhaps) yet in reality are just furry technoqueers.

DAVID: My answer is that for the most part we are invisible to straight people. I think most gay people are still seen by the straight world in the old stereotypes. When I mention Bears to straights who are pretty cool, they don't even know what I'm talking about.

MICHAEL: But do you think that Bears are at all visible as gay to straight people? They just look like older men. There is nothing gay about the look to those who don't know.

RON: What impact have the Bears had on queer culture at large?

MICHAEL: I don't think there is a great deal of impact by Bears on gay culture. I think that what we call gay culture is actually an enormous set of overlapping subcultures that have little impact on one another. I do think that the importance of Bears and Bear culture is that it shows that gay culture is growing and becoming more and more interesting with age. And that is great, it is a sign of maturity.

DAVID: I think with some of my students that they are often more comfortable with a greater range of what it means to be gay and seem to have a less stereotyped notion of what they have to live up to. That might be a response to Bear culture, but I have never heard them speak of it. They seem to be very oblivious to the idea. In fact the only gay person under 30 who has ever mentioned Bear culture to me is my niece [Sharon Bergman, see chapter 22] and her girlfriend, who think of themselves as lady Bears.

MICHAEL: I also think that gay male culture has an enormous capacity to reinvent and self-invent. There is a chapter in my book, *The Pleasure Principle*, that charts how the gay male body changed how straight men viewed their own bodies. I think that the capacity to invent the Bear has shown straight culture—just as the clone and the daddy and other gay types did—that men can be any number of things. And more importantly that that image can be sexy.

DAVID: Gay men are always showing straight men how to look at themselves. Look at James Dean and any number of gay movie stars who came to represent American maleness.

RON: And that's the impact that Bears had—they made visible to the larger gay culture a far greater range of images, and thereby broke through the contemporary gay male beauty code.

MICHAEL: I think that gay men and gay sensibility have usually paved the way for how Americans think about a whole range of body types and images. But this is always complicated. The reality is that the Marlboro Man—as an image, and I suspect as a model—came out of certain gay types of the 1960s and '70s. He can also be seen as a early proto-Bear. But that would not have had the impact it did if it were not connected to a major advertising campaign put together by the cigarette industry. The image may have started out gay, but its effect was through a mainstream venue. The same with James Dean—his was a gay image, but developed through the Hollywood studio system. I think that at this point in history—as with all social trends that are media-influenced—what causes what is the most interesting question.

RON: You mean, did the individuals who were Bears create the magazine that created the groups and thus the subculture, or some other way around?

MICHAEL: As David said earlier, Bears did not come out of nowhere. And Bears have been commercialized from the beginning. There would be no "movement" without the magazines.

RON: But you stated earlier, Michael, that the Bear 'zines do not comprise a movement by themselves. You don't think that the Bear bulletin board groups along with the Bear bars and the Bear Hug groups helped the Bear culture to spread far and fast?

MICHAEL: Sure, the bulletin boards did, but the magazines started it. And kept it going with products and videos and on and on. It became marketing, like everything else in U.S. culture.

RON: How do you feel about the emerging under-40 Bear groups calling themselves Gen-X Bears?

MICHAEL: Gen-X Bears are another spin-off, another market.

DAVID: It is very important that they are not locked off by age groups. One of the most marvelous parts of the *Loon* books was their celebration of intergenerational sex. What I think is very harmful in contemporary gay society is the separation of age groups. Gay bars are now much more age differentiated than they were when I was coming out. Too much of American society is about finding a niche for yourself, a small place where you can feel safe, a gated community. Gay life follows that path too, and one would hope that Bear culture, which had resisted this, would not fall under the spell of having different age groups.

MICHAEL: NAMBLA [North American Man-Boy Love Association] Bears? ;-)

DAVID: NAMBLA is about questions of the age of consent. I don't mean to raise that issue here. But I think it is not a good thing when 20-year-olds know only other 20-year-olds, that 40-year-olds have no contact with men younger and older.

MICHAEL: I agree. In my life I've always had friends who were much older and much younger. And David, you're right, this is more of an American problem than a gay one. I suspect that gay life is far more age-stratified than straight life. But I want to point out that in the current political atmosphere the praise of intergenerational sex in the *Loon* books looks very suspect. Let's face it, several of Oscar Wilde's tricks and part-time boyfriends were under the age of 17. If Wilde lived now and was arrested, he would not be a gay martyr but would be condemned as a boy lover, a pedophile, and a sexual predator. Part of the elusive myth of freedom that the *Loon* books promote also deals with the freedom of young people to have sex with older people—something that we as a community find increasingly difficult to discuss.

RON: As David touched on earlier, there has been some discussion on the topic of women as Bears—primarily lesbians, I believe—who self-identify as Bears, relating to other perceived qualities of bears, such as nurturance and protection of loved ones.

MICHAEL: I wonder how many. This seems totally idiosyncratic with little resonance for most women.

DAVID: I'm in no position to speak about "most women," but I do sense greater visibility of women who are crossing gender lines, queering the boundaries of maleness, and my impression is that "Bearness" might have a particular appeal for such women. I would welcome it. The presence of women in Bear groups might be helpful, but I think it would be resisted by the men. But these women are strong, and they are likely to outlast the resistance of the men.

MICHAEL: Bear groups seem to be based on sexual cruising and flirting. Why would women help the group?

RON: Besides, there's resistance to non-Bear types—let alone women of any sort—within Bear groups.

DAVID: Because they might break down the cliquishness and insularity of Bearclubs. Besides, when there have been women at bars at the same time as Bears are gathering, I haven't noticed any diminution of the cruising or even of sex. My impression is that the women who go to such bars (and admittedly the number is small) are ones that, rather than discourage cruising between men, enjoy the greater sexual freedom they find there.

MICHAEL: This brings up the question: what do Bears really have in common except an attraction to one another and the desire to be in a group of like-minded and like-bodied people? Which is not a necessarily bad thing—but what do they have in common?

RON: Perhaps they share the same class or at least the same class values—or the illusion of shared class values?

MICHAEL: Do you mean class as in economic class? I find that hard to believe. And if you are implying that class value—and I am not sure what that means in the context of the U.S. and its history and economy—are things like not dressing or acting middle-class, that strikes me as, well, superficial, and sort of insulting to working-class men who have to dress that way because they don't have enough money to dress up. I still wonder what Bears have in common except a body type. Which again is a fine thing to have in common. But it seems Bearclubs are like restricted country clubs: No thin people need apply?

RON: But Bears don't necessarily have a common body type. Although I'm trim, I've never felt out of place in a Bear space—at least not because of my body type. Certainly I've never gone to a Bear event or a Bear space and felt, Oh, I'm not fat enough or hairy enough. In contrast with predominant media images and dance-bar attitudes, you will find people in the Bear groups who are thin and clean-shaven and smooth-bodied—just not usually with all of those characteristics.

DAVID: We must distinguish between Bear groups as they are and how they might be. I would like to see Bears as a force of resistance against the fashion industry, the style industry, and other types of classist ways of separating people. It would be nice to find in the gay world a group whose aim was inclusion between and among genders. I think that would be the attraction for women to join Bear groups, and it might be a source of attraction for men.

MICHAEL: Sorry to be cynical, but good luck. If we have seen anything it has been a desire for Bears to become fashionable. What else does *Bear* magazine promote?

DAVID: I hardly think that anyone would call *Bear* magazine fashionable, although it could be said to celebrate a certain style. It doesn't have the circulation of *Out* or *The Advocate*, which are clearly small mass-market journals.

MICHAEL: Of course, *Bear* magazine is not fashionable in the sense that Calvin Klein is fashionable, but it is trying to celebrate, promote, and market a style and a look. It exists—and presumably makes money—by selling that look. If Calvin Klein or Ralph Lauren started a Bear line next season—not an impossible thought in an age when the economics of the industry cause fashions to change so quickly—Bears would be in.

RON: There has been some mobilization around AIDS, but otherwise Bears are hardly political creatures.

MICHAEL: I do think that there is a patina of anticlass bias in Bear culture, but this is actually a fantasy of working-class life. It's an idealization that implies that the working class is more masculine and natural than those of lesser influence and wealth and looks. But this is a fantasy, and one that is totally at odds with real people's real lives.

RON: Unfortunately, Bearclubs tend to further stratify their members into inner circles—the A-Bears—and the rest of the group. Bear contests idealize pretty-boy Bears—sometimes called glamour Bears—over the rest of the unfortunate plain-Jane Bears. It's the same old looksism all over again.

MICHAEL: My point exactly. Bear culture, like all socially constructed cultures based on certain identifiable attributes, becomes hierarchical.

DAVID: Yes, Bears are becoming more and more like everyone else. They are the sweater queens of the '90s, but instead of wearing their angora over their bodies, the fur is applied directly to the skin.

RON: Very good. Final comments?

MICHAEL: I am glad that in this increasingly mandated world of sexual and body conformity, Bears have created a new and approved way for gay men to look. The point, it seems to be, is to create endless ways for people to look and to make sure that no matter how someone looks, they are not ostracized, ignored, or discriminated against.

DAVID: Bear life, like gay life in general, is part of American culture, not separate from it. And it has the same limitations and problems as American culture. Insofar as Bears have become exclusive and hierarchical, it is because American culture is. Bear culture denies this because America denies its classist base. I think Michael and I are in virtual agreement.

Chapter 4
Bear Essentials: Bear Spirit in Community
~ A Discussion With Al Cotton,
Alex Damman, and Jim Mitulski ~

AL COTTON is an Alabama native who moved to Atlanta in 1983. He holds a BA in English and history from Huntington College in Montgomery, Alabama, and a Masters in English from Vanderbilt University. He has helped to start four gay community publications in Atlanta: He was founding editor of *Visionary: The Newsletter of Gay Spirit Visions* and founding co-editor of the *Amethyst* literary journal. He has written a general interest column and a book review column for *Southern Voice*. His work has also appeared in *White Crane Journal* and the *Gay & Lesbian Review*. He was a member of the Gay Spirit Visions planning committee for eight years and is currently Atlanta's Body Electric coordinator. He has been a practitioner of Shambhala Training meditation since 1995.

When ALEX DAMMAN became an ovo-lacto vegetarian at age 11, he just knew that his life was destined to be a series of conflicts with the dominant culture. This has involved living in Kansas, Missouri, New Jersey, Virginia, Maryland, North Carolina, and Illinois; helping to found the intentional community Acorn in Cuckoo, Virginia; getting degrees in math, computer science, and landscape design; being fascinated by plants and permaculture; making a living by working for telecommunications and utility companies; buying a farm for a custom home and long-range plant projects; and riding his BMW motorcycle. For the last 10 years he has attended Faerie gatherings with the circles at Short

Mountain Sanctuary, Tennessee; the New York circle; Faerie Camp Destiny, Vermont; and Circle Star, California, not to mention Rainbow Family Tribe national gatherings and others. He currently works as a computer consultant in Peoria, Illinois, and is extremely available.

Rev. JIM MITULSKI has been pastor of Metropolitan Community Church of San Francisco since 1986. In January 1998 the congregation voted to make him Senior Pastor. Before MCC San Francisco, he was associate pastor of the MCC in New York City's Greenwich Village. Rev. Mitulski has been an activist for gay and lesbian civil rights and for the right to marry. He attracted national attention in August 1996 while distributing medical marijuana at MCC/San Francisco to people with AIDS and other illnesses. Jim has also been interviewed extensively about his remarkable success with the new protease inhibitor treatments for AIDS. He has a bachelor's degree from Columbia University, a master of divinity degree from Pacific School of Religion in Berkeley, California, and was a Merrill Fellow at the Harvard Divinity School in Cambridge, Massachusetts. He is currently a doctoral student at San Francisco Theological Seminary.

The Old Testament (*Proverbs* 18:14) offers a concise appreciation of the preeminence of self-esteem among virtues: "The spirit of a man will sustain his infirmity; but a wounded spirit who can bear?" The double-entendre aside, this passage speaks volumes about men in the Bear community, many whose spirits have been wounded or broken by homophobia and body fascism.

If a man has proper self-esteem devoid of egoism—that is, if he feels good about his essential nature—then he will most likely feel positively about his self-image, regardless of what body type he may be: hairy, hefty, or even unhandsome. Conversely, if a man doubts his innate self-worth because of negative family, cultural, religious, or societal messages, no amount of money, power, status, sex, or food will fill the hole of that bottomless pit of the soul.

Repeatedly in my encounters and interviews with Bears from around the world, men who were, in my opinion, attractive and desirable, confessed to a lack of self-esteem. At IBR 2000 I attended an affinity group led by Craig Byrnes on Bear Self-esteem. The participants, one by one, spoke of the terrible disparagement they suffered at the hands of their tormentors—from their early youth until the present day—based on their looks. Hearing these men's experiences confirmed my intuition that many, if not most, Bears have rarely, if ever, had their basic natures affirmed in a positive, holistic, unconditional manner—until they came into contact with the Bear community of men.

My experience in Craig's workshop also clearly demonstrated to me the need for open discussion of such issues in the Bear community. Bears are in need of healing on many levels—personal, community, and cultural—and I hope that conversations, such as Bear Self-esteem and the online discussion recorded here, serve as chicken soup (or whatever the Bearish equivalent may be) for the wounded Bear soul.

RON: First, let's get a little background. Jim, how and when did you first learn about Bears?

JIM: I think sometime during the height of the AIDS years here—maybe early '90s, or even before. The Bear culture seemed a permutation of the leather community, centered on the Lone Star, principally. And it was a distinct outgrowth of the AIDS years—a curious affirmation of the male body during a period when our bodies were changing. "Bear" was in some quarters a moniker that was greeted with some derision. At times, both younger guys as well as peers my age described the Bear scene as an excuse for not conforming to the "right" image.

AL: As for me, I'm fairly certain my connection was through *Bear* magazine. I know I have issue number 10 or 12 at home, so that would be a clue as to when [1989-90]. When I first connected with the magazine, I got a sense that these guys in the magazine looked like guys I might actually see in a bar—not the buffed and pumped porn stars that were completely unattainable. I didn't have words for it then, but in retrospect it feels as if we as gay men were shifting from looking for an erotic ideal to eroticizing things that were attainable—yet still derided.

RON: Still very much scorned, yes.

JIM: Al, you may feel that Bear culture is not porn-driven or depicted, but the first Bear porn from Brush Creek I saw changed porn for me from depiction of fantasy to that of reality.

AL: It certainly started out that way, although I'm not sure it hasn't been corrupted of its reality element.

RON: The whole shtick of early *Bear* magazine images was about amateur, non-professional models—real men. Alex, how did "Bear" first enter your awareness?

ALEX: I became aware of Bears at some point in the late 1980s because it overlapped my own tastes fairly well. I joined New England Bears in 1993. I went to a winter run in Provincetown. I realized that some people are heavily into Beardom as their personal culture.

AL: I've seen it go from being an identification to an obsession pretty quickly.

RON: Perhaps that speaks to how desperately some Bear-type men long to find a community to belong to.

AL: Yes, to come out and still be rejected because of your body type can be incredibly devastating.

ALEX: I tend to just be—to discover myself and see what community is out there.

RON: Jim, do you associate with the Bear community in San Francisco at all?

JIM: I think the Bear community might possibly be more assimilated here. There are Bear bars, Bear coffee shops, and even Bear gyms—we are everywhere. Although I don't belong to a Bearclub, I do know lots of Bears, and I've been to Bearsex parties, some of which were quite large.

AL: I never joined a Bearclub. I was in a leather club once, and vowed never again to vote on anyone's bylaws.

RON: Ugh, I agree, Al. Nothing makes me feel less sexy than bylaws, although I do enjoy the camaraderie of the clubs otherwise.

AL: Jim, I think you are using "corrupted" and "assimilated" to mean something similar.

JIM: Perhaps I romanticize, but I think there's something unbearlike in overly structured ways of affiliating—are Bears more non-conformist, more resistant to the culture of clubs and organizations?

ALEX: Every group has its share of people who are only comfortable with a high degree of control.

AL: Well, Bears are not pack animals, so that would make some archetypal sense, I think. *G*

RON: Good point, Al. Four-legged bears tend to hang in smaller kinship groups.

JIM: It is interesting to go to large dance parties (1,000-plus guys, many partying) and observe how Bears congregate in one area and other types elsewhere. It's kind of thrilling to be in that arena, which typically glorifies a different body type, to be dancing shirtless with a bunch of other Bears.

ALEX: It's something like people who ask on the Bears Mailing List, "Who here knits?" I happen to, but feel plenty splintered already.

AL: I was rather amazed to see a "Bear coffeehouse" in San Francisco. Talk about honing in on a very fine point—that level of specialization isn't available in many places.

RON: Bears perhaps have become specialized in the same way the rest of American cultures have, especially GLBTQ cultures. Specialized may in this case mean the same as corrupted or assimilated.

AL: Yeah, we're sort of fencing in an elusive concept with these words.

RON: I'd like us to look at how Bears manifest gay masculinity, especially in terms of community. Would any of you agree to the idea of there seeming to be a certain essence of Beardom?

JIM: Essence of Beardom—my favorite scent! Sweat, the natural male body smell.

RON: *Bear* magazine stated it initially as "Masculinity without the trappings," although it may not engender those same ideals now. Is there something more to Beardom than this, some essence that we might call "Bear spirit"?

JIM: "Trappings" is a great multivalent word to use with Bears—what Bear likes to be trapped in a particular construction of masculinity?

AL: I always saw that slogan as a slam at the sort of elaborate masculinity or effeminate masculinity of other people—those were the traps, I thought.

RON: Perhaps Bearness itself is the essential substance—some sort of distilled masculinity.

ALEX: I do think that the foremost reason people get involved with Bears is personal horniness. What they find when they get there is people who have had similar experiences of rejection and puzzlement at what is worshipped by gay men.

AL: I wonder if Bear hasn't created just another trap.

ALEX: Trappings such as beads can be quite fetching.

AL: *LOL*

JIM: We don't simply like Bears, though, because we have been rejected by other norms—I like Bears because of how they look, taste, feel, and act.

AL: It's really hard to define masculinity in a particular way, and then not come to objectify that definition.

RON: That reminds me of an Eastern spiritual concept of "golden handcuffs"—giving up one limited identification just to step into another. Is anything special about being a Bear that might mean greater freedom, sexually or in any other way?

AL: I'm not so Buddhist that I can give up personal identifications, but there's a point where they do limit you in ways that I don't find healthy.

JIM: Affirming Bear looks has a spiritual dimension—all men, not just certain types, are made "in the image and likeness of god," to quote *Genesis*—Bearness is an aspect of divinity.

RON: Can you describe or define that aspect of divinity, Jim?

JIM: Bear bodies—large, hairy, or simply unadorned—are the least distant from how we are created. In other words, divinity is real humanity.

AL: I think "Bear" as a definition only works as a definition in opposition to a dominant gay culture that excludes Bears. For example, when I explain it to someone unfamiliar with the concept, I always have to give the cultural context in which the need for Bearness arose.

JIM: I don't entirely agree, Al. Bearness is not a reaction; constructions of masculinity are reactions. Bear is the origin, how men really are, uncorrupt and unaltered. Bearness represents a return to ourselves, not an alternative identity.

AL: But it does seem to me that Bears would not have arisen if there hadn't been body-type discrimination in the gay community at large.

RON: That's the age-old riddle: Which came first, the chicken or the Bear? Seriously, though, I'd like to get back to the idea of archetypal bear qualities. Are there archetypal or symbolic aspects of four-legged bears that you identify with?

AL: A grounded, down-to-earthness would be my main bear identifier.

ALEX: The facial hair aspect of Bears is vital. I am also attracted to guys who have unusually long or short head hair or other interesting hair changes such as a balding or shaved head.

JIM: This may mark me as a Bear essentialist—but I think Bear identity is inevitable: The more that we as men learn to love ourselves, the more Bearlike we become.

AL: *LOL* The Bear Essentials!

RON: Well, what about less obvious physical characteristics beyond facial and body hair and girth?

ALEX: I consider Bears in the process of discovery of their natures, tuning in to what is inside us.

AL: Well, there are lots of guys who have beards who don't have what I would consider a Bear personality at all.

RON: True, but for some of us, there's something far deeper, more soulful, to our Bearness than being just another furry face. Might that deeper meaning relate to the four-legged types? What I mean is qualities such as fierce protection of one's charges, the regularity of seasonal cycles, being top-feeders, resourcefulness in Nature, and the like.

JIM: For example: hibernation is a spiritual concept, an intentional downtime in which we prepare for a period of growth, activity, and creativity.

ALEX: Having a totem animal (or favorite cartoon character or pro wrestler) remains a useful concept. I am plenty lumbering enough and should probably seek otters!

AL: Alex, I appreciate you desolemnizing the concept of totem animals very much.

ALEX: Seeking out qualities that you want to adopt is a good process. It means that you are tuning in to something larger than your human existence.

JIM: Is there not also an outlaw character, a ferocity, a passionate quality which in its negative manifestation can be antisocial? Also, big appetites, more than just for food. Appetite is a metaphor for desiring larger-than-life experience.

RON: Such as big sexual appetites.

JIM: A gruff exterior. Are Bears less emotionally expressive than some other men? Or are we more expressive—louder, if you will? Also, Bears socialize in bearlike habitats—outdoors or in bars or sex club venues that resemble caves. Bears go to the mountains, not the seashore (someone's Provincetown experience notwithstanding).

AL: I don't take "Bearness" that far because I don't think gay men are around actual bears enough to be familiar with their characteristics. It's not much more than a cartoon, to echo Alex's joke.

RON: Good point, Al. Most Bears don't consciously take it that far. But I wonder if part of the attraction to Bears or Bearness might consist of unconscious connections to such archetypal qualities.

AL: Personally, I do identify with the hibernating quality of bears, but I don't think that correlates with what gay men define as Bears.

ALEX: There could have been any icon, say, the peanut (the plant is actually hairy, I believe), and we would have all rallied 'round.

RON: Peanut Pride! Do you think, perhaps, that identifying with Bears has helped some men to get in touch with that totemic part of themselves?

AL: Well, perhaps some, but for most, the farthest it goes is into T-shirt purchases, I think!

RON: So are Bears just hairy urban queers? Or is there something more?

AL: Well, at least that much we can agree on!

JIM: So reductionist! Possibly true, but I hate to concede that.

ALEX: I don't think of Beardom solely as an urban phenomenon.

RON: Alex, I'd be interested in hearing how you compare the spiritual fiber of Bears to that of the Radical Faeries.

ALEX: Clearly the spiritual aspect of Radical Faeries is more explicit and is expressed through ritual that you can participate in. As I said, Bears are in search of their true natural identities, and Faeries are also in search of the most charming and amusing expression of their natures.

AL: I don't know many Bears who think of themselves as being in search of their true identity. I think, when they find the Bear community, they think they've found it. For them, Bear is the end of the search, not the beginning.

ALEX: Humans are always looking, searching, seeking, finding.

JIM: We may be ascribing more intentionality or consciousness to Bear culture than is sometimes present.

RON: Bears (the four-legged kind) are the greatest foragers of the forest. Is an interest in spiritual or interior life completely separate from most men's Bearness? Excluding present company, of course.

AL: My online handle is Bear Seeker, and the profile says, "I am a Bear and a seeker, though not always seeking Bears." I don't think Bears are any more or less likely than anyone else to seek whatever it is that we are seeking.

ALEX: I feel that interior life is separate from Beardom, which is largely a social connection phenomenon.

RON: But aren't the Radical Faeries a social phenomenon?

ALEX: Faeries probably exist on more levels, since there is definitely a tribal identity, which is a stronger modus operandi than Bears meeting each other socially.

AL: I still want to go back to the "corrupted-assimilated" point from earlier. I think Bearness, when it started, had a strong component of personal reclaiming of erotic power or sexual connection.

JIM: A Bear metaphysics.

AL: Almost every identity starts from a place of authenticity, and then becomes corrupted by the way our media-driven and capitalist culture turns it into a niche that it can market. Bearness started as an authentic response to a culture that objectified and idealized one type of gay person. But it's almost inevitable that if you come up with another choice, it will get objectified too. Now you can buy Bear porn that objectifies us just as much as regular porn or gay porn objectifies its subject.

In that sense (which is very Buddhist at its root), any identity moves away from being an authentic expression toward being a niche version of the same stereotype-archetype that you started with. That's why I feel objectified, sometimes, when people go crazy over the hair on my back, just as much as women do when men ogle their breasts.

RON: Let's refocus now on how Bears form community and how those communities compare with other gay subcultures.

JIM: The impulse to form community rather than living solely or in pairs in isolation, is intrinsically spiritual. Bears are often seeking more than a husband, and Bear marriage is sometimes more complex than some forms of gay marriage. Bear marriages seem more like multiple-branched families.

ALEX: Yes, that is a good point. That is a very striking and wonderful way of putting it, but these processes have a point of view centered on the self, different from a more universal cosmology that people's spiritual lives usually try to approach.

RON: Do Bears form community in unique ways?

AL: I don't know of any unique ways. There are bars, runs, relationships. They use much the same patterns that leather groups use, so I wouldn't call it unique, though it may be unique to those two subcultures.

ALEX: I think that being a Bear helps to filter down the crush of humanity so that you can have constraints in choosing your circle of friends.

JIM: I wonder if Bear men are gender separatists, not out of misogyny but out of a preference to socialize with other men. This doesn't unfortunately translate into the dictum that Bear men are less sexist, but

I think it's a less cogendered communal existence.

AL: One does see women in the leather community, though it seems very few actually try to infiltrate the Bear world. Since masculinity is the focus, it sort of defines women out of the picture.

ALEX: Yes, I agree.

JIM: Bear community also has a healing dimension, not just from the exclusions we experience as adults in the gay community, but also as a corrective to childhood or adolescent exclusions.

AL: The great charge I got was from being among a group of men who define my body type as being attractive. I didn't feel like there was only one person in the bar that I was attracted to, and yet wonder if my body type disqualified him from being interested in me.

ALEX: I agree that Bears are going to individually find their own favorite aspects of being involved in Bear community.

JIM: It's tempting to question whether there is a Bear identity. The more we deconstruct it, the more I wonder if it is so different from the experience of other gay men. Still, there is something unmistakable about it.

RON: Yes, Jim, exactly as Al was describing his experience of the great charge. That experience has got to be greater than a mere ego-rush at being objectified. I think most of the Bear-identified men I know have had that same feeling. So perhaps in the final analysis, we're better off talking about "the Bear experience," rather than "Bear identity."

AL: I like that much better.

ALEX: That is much more meaningful to me.

JIM: I am uncomfortable with the notion of Bear ontology, in philosophical terms. However, we did all arrive in the Bear community for reasons, many of them shared. For me, whether this is urban (San Franciscan) or common, it is inextricably linked to the HIV experience in addition to the other experiences we've referenced.

AL: Even if "Bear identity" stands for very little, the Bear experience still happens on a regular basis. When it does, it transforms the sexual self-image of hairy, stocky guys who have come to believe that they are erotically untouchable by the rest of their community and who come to discover, almost miraculously, that they're not. It's in each man's Bear experience where the magic still happens.

PART TWO

BEAR HISTORY AND EVOLUTION

Chapter 5
The Birth of Girth & Mirth
~ An Interview With Reed Wilgoren ~

More than a decade before Bears and grizzlies and cubs were even a twinkle in some gay men's eyes, there was Girth & Mirth, the now-international organization for big men and their admirers. Yet even before that, one such big man, REED WILGOREN, came out into gay life the year after he graduated high school in Boston in 1969, the same year as the Stonewall Revolution.

Reed quickly became involved with the informal network of chubbies and chasers on the East Coast. When he moved to the San Francisco Bay area in the mid '70s, he was at the forefront of the network that was to become the first Girth & Mirth group there. When Reed later returned to Boston, he also founded Girth & Mirth of New England.

Following a lead from Les Wright, I contacted Reed and we made arrangements for an interview at his home north of Boston. Meanwhile, I contacted some of Reed's cohorts from the early San Francisco Girth & Mirth days for additional background. When Reed and I finally met to talk about those pioneering days, I was delighted to discover that Reed is not only a handsome and gentle fellow but also an articulate and funny storyteller.

I feel it's important that self-identified Bears understand there's a context in which the Bear subculture they enjoy today—the social clubs, the events, and such—had its source, not just in chubby and chaser groups, but in the early gay liberation movement. Part of these gay pioneers' initial work with Girth & Mirth was not simply to socialize; it was part of a whole culture of liberationist activity. Girth & Mirth was active before any mainstream fat-acceptance groups; in fact, I should point out that the groundbreaking book, *Fat Is a Feminist Issue*, didn't come out until 1978, two years after the founding of Girth & Mirth.

RON: First of all, where did you grow up and go to school?

REED: I grew up in the Allston-Brighton area [of Boston], and graduated Brighton High. Then I lived in the Brighton area well into the '60s. I came out into gay life in 1969, the year after I graduated high school, probably at 18 or 19 years old, and mostly lived on my own ever since. Then I worked and went to school in the Boston area until I moved to California.

RON: What was gay Boston like then? What was your main venue for meeting folks?

REED: People, even back in school, always said there were places where gay people hung out. They would say uncomplimentary things like "Oh, that's where the fags hang out." In those days there was a bar called The Punchbowl, which was closed by the time I came out, and two others called The Other Side and Jacques' [both since closed], which were in the Bay Village area of Boston. Those bars [had that reputation], so when I decided to come out and look I went to The Other Side, which was formerly The Punchbowl crowd of people. That was a very eventful evening, to say the least.

RON: [laughs] It must have been, judging from your smile! Was coming out relatively easy for you?

REED: Yes, and no. I knew that this was what I had tendencies to do, although I'd had relationships with women all through school—when I was a junior in high school, I was almost engaged, much to my parents' delight! Then I went the other way, and I decided to come out in 1969. When I went into the bar that night, I encountered a very varied group of people—lesbian women, older and younger gay men, drag queens, transvestites, the whole nine yards.

RON: What was the hard part?

REED: The difficult part was that people were telling me, "You're a good-looking fellow, but you're overweight, you're a big man. That's going to be held against you, coming out in the gay world."

RON: How big were you then?

REED: When I came out, I was perhaps 200-225 pounds. I had a football player–size build. I did in fact play football in high school.

RON: Was it doubly hard being gay and being heavy? It was still very much stigmatized then.

REED: Exactly. It was difficult, not so much because there was shame at my size but because of the reaction I got from other gay people in the bars and community. They considered it a stumbling block. There was always that unspoken feeling, "Oh, well, jeez, you're really nice, and you're really nice looking, but you're so big." Only slim gay men were considered attractive in those days.

My first night out, the first man that I met in the bar was very gay, very out, but also had a cultured side. He was a schoolteacher, and he was determined to show me around. He said, "If you want to put yourself in my hands for the evening, I'll show you the ropes." So we went all around Bay Village. We went from The Other Side to Jacques' to see a drag show, and from there we went to...oh, the other bar that just closed down [in 1998]...

RON: Napoleon's?

REED: Napoleon's. It was very relaxing and clean, with a group of people definitely varied in age and size. Instantly I felt more comfortable there. Then from there we went on sort of a driving tour around Boston. This fellow, Jim, showed me the cruising areas, the other bars, where to go, where not to go...

RON: Like the Fens...

REED: The Fens, and the Combat Zone—we went to some bars down there. He showed me an area that was referred to as "Vaseline Corner" [also called "Vaseline Alley"]. That was the corner where you went after the bars closed if you were really desperately looking for something, and hung around. People would drive by and see if you were what they were looking for for the evening, and you'd see if they were what you were looking for.

RON: Did you score that first night?

REED: No.

RON: You were just...shopping?

REED: Shopping, yes. So, Jim spent the rest of the evening with me until he drove me home. I considered myself fortunate to meet somebody as kind, decent, and trustworthy as him to hang out with my first night in gay life in Boston. My experience wasn't bad because of him.

However, he said negative things about my size, such as that it would be difficult as a big man to meet people.

RON: Did you take that message to heart—

REED: Somewhat—

RON: Or were you able to just let it go?

REED: Probably, to some extent. I didn't think much of it.

REED: At The Other Side, there was a piano player and singer, Ellie Boswell, who sang blues and all kinds of music. She was a big black woman, and she told me, "Some night, somebody will come in here and you will be the one that they are looking for, and everything you think about your size and what you look like will mean nothing. I hope I'm here when it happens." I replied, "Ellie, you're an eternal optimist. I'm taking your word that this will happen." And about three weeks later, it did happen—right at her piano!

RON: Great! Please tell me about that. You were at the bar, near Ellie at the piano?

REED: Yes, this man walked in the door, turned his head, and spotted me, and it was like somebody discovering cheesecake for the first time. And he looked at me with every bit as much desire.

RON: Discovering cheesecake—I love that analogy!

REED: He wasn't too hard to look at himself. He was very well dressed, very handsome. When I was younger, I hoped in my heart of hearts that I would find somebody older than myself, and Bob was certainly that. He walked over to me, offered to buy me a drink, chatted with me for half an hour or so, and then proceeded to unbutton my shirt, maybe halfway down. Ellie, the piano player, was watching all of this, and making little subtle eyes at me in the background, and then launched into one of her blues songs which she had composed herself, which had a lot of gay innuendoes. The song was entitled "Hot Nuts," and they *were* very hot for both Bob and me at that point.

RON: She played that song just for you.

REED: Yes. Being a big gay man and being young and inexperienced, I never in my life had anybody come after me like that. I discovered what a chubby chaser was, and how that would affect my life.

Well, it was a very eventful night because this man, Bob, invited me to go with him to Napoleon's, to hook up with some other friends of his. I had no idea that I was about to enter the most notorious circle of chubby chasers. In the old days, chubby chasers existed all over the country.

This was pre–Girth & Mirth, pre-Bear. This was a telephone and mail network of chubbies and chasers, and this fellow Bob and the people he introduced to me in the other bar were the key players on the East Coast. And I was the innocent young big guy about to be devoured, literally, in their midst.

RON: They used that phrase, "chubby chaser," themselves?

REED: Yes, that was the term of that era, and there were bars in all major cities—New York, San Francisco, Los Angeles, and other places—that were known to be chubby and chubby chaser bars per se.

RON: Was it then a particularly gay term, or something that women and straights would have used?

REED: It has spilled over into those groups now, but back then it was pretty much considered a gay term for big men and the guys who like them.

RON: So, this informal network of big gay men preceded not only the Bears but also the entire fat-acceptance movement in America. Please continue now.

REED: When I walked into Napoleon's with Bob that night, he introduced me to his friends, and we proceeded to go to the upstairs bar, which was what we then called a "conversational bar"—very low-key music, a place to meet people in a very informal setting. As we began going up the steps, Bob walking in front of me, another man whom I didn't know at all, who'd been sort of lurking in the shadows, was following me and feeling me up! This man was destined to become my first lover. [*Both laugh*]

RON: Very interesting! And his name?

REED: His name is Harvey; he's now living in the San Francisco Bay area. I came into his life at a very precarious time: His gay life was very much closeted, and I was so young. It was all very exciting for me, but he had to be very wary of what we were doing. And I was scared myself. I'd never been alone with a man before that evening, and it seemed to be all happening to me at once. At one point, Harvey was on one side of me and Bob was on the other, and they were both running their hands all over my body from my head all the way below my waist down to my knees and back up again. I felt just like the expression, "I didn't know whether to shit or go blind."

RON: Stonewall hadn't even happened or had just happened months before.

REED: No, none of that. And then they introduced me to the rest of the crowd, and they consisted of Bob's lover, Taylor Reed—an actor and singer on Broadway from the [entertainer] Jimmy Coco era who has since passed away (as has Bob)—and a few other people. So they invited me to go back to their hotel room. That was a whole other part of the evening.

RON: I see. [*Laughs*]

REED: They took me to a hotel called The Avery right in the middle of the Combat Zone, where you could meet anyone from a businessman to a transvestite to a prostitute and everything in between. They had very clean, decent rooms where you could have an inexpensive fling. So they took me to their room, and I had no idea what was in mind, but they knew. They proceeded to orchestrate this orgy in the room.

RON: With just the three of you? Or with more?

REED: There were five of us: Bob, who had initially met me at The Other Side; Harvey, who was to become my first lover; Bob's lover; and another friend. They were all in the room, wanting me in their respective ways, or rather wanting to have their way with me, as it were. I made it very clear that that wasn't going to happen but I was still curious enough to engage in part of the evening, doing what I felt comfortable doing. When I was no longer comfortable, then I asked to leave, and Harvey drove me home, but I didn't let him take me right to my house. I had him drop me off a block away at a strange house because I didn't want him to know where I lived with my parents.

RON: I don't think it was an uncommon gambit in those days, dropping off a block away. I remember doing the same thing in college.

REED: But I was never the same after that evening.

RON: It's amazing that, at least so far, you had such a happy story. You were affirmed very early in the coming-out process.

REED: Yes. Well, Harvey and I became quite involved, spending all of our free time together—vacations, weekends away to Provincetown, Vermont, New York City. We had a very illicit romance for maybe four years. And I was growing as a gay man and a big man through my experiences with him along the road. Eventually I realized that he wasn't ready to have a lover and that it was time to move on to something else in my life. He said, "If things don't work out between us, I hope that we'll remain friends. And I'll also give you other introductions to other chubby chasers and other people I know on the West Coast, if that's what you're looking for."

RON: In the meantime, though, you had your entrée into this world pretty much all the way up the Eastern Seaboard.

REED: Yes. And they were a pretty affluent group of people.

[Reed's first lover, Harvey, later introduced him to "one of the most notorious chubby chasers in the country," Tony diGenova, who invited Reed to stay with him in his posh Oakland house. So, in the early '70s, Reed quit his job in Boston and moved to Oakland, where eventually he met his next lover, Bob.]

RON: So, what was your life like then?

REED: I was unemployed, young—19 to 20 years old—big, and good-looking to whomever was looking for a big young man at that time. And as far as chubby chasers were concerned, during that period in San Francisco, the world was my oyster. Ha! I never realized that I would meet so many significant people for friendship, fun, and sex, all of which would then also evolve into a picture-perfect relationship with my lover Bob (who since then passed away from a heart condition), and everything else that went along with it, from 1971 to '85 and the coming of AIDS....

RON: When did you move in with Bob?

REED: In 1973.

RON: And you were together for six years.

REED: Yes. A couple of years after I met Bob, Girth & Mirth came about. Charlie Brown, the founder of the group, put an ad in a gay newspaper eliciting interest in a big men's organization.

RON: I spoke with Charlie on the phone, actually. By his telling of the incident, it was in February 1976 that he took out an ad in the *Berkeley Barb*. He described it to me: He had gone in there with a friend, to help his friend place an ad, and on kind of a joke, or dare, Charlie decided to place an ad himself. He titled his ad "Chubbies and Chasers, Unite!" And he called it a "clarion call."

REED: And clarion it was. It was like, "Telephone, tell a friend, tell any chubby chaser and chubby that you know!" This was a Saturday or Sunday morning, and people were still home in their robes and slippers, drinking coffee and reading the morning paper when they got the call. It was like electricity went through everyone, thinking, *Finally! It's happened!*

RON: So everyone was calling everybody else, asking, "Have you heard? Have you heard about this?"

REED: It was just amazing! What excitement it stirred up in all of us in the Bay area at that moment!

RON: You jammed the lines of area code 415, right?

REED: And the person who had called me had already called Charlie Brown and his lover and spoken to them, and everyone was just brimming over with enthusiasm and anticipation as to what we were going to do with this. And within a very short time, we organized our very first meeting in San Francisco. The core group of people that showed up was already friends and had been in this network of chubbies and chasers, pre–Charlie Brown, but of course, had Charlie not put this ad out, we never would have been. So he was definitely in the forefront of Girth & Mirth.

RON: There was already a network there, but it was—

REED: Loosely organized.

RON: Yes, an informal network. And the ad served to give it some cohesion. Charlie said to me, "I get credited far more than I should."

REED: He's still a very modest man, and very boyish in his own right, although he's now in his late 40s. He's still very shy and doesn't give himself enough credit for what he did to change the course of events for big men and, eventually, Bears.

RON: So, please continue with your story from there.

REED: Well, Bob and I went to the first meeting and were amazed at how many of our own friends showed up that night. As we looked around the room, we realized that, other than Charlie and his lover, we knew almost everybody there. We had a very interesting evening indeed, exchanging ideas, discussing where we wanted to go. We collected enough money that night just to give the bar owner something for his trouble. We also did come up with the name Girth & Mirth that night.

RON: So, aside from the connotation of the words *mirth* and *gay*, you had Santa Claus for an archetype?

REED: Exactly. Big and jolly and bearded as well. A segue to Bears, actually.

RON: How did the organization become formalized? Did you appoint officers, and a council, and have regular meetings and the like?

REED: Yes, we set up officers, and planned meetings in people's homes, and picnics and outings. About a year or two after we organized, we decided to participate in the first real Gay Day parade in San Francisco.

RON: Was that the same year—1976?

REED: Yeah, right around then, May or June of '76. I'd bought a '64 Ford Galaxy convertible and was restoring it when they asked Bob and I if we'd enter my car as the Girth & Mirth float. I would be the chubby and Bob would be the chubby chaser, sitting up on the back of the convertible, and Tony diGenova would be the driver, and his then-lover was the passenger.

I did not know what to expect, but when we pulled out into the mainstream of the parade onto Market Street, it seemed like, for that moment in my life, the whole world was gay, and we were an incredibly significant part of it all. We had no idea how it was going to change all of our lives as big men and eventually as Bears. It was truly amazing how well we were accepted and encouraged to be there at that moment! We were in tears, and we were smiling, we were laughing, crying, all through the whole parade. It was a very moving experience—and still feels so, even to talk about it at this moment...

RON: I can tell.

REED: The following year we actually made a real statement and had an information booth set up to disseminate written information because we already had a newsletter organized by '77.

RON: Great. So did the group then expand exponentially?

REED: Well, we had an ongoing ad running in the *Berkeley Barb*, and the gay weekly newspaper *Bay Area Reporter* listed us as a viable group along with the meeting places and times, which always varied. We started off at just one bar, but then, over the years, met in many different places, other bars, churches, meeting halls, and various places in the city. Finding a meeting place there that was affordable and accepting of our group was not easy in those days. There were no formally organized gay and lesbian centers or anything like that. We had to fend for ourselves. But eventually we were more financially viable and could afford a better meeting place, and our activities became more organized.

RON: Did you and the other San Francisco men contact your friends back east in New York when your group was formed?

REED: Oh, definitely! It spread like wildfire all across the country, through this already established network, as I said, of people, mostly friends, who were chubbies and chubby chasers.

RON: I'd like to add another voice to the oral history here, if I may, from the Girth & Mirth New York Web site [www.gandmny.com]:

"In the mid 1970's there was an unauthorized list of big men and their admirers that was being circulated throughout the U.S. Used solely for contact it was a list some of us found ourselves embarrassed, and pissed off, to have been included on. This list, however, was the primary source with which the eventual founders contacted people who lived in the New York tristate area to inquire if there might be an interest in participating in the formation of a club. They also networked with their own private contacts, using the little black books of friends and acquaintances. Three of these founders, Ernie Harff, Ed Plunkett, and Ben Schack, are still active members of G&M New York."

REED: Ernie Harff just passed away a week or two ago [November 1999]. The other two people are still involved and living.... The next group to come about was the New York group.

RON: Right, which, according to their Web site, started up in June 1978.

REED: There was a solid core group of chubbies and chasers already in place in New York, just waiting for something like this to happen. This group had many more affluent members, much like Tony diGenova in San Francisco, who were icons of the big men's and chubby chasers' world. And because they had money to put into this effort, the New York group became, and still is, one the largest Girth & Mirth contingents around the country.

After New York got going, we decided to have the first Convergence.

RON: The ABC [Affiliated Bigmen's Clubs] Web site says that "[i]n 1986 the first ABC sanctioned Convergence was held in Seattle and in 1988 G&M New York was its host." So, from what I can tell there were several less formal Convergences before this. Is that correct?

REED: Yes. There have been many Convergences held across the country, most of which I try to go to—at least every other one.

RON: The current President of ABC, Aron Ahoronian, told me about EBMC [Europe Big Men's Clubs], which is a very strong association centered out of Belgium.

REED: Yes. They have their event right around Valentine's Day, I believe.

RON: What were the early Convergence gatherings like? Was it basically just "social hour" for 2½ days?

REED: Well, socializing, and a lot of sexual contacts made too. It was a place where big men and their admirers could really let their hair down and be what they wanted to be. The environment allowed big men to feel the elation of all these guys really seeking, loving, and appreciating them for who they were, as well as their size.

RON: They could let out their belts a couple notches, so to speak?

REED: Yes, exactly. The chubby chasers, the admirers of big men, could also be in an environment where they didn't feel like freaks or out of the ordinary. They could also admit to and freely demonstrate their admiration of other big guys in this open environment and know that they had the support and the numbers. Being able to act that free together was a tremendous feeling.

RON: You said that at that time there was a fairly rigid stereotype of what gay men were supposed to look like, and how they acted.

REED: Exactly. The advent of big men was something that definitely needed to happen.

RON: This was before there were "Castro clones" or "leather daddies," right?

REED: Yes. When we became visible, in cities like San Francisco and New York, it wasn't always with open arms. There were many nasty comments made in those days by the "body beautiful" types, and those looking for them, when they saw us en masse. It was like, "What is this?"

RON: Can you give an example?

REED: I remember a group of us walking down Castro at 18th—pretty much in the heart of the Castro—and there was a very popular bar there called The Elephant Walk, and it opened onto the sidewalk. We came to the corner and were looking around, and somebody made a comment, called me a "fat slob" or a "fat pig." And the group heard and acknowledged it but didn't say anything back. Well, I stepped back and found the person in the window within hand's reach, and I said to this person, "Would you like to repeat what you said, to me and to us, again?"

RON: How brave! What happened?

REED: I said to him, "I don't think that was a very complimentary thing to say. Would you like to repeat it again?" He said, "No, I wouldn't," and just quietly shrank down into his chair. I think my girth definitely put a little fear into him as a physical threat, although a physical confrontation was not what I had in mind. Still, that comment definitely needed to be addressed right then.

RON: That's a wonderful story. It was great that you stood up for yourself, yourselves—

REED: As time went on, the more we were seen and thus became a viable group within the City, the more we were accepted and welcomed by other gay men in other clubs. "Oh, wow, here's the Girth & Mirth crowd, let's welcome them."

That was definitely a crossover point, a goal to reach: to not look like the Castro clones, to be able to walk down the street as a big man with your lover, and to hug and kiss and have him run his hands all over your body.

RON: To have as much pride as the next gay man is very important. Anyway, after the New York group got underway, and there were other clubs that formed around the country, how involved were you with the organization of the Bay area and other groups?

REED: Originally I was a Board member and a planning person for the San Francisco group. When I started my own group here in Boston in 1985–1986, I became their ABC rep.

RON: You moved back in 1985?

REED: Yes. I thought that starting Girth & Mirth of New England would be a vehicle to reintroduce myself into gay life in Boston, since being gone for 14 years, I pretty much had to start all over again. It was a great vehicle for making friends and establishing a lifestyle.

RON: How did you go about setting up the group here in Boston?

REED: I contacted somebody at [Boston gay newsweekly] *Bay Windows,* and they did a cover story, complete with a picture of me, that went all the way back from the beginning of Girth & Mirth in San Francisco through my moving here and starting a group here in Boston. They were extremely helpful.

Girth & Mirth of New England was a thriving, viable club from '86 through '91. Our first Convergence in Boston was very successful. Unfortunately, after that event the group headed into a downhill spiral: We lost meeting places and our population of members, and it just whittled down to the point where we couldn't stay in operation any more. But just as we were becoming almost nonexistent, the New England Bears came into existence.

RON: Bill Sanderson's group, which started around 1992.

REED: Yes. The Bear movement had become very visible and viable here and in other cities. A lot of Girth & Mirth of New England members spilled over into the New England Bears. We were happy that, even though we were breaking up, there would be some continuity for us. Even though it wasn't Girth & Mirth, there was a place for us to go. Yet there was quite a big difference between the Bears and Girth & Mirth.

RON: How so?

REED: When the group started, if you sat a big man up next to a Bear, you'd see a difference—in size and age and mindset. Now, of course, it's changed a lot over the years. As the Bear groups progressed, they included other bigger men, older men, men of different nationalities and backgrounds. Still, in the early days they were very typecast.

I belong to several different groups now. When I celebrated my fiftieth in July, I went to some of the Bear meetings in San Francisco. I also went to my first Bear Hug party, which was really neat because people came together in a meeting place that could range from social to sexual and everything in between.

Of course, not everyone in these groups is looking for a particular type, but some of them are very typecasting. Some big men won't think of another big man as attractive; they're only looking for, say, a young jock type, chasers, or Bears. Then there are other big men that, like myself, cross over a wide spectrum. I'm physically attracted to folks anywhere from 25 years old, 150 pounds, all the way up to men in their sixties, maybe 350 to 400 pounds. It depends on who the person is and what they're all about.

RON: Do you feel that the Bear groups largely absorbed Girth & Mirth men?

REED: Somewhat. I found it kind of difficult to cross over into that group, to be honest with you. Coming from my own personal life experience and being very well accepted socially and sexually as a big man, then going into Bear groups was definitely quite a different experience for me. I felt, and still do feel sometimes, that age and size are definitely a discriminatory factor with Bears. It's lessening, though: Those attitudes in general have improved greatly.

RON: I would hope so.

REED: People are still coming out into this whole scene; Bears and big men and their admirers need to have this acceptance. Moreover, there needs to be a place for us in gay society as well as society in general, for now and for the future. Just as people are coming out every day—men and women realizing their sexuality—new Bears and new chubbies and new chasers are also evolving in the world. There have to be people waiting to embrace them and show them the way, much as people showed me the way, who helped me to become what I am and who I am today.

Chapter 6
Bearness's Beautiful Big Blank:
Tracing the Genome of Ursomasculinity
~ An Interview With Jack Fritscher ~

JACK FRITSCHER has stood at the forefront of gay men's culture and erotica for more than 20 years. Twenty of his 400 published stories, and 40 of the 125 videos he's written, directed, and photographed, are Bear themed. Jack received his Ph.D. in American Literature from Loyola University of Chicago and taught journalism and creative writing at several Midwestern universities. He served as founding San Francisco editor in chief of *Drummer*. In 1979, after writing his groundbreaking book *Leather Blues*, he founded the quarterly *MAN2MAN*, the first 'zine of the 1980s. In 1981, he established the Bay area tabloid *California Action Guide*. His nonfiction, literary fiction, and comic erotic fiction have received both critical acclaim and an international cult following. His epic novel, *Some Dance to Remember*, has been called "the gay *Gone with the Wind*," and is the fiction counterpart of *Mapplethorpe: Assault with a Deadly Camera*. Five anthologies also collect his writing and photography, as well as *The Journal of Popular Culture*, *In Touch*, *Honcho*, *Uncut*, *International Leatherman*, and *Hombres Latinos*, to name a few periodicals. He brings a loving ear, erotic eye, and lyric voice to American gay popular culture and is an archivist active in researching, recording, and preserving the heritage of gay history. He and his partner of more than 20 years, Palm Drive publisher Mark Hemry, were married in a civil union in Vermont. He was recently given a Pioneer Survivor award by the Pioneer Survivor Society of San Francisco. Discover much more at www.JackFritscher.com.

Bear-type gay men existed, of course, long before the moniker *bear* came into any sort of popular gay usage. In examining the roots of the big furry beast, I wanted to include the voice of someone who knew first-hand the pop-culture 1970s precedents to the explosion of the San Francisco Bear phenomenon in the late 1980s. That man is Jack Fritscher, who was involved with Richard Bulger and Chris Nelson, cofounders of *Bear* magazine, and the San Francisco South of Market scene (see the Vafiades interview, chapter 7, and Jack's foreword to *The Bear Book II*).

Aside from being revelatory, my interview with this gay Bear pioneer, like two bears romping in the woods, was filled with playful and creative glee. To wit: Jack defined "homomasculinity" in '80s San Francisco gayspeak as a term and a lifestyle for masculine-identified gay men and, improvising on his wonderful neologism, I coined "ursomasculinity" to refer to the existence of Bearish masculinity ("urso" is Latin for "bear"). As we continued tracing the various antecedents to the Bear image, Jack then upped the ante and cleverly invented "urso-ur-masculinity" (the prefix "ur-" means "prototypical"). Incidentally, Jack asked that his last name be used for clarity here in the dialogue lead-ins.

Jack and I began our oral-history telephone interview by discussing the pop-culture significance of monthly gay magazines ("Magazines reflect and grab readers harder, deeper, faster than books," he stated) such as *Drummer* and *Bear*, and then we launched into, as Jack called it, our "Bear roots vérité."

RON: Jack, what was *Drummer* like when you started working there as editor in chief?

FRITSCHER: *Drummer* first published in 1975, and when I first came aboard officially in June 1977, it had struggled to publish about 14 issues. It was like a stillborn baby that wasn't breathing. Harold Cox, publisher of *Checkmate* magazine, *Drummer*'s virtual successor, said that I slapped *Drummer* with an identity and made it cry, scream, shout, and kick.

In the early issues, I was involved first as a freelance writer and photographer, introducing my friends into *Drummer*: photographer Jim

Stewart; artist Tom Hinde; my domestic lover and photography business partner, David Sparrow; my bicoastal lover, photographer Robert Mapplethorpe; and my creative partner, video artist David Hurles of Old Reliable fame. My friend, the wonderful Bear-pec artist A. Jay, the art director for *Drummer*, begged me to take the job. Suddenly, because of my years of journalism and magazine experience, I became *Drummer's* founding San Francisco editor.

RON: What other work were you doing at the time?

FRITSCHER: Always writing. I am a gonzo journalist after the New Journalism of writers like Tom Wolfe and George Plimpton in the '60s: you must participate in what you write about. That's very Hemingwayesque, but also the way of the true pop culture analyst. My fiction was first published in magazines when I was 19 in 1958. I wrote the first leather novel, *Leather Blues*, with two overtly Bearish characters, in 1972. In 1976, I began writing for Kaiser Engineers in the San Francisco Bay area and ran their marketing and proposals departments. Before that, I was an associate professor with tenure at a university, so I am allowed to make cracks about academics. Pertinent here is the fact that in 1968 I was one of the founding members of the American Popular Culture Association, so I was prepared for the outbreak of gay culture after Stonewall in 1969.

RON: Did you ever feel overqualified to be editing *Drummer*?

FRITSCHER: No. Only the terminally vain, the lazy, and the untalented say they're overqualified. "Those who can't, teach, and those who can, do." I taught writing and journalism at university and am fully credentialed to this day to teach university. *But what could be better than being editor and chief writer of a new magazine in a new culture that is just discovering its identity?* Put that last sentence in italics. Identity was exactly what I had in mind.

RON: How did this ursomasculinity (to improvise on your wonderful word *homomasculinity*) develop? Did you see it birthing itself upon *Drummer's* pages as well as the culture around you?

FRITSCHER: What I'm going to tell you here is, in a sense, a personal history and not academic theory-query. This stuff happened to me or I helped it happen. I'm not taking a territorial piss on this stuff, because you can't copyright a concept. The dates when someone actually first does something, however, are objective, and so by objectively examining materials in print—left behind like bear tracks in the woods—I can point to the who-what-where-when-and-how this "Bear" concept evolved.

I didn't invent leather or cigars or jockstraps or Bears, but I took those words as concepts and pulled them out of generic masculinity and fetishized them into homomasculinity for gay men. While many gay men may have had an opinion about or a secret turn-on to cigars, by my writing the first cigar fetish article in the gay press, suddenly there were "smoke signals." A measurable phenomenon began to appear in the gay bars right away and in the letters to the editor and the personals the next issue. A sociologist could see cause and effect happening.

RON: So *Drummer* had its pulse on the crotch of homomasculine America.

FRITSCHER: Everybody was reading *Drummer* because it was the only magazine for masculine-identified men. It was the third glossy format magazine founded after Stonewall. The rest were like *Blue Boy* or *Queen's Quarterly*.

RON: The others had very little news or editorial content.

FRITSCHER: They were mostly pictures and jokes—sweater jokes, camp jokes, and men pretending they were girly, or doing that sort of self-hating satire of masculinity gay men were at the time prone to, actually referring to themselves as "friends of Dorothy." Basically, gay male self-hatred of the masculine animus comes from straight people's stereotype that gay men are not real men, are girly, effeminate, and maybe even, a third sex.

This is why I like the concept of "Bear." And this is my original analysis and definition which you might put in italics for any reader skimming: *Bear is a concept so receptively blank that as a label it welcomes and absorbs all masculine fantasies, fetishes, identities, and body types.* "Bear" is all-inclusive.

RON: The Bear archetype is based on one of those themes that you extracted from the fabric of homomasculine life.

FRITSCHER: It was. *Drummer* was a hot-center lightning rod of masculine-identified homosexuality trying to differentiate itself from the sweater sissyness of the stereotype that straight people always perceived gay men to be. Ultimately, Bears are a masculine retort to that kind of effeminate stereotype which people feel they can control like they think they can control women.

Recently a very big Bear I know moved to Hubbub, Texas. He looks so much like every other guy at the WalMart that he was perceived as straight. When he finally said, "Get over it! I'm gay," the straight folks in Hubbub said, "You can't be gay. You're too old, hairy, and fat," as if only the young, hairless, and wispy can be gay. That's the stereotype some straight people use to measure queers.

RON: It's an all-pervasive misconception of gay masculinity. Can you identify in mainstream American culture what then happened so that finally homomasculine activity and attitude could be teased out from the—as you so succinctly coined it—gaystream?

FRITSCHER: In the immortal words of *The Rocky Horror Picture Show*, "Let's do the time warp again." Time-travel back in pop culture. The gay men who came out in the golden age of gay liberation in the '70s all watched the same movies and TV as boys in the '50s and '60s. Adult gay men in the '70s all shared a common adolescence that affected their erotic psyches, fantasies, and ideals.

In tracing and mapping a Bear gene, I think the very DNA for the generation of gays who arrived at the concept of Bear emanates from the 1950s with movies like *Quo Vadis*, Steve Reeves, and gladiator movies. These images of men dramatized powerful men with bodies carved with muscle, or gigantic in size, with heroes bearded, and villains bearded and matted with body hair. In 1951 *Quo Vadis* was the most awaited movie of its day. All the strength of that movie was in the big-hearted gladiator named Ursus. American boys became fascinated by the arena, nearly naked men, and gladiatorial combat. Fast-forward to Mr. America, Steve Reeves, in the late '50s, wearing a beard and fighting off other muscle guys hairier and beefier than the very refined Reeves himself. Those *Hercules* movies fed directly into the mixture comprising today's musclebears.

At the same time on TV, boys were stunned week after week watching Bear prototype Clint Walker in *Cheyenne* (1955-63). The straight, hairy Walker developed his overt Bearishness in movies like *The Night of the Grizzly*. Those boys watching Walker for eight years became the first adult males after Stonewall in the '70s—so there's no wonder that Walker's lumberjack look was the basis of the Castro clone look, which started out more Clint than clone.

The '60s ended innocence. The '70s, an age of liberation, introduced men as—thank God—sex objects in the centerfolds of magazines ostensibly for the pleasure of liberated women. Hee hee. *Cosmopolitan* and *Playgirl* featured some incredible hairy men, like Burt Reynolds, Joe

Namath, and Russ Francis, the famous pro-football star who also wrestled.

So many pop-culture athletes figure here as well. To cite but one example, there's the *Cosmo* model, quarterback Terry Bradshaw, who has gained the proportions of a large-sized Bear: hairy, bald, and—to pop culture straight cheers—one of the sexiest men alive. In the '70s, Bradshaw was young, hairy, balding, and built, and featured as a hunk in women's magazines. That meant all of us men could be free with our bodies.

Male icons of the '70s, like those already mentioned, as well as Joe Namath, O.J. Simpson, and Ted Turner, brought a wholesome sexiness to American masculinity, far unlike the '60s uptight John Wayne or Ronald Reagan or urbane Cary Grant. The '70s showed men as sexy, rough, natural. Grooming no longer meant clipping, shaving, and cutting hair. Men's looks changed as drastically as sexual mores. Listen to the Top-Ten theme song from the musical *Hair*, glorifying hairiness forbidden by the crewcut U.S. army and the chest-shaving stars of Hollywood. Pop culture embraced liberation and revolution at the same time by depuritanizing and celebrating the secondary sexual characteristics of the male. That is the pop culture birth of Bear.

Bear celebrates the secondary sexual characteristics of the male: facial hair, body hair, proportional size, baldness—all those things that Delilah wives don't like because they want their Samson husbands to cut their hair, get cleaned up, put on ties, shave their backs, shave their chests, get rid of all that nasty forearm hair with Nair, wear toupees...

RON: And graying hair as well. There were also Richard Amory's *Song of the Loon* books from the late '60s, which was made into a film as well, in 1970.

FRITSCHER: That, of course, collides into the '70s first gay films, directed by Wakefield Poole, which tilted from the blond and hair-free *Boys in the Sand* to the bearded, rough, handballing film *Moving*.

Out of those secondary sexual characteristics came the cult of "real men." I don't mean real men in the sense that straights use the expression but in the sense of a natural man. In the '70s, for the first time, you were allowed to be "natural" rather than "normal."

Bears physically signify everything that the pussy-whipped PC [politically correct] norm is against. Think of Bear drawings in the wide range of Bear-themed magazines. How do Bear artists draw Bears? The PC despise the white male in the trailer park with the gun. That redneck archetype, armed with gun and knife, gone hunting, is a major erotic symbol of Bear life. Most Bears would die to live in a mobile home park with a gun and a Hog [a Harley-Davidson]. That kind of man can be as hairy, bikerish, and free as he wants. Isn't that the gay Bear magazine ideal?

Actually, I love that we're getting in our Bear mags a non-elitist honesty coming from people's fantasies. Bears are gay people's princes, who vocalize the song of the Bear for lost homomasculinity.

RON: But let's return to tracing the Bear lineage.

FRITSCHER: Like Wakefield Poole, the Gage Brothers, who followed him in the film trilogy *Kansas City Trucking*, *El Paso Wrecking Company*, and *L.A. Tool and Die*, had the greatest homomasculine movie titles ever. In one of the early issues of *Drummer*, the first Daddy Bear, Richard Locke, called the famous leather sadist Fred Halsted a "real teddy bear" after they finished shooting *L.A. Tool and Die*. So, as early as 1977 you have one famous porn star calling another one a teddy bear, even though Fred Halsted's hypermasculinity in no way denoted Bearishness.

Bears began to differentiate themselves for me with porn star Richard Locke, who was the perfect model for the coming Bear movement. In an interview in *Drummer*, my first question—hilarious now—to him was, "Now that you are 37, what do you think will happen to your porn star career?" Richard had a touch of gray in his mustache then, and 37 in gay San Francisco years was old. Gay liberation, like all the revolutions of the '60s and '70s, was a youth culture. Because I was the same age as Richard Locke, I was pedaling fast to prepare for turning 40 myself.

In 1978, there was a film called *In Praise of Older Women*. What a great theme to inject in *Drummer*: "In Praise of Older Men." Cope with the inevitable, I figured, because all the hot guys out on Folsom and Castro are going to be older eventually. I wondered, "What kind of image can they grow gracefully into: What kind of light can I as an editor and writer beam into the end of this tunnel?" So I pumped (journalistically) Richard Locke into the sparkling new icon of a "daddy," which begat "daddy's boy." With Locke's drop-dead good looks, personality, and performances in the Gage trilogy, the campaign made Locke legendary. As soon as that interview was published, men engaged in the national gay conversation suddenly felt better about turning 30 or 40 or

50. Men can be hot whatever decade they're in.

Locke, along with Colt's Ledermeister, Paul Garrior, were the first icons of real men in the homomasculine lifestyle that led to the Bear lifestyle. Ledermeister is the original-recipe mockup of the hairy gay Bear. Subtract the twinkies, clones, fluff, and drag—in the '70s, gay men came out who were purely about masculinity as an absolute, not as reciprocal to anything else. The movement, rather respectfully, actually, left the twinkies, clones, and drags to their alternative lifestyle. Masculinity was the celebration of the day.

RON: So let's fast-forward in our written docudrama of Bear vérité.

FRITSCHER: The mid-20th-century images of straight-media hunks translated into the most famous early Colt and Target Studio's Bear god model, Ledermeister. At the same time, Bearish artists like Lugar at Colt and Target, Rex in his Rexwerk, and Domino in New York showcased hairy men.

Then British artist Bill Ward, with his handsome-as-Colt characters Drum and King in *Drummer*, truly penned the emerging fantasy of the dominant musclebear. Cavello often drew hairy men, but his drawings—for all their WeHo [West Hollywood] S&M—are very pretty George Petty. The Hun is one American artist whose work has chased the popular taste for Bear. As Bears arose, the Hun's drawings showed men transmorphing out of lumberjack into Bear. Plus the Hun dramatizes black men as Bears the way Domino goes for ethnicity of Latino, Greek, Italian, and Irish.

Alongside those men and Chuck Arnett, who inked those Red Star Saloon primal drawings of Bears prowling after midnight, the South-of-Market artist who did the most for Bearish hair was, of course, A. Jay (Al Shapiro). A. Jay was the ur-cartoonist in *Queen's Quarterly* and then in *Drummer* who did a nipple-and-fur comic strip called "The Super Adventures of Harry Chess."

RON: There was also Tim Barela, who began penning *Leonard & Larry* in 1984. In a different context, but still part of the Bear artist cultural landscape.

FRITSCHER: Tim is a fun cartoonist-comedian, like A. Jay. My list is more to note the early artists whose work years later is taken for granted as if it were always there, and is community property. Tom of Finland included hairy men, but Domino and Bill Ward roughed up the final image out of Tom's cleaner lines. For the pop-art history fun of it, compare four drawings of lumberjacks by Tom, the Hun, Domino, and Bill Ward.

I'm trying to point out the evolution of some of these early people because it parallels the emergence of different *Drummer* fetishes: cigars, bondage, leather, tits, fists, ballwork, tattoos, piercings, whatever. I didn't invent those things, but I was the first to codify them into concepts in dedicated articles, photo layouts, or covers, and bring them into pop focus. The fetishes were lurking in the gay psyche, like the Bear fetish, but no one had ever formalized them in print before. Every gay magazine since 1978 repeats those first fetishes. Nobody's come up with any new fetish or male look because there are only so many things you can do with your body.

RON: Your description of how each of these aspects of masculinity was brought out of the closet and into pop consciousness strikes me as there being a face put onto gay men, a de-anonymizing of gay men. Giving gay men a vehicle to articulate their own voices was vastly empowering.

FRITSCHER: Everybody talks about gay liberation, but one real thing in actual gay liberation was to liberate the men who were men, homomasculine men, because that was the ultimate goal of '70s gay lib.

RON: Liberating masculinity was the whole point of it?

FRITSCHER: The historical point in the '70s was to liberate everybody who was gay or lesbian in every shade of being gay and lesbian. But the hardest thing to be today in America is a man. The hardest thing to be in the world has always been a man. You can man-bash on commercials and talk shows and in Lilith songs. But if you turned that around and bashed women or blacks or homosexuals like that, there would be people writing letters and up in arms and demonstrating in a Million Whatever March on the Capitol. But bashing men seems to be perfectly fine. Making men the villains because you feel put-upon is stupid, like blaming your father because you are experiencing the downside of the human condition. Tough tits. Trashing masculinity leaves gay men nowhere to go as they try to escape the syndrome of sissy-fag Judy-Judy-Judyness.

Gay men are called by nature's genes and by a personal inner voice to celebrate masculinity, man to man, without breeding. Guys who are male act like guys unless they are coerced into effeminacy by straights or into "sensitivity" by PC agenda.

RON: So how did this previously submerged theme of ursomasculinity develop and sprout in the '80s?

FRITSCHER: When *Drummer* changed hands in 1987, new publisher Tony DeBlase did much for Bears. He was a wonderful publisher of *Drummer*. I gave Tony a list of concepts that could be done for upcoming issues of *Drummer*. He immediately went for my Bears and mountain men theme, which I wanted to enlarge from *Bear*'s small 'zine size to large-format *Drummer*.

Actually, issue no. 119 is the first full glossy magazine presentation ever of Bears, including the first-ever Bear-themed feature article, "How to Hunt Buckskin Leather Mountain Men and Live Among the Bears!" as expository analysis. That issue is full of Palm Drive photography of Bears, including the model John Muir from the cover and centerfold of the first issue of *Bear*.

Bear historians need to look at *Drummer*'s seminal issues no. 19–30, and no. 119; the two-year, eight-issue run of the quarterly *MAN2MAN*; and the San Francisco tabloid, *California Action Guide*, where for the first time anywhere, I put on the large-format cover the huge words BEARS: HAIR FETISH RANCH, with a two-page feature article inside.

RON: That came out five years before *Bear* magazine first published.

FRITSCHER: Bear was a consciousness whose time had come, because the gay population was aging. Slender, hairless, 20-somethings found that their bodies in their thirties were growing more hair than they had before and they were losing some of their slender body shape. They were turning into their own fathers. So physical genetic XY-ness drove men into the Bear cave. It was a new way to identify oneself. Sissyness had always been about doing your mother's act. Bearness is about doing the best of your father's act.

For some of us who were there and experienced this, we outed our own personal erotic desires, fantasies, and sex lives, and mainlined them into the gaystream, the manstream (no *i*), and the Bearstream.

RON: Bearness also embraced an ideal that also demonstrated that you don't have to have a big dick to be an erotic gay man.

FRITSCHER: Well, that's one of the noncompetitive things about Bears. Bearness is not about dicks. That works as part of Bearness's beautiful big blank that includes all sizes, types, and trips, because it allows men, no matter how they're hung, to participate without feeling something is inferior about themselves.

Let's simplify the equation here. What *Bear* magazine did for hairy guys (and Richard [Bulger, *Bear* magazine publisher] didn't mean overweight Bears, by the way) was to pull together out of the zeitgeist a certain image.

Bear culture came out as the magazine *Bear*, flying on a concept based on all the activity, writing, thought, and photographs of the Bearish men that had gone on before. Richard Bulger was trying to find a niche and fill it, get laid, and make some money. So, Richard, finding a slice of the pie, chose Bears. He could just as easily have chosen husky men, as someone else did with *Husky* magazine, which imitated both *MAN2MAN* and *Bear.* As it was, Richard told publisher Mark Hemry he chose *MAN2MAN* as his model.

RON: "Bear" corresponded with Richard's own physical description, as well his preferential description.

FRITSCHER: Actually, Richard wrote in *Bear* that he did not consider himself a Bear. Yet out of his genetic makeup and style of living, what he did was to find something to objectify and glorify by putting it into print. Nothing wrong with that, because we create out of who we are. And he was mentally one of the Bears, absorbing Bear culture, reading the Bear demographic possibilities, and merchandising a mag to that culture. Richard Bulger took Bearness and ratcheted the requirements down a few notches so that it would accommodate the more relaxed, more natural look. He folded in the aging hippie thing.

RON: And the biker image. He synthesized these elements in order to make it accessible. Also, I suspect, in order to get models he could afford!

FRITSCHER: Richard made it appeal to a wider audience, an underserved demographic niche, so that he could sell magazines. Nothing wrong with that. *Bear* magazine is a marketing phenom appropriate to the sunny capitalism of gay lib. *Bear* and *American Bear* have become a wonderful business that makes a lot of people happy, and that's a wonderful thing because most gay magazines don't make people happy. Most mags are full of politics, disease, and agenda, and sometimes even details we need to know about, but they're not part of erotic fantasy. The Bear cult in the age of AIDS has given relief because Bears offer an image of robust health in a time of the "thin disease." In order to combat something as horrific as AIDS, we need the wonderful look of full-blown Bears.

Oddly enough, Chris Nelson's studio wasn't called Bear, it was called

Brahma. They were working with both the bull and bear thing and trying to rope as much concept together as they could. "Bull" could have caught fire as easily as "Bear."

RON: Tell me more about your interactions with Richard and Chris and the salons that Richard used to have.

FRITSCHER: Well, I call the get-togethers that Richard hosted "salons," although they never called them that. But Richard ran a salon just like David Hurles at Old Reliable and I at *Drummer*. Richard would have these models and wannabe models stop by his place and hang out. He had a kind of open door policy; he would shoot casual videos in his bedroom or in his shower. Some Bear models we shared were John Muir, Sonny Butts, and Jason Steele. Richard never went on location. I always took models on location, because I wanted to get their different energy in different places.

RON: Are you talking about his home base at the Firehouse in the Mission, where he lived with Chris and had the *Bear* offices?

FRITSCHER: Not at first. Initially, his salon was his living quarters in a former storefront near Church Street. I loved those open-door policies in the '70s. Everybody had them.

RON: What was your personal take on Richard? Where was his head, and what were his aspirations? Do you think he expected this to take off in the way it did?

FRITSCHER: I think Richard started *Bear* as a device, as often happens, to get laid. Then it took on a life of its own. Photography is a reliable way to get beautiful guys to take their clothes off. Old Reliable was doing it with straight street hustlers out of the Old Crow hustler bar on Market. Richard and Chris were shooting normal gay men from the Ambush. The gay press at first did not understand either photographer. Every editor refused Old Reliable until I broke him wide open in *Drummer* in 1978. Outside of *Drummer*, no editor would touch Bearish men, until Richard Bulger dared to open *Bear* magazine in 1987.

I'm not privy to what his business thoughts were, other than that he asked Mark Hemry and me how we produced *MAN2MAN*, so he could produce *Bear*; who we used for printers, mechanical information, distribution. Of course, everybody who starts a gay magazine eventually gets offers from somebody to buy it, whether from somebody gay or from the Mafia.

RON: Please tell me about your interactions with Chris.

FRITSCHER: My relationship with Chris Nelson was almost totally silent. I can't remember him ever speaking. He was extremely talented and knew what he was doing. When he shot me for a photo spread in one of the early issues of Bear, it was a very nondirected shoot. He was distant and far away. He even kept the camera far away. Maybe it was just me, but I think he knew I'd have some sort of sense of what I wanted to do. Essentially, I was just turned loose in front of the camera. He captured this impromptu performance art with his more formal still camera.

Look at the absolutely archetypal cover of *The Bear Cult*, Chris Nelson's coffee-table book of photographs: a guy in jeans and boots with his shirt off standing by a car from under which another guy's boots stick out. That's romantic and existential. Notice the sense of humor that comes through: the shirtless Bear standing next to a car, with a leg coming from underneath the car, obscuring the license plate. Now that's a Bear in a Bear situation: two guys, a combustion engine, a crotch objectified and deliciously detached from a person.

RON: Accentuated by the grimy hand of the guy underneath the car visibly holding a wrench and grasping the leg of the man standing up. The diversity of Bear images in *The Bear Cult* shows all the body types of Bears, from skinny, hairy boys to heavyweight grizzlies, as well as Bears of all colors.

FRITSCHER: *The Bear Cult* contains a diversity of Bears in weight and ethnicity and shows the first principle, that you don't have to be thin or fat to be a Bear. One of the photographs in the book that captures Bearness and masculinity is page 10: John Muir.

RON: That's Chris's choice for the first portrait in the book.

FRITSCHER: It's an absolutely incredible portrait, so much so that we received permission years ago to use it on a Palm Drive brochure. So that's how aligned Richard and I were. We were on the same page doing the same thing. He called his gig *Bear* (1987) and we called ours *MAN2MAN* magazine (1980), the *California Action Guide* (1982), and Palm Drive Video (1984).

As much as I love Ted [Edward Lucie-Smith], in his introduction to Chris's book, he focused on Richard Bulger as if Bearness dawned full-blown from *Bear*. In actuality, *Bear* magazine emerged from a Bearness that had already existed for at least 15 years before the magazine.

RON: Let's return to tracing the genesis of the Bear. What is your take on how the Bear-themed media has evolved? Do you see any particular trends?

FRITSCHER: Again, it's the democratizing out of the personal ads through *Tough Customers* into *MAN2MAN* so that you now have a better reflection of real people rather than models. It really pains me when I see, in *Bear* or other magazines, pictures consisting of nothing more than video models who are put in to fill pages because their video producer wants to get free advertising. Those video models are hired for three hours to go fuck somebody. They have nothing to do with culture per se. It hurts the real culture because they aren't real.

RON: Do you mean that these models go from amateur to professional after that initial time?

FRITSCHER: No, I mean they go from real to false. What is amateur and what is professional? To the straight world, anything gay is amateur. Our magazines are amateur, gay publishing of books is amateur. What we're doing in your book is amateur to the straight world because they won't even review it. They don't have categories for it. Your book, however, is very real. You're getting real conversation out all the people in your book, and that is what you want: a book vérité. Bear vérité is what you want, and I'm trying to give you Bear vérité in terms of how Bear threads its pop culture way through gay culture as a masculine piece of DNA mapping the genome of Bear.

People can take from it what they want or add to it what they want, but Bears have proceeded through this march, this long gay parade that comes down from 1969; well, before that of course, but let's just say from 1969. We're all marching together and Bears are one very specific contingent in that. These magazines right now continue to feature an explicit group but how long they can continue, I don't know. I think they will be supplanted by the Internet because at the same time you're talking about Bear culture like it's *Bear* magazine, but it happens not to be *Bear* magazine because it happens to be Bear videos that fund that magazine.

RON: It seems to me that the vast majority of Bear culture lives off the page and outside the VCR. It lives in the Bearclubs and Bear Web sites and the Bear runs and confabs.

FRITSCHER: Now that's a real Bear experience, going off with another predictable Bear from some convention so that you can hug. Cool. I'm not knocking it, but why not get an unpredictable Bear, a straight guy, and do all this Bear stuff (wrestling, biking, eating) with him, especially if he knows what he's doing and he brings to you all the authenticity of the police force or the Marine Corps or the WWF and lays it on top of you, because you fantasize about wrestlers, bikers, and jarheads? Bring on the real thing, not the gay imitation. Not all Bear eros is actual sex. How narrow.

RON: But most gay Bears wouldn't act upon their desire for that kind of sex. They'd be too intimidated.

FRITSCHER: Then they're not really Bears, because being a Bear is a state of mind, and if you're afraid of the real thing, you're not a Bear. That's the test! Get it? I always love it when people say they are gay and shy. How can you be shy after you've dared to come out? For God's sake, what else is there to be shy about? If you're a Bear and afraid then you're not really a Bear, although you might look like one.

If you don't have the courage of your convictions, then you don't deserve to be gay, or a Bear, or a man, or anything. That is what it is to be grown up, to go get what you want.

RON: I don't think most people do that, gay or straight. Most people don't think they can live their fantasies.

FRITSCHER: If you don't live your fantasies, you're a failure. And a fool. Getting what you want is not living a fantasy; it's actualizing your potential. Remember, ultimately nobody gives a good goddamn what you do. Nobody's watching, unless you're Mr. Clinton and the right-wing coup wants to get you on everything—but if he weren't the most powerful person in the world, they wouldn't care. You can do whatever you want because nobody cares what you do—I'm talking about you personally and me personally. Nobody gives a fine fuck. I could go fuck somebody in the street and outside of people crying, "Omigod, the children, the children," nobody cares at all. So to be intimidated is not part of the archetypal Bear ideal. A Bear should be the intimidating one. I think [author and sexpert] Susie Bright is a Bear.

RON: Absolutely.

FRITSCHER: But she doesn't intimidate me and I don't intimidate her. We can stand up on our hind legs and roar at each other, which is wonderful. So it's not even about gender.

RON: Certainly, courage and fortitude have nothing to do with what you have between your legs.

FRITSCHER: Right, and if we don't take the analog and internalize what Bear is, or what leather is, or muscle, and find out what Bear or leather or muscle is to us psychologically and spiritually, it's just a fashion, a style, an affectation from which we've learned nothing. Like leathers bought in the back of a bar.

RON: That's exactly the point about Bear spirit, that there has to be some sort of internal identification.

FRITSCHER: It's completely necessary because without internalizing it, there's no point to it. If it's just an external, physical thing, you're not going to be a very good Bear playmate because you don't understand it. Even if you look like the ideal Bear, such as Jack Radcliffe or Chris Duffy, it doesn't make any difference internally.

I didn't turn out looking like these people either, but on the inside, I can turn on the switch and be the Bear; I can turn on the switch and be the bodybuilder. I can turn on the switch and be the sadistic leather top. I could turn on the switch and be the masochistic bottom if I could just find someone to be the top. But with all these shy Bears running around, what good are they? Underneath them all is Ms. Piggy. [*Both laugh*]

There's nothing worse than seeing a big brute doing all this standing and posing at a Bear convention or in a Bear bar, only to then watch him pirouette out the door. Talk about a fall from platonic grace! Even though I'm just saying that to be funny, truly, if the Bear isn't the totem animal on the shield of the tribe, and if you don't live the Bearishness of being Bear, then you are only a faux Bear. A fairy in a fake fur coat. You're faking Bear and you do Bears a disservice.

Some men, who have nowhere else to turn for acceptance of their avoirdupois, suddenly christen themselves Bear. And every day the measure goes up on what weight a Bear is before he becomes a chubby. And that's fine. I'm not criticizing anybody. I'm just positing an existential analysis of the situation. A man's health is his very best possession. Nobody should betray his health in the name of being a Bear.

RON: This is also characteristic of the human condition, in general, and the condition of being an American: most people will choose to buy the Bear T-shirt and wear it on the outside without internalizing any of the inner qualities of the bear.

FRITSCHER: Exactly. "Bear" has appeal because it's not exclusionary. It includes anybody who wants to call themselves Bear or have Bear spirit. Unfortunately, it's a cheap way to pull off an image. If it's just image, fine. But I'm interested in the essential Bear, just like the essential leatherman and the essential bodybuilder. If you go into any crowd of Bears, you'll see mostly a bunch of stereotypes, rather than an archetype. Now, all those stereotypes could move toward the archetype, could transform themselves into the archetype by meditating on it, by thinking about it, by spiritualizing themselves and walking into that identity. But most gay men don't even know how to walk like a man! I mean, there needs to be a butch academy—not in the bad sense of butch, but to overcome the self-hating effeminacy and PC-whipped passivity lived as lifestyle by some gay men.

RON: Oh, you mean just like they opened up schools for gay men to learn how to do drag.

FRITSCHER: Ugh. PC apparatchiks in the gay press sometimes misunderstand comments that I make, such as, "Men are valid. Masculinity is valid." It drives them crazy because they think I'm attacking them and their sweaters. They have every right to be girly men. Yet I'm not talking about them; I'm talking about the other side of being gay, which is about expressing a masculine, sexual way of being. There's no worse insult to a woman than drag, because all that drag does is point up the stereotypical worse things that women do, because it emphasizes the superficial things.

RON: All the makeup, glitter, big hair, and heaving bodices. Usually it takes place within an extremely hateful and fearsome environment.

FRITSCHER: Right. Drag embraces all the things that women themselves eschew—makeup, bras, dresses, and everything that has been out of style for 40 years. Again, that's fine if somebody wants to do it, but that's not what being Bear is about. Being Bear is choosing to be a certain way, about honoring a certain way that you are in and of yourself. And if you really identify as being Bear—and I think it is a good way to get laid—then you're going to have to investigate the Bearishness of yourself and what it is to be Bear. The "incredible lightness of being Bear," right?

RON: Or perhaps the incredible heft of being Bear, as the case may be. But what you're speaking of is Bearness as a life path, like the path of the warrior.

There's a marvelous book, unfortunately out of print, called *The Sacred Paw: The Bear in History, Myth, and Literature.* The number of points of commonality between four-legged creatures and humans is amazing. We could be taking from this identification a wealth of meaning to serve our own personal transformation. Yet if you ask most men who identify as Bears what they feel they have in common with the four-legged creature—which I did while researching this book—all they can think of is the hair, maybe the girth. Not a word about strength, endurance, speed, courage, fierceness, appetite. In fact, most Bears think bears are slow, dumb, fat animals.

FRITSCHER: They think bears are fat, but bears are big, they're not fat.

RON: They can store sometimes as much as a half a foot of fat.

FRITSCHER: Because they hibernate. We don't. There's a point where anthropomorphism fails. You might also want to mention the [also out of print] book *Bulls through the Ages* by Ralph Whitlock, because in a sense it does the same things, taking the bull identification on the shield as an archetypal icon in the gay tribe. There are all these different creatures that gay men can turn to, to objectify these internal characteristics.

The bear concept is a mode of expression that can be used archetypically or stereotypically and it's a handle on human psychology. It's a way to take all the negatives associated with homosexuality and turn them into positives. Thus, men no longer think they have to be either effeminate like sweater kveens or hard like leathermen, although both stereotypes are misconceptions, too.

RON: Perhaps by moving outside of oneself into the bear archetype, one gains perspective on being a true human, or man. That has potential for being truly liberating. How you might see the Bear phenomenon evolving in the future?

FRITSCHER: I think it is time now for the archiving of Bear to begin. Your book is one of the first to go into gathering some of this together, but even so you're getting people talking. Somebody needs to start gathering the primary materials of Beardom together like photographs, videos, and magazines. If anybody really wants to pursue this, they should start looking at the images in some of the magazines that have existed for years and especially look at the videos.

RON: Regarding the idea for a serious archiving effort, I would agree, but absent some kind of endowment, I don't see that happening. We need to be better endowed.

FRITSCHER: No pun intended. Well, leatherarchives.org is supported by the Leather Archives, which in six years has gone from zero to having a wonderful building and thousands of dollars sent to it by guys who send money to things like that. And beararchives.com could be funded by the Bear Archives, which could be started by somebody who gets a grant or just puts out a newsletter.

RON: To accomplish that kind of task requires—

FRITSCHER: A fund-raising effort by somebody who is going to organize it and be legit and include everything from oral history, magazine and book writing, videos, and seminars to the philosophy, psychology, teleology, and spirituality of Bearness.

RON: Among subculture Bears, however, there's tremendous resistance to any kind of organization. They feel it's antithetical to what Bearness is all about, as if it was only about being hairy homo homeboys. Once when I posted onto the BML [Bears Mailing List] the idea of having a Bear leadership conference, I received so much negative mail, there was so little support for it, maybe 10 to one. People just thought it was the most ridiculous thing in the world.

FRITSCHER: Because who wants to join anything and have it talked to death? I mean, I wouldn't get involved in it. I hate that sort of stuff, I really do, but that doesn't mean it shouldn't be done. But there has to be the right kind of person, the right personality. Like any project, it is a projection of the one person whose personality pulls it together, just like Richard Bulger pulled together *Bear*.

It comes out of somebody wanting to do that, but you can't really organize the masses to contribute to your project. They don't want to do it. It's like me in the '70s trying to pull *Drummer* into focus. I wrote nearly every word in it and took nearly every photograph and begged every artist who ever drew anything to "Please draw me something for *Drummer*," because everybody was having sex. Nobody wanted to stop fucking long enough to contribute, but they all wanted to have *Drummer* in their hands as soon as it came out, so in between having sex in the baths and backrooms and on the streets, they would have something more to jerk off to at night when they were home alone recuperating. That's when your Bears live inside their VCRs, magazines, and books. Recuperating. Hibernating.

These things happen because the time is ripe and then an individual who is right for it pulls it together.

RON: Well, let's hope someone will come forward to take up that work.

FRITSCHER: It's like all my work. That's what I do. I try to gather oral history. I had a grant in 1972 to do an oral history of Sam Steward. That's all on audio tape. All these bits and pieces that float through the filing cabinets and all that, a kind of www.JackFritscher.com archive; but one day it will be part of a larger library. It includes gay literature, gay culture, gay history, and much more. Right now it's going out over the Internet and in a series of books, which in the next couple of years will timeline everything together. All the work that you and Les Wright are doing is wonderful, but one day we'll all be a dusty chapter in Bear archives. One day we'll just be a footnote in the larger picture of Bear. *Ursus horribilis* will eat everything that is now and move on to the next thing in the future.

RON: Bears don't eat their young, I think.

FRITSCHER: Gay ones do. And their old. [*Both laugh*] That reminds me of the dustup over the use of the word "Bear." There was a bunch of people fighting over the use of the word "Bear" about 10 years ago. Somebody asked me what I thought of it, and I said, "I used Bear in the first issue of *MAN2MAN* in December 1979/January 1980 before any of you came to town. So [*blows a raspberry*]! You can do what you want, but your antecedents are here. You didn't think it up, nor did I think it up, it was something that was there, but I articulated it first." Everybody backed down. Emerson said, "We're all pygmies standing on the shoulders of giants." So we all just take what went before and fold it into the new way things are.

It will be interesting to see where Bears will be by 2003. Some 16-year-old guy, who will be 19 in three years, will pick up your book and look at it, and suddenly the light bulb will go on over his head, and a whole new way of being Bear will emerge. Some actor, some player will come along and change the Bear look. Just as the ways of being gay and the ways of being male change, the way of being Bear will change as well. We're not at "Full *Ursus*" yet!

CHAPTER 7
THE RAINBOW MC AND THE OLD LONE STAR
~ A DISCUSSION WITH PETE VAFIADES ~

"BONSAI PETE" VAFIADES was born in the Bangor, Maine, area. He left Maine at age 20 to seek a place where he could be more at peace with himself and to pursue his quest: "homos and hort" (horticulture). Friends gave him the nickname "Bonsai Pete" because of his love of the art of bonsai—the miniaturization of trees. At UCLA, he earned a degree in landscape architecture. While visiting the San Francisco Bay area, its magic cast a spell on him. In just a few short weeks after returning from vacation, he landed his first job over the phone working for a plant rental company, and moved to San Francisco in 1979. Pete is now the manager of the Hole in the Wall Saloon in the South of Market (SoMa) area of San Francisco.

Part of the genesis of Bear identity—or at least of Bear commercialization that became "Bear Disney"—centers on the alliance of two Bears with ambitious Bear-based businesses in San Francisco in the late 1980s: Rick Redewill, the original owner of the Bear bar Lone Star Saloon, and Richard Bulger, the publisher and cofounder (with photographer Chris Nelson doing business as Brahma Studios) of *Bear* magazine. Although it's clear that gay Bears existed before this time, in some ways the friendship and business alliance between these two men formed a ground zero for Bears and Beardom as it's known around the world.

I should point out here that San Francisco gay culture of that time embraced its bars as centers of gay men's lives. The significance of the bars may not be easily perceived outside the context of the pleasure-seeking culture of 1980s gay bar life. It is important to understand, though, the way that gay men networked and formed attractions, friendships, business alliances, and communities inside these settings. Bar owners such as Rick Redewill were seen as community leaders. During that time—following the closure of all gay San Francisco baths—the Lone Star functioned as a kind of Bear community center that attracted a wealth of creative gay men's culture: visual arts, writing, music, sex, even sports. The fact that it served as a nexus for such a plethora of culture at perhaps the height of the onslaught of AIDS deaths is a matter of wonder.

There were certainly other cultural sources forming the mold of the early San Francisco Bear identity, however, more than just these two men and their businesses. One, for example, was the Bear Hugs sex party scene, which Les Wright has written about extensively elsewhere. Another was the South of Market leather and biker crowd that fed both the Lone Star and *Bear* magazine scenes, both personally and professionally.

Luke Mauerman wrote an excellent history-of-sorts of *Bear* magazine for *The Bear Book*. My interview with Rainbow Motorcycle Club member and *Drummer* editor Jack Fritscher (chapter 6), as well as his foreword to *The Bear Book II* provides additional *Bear* magazine background, so I have tried not to chronicle much of that part of the story here. Likewise, I refer readers interested in discovering more about 1980s early-AIDS San Francisco to Geoff Mains's *Urban Aboriginals* and *Gentle Warriors* as well as Jack Fritscher's *Some Dance to Remember*.

I arrived on the scene after both the bar and the magazine were under way (although still fledgling, the bar more so than the magazine). I've always associated the two businessmen with the biker leathermen of SoMa. Undoubtedly the motorcycle club with members in closest proximity to both Redewill and Bulger was the Rainbow MC [Motorcycle Club].

Bonsai Pete was in the thick of this SoMa Bear soup, having worked at the Ambush, considered to be the Lone Star's predecessor, and then bartending at the original and second Lone Star incarnations. As well, he had been a Rainbow MC member for those many years. Although he knew many of the players at Brush Creek Media, the daddy organization owning *Bear* magazine, my conversation with Bonsai Pete focused primarily on the SoMa scene, the Rainbow MC, and the Lone Star.

This interview differs from most in that I have provided substantial personal information and views based on my own experiences in and around the Lone Star. I created graphics and promotional pieces for the Lone Star and rented an apartment from Rick Redewill. Pete and I were good friends during much of the time I lived in San Francisco, and this conversational style of interviewing seems entirely appropriate for what in actuality is two pals shooting the breeze about the good old days.

RON: When you arrived in San Francisco in 1979, were you attracted to Bear types even then?

PETE: I have always been primarily attracted to others who are male or homomasculine, as we now know it. I was always on the hunt for men that were men: furry, hunky, virile, horny, masculine gay men.

RON: Can you describe gay life in San Francisco back then? Were you finally able to find the kind of men you were searching for?

PETE: Oh, yeah. So many...so very many...I was in heaven and realized it. Every night then was like a Saturday night now. The alleys and streets were always full of nothing but gay, homomasculine, tough-dude types.

RON: Please describe the SoMa scene back then.

PETE: The term SoMa had not yet been introduced. The South of Market, or South of the Slot district, as we called it then, was much less inhabited in those days. The daytime was mostly active with warehouse workers and truck drivers, a few restaurants, and no retail anything at all. The nighttime was a different scene altogether. The bars were filled from early evening on until two o'clock A.M. The men came from everywhere and there were twice as many gay establishments.

RON: Had the leather scene already established its "center" there?

PETE: Yes, totally, but with no realization by the straight world.

RON: Where did you hang out most in the early '80s?

PETE: The Ambush, the Eagle on Sundays, the Brig on weekend nights, and Bootcamp after hours.

RON: Where did the bikers hang out?

PETE: All bars had bikers hanging out, the way I remember it.

RON: Sounds good. Did you own a ride then?

PETE: Oh, yeah! I had a Honda 650—nothing much of an image or icon but it looked and ran real well, and I spent many hours maintaining and keeping it repaired myself.

RON: When and how did you first connect with the Rainbow MC?

PETE: One Sunday afternoon in the spring of 1981, I was out cruising on the Eagle terrace, and noticed this group of bros [brothers] who were sucking down brews and passing around joints. They were by far the most animated and seductive bunch of men I'd ever seen. As I listened and hung out with them I became aware that these guys were not of the regular type of homosexual—or even of the regular type of Homo sapiens. In fact, as I came to know them better, I found out that they all were actually artists of every sort.

RON: Such as...

PETE: Ronald Johnson was the poet who wrote "Ark," which is the longest poem in history. Jack Sharpless was another published poet. Peter Hartman was a music composer and choreographer, and was responsible for 544 Natoma, a cutting-edge performance arts studio for the most unusual and gripping sex-art performances. There were several artists who expressed through brush and canvas—Jimbo and Mario and Hoot and Billy and Kenny. Kenny Davis, the founder of the RMC, wasn't there then that first time. Also not present was the very well known writer Jack Fritscher, who undoubtedly wrote the definition of, if not even invented, the word *homomasculine*. I met both Kenny and Jack another time, though.

RON: How did the group get started?

PETE: The RMC was started as a mock, gay, Hells Angels kind of club, in 1972, I think. The original members were fed up with the typical gay bike club scene with its officers, dues, meetings, and pressed and starched uniforms: rules, rules, and more rules. The Rainbows' idea was to loosely form a club of tough guys who looked the part and to show up at all the other bike club events and kinda make fun of the sissy clubs. They tried to make some kind of scene everywhere they gathered—always in good fun, though, never harmful in a physical sense. Their very presence always drew attention to their circle and the fooling around in the circle was always hot, with pissing on everything and everyone a main event, as well as other perverted acts of debauchery and so forth.

RON: One thing I remember about the Rainbows was their fondness for golden showers [pissing]. There's even a picture in Geoff Mains's book, *Urban Aboriginals*, prefacing the chapter on golden showers, of guys standing around an RMC jacket.

PETE: Theoretically, or supposedly, the Rainbows were into that, yeah. That's what became like the public image, but some of 'em were into it and some of 'em weren't!

RON: Didn't they have buttons made up, saying, "Let us spray"?

PETE: Yes, but the buttons had less to do with pissing than the fact that we made five or six new members all at once at a Satyrs' [MC] Run. During the year previous to those buttons, five or six members died, and we had what we called "a litter"—and so the "let us spray" button referred to our bringing in all those new members at once.

RON: Was pissing on new pledges or their jackets part of the initiation?

PETE: There certainly always was an area set aside for that, if they wanted to be, yes.

RON: Maybe not by rules so much as by tradition.

PETE: Yeah, it became a tradition, and it definitely still is.

RON: What sort of events did the Rainbows have?

PETE: They didn't do anything other than have a few parties, mostly at the Brig—actually, it was the No Name then, when the Rainbows first started. The parties were notorious for being outrageously sexually liberated and sleazy and nasty. The Rainbows always crashed everybody else's parties: that way they didn't have to organize to the degree of having a president, treasurer, a bank account, or anything like that. They let other people organize the parties and then stepped in on those! But they were always welcome and always a crowd magnet. Still are.

RON: Tell me more about the Satyrs Motorcycle Run. The Satyrs MC is a gay motorcycle club, right?

PETE: Yes, Satyrs is the oldest gay motorcycle club—over 40 years old—based out of Los Angeles. The Satyrs Run was absolutely the Rainbows' main event, held in the Sierras, about 8,000 feet up, in a really beautiful spot. Mostly, but not only, bikes would come; between 150 and 300 people would show up. The Satyrs MC had the main camp, with the kitchen, all the utilities and supplies, and everything. The Rainbows sort of supplied the party. We had our own camping area adjacent to theirs, and it would become the run within the run, and we'd get our rainbow flag up there.

RON: But you interacted with the rest of the run participants, right?

PETE: Oh, yeah, completely. The whole purpose of the Rainbows being there was to spread camaraderie, contrary to popular belief.

RON: Why do you say "contrary to popular belief"?

PETE: When I first started going 20 years ago, it seemed like the Rainbows were the scourge of the whole event. Everybody acted afraid of them, or talked badly of them, but as the years went on attitudes all changed to the point that Satyrs have become Rainbows and Rainbows have become Satyrs now. Totally different feel to the event.

RON: In its heyday, about how many members did the Rainbows have?

PETE: The Rainbows have always maintained a steady 13- to 16-member base, and that's where we still are.

RON: So you must be one of the long-standing members of the Rainbows. Who else has been around as long as you?

PETE: Just Jack Fritscher, John Frizzell, and Jim Housley, as far as I can remember.

RON: So that leads us up into the time of the Ambush, which a lot of people consider to be the Lone Star's predecessor.

PETE: Right. The Ambush was located across the street from the current location of the Lone Star on Harrison Street. They had only a beer and wine license; it wasn't a full liquor bar. The first floor had a pool table in the main bar, and art shows that would change regularly, like every other week or every month, for local artists to show and sell their work. On the second floor was a restaurant and card tables, and the third floor had a little store, which sold various sundry items such as tobacco, and a tattoo parlor.

I worked at the Ambush for about two weeks before it closed in '87. They hired me to help clean, actually. I did a couple of art shows there too with my bonsai, which was kind of different for that place.

RON: What did you and the other Ambush men do when it closed? To my understanding, there was a kind of diaspora of the Ambush people. Some went to My Place and some to the Powerhouse and some to the Eagle.

PETE: Most of the core group moved to My Place, which was called Folsom New World at the time. A few people also went to the Watering Hole at Hallam Place and Folsom Street, but definitely the core group from the Ambush and everybody who eventually went to the Lone Star went to the My Place bar.

RON: So sometime in there you met Rick Redewill, the original owner of the Lone Star. How did you meet?

PETE: Some basement somewhere. [*Ron laughs*] I was looking for work when I met him at the Slot Hotel, and he was looking for somebody to paint apartments in this building he'd just bought. I did that for him, and we just got to be good friends from then on. But when he started the Lone Star Saloon he asked me to bartend for him.

RON: Rick had a talent for spotting and hiring bartenders that fit the image of the bar that he wanted. He often picked from among his friends.

PETE: Exactly, he tried to pick working-class, blue-collar guys, not real show-bunnies, so to speak.

RON: Right, men like the Rainbows. So Rick had been looking for a place, and then he found and rented the space at 1098 Howard.

PETE: Seventh Street and Howard, yeah.

RON: Did you help Rick fix the place up? I'm curious because by the time I first went to the bar, there was already all of this hardware and stuff on the walls.

PETE: Yes, I helped decorate that. It all came together really quick because Rick said, "We don't have enough things, we don't have enough stuff!" So we put the word out and in no time there was an overabundance of things. People were really willing to help with that.

RON: So the fledgling community in a sense really helped to create the atmosphere of the bar. What was it like at the beginning?

PETE: It was very exciting. We had a couple of pre-opening parties, and the first one was quite small and intimate.

RON: Small and intimate—meaning dark and sleazy, of course. Do you recall when that was?

PETE: The first pre-opening party was about June 30th. Then the official opening of the bar was July Fourth week, as I recall.

The next event must have been Dore Alley Street Fair. I went out soliciting for business in public. I made a giant star-shaped sign on a pole and just wrote LONE STAR SALOON and the address on one side, and then on the other side, ROCK & ROLL and put on my best garb and went out. And it was like the Pied Piper or whatever: When I came back, there were a zillion people behind me! The place was crammed, bodies everywhere. God, it was just jammed. It was great fun.

Of course, the Rainbows also had a giant 17th anniversary party there. We called it an "anniversary riot." There were just too many people for the place to fit 'em all in. And I remember that party was when everybody made "the noise" that could be heard for blocks around, everybody was just screaming, to the point where you could go two blocks away and still hear the hum from the place. It was really weird.

RON: The Man-buzz.

PETE: That was kind of like the Rainbow's send-off for Rick—or maybe more like a get-off-the-ground party. It really helped to establish the Lone Star.

RON: A barwarming, maybe.

PETE: Next we had a cigar party. We decided to be the host for the cigar club, The Hot Ash Club, on Thursday nights. That was certainly a heyday for them as well. I recall the first Hot Ash party was outrageous. The Fire Department came, the smoke was billowing out of the bar so thick. People had to step outside to breathe, the smoke was just too overpowering. That was fun.

RON: I remember showing up for one of those nights—the smoke was unbearable. It wasn't a big space to begin with. Of course, there was the Lone Star slogan, or cheer, maybe: "Close the Fuckin' Door."

PETE: Right, which was on the back of the first T-shirt. That saying was due to the fact the bar was a few feet down; when you walked in the door you had to come down a few steps. The door faced west-southwest, and so if you were in the bar and you would open that door and the sun would just glare in your face.

RON: In the afternoon during Happy Hour. Was that a double door?

PETE: Yeah, it was. The door didn't close itself, either. It opened and would stay open. So everybody would scream, "Close the fuckin' door," and that became the motto.

RON: It was so hard to try to enter the bar without falling down the stairs, because if you came in from that bright sunlight you needed at least a minute for your eyes to adjust!

PETE: Nothing like making an entrance. Those doors had no mercy for anyone, inside or out.

RON: A guy named Sal, who as it turned out was working in a type shop where I later got a job, did the first T-shirts. Neither Sal nor Rick could find the artwork, so I had to redesign it when Rick wanted them reprinted.

PETE: Yeah, I remember that.

RON: I also painted the star on the front of the building.

PETE: That's right, I remember that too. Remember the star that we did first? Rick wanted the star on the building, and I and (I guess) Lyn Light did it with fake blood, stage blood. The next day there was this trail of ants carrying the star away down the sidewalk. Rick was not amused, if I recall, but we thought it was hilarious. Then you came and painted the real one.

RON: I had a part-time job in the city at the time and was living in Emeryville. I heard about the Lone Star from a guy I met at the Pilsner Inn [bar near the Castro] named Roger, who told me, "You should definitely check the Lone Star out because the kind of guys that you like will be there." And he was completely correct.

When I met Rick I asked him if he needed any help in terms of ads or graphics and the like, and he said, "Well, can you paint this star?" It seemed easy, but it took me several tries to get the proportions and angles right.

PETE: Stars aren't as easy as they would appear. Something odd about a star.

RON: Sure is. You mentioned Lyn Light. Was he working there at the time?

PETE: Yeah, Lyn Light, and JoeBear Golini was probably there by then. And Ron Brewer.

RON: Right. Ron eventually won a major leather title, right?

PETE: Yeah, and then he moved to Arizona.

RON: And then we lost him to AIDS. When I started coming to the bar regularly, I was very quiet and would just sit by myself most times. Ron was an outrageous provocateur and he would throw handfuls of ice across the bar at me, trying to get me roused up.

PETE: Who else was around in those days? There was Rick's lover then, Ken Stanley, who didn't really work at the bar, but he certainly helped with setting it up. But Rick was pretty much proprietor and manager at first.

RON: It was still a pretty small place. There was just one pool table and not much room around it.

PETE: Actually, it was a downsized pool table. The cellar door was fun too: a trapdoor in the back part of the bar. Down there was liquor storage and other supplies and Rick's office. You had to make everybody get off to open it. Then you'd sort of drop straight down into it and pray that nobody fell in.

RON: How much time was there before the big earthquake?

PETE: It was just three months. Or three and a half months, perhaps.

RON: Were there theme parties at the old place?

PETE: The one theme party was a Friday the 13th party in October, and the theme for it was "macabre," so to speak, getting ready for Halloween. We decorated the whole place in sheets and surgical gloves. I don't know what the point was behind all of this exactly, but it was just weird enough.

RON: So that Friday the 13th party was just a few days before the earthquake, which took place the following Tuesday, October 17th, 1989. I'd just turned 31.

PETE: I remember that even before the earthquake, Rick was becoming "over it" already. Right before the earthquake, he was saying, "Well, what are we going to do? There's not enough space and we need a full liquor license." His attitude was, "What are we going to do? This place is already a success and I'm bored." He wanted more.

RON: So then we get to the Loma Prieta earthquake, which rocked through the San Francisco Bay area, severely damaging the Lone Star building. Within days the building was condemned.

PETE: When I got there, hours after the quake hit, the police wouldn't let anyone in. The funny thing was that the cops had no clue that anybody was in there. So we hung around there until, eventually, the cops left. When we got in there, it was just like being in a movie. The whole scene was...

RON: Surreal. Kind of like *The Poseidon Adventure*, with everything upside-down.

PETE: Yeah! A hole had opened up in the middle of the floor, and the cooler was tipped over and half-sunk into the basement. All the beer in the cooler had been retrieved, and Rick was saying, "Well, just drink it! Drink it! Drink it all! Because that's all we can do with it." After a while, we started moving things out of the bar as quickly as possible because the cops were supposed to return, and we knew they would not let us in there any more.

RON: It was very dangerous for you guys to stay in there.

PETE: I guess, but that building sat there for another month or two afterward, and I was in and out of it a hundred times, but you're right, theoretically it was dangerous. [*Both laugh*]

RON: I guess danger is relative. Especially if you have a cooler full of beer you have to drink.

PETE: Exactly. I remember the apartments upstairs, which each had a very short clawfoot bathtub. They were really cool little tubs. After the quake, when we were walking through the whole building, I remember seeing that the plumbing had stayed where it should have have been. All the bathtubs were floating up in the air on their drainpipes because the whole building had settled several feet, but all the plumbing was intact. That was so weird looking, that was really strange.

RON: What was salvaged?

PETE: Pretty much everything. We couldn't get the cooler out but we got out the pool table, the cash registers, the decorations, and all the important things. We moved all the stuff over to the basement of Rick's house.

RON: Over the next six months, Rick took me to look at several prospective spaces. A few of the spaces seemed promising, and he tried to acquire them, but they kept falling through for one or another reasons. He looked at the old Ambush space, I think. And then there was a sewing shop.

PETE: That's the one he got, finally, the summer after that October. We were open for business in July or August of the following year, 1990.

RON: So, that would make it about 10 months. I think he was really pushing to have it up and open by the time of the summer street fairs. In the meantime, though, he had the build-out. They first built the front bar, which, initially I think, was very simple. And then they built a small room used for a store.

PETE: Yeah, we called it the Cotton Gin because it was full of cotton T-shirts.

RON: Rick was really getting into the whole idea of "tourist product sales" of Lone Star items like T-shirts and belts and posters at that point. I remember his eyes widening with excitement as he described how much merchandising profit *Bear* magazine was making—and he wanted to carve out a piece of that for himself. I think he realized then that there was a real promotional opportunity, and I think he was also encouraged at that point by Richard Bulger.

PETE: Richard Bulger, the publisher of *Bear* magazine. That whole thing was coinciding, definitely.

RON: Let's talk about the friendship between Rick and Richard. Do you know how the two of them met?

PETE: Richard came into the old bar and asked if he could sell his magazines there, as I recall.

RON: They also had friends in common and were roughly the same age, I believe. Richard started the magazine in '87 and put out about half a dozen issues before the old bar opened. The alliance between them wasn't just professional, however; they had palled around and partied together.

PETE: When the earthquake hit, Richard felt terrible that the Lone Star was gone—not only for Rick in that he didn't have a business, but also because we didn't have a place to hang out anymore. Rick had just printed all those T-shirts and felt like they were useless. Then Richard offered to run an ad in the magazine. It was almost like "contribute to the Lone Star Fund" charity or something.

RON: There was a short article in issue no. 11, which showed Bear icon Jack Radcliffe on the cover for the first time. There also was a display ad that was pretty outrageous, when you think about it:

> *Lone Star Saloon*
> *Physically Destroyed October 17, 1989*
> *But The Spirit Lives On*
> *Lone Star Memorial T-Shirts*
> *Proceeds to Lone Star Relocation Project*

They were making out to be like some sort of charity!

PETE: That was what really brought the place to legendary status, so to speak.

RON: You're absolutely right, Pete. The back cover of that issue also had Chris Nelson's classic picture of the group in front of the quaked-out Lone Star. Chris later made that the lead image in his book *The Bear Cult*. It shows Joe Banks and John Gardiner, Terry, and JoeBear. You're shown monkeying around on the scaffolding. Steve Kasper, a Rainbow and a *Bear* magazine coverman, whom I worked for on and off doing gardening, is holding up Buddy's IV bag—I guess Steve had sprung Buddy from the hospital. And there's some other guys as well. The morning of the photo, Kasper had called to tell me it was happening, but it was drizzling and I didn't want to ride my motorcycle all the way around the bay (I was in the East Bay and the Bay Bridge was closed) just for the photo.

But that photo is evocative of nothing so much as a group of orphans standing in the rain in the shadow of their irreparably damaged orphanage.

PETE: And so lots and lots of orders for T-shirts came through the mail and people were in touch all the time wanting to know because the article also mentioned that the new one would be opening, but nobody knew exactly when or where.

RON: The new bar got a national reputation due to its exposure in *Bear* magazine. After it opened Rick asked me to put together a newsletter. He told me that he had already a mailing list of several hundred, mostly outside the Bay area. I also think he got names from Richard's magazine's list, too.

PETE: The reopening of the bar seemed very connected with the Bear thing, I guess, because *Bear* magazine was the main source of news about it.

RON: A lot of this "significant coincident" has to do with Rick's friendship with Richard. Rick was trying to create the image of the nasty little biker bar with an international reputation, and his shrewd alliance with Richard made that happen. If they hadn't been friends or even friendly, I doubt the Lone Star could have hitched its wagon to the magazine's star.

On the other hand, the earthquake event provided the magazine's first real news, the first editorial content that addressed a community of men who identified as or with Bears. Not only was there an identifiable group of these Bear men, they had a cause! They'd suffered displacement in the earthquake—although it's kind of silly to think of these middle-aged hairy homos as some sort of deprived orphans in need of, like you said, a charitable fund so they could have a place to drink and carouse. Bar life in the city (and elsewhere) was important in the way that gay men form community—which is not so much the case in gay life today—and the earthquake was the adversity out of which this first Bear community was forged.

Meanwhile, back at the ranch—even before the new Lone Star was open to the public, Rick held several pre-opening parties, by invitation.

PETE: Basically it was Rick's way of keeping his old patrons and friends in touch.

RON: JoeBear became the first hired manager at the new Lone Star, right?

PETE: Yes. JoeBear had been managing a bar in the Haight. Rick had no experience whatsoever with liquor, and he wanted JoeBear's experience with the liquor distributors and setting up the bar. JoeBear did a very good job with all that, and with all of us. Many of us weren't really bartenders; some had never even bartended.

RON: Other than bartending, you did other work around the bar, right?

PETE: Decorative type of stuff, like non-flower flower arrangements.

RON: Very cutting-edge. Describe some of those things that you did, Pete.

PETE: Very industrial, lots of rust and odd metal objects. Rick gave me the center spot behind the bar, which had a nice spotlight. That became my space. I did a spring arrangement in the springtime, which was all these coil springs from the front ends of cars welded onto stakes and put in a metal bucket. That was a joke that everybody got and thought was cool. The one with the coils was one of my favorites.

RON: I always was amazed by your mechanico-floral centerpieces behind the bar. Always the sublime counterpoised with the mundane. In particular, I remember one Valentine's Day you had a prominent black leather heart with a rusty chainsaw arrowed through it, hung over a tastefully dripped pool of red. And what else were you doing at the new bar?

PETE: Decorating the patio was one of the things that I liked. I used to get these huge junky hunks of metal, like gears and booms and hooks and stuff like that, and drag them out to that patio.

RON: Rick was great in that way: he'd let the creative people like yourself and Steve Stafford and, to a much lesser extent, myself, do our thing that way. He was creative to the extent of recognizing other people's talents.

PETE: Rick always maintained that he did not have any creative talent himself, although I think certainly he overlooked the fact that he was the major engineer himself of the whole thing. He was able to pick the people, and he was more than willing to let other people do their thing to create a cool atmosphere. For instance, the Lone Star also did art shows like the Ambush had done.

RON: Over the years dozens of people have exhibited there. It's remarkable, if you think about it, that we're talking about a bar, not an art gallery. Plus there was the SHADES Project, which Willie Watson, Richard Carron, and Tucker Finn began, which had professional and amateur artists alike create images on window shades, which would then be auctioned off to benefit the AIDS Emergency Fund. When did Steve

Stafford pop onto the scene? He was a Rainbow, right?

PETE: He became a Rainbow the last year he was alive. Steve met Rick just before the new bar opened, and from there he drew the first poster for the Lone Star.

RON: Featuring the guy with the anvil—the "Second Opening" poster.

PETE: The whole Russian thing.

RON: Rick even had shirts made with the name of the bar in Cyrillic. Then Steve started to design T-shirts and other promotional stuff. He also came on bartending, too, at some point.

PETE: Later on he did. He didn't want to at first, but then Rick convinced him. Then the got the job at *Bear*, which was a good thing.

RON: He was first the art director, then the managing editor there, after Frank Strona. But back at the bar in the first year, Rick tried hard to create, in a sense, programming for the bar, so that every day there was something going on. On the weekends we started the beer busts, which were almost always benefits right from the outset.

PETE: The receptions for the art shows were Wednesday nights.

RON: Thursday nights were *The Simpsons*, and the last Thursday of each month was Cigar Night.

PETE: Tuesday night was pool league. And we always had a softball team.

RON: Right, what was the name of the team?

PETE: The Cockstars. That didn't happen until after Rick's second bar, Cocktails, was open, or at least I don't recall there being a softball team prior to that. But Cocktails was not for long, either.

RON: As soon as Rick had finished building the back bar on the patio at the Lone Star, he started looking around for a new venue. Why was that? Why wasn't one bar enough for him?

PETE: Rick had realized he was ill at that point—but he developed what they call the Sarah Winchester syndrome. [Sarah Winchester was an eccentric woman who believed she would stay alive as long as she continued to renovate her house.] You just keep building and building and building, thinking that you'll never die. So he was definitely looking for something, and he was now ready for something a little more active along the lines of—

RON: Something mainstream?

PETE: He wanted to do something after-hours, too, which he couldn't do at the Lone Star.

[Rick Redewill and the staff of the Lone Star siphoned off much of the energy into the preparations for the opening of Cocktails, but it became immediately obvious that the new bar was not going to be a venue nearly as successful as the Lone Star. Ron, who had been hired as a bartender at Cocktails, was laid off two weeks after it opened. Following a coup of the manager's position from JoeBear by the less-qualified Lyn Light, Pete left the Lone Star for over a year. Steven Stafford left the Lone Star to work for Richard Bulger as *Bear* magazine's managing editor. Sapped by the strain of opening Cocktails, Rick's failing health put him in the hospital for weeks and then in recovery, which severely limited his direct involvement in both businesses. The Lone Star, which had been on autopilot and paying all the bills, saw a downturn in business and morale. Lyn's health, as well as that of his lover, Jerry, who worked at the bar, and Steve Stafford's was failing. As Rick became more and more ill, he started looking for someone to buy the Lone Star. Many bar patrons were also becoming sick and dying.]

RON: Finally, Rick passed away on April 14, 1993, just days after he signed a deal to sell the bar. Lyn Light died only a couple of months later. Steve Stafford died a year after Rick, I believe, and then Richard Bulger sold Brush Creek Media at the end of '94. Rick Redewill's death signalled the end of an era. It was a very sad time, probably the height at which we were losing people to AIDS. The Rainbows had also lost several guys.

PETE: Yes, there was Michael Martin, Hoot Jenkins, Jack Sharpless, Steve Kasper, and my former lover, Gary Bell—all about the same time.

RON: After Rick died, the bar went into purgatory. Originally three men bought it from Rick, but then there were problems between them, and, after a legal tussle, one of them got the business solo.

PETE: Kevin Owens, who's from a great big Texas family company, owns it now. Kevin took over about two years after Rick died.

RON: In the meantime what happened with the theme nights and all the other stuff? Was all that forgotten?

PETE: No, I don't think it was all forgotten, but they certainly don't do them like we used to. And they have certainly concentrated on the Bear thing now. It's totally a Bear bar, 100%. During the big IBR [International Bear Rendezvous] in February, the Lone Star is at the epicenter of that event.

One of Rick's wants was to develop the retail thing, and Kevin has done that fully. They have a full Lone Star merchandise store upstairs and go all over the country to different Bear events to sell their merchandise.

RON: They have a little cottage industry going on. Or not so little, as the case may be.

PETE: Totally. I think there's an online store, too.

RON: Yes, there is. They've really developed that aspect of the business, which is, well, enterprising of them. As my friend Mike calls it, it's like "Bear Disneyland." Does the Lone Star still attract the motorcycle crowd?

PETE: There are always bikes out there, absolutely, but you'll find bikes in front of all the bars still.

RON: Well, the Lone Star sure isn't the same place it was when we were there. When I was in San Francisco for IBR 2000, I didn't go to the Lone Star at night, when it was packed tits to ass. I went in the afternoons and on the Monday night following IBR. They still had the sign that I painted with Steve Stafford out there on the back patio wall. The place felt familiar and comfortable as ever, but it no longer felt magical in the same way at all.

PETE: Well, an awful lot of energy has been drained out of there. Still, I hope that younger people, or ones just getting into the life, can find the kind of niche that we once had. The best that you can have is memories that you're fond of from one time or another. Those memories and times certainly are some of my fondest.

RON: Same here, pal.

CHAPTER 8
FROM CULT TO SUBCULTURE TO COUTURE:
EVOLVING BEAR COMMUNITY
~ A DISCUSSION WITH LES WRIGHT ~

LES WRIGHT was the firstborn of a family of day laborers and rail-road workers in Syracuse, New York, in 1953. First a student at SUNY, Albany, he spent the 1970s as an expatriate studying at German universities (the origins of his gay left activism), then spent 14 years in "gay finishing school," residing in San Francisco's Castro district while completing his Ph.D. in Comparative Literature at UC Berkeley. He has trained formally as a German, Russian, and American Studies scholar, and as a community-based gay cultural historian. As a long-term survivor of multiple trauma and various forms of "social death" (incest, addiction, homelessness, HIV/AIDS), Les has also trained to become a certified thanatologist, examining the traumatizing effects of being queer in heteronormative societies. He is the founder-curator of the Bear History Project, editor of the groundbreaking *The Bear Book*, vols. I & II, lead curator of Bear Icons Exhibitions I & II, author of numerous articles, and currently a teacher of Cultural Studies at Mount Ida College in the Boston area.

Where do we locate Bear community? There are probably far too few self-identified Bears to ever constitute a Bear ghetto, but are Bears destined to be a community in diaspora, floating somewhere between major urban area Bearclubs, rural outposts, and the Internet?

Few have observed the emergence and flourishing of Bear subculture with the methodical perseverance and hopeful vision of Les Wright, who in many ways embodies the higher qualities, aside from his Bearish physical presence, that I associate with being a Bear—especially his playfulness and sense of Bear brotherhood.

When Les and I met at a 1988 meeting of a sane and sober leather-BDSM group in San Francisco, the Trusted Servants, we shared almost immediately that sense of brotherhood, as well as a barely stated understanding that our participation in Bear community was something that had changed our lives. While Les pursued his Bear social contacts at the Bear Hugs sex parties, I followed mine at the Lone Star Saloon—yet whenever we'd run into each other on the street, we felt a similar spirit of excitement at the creation of this new community.

Coincidentally, we both left San Francisco in the early '90s to move to Boston, which is where our mutual interest in Bear culture turned from a rather intense physical participation to more intellectual pursuits. I was honored when Les asked me to contribute to both of *The Bear Books*; naturally, when the time came to put together *Bears on Bears*, I turned to Les in an online discussion to help me unpack some tough questions about the state of Beardom.

RON: How do you apply your skills as a scholar to the Bear subculture?

LES: At this point I am mostly interested in what has turned into this gargantuan Bear Icons project—of questioning and challenging by various aesthetic and theoretical means current social ideas of what masculinity is—shaking complacent thinking up a bit.

The Bear Icons project began as a complementary project, a visual supplement to *The Bear Book*, since the publisher, Haworth Press, was not equipped to publish a lot of artwork or other visuals. So, what started out as a virtual art show transformed into an actual, evolving art exhibition—in New York City (1999) and in Boston (2000). From there, T.J. Norris and I have been looking at taking on tour a sort of Bear version of the pivotal photo exhibit "The Family of Man."

RON: I can see that Bear Icons would reflect your sensibilities. Why does it seem so important to concentrate on the visual aspect of the subculture?

LES: Well, it's a question of what's compelling. I'm interested in how self-identifying Bears look, how they see themselves, the vast range, from folk pornographic to edgy and all the crazy and vivid visions that Bear-oriented artists and photographers have.

On the other hand, a lot of Bear history boils down to another version of the identity politics I experienced during the days of gay liberation.

RON: Please clarify that.

LES: I feel I have peaked on Bears as a social novelty.

RON: Personally?

LES: Yes. I have seen Bear groups, clubs, and commercial ventures devolve into the same in-group/out-group wrangling and cynical sabotaging of the perceived competition. The fleeting moment of utopian alternative—which is what originally got me caught up in the Bear stuff—has largely dissipated. The best of activities today that Bears engage in arise out of genuine desire to serve a greater good, to do civic good deeds in the name of Bear community.

While I have been moving away from Bear-specific research, I have become much more interested in questions of the social construction of masculinity, of who and what we find attractive—how erotic desire works. I have also been exploring very pressing questions about the relationship between masculinity and violence in our society. And that brings my Bear work full circle to the other big area that I have been rummaging around in for many years, namely sexual violence, homophobia, trauma, and its effects on long-term survival.

It's a wonder anyone turns out reasonably well-adjusted, given the amount of trauma that parents, communities, and American society perpetrates upon little kids. So, I have started to look at Bears as a response to being ostracized and traumatized by the gay mainstream.

RON: Do you feel there is, or at least could be, a Bear political agenda?

LES: I think there could be, and there should be, some kind of Bear political agenda.

RON: What might it consist of? The first item that comes to mind is advocacy for gay (and mainstream) media to produce greater diversity of images.

LES: The media shape us at least as much as they reflect us. Those who have the power to decide what goes in and what stays out are the folks wielding that political power. The gay media are actually extremely conservative.

RON: They're only as liberal as the conservative companies that own them, as the saying goes.

LES: The notion of serving society, as constituted in the social democracies of western Europe, is anathema to most Americans. Liberal democracy is equated with free-enterprise capitalism, which is equated with freedom (of consumer choice). There is no sense of responsibility or duty or even fellow-feeling in our society, by and large.

RON: Please apply this to the current situation in Bear subculture.

LES: Now, within the context of Bear community this means something like "You have value as a person as long as I want something from you." In other words, "Buy my stuff, give me sex, validate me and, if I like you, I'll say nice things about you too." And underneath that message is this whole undercurrent of internalized homophobia that pervades very nearly all the queer community and screws things up as well. So, there is that multidimensional consumer dynamic that people tend to be very blind to.

RON: How does that manifest in Bear culture?

LES: Well, the obvious way is the whole hierarchy of Bear beauty. I am shocked still when I hear a Bear talking about self-acceptance and the idea of "bigger is better" one moment, and then in the next moment making a mad dash for some young, buffed, muscled guy. You know, the ideal vs. real dichotomy: "I know what I want, but I'll take what I can get." I think of this as Bears becoming conscious of their own sexual capital.

RON: And, I hope, getting a better exchange rate. But why fault Bears in particular for falling short of their ideals? Hell, why shouldn't Bears be objectifying and objectified, like everyone else in this culture?

LES: Some Bears actually have unique sexual preferences, but the magazines propagate specific ideals. I am as romantic and idealistic as they come—a naive fool, probably—so a lot of my criticism of others applies at least as much to myself. But I take issue with double standards. And I am extremely uncomfortable with the sexual capital self-knowledge thing.

RON: It's very difficult to tease out and improve one's self-esteem without increasing one's knowledge of one's own sexual capital.

LES: The magazines put in what people will buy. So you can't blame the magazine publishers for promoting their idealized Bears—after all, that is what people are willing to spend money on.

RON: Addressing the virtual invisibility of Bears of color—in Bear media and at Bear events—might be another agenda item.

LES: There is no one absolute standard for beauty. It's surprisingly variable.

RON: Right, which makes gay body-fashion fascism even more insidious. Beardom seems an emergent masculinity that lost its way somewhere in all of this.

LES: That would be true if there had been an intent, a concerted attempt. Masculinity is a fetishized consumer object in our culture.

RON: And as such, it would be an easy target for Bears to organize to attack it, or at least criticize it. What's your perspective on Gen-X Bears (GXBs)? They seem very organized and much more interested in making a social difference.

LES: I'm not that versed in the GXB scene. I think a profound difference is that they are the first gay generation to grow up with a whole socially integrated support system, or at least knowledge of a preexisting gay community and identity. That must be very odd.

RON: Odd, perhaps, to those of us who came of age after Stonewall and before AIDS. The leather community doesn't really serve that function.

LES: True, the leather community no longer serves that initiation function. In the '60s you needed a gay insider to initiate you into the subculture; in the '40s it was even more difficult to make your way into the life. So what kind of gay existence do Gen-Xers come out into? A lot of media, reference and resource books, and local and national support groups. Since they have no need to create community from scratch, maybe some of what GXBs have, and are, comes from having a leg up, and not having to start at square one as the generation before them had to. GXBs did not enter this world with laws against homosexuality, the American Psychiatric Association declaring us mentally ill, police raids, and your name in the papers—

RON: Yes, but they came out into AIDS culture, too.

LES: True, Gen-Xers came out into a world filled with AIDS, and a dawning Bear subculture. I think the newness of Beardom may have been some of the draw. Gen-X Bears emerged at a pivotal point: these men came out as gay but discovered they did not fit the preferred images, and along came older gay men who were models of self-acceptance.

RON: Finding ideal images to which Gen-X Bears can relate and pattern must promote greatly their self-esteem.

LES: Precisely. I think they have far more self-esteem than earlier generations, and they get early Beardom as a role model without the emotional baggage. They have the option to reject those who tell them they "don't look right" for the gay world, whereas the first-wave Bears had to and still are fighting a lot of internalized negative self-image problems because there was no alternative in the past.

RON: Fighting ageism might be another point of political rallying for Bears.

LES: Yes, and with the Baby Boom generation aging, I think that is almost inevitable, don't you?

RON: Well, in view of Bear youth adding themselves to the ever-burgeoning Bear community, one has to wonder what this means in terms of Bears' assimilation into the gaystream, as well as into the straight mainstream. Have Bears always been destined to be a community in diaspora, without a solid core of identity?

LES: I have two thoughts at the moment on this. First is the whole concept of community—gay, queer, Bear. As a community we are not that old, and so I wonder if we will continue to exist with a community consciousness or identity. To use a clichéd comparison, if you are visibly marked as different (e.g. black), then outside forces will see to it that this sense of community in diaspora goes on, but if the shared culture is lost (e.g., assimilated Jews), are you then still in community, even if in diaspora?

RON: Are you speaking of the relationship of identity to community?

LES: In view of what I have read and not experienced directly, the new generations of queer youth desire full assimilation into mainstream society. Some reject the label of gay or queer identity: it would be hard to have a sense of community with people who do not see themselves as being like you or me.

RON: Right. By definition, community cannot exist without a unitive identity.

LES: Exactly. But is this media hype, folks fishing for a new angle, or a real and profound shift on the cusp of happening?

RON: In this case, though, Bear youth do identify with the community—at least to some extent. What about the growing number of men who tried the Bearclub thing and got turned off by the cliques or the A-Bear, musclebear, glam Bear worship?

LES: And are now former Bears?

RON: Well, for the last five years I've been calling them postbears.

LES: Well, are there really any ex-gays?

RON: Ah! but ex-gay is not at all postgay!

LES: And the difference is...?

RON: I was afraid you'd ask that. In a nutshell: postgay seems a primarily self-motivated identity change, whereas ex-gay stems from psychological pressure exerted from insidious outside religious-right hetero sources. Being ex-gay is about rejecting in toto homosex and gay culture; postgay represents a willing shift away from solely homosex and gay culture toward a desire for fluidity of sexual or gender identity leading to utter integration into straight society.

LES: It seems that there are several different gay consciousness generations all commingling, and we tend not to notice them so much. We do speak in terms of gay generations, and arbitrarily distinguish pre-Stonewall, Stonewall, AIDS era, and so on.

RON: Plus "queer" and "questioning"—these are men in differing gay-bi "cohorts," as Eric Rofes would put it.

LES: We have some queer youth who say they are postgay and see queerness as a small aspect of their identity. We also have Bear youth, who are building a great deal of their identity on being homoerotically included and specifically identifying with gay Bears. Now, these two individuals may be of the same cohort, but they are living in very different generations of gay consciousness.

We are a conscious community, more in the utopian tradition of people who have chosen to come together. Any diaspora consciousness requires that we first have a sense of community.

RON: True.

LES: Plenty of queer folk don't have that to begin with, let alone the youth who now have no memory of the old culture or speak the old language of oppression. Bear youth may be young gay men who feel oppressed within their own community of queers. Yet it's diametrically opposite of those queer youth who reject the label of "gay" to avoid anti-gay oppression.

RON: So, for such a Bear-identified youth who also sees himself as postgay, isn't there some kind of essential inner conflict set up? Or are gay youths today open enough to incorporate these things? It's hard to say in theory, perhaps.

LES: I must share an example from the recent past with a long-standing gay friend of mine: I knew K. for many years in San Francisco. After breaking up with his second lover—a very painful and messy affair, "monogamous," but the lover infected K. with HIV—K. lost his job and his house, threw in the towel around 1990, and returned home to Middle America. He did tons of AIDS activist work for his state, grew weary of all this, and then the last of his male gay friends in San Francisco died. He became emotionally attached to a woman and the two of them got married a year ago.

Now, K. is still gay (at least in my mind), has written some interesting apologia to me about all this, but says he is now far happier than ever, married to a woman and fully reintegrated into straight society. In fact, he says he wishes he had done this years ago. My understanding is that it's either non- or low-sexual, but it's really about his rejection of a gay social identity and living in a gay community, which he has rejected completely. But is he still gay? Or maybe bi?

RON: Interesting puzzle. Does he still play Barbra Streisand albums?

LES: I think so...

RON: Well, there you go!

LES: Anyway, here's the rest of the analogy. If I compare my experiences of gay men in urban community with living out here in the sticks, where some guys (Bears) are closeted, to varying degrees, a few have that full-blown urban-style gay identity, and some identify as "just regular Joes" who like to fuck with men. The attitude is, "My having sex with men is not connected with faggots and faggotry."

So we come back to the question of who is a Bear, and creating or identifying with Bear community. Some guys living out this way, who completely reject homosexuals and "their lifestyle," kind of slip in the back door by messing around with a local Bear or two.

RON: You mean MSMs—men who have sex with men but who don't necessarily identify as gay or bisexual.

LES: There are tons of guys out there interested in fucking but not in being in any way identified as gay or as a Bear. So when the postgay generation comes along, we still have this kind of pre-Stonewall closeted and even nonsocial identity regular Joe folks. The (very postmodernist) question in my mind is: When postgay youth rejects the label, presumably this enables more men to have sex with men without fear of being labeled gay. Is this progressing forward, or a major reactive slide backward, or what?

It's kind of like this linear progression through time, where men have always had sex with men, and we have this bubble that bulges between the 19th and 20th centuries and then disappears again—the bubble representing the moment of gay identity.

RON: So Bears are a sub-bubble?

LES: Only the very best of them! But seriously, we have this broadening splay of directions that homoerotically inclined men can now choose among. They can be old-fashioned closeted, out, in community or not, or postgay, queer, or postqueer. Bears are a postmodern phenomenon: mix and match, make up your own rules, use stuff from all different places in culture and history.

RON: Beardom still exists as an emergent masculinity, but how long that might last is hard to say.

LES: It's all up for grabs. Bears, by defining ourselves as gay and masculine, deconstruct the whole notion treasured by mainstream society that gay men aren't really men and therefore justify persecution, or social intolerance. I think Bears are to mainstream society what drag queens are to the gay rights movement—only in exactly the opposite socio-sexual term.

RON: I agree. The most notable parallel between Bears breaking down masculine and feminine concepts seems to me to be transpersons, who really queer our masculinity as we know it.

LES: Yes, our culture pivots on either/or duality. Bears do not fit neatly in any of the dualistic categories, and I think that not fitting in to a square hole, not even being a round peg, makes a lot of people crazy.

Part Three

Bear Icons and Celeb-bear-ties

CHAPTER 9
WHAT MAKES A BEAR PORN LEGEND?
~ AN INTERVIEW WITH JACK RADCLIFFE ~

"JACK RADCLIFFE," as he's known to tens of thousands of admirers, is the man most preeminently thought of as a Bear icon. He has been a featured Brush Creek Media model since the early days of *Bear* magazine, and his image also appeared in Chris Nelson's classic *The Bear Cult*. Aside from being a veritable pinup Bear, Jack has starred in a load of videos, including *Uncut Footage*, *Bear Palm Springs Vacation*, *Leather Bears at Play*, *Big Bear Trucking Company*, and *Bear Sex Party*. His physical image—tall, handsome, furry, muscular, with sparkling brown eyes—has been so popular with the Bear set that he's been featured in his very own calendar as well.

Jack, in his late thirties, at 6 foot 2 and 240 pounds, has been reluctant to admit his status as an icon. More than that, he proved to be a somewhat elusive Bear, as his work is quite demanding. But after repeated attempts, I managed to capture him via telephone for this glimpse of the soft, furry underbelly of the beast.

RON: Jack, tell us a little bit about your background, where you grew up, and about your family.

JACK: I grew up on Staten Island in New York City, with two parents and a brother and sister.

RON: Are your parents still living? Are you still close with your family?

JACK: Yes, they're both alive, and we're fairly close.

RON: Do they know about your life in porn?

JACK: Yes.

RON: Do you know if they've seen any of your pictures?

JACK: I don't know. I know I've told my mother about it, but has she gone out and seen it? I really don't know. I doubt it. I've told my brother about it. He's gay, so there's a good possibility he's seen my pictures somewhere, browsing the Web. He's younger and lives in North Carolina.

RON: Did you go to school also in Staten Island?

JACK: Only up to high school. I went to college up in Buffalo, New York. I've got two degrees: one in math and one in physics.

RON: In physics. Really? I'm impressed. Why did you pursue physics?

JACK: I enjoy it.

RON: Is it applicable to your work now?

JACK: The concepts, in terms of figuring things out, and the methodologies are useful. Is it useful to know how particles collide? Not necessarily.

RON: But the mental or intellectual discipline was useful?

JACK: Right.

RON: Please say something about your current work.

JACK: Basically I'm a computer programmer.

RON: And you co-own a software company at present?

JACK: It's more like a software consulting company. It's very demanding work—sometimes I put in 10 to 12 hours a day. We have about nine or 10 employees.

RON: Do the folks at work know about your photo and video appearances?

JACK: I don't ask, I don't know.

RON: They don't ask, you don't tell. [*Both laugh*] So, to return to your personal history: After you finished college in Buffalo you moved to Denver.

JACK: Right.

RON: And how long were you in Denver?

JACK: I was in Denver for about six, seven years.

RON: Before you came to San Francisco.

JACK: Right.

RON: When did you come out?

JACK: I came out when I left college in '83. That was the summer when I was moving from Buffalo to Denver and I really got to explore then.

RON: That was after college. But before that, had you dated women?

JACK: No. I've never been with a woman.

RON: How long have you worn a beard?

JACK: Pretty much since I could grow one.

RON: Have you always thought of yourself as a Bear?

JACK: Actually, the concept didn't enter my mind until the *Bear* magazine editor had sent me a copy of the magazine. I'd met one of Richard's employees when I was working at a bar in Denver, and he told me about the magazine. His name was Congo.

RON: Congo Moore, who did sales and marketing for *Bear* early on.

JACK: He told me about the magazine and all that was going on with it. He said he'd like to take some pictures, and then he sent me a copy or two to look at.

RON: I remember seeing in one of the early *Bear* magazines a pictorial feature on Denver that included several photos of you, including one with your dick hanging out of your shorts, with the headline, "Here's What Awaits You in Denver."

JACK: Yeah. Issue no. 9 was the very first issue I was in.

RON: In issue no. 10 you were already featured in an ad on the inside front cover for Chris's Brahma Studios—which was odd, considering that they didn't make you a coverman or give you a photo spread of your own until the next issue, no. 11. In any case, you moved rather fast through their ranks.

JACK: You think so?

RON: To me it seems pretty darn quick, yes. How did you feel during your first photo shoot? Were you nervous?

JACK: Yes! [*Both laugh*]

RON: But not shy.

JACK: Yes, I was shy.

RON: Were you particularly shy as a kid or a young man?

JACK: Oh, yeah. I still am!

RON: But there's a difference between shyness and modesty.

JACK: Well, I don't walk around showing myself off at every opportunity. I rarely, rarely go out, and when I do, I don't randomly walk up to people and say, "Hi, how are you? Blahblahblah." I just sort of hang around and if people talk with me, I'll talk with them. And that's about it. I'm not an outgoing, gregarious person, so I do see myself as being rather shy. When I'm doing a photo shoot or a movie, I'm usually dealing with just one or two other people, and I'm more just in the moment of the thing, so I just deal with the moment.

RON: Do you have to work at being outgoing?

JACK: Definitely.

RON: Did you have a poor self-image of yourself as a kid, like a lot of Bears?

JACK: Oh, yeah, absolutely. I was fat and ugly.

RON: You really felt that way? Did you have a weight problem when you were young?

JACK: Yes, I was definitely big.

RON: So did exposing yourself in *Bear* help you overcome that shyness?

JACK: Mmm, not really.

RON: Do you feel that your contact with the Bear community has helped to improve your self-esteem?

JACK: Well, I think the attention has helped that somewhat and has helped make me feel better about myself, but I still do feel that I'm not the hottest guy out there in the world. I'm just sort of OK. There are guys who are much, much hotter than I am. Feeling this way doesn't let any of the attention I get go to my head. Also, in the normal course of getting older and doing my workaday life, I've learned to deal with not being quite so painfully shy and dealing with people in groups.

RON: So you don't at all buy the shtick of Jack Radcliffe being likened unto a Bear god.

JACK: I don't think so at all! [*Laughs*] I'm just a regular guy.

RON: You don't identify with the character "Jack" in that way.

JACK: I don't think that either I or "Jack" are some sort of Bear god. I appreciate that people use me as somewhat of a role model or a comparison—I'm flattered by that—but I don't think I'm the defining object of what a Bear should be.

RON: Is there a way you would define that?

JACK: I think that is each person's own opinion or decision that they have to make. Let's get real—I can't decide for a group, and I don't think anyone can decide for a whole subculture. It's what each person makes of it for himself.

RON: Very true. How did you choose your screen name?

JACK: It honestly just came out of thin air. I only wanted something that sounded masculine and "normal" and not like some porn name.

RON: Not obviously sexualized, like "Rod Everhard."

JACK: Right.

RON: Was it a big leap for you to go from still photos to video?

JACK: I shot my first video at the same time we did the photo shoot. It was very much part of the same process for me. I hardly had the first clue what I was supposed to do, but Chris [Nelson, the photographer] and Richard [Bulger, the publisher] basically just said, "Do this. Do that." And I was like, "I'm here, Richard, you're paying me to do whatever." And I did what everybody said to do, and that was it.

RON: Both of them were excellent at making models feel comfortable. How was the transition from solo to the "interactive" videos, so to speak?

JACK: Well, they contacted me a few years later and asked me, "Do you want to do a group video?" And I was like, "Sure." It really wasn't that big a deal.

RON: Did it also feel awkward or uncomfortable at first?

JACK: The whole experience was very new. It was different, you know, working with people and still trying to take direction and do stuff, but it was fun. If I hadn't enjoyed it, I wouldn't have continued it.

RON: Of course not. There was an ongoing joke, while you and several other Brush Creek models tended bar at the Lone Star, that the bartenders there posed for *Bear* because it doubled their tips. Was that true?

JACK: I wish. [*Both laugh*] It may have increased tips somewhat, but only from some of the people. The way a bartender makes better tips is, of course, to be personable and to remember people's names and what they drink and such. Just because they're in a magazine doesn't have a whole lot of effect.

RON: Is that so?

JACK: It's more for the people who come into the bar from out of town and say, "Oh! I've seen you!" [*Laughs*]

RON: Right. I imagine you got quite a bit of that as well, too.

JACK: Some, of course.

RON: But for the regulars, that wasn't the case.

JACK: No, I don't think so. At least that's my perception.

RON: Still, the appearance of *Bear* models enhanced the bar's business. What did you enjoy most about bartending at the Lone Star? Was it just the money?

JACK: Part of it was that I needed the money, but also I was just meeting people and liked having that little social outlet. I tend to be fairly quiet and reserved. It was fun to meet people and get to know them. But the main driving force back then was the money. I was new to the city, and I just needed some extra cash.

RON: Right. Did you find that bartending really forced you to be more gregarious?

JACK: Definitely. I'm still not so terribly outgoing. But then, even as a bartender, I wasn't as outgoing as most bartenders are. But it forced me to be more outgoing than I normally was.

RON: Over time, as your popularity has soared, your face and body have become very well known among Bears worldwide. Does it ever feel weird to know that thousands of men have jacked off looking at your image?

JACK: [*Laughs*] You think so?

RON: Absolutely. Do you not think that's the case?

JACK: It's not like I go around thinking about it, quite honestly. It's very flattering because I don't think that I'm all that special myself. Do I think it's weird? No, not at all. That's exactly what I expect people to do with that, anyway. It's just sort of what happens. What do I think about it and the fact that it's me? It's kind of fun and exciting that people are, you know, getting off on me, possibly, the same way I've gotten off on other people.

RON: Are there any particular models that come to mind whom you find particularly attractive now, or have found attractive in the past?

JACK: Well, for me, I tend to go more for men with muscular builds, and men who are hairy. I've always liked Carl Hardwick. He's a good example. And Pete Kuzak. I dig men like that, who are basically muscular and also hairy.

RON: Is there anyone you admired in your younger years that comes to mind, such as Al Parker?

JACK: Well, Al Parker was obviously good. Not that I can think of anyone off the top of my head. We're talking a long time ago. [*Both laugh*]

RON: That was a whole other generation of porn stars then.

JACK: Back in the late '70s and early '80s, I liked movies such as *L.A. Tool and Die* and others like that.

RON: Right, the Gage Brothers' movies.

JACK: Many of their models were masculine and felt comfortable with facial hair and body hair and stuff like that. Also, the Colt models I found very, very attractive.

RON: In a relationship with a lover or partner, what sort of man do you find attractive, both physically and nonphysically?

JACK: Physically, I like people with a very good build. I like facial hair. I like, generally speaking, men with a masculine demeanor and who are self-assured.

RON: Is body hair not much of a fetish for you?

JACK: I like body hair, but it's not crucial for me.

RON: Have your tastes always run this way?

JACK: Sure have. Part of being attracted to someone is more than just physical. For me, someone can be physically gorgeous, but if they open their mouth and sound completely stupid, it just blows the whole picture.

RON: Sure. What sort of nonphysical characteristics do you look for in a lover or a partner?

JACK: Well, I like men who are confident, self-assured, intelligent, and polite. All that kind of stuff.

RON: What do you do to relax?

JACK: I like to do a lot of stuff outdoors.

RON: You mean hiking or cycling?

JACK: Hiking or just going to the beach, going to the mountains to ski, scuba diving, stuff like that.

RON: So you enjoy outdoors activities. What sort of music do you like to listen to?

JACK: Generally, rock, or, more lately, country/western.

RON: Really? Do you two-step?

JACK: Yes.

RON: How long have you been doing that?

JACK: Oh, for years. I learned to two-step back in Denver.

RON: I must say, you look great in a cowboy hat. May I ask, what's your favorite food?

JACK: [*Laughs*] Well...probably a good steak.

RON: Now, let's say that you and I are on a date. We've had a nice steak dinner and a bottle of wine, gone out two-stepping, and had a great time so far. Then we go over to your apartment and start to get comfortable. Tell me, Jack, what can I do to really, really turn you on?

JACK: [*Laughs*] Um...

RON: What really turns your crank?

JACK: What's my magic button?

RON: That would be the question.

JACK: Heh heh—for me, it probably would be my nipples. If you play with those, they just take over.

RON: That's very good to know. Earlier you were saying that you didn't think that you were all that hot. If there were one thing that you could change about your appearance, what would it be?

JACK: Yikes. I've always wanted to be leaner. I know that must sound horrible.

RON: Well, I suspect that a lot of your fans wouldn't really want you to get too much leaner.

JACK: Maybe not too much leaner, but I'm sure they'd all love it if I got even bigger. [*Both laugh*]

RON: Yes, I think you're right. Do you hit the gym regularly?

JACK: Oh, yeah, definitely. Five or six times a week.

RON: Are there any particular things that you're working on at the moment at the gym? Or do you try to vary your workout?

JACK: My gym routine's all geared toward getting more muscular. I know I'm never gonna have that type of perfect, chiseled physique, but it's more about thickness and size for me.

RON: Do you get a lot of fan mail?

JACK: A fair amount. I don't know what other people may get, but I probably get on average a dozen pieces of mail or E-mail per day.

RON: That seems like a lot to me. But then, I don't know what to compare it to. I never get fan mail. [*Both laugh*] So what kind of things do people write in their letters and E-mails?

JACK: They're all generally very polite and nice, and they say that they like the way I look, and they're glad that I have a lot of pictures of me to go around. Once in a while you get the people who say that looking at me helped them realize what they liked. I especially enjoy hearing from folks who are just coming out and are kind of interested in men, but maybe didn't like what they were seeing in the "normal" sort of porno magazines. Then they saw a picture of me and said, "Oh! That's what I like. Now I see that there's something out there like that." And they tend to appreciate that.

RON: How does that make you feel, to know that you've helped certain men to come out?

JACK: [*Laughs*] Flattered. Very flattered.

RON: That's great. Are you able to respond to most of the fan mail?

JACK: I try to respond, although I don't have time to be very verbose. I'm not a big writer anyway, but I answer the E-mails. I say at least "Thank you." I try to answer their questions. I'm not really big on sending pictures because basically all the studios own pictures of me—if I send pictures out, the studios and photographers get angry. Plus, it's all over the Web so the images are available there as well.

RON: Do you get a lot of fan mail from folks in outlying areas?

JACK: I get fan mail from everywhere! [*Both laugh*] People write to me from all over the country, all over the world. It really amazes me from where I get E-mail. So, it's always interesting and sometimes surprising. Sometimes I'll get a person that wants to have long, in-depth conversations or wants to know every single aspect of my life, and that I'm not very comfortable with. I'm willing to be friendly and polite and do what I can.

RON: Do you mean in person?

JACK: Through E-mail.

RON: Well, that's what interviews like these are for. So you can tell your fans everything, just once. [*Both laugh*]

JACK: Right, but there are people that want to know very in-depth things: What do I eat? When do I go to sleep? How often do I take a dump? Stuff like that.

RON: That's a bit much.

JACK: Absolutely.

RON: I wonder what level of privacy you can expect as a porn star. Some people, myself included, would have a difficult time putting out pictures of themselves, not knowing where they're going to end up. Particularly with the Web now, one can't exert any kind of control over where the images go.

JACK: Yes.

RON: Is the fact that you can't control where your image is used something that matters to you at all?

JACK: Not particularly. It's the same thing when you have pictures taken of you for magazines. You have no control over where they show up or how they get used. So now the fact that I'm completely available on the Web really is immaterial.

RON: Is it difficult for you to find privacy when you go out, say, for a beer at the Lone Star? Or when you're travelling?

JACK: Not at all. If anything, it's nice to have someone recognize me and to have someone to talk to. If I'm in the middle of something and it's inconvenient, if I'm not necessarily available to talk, I'll tell the person and usually that's it. But when it gets down to finding privacy, no, I really don't have an issue with that. Or at least I haven't had any problems with it so far.

RON: You're not bothered by leering, gawking fans distracting you when you're trying to have a private conversation?

JACK: Not really. As long as they're not, like, in my face and asking questions and being rude or impolite. When that becomes an issue, then I simply ask them to, you know, please go away. [*Both laugh*] But that's happened so rarely that, generally speaking, interruptions really don't offend me.

RON: You rarely have to deal with unruly admirers.

JACK: Rarely, yes.

RON: That's good. How do you view the growth of Bear subculture over the past decade or so?

JACK: What do you mean?

RON: The Bear phenomenon is obviously something that you've watched grow from its initial stages into quite a burgeoning subculture. It has opened up sexuality for a lot of men.

JACK: It certainly has.

RON: Do you have any particular observations about the evolving form of the Bear subculture or the community? Are you pleased to see that it's growing in this way?

JACK: Yes, I'm glad to see it's continuing to grow. I think that there was a distinct void there. There were many men—especially those not living in the major cities—who felt that they were just normal, ordinary guys who felt somewhat excluded because they didn't necessarily meet the standards of what's displayed in all the magazines and videos as gay men.

RON: They didn't fit the idealized gay male stereotype.

JACK: Exactly: the "ideal" man, with the smooth, clean-shaven, young, very clean, perfect body—that kind of look.

RON: Right.

JACK: So, I think that the Bear movement has allowed people who may not think of themselves as the perfect person or as having a perfect body to be accepted and to be able to revel in that and to enjoy themselves, which is what's important. You know, I feel the most important thing is that people must be comfortable with themselves and who and what they are. They have to understand that whatever other people think really doesn't matter.

It's good to see that the Bear community has grown and that, generally speaking, it's very accepting in terms of who they bring in. You know, you don't have to necessarily be hairy or big, you can be a little cub that likes to hang out with Bear guys, or you can be really, really muscular, and that's great, too.

RON: You mention little cubs and really muscular guys. Elsewhere you've gone on the record as being somewhat critical of heavily obese men.

JACK: Again, I'd like to say that that decision is up to each individual person. I'd like to think that each person would strive to be as healthy as possible. Those who strive to get into conditions that are unhealthy may want to ask themselves if it's wise or if it indicates that there may be some other deeper problem. Still, I feel strongly that each person should be happy with who and what they are, and should strive to be healthy. Now, healthy doesn't mean that you've got to be skinny or super-muscular or anything cast in stone—it's what's right for you. Those who are dangerously obese or unhealthily overweight should strive to rectify that, only for their own good and for the people who care for them.

RON: Do you feel that Bears are less exclusionary than in other parts of gay life?

JACK: Yes, especially in comparison to some of the more demanding subcultures, such as the drag queen culture or the leather subculture, which I feel tend to be stricter and more rigid in their stereotypes and judgments of what it deems as acceptable looks and behavior. The Bear community is far more accepting in the way that it says to everyone, "We don't care. We all appreciate each other and that's what counts." So, I think the advent of the Bear subculture was an opportunity that needed to be fulfilled, and I'm glad that it came about.

RON: What do you like least about the Bear phenomenon?

JACK: In terms of what?

RON: What do you find the most disappointing or upsetting, in terms of attitudes, trends, kitschy stuff, or anything else?

JACK: The only thing that I find a bit much is that it seems to have gotten very commercial. People seem to be hot on the lookout how to make money off the Bear subculture, from shirts and merchandise to pay Web site or other schemes.

RON: So the merchandising bothers you somewhat, although Brush Creek merchandises your image?

JACK: Yes, it just seems that things have gotten more and more commercial. So many different ways of trying to extract money out of people just because they're Bear. So, that's pretty disturbing, but I guess people will look to find ways to make money, no matter what and where. So, I guess it was bound to happen. It just seems a bit much at times.

RON: What do you like best about Bear subculture?

JACK: Basically, that they're just a bunch of regular, masculine guys and they're just looking for other masculine guys to get to know and be comfortable with.

RON: Great. If there's one thing that you could say to all your fans, what would it be?

JACK: "Thanks." [*Both laugh*]

RON: Short and sweet. Ten years from now, what do you see yourself doing in life? Do you see yourself continuing to model?

JACK: I still plan on working and making money from my regular occupation. In terms of modeling, I guess as long as people find me attractive, then I'll probably do something. I do it partly for the fun and partly for the money, but, you know, if I were to ever get a sense that people felt it was old and tired, or if they weren't still interested in looking at me, I would probably stop it.

RON: Thank you for your time. Any final comments?

JACK: All I can say is that I've had a great time modeling, and everyone has been wonderful. I look forward to doing more of it and enjoying it.

CHAPTER 10
LET THE LAUGHING BEAR LEAD
~ AN INTERVIEW WITH RICK TROMBLY ~

The Honorable RICK TROMBLY is an openly gay Democratic state senator serving his first term representing District 7 from Boscawen, New Hampshire. He holds the leadership position of majority whip in the senate. Before his election to the senate, Trombly served 16 years in the New Hampshire house of representatives. Four of those years he was the house Democratic leader. He has been an active civic leader in his hometown district, serving as a selectman and moderator for the town of Boscawen, and as an active member of the Merrimack Valley School District serving as the district moderator. He also serves on the Democratic National Committee. Rick holds degrees from the University of New Hampshire and Franklin Pierce Law Center and is a partner in the law firm Vanacore, Nielsen, & Trombly in Concord. His Senatorial priorities include lowering property taxes by reforming education funding, health care reform, and campaign finance reform.

In a 1999 newspaper photograph of New Hampshire's five openly gay legislators, one of the figures caught my eye—a big, tall, dark-bearded Bear, of course. The Bear turned out to be the Honorable Rick Trombly, who was elected to the New Hampshire state senate in a somewhat controversial election. I was interested in meeting Rick to ask him about how he might relate being a Bear to his life in politics.

(A noteworthy Bearish political incident: During the 2000 U.S. presidential campaign, after an aide to Democratic vice-presidential candidate Joe Lieberman suggested the senator should hide some chest hair peeking out of his shirt before a television taping, Lieberman demurred, saying, "There is a constituency for chest hair.")

Despite Rick's demanding schedule as a legislator and lawyer in a busy private practice, he agreed to an interview. We met in his law office in beautiful Concord, New Hampshire, where he spoke to me of his state's impressive gay-rights legislation, which he has been instrumental in attaining. Eventually, of course, the topic turned to Bears.

RON: Let's talk about Bears.

RICK: Sure. Bears, Bears, Bears. [*Laughs*] "Woof." It's just great that a Bear goes "Woof." Whoever invented that word, I want to meet him (or her). It seems to have spread to the non-Bear community, because I have some other friends who use that term now.

RON: I've even heard of straight women using that expression about men. Presumably straight men, I guess. In our phone conversation earlier, you said to me that you think it's obvious that you're a Bear, but in your own mind, what do you feel makes you a Bear?

RICK: First of all, there are certain physical aspects that make me a Bear. I would consider height and weight, volume, proportionality, and obviously hairiness as well. Although there are smaller Bears—I guess they're called cubs, or whatever. So, as far as the physical aspects, I have them all down pat.

RON: Have you always worn a beard?

RICK: I had my beard in college, but it was quite different! I had lots of hair, and it was big and bushy, believe it or not.

And then of course there's attitude—and please allow me to be completely general, but it's my definition—I think Bears tend to be happier people, in terms of being more willing to laugh. I think they laugh more heartily. Bears, Bears, Bears. [*Laughs*]

I think that Bears are generally outside of the mainstream. When you say "gay," most people don't think "Bear." It's as if we're sort of grazing on the side of the riverbank while gay life flows along. In gay life it seems that there are Bears and then there are what most people think of as stereotypical gay men.

The image of attractiveness to most people is not the Bear image. This indoctrination is exactly what Madison Avenue does. And many Bears are people who grew up heavy, or not blond, or not smooth. I think people who grow up being different on any basis tend to be more accepting of other people who are different, such as people who are handicapped or emotionally not fully developed.

Bears look at the world in a different way because I believe there is discrimination—I'm not saying of civil rights—based on size in this society. They're the ones who—whether female or male—get picked on, are not expected to achieve, and don't get the great jobs right off. For these reasons I think they have a different outlook on life; they're more sympathetic to others. I think Bears are jovial and more accepting. Loyal, too.

RON: When did you first become aware of the whole construct of Bearness?

RICK: Well, I would probably say mid to late '80s. I noticed that in the late '80s, when AIDS was hitting the gay community hardest and people were wasting because they were ill, big men were seen as healthy, or at least healthier. People started paying more attention in those days to Bears, when magazines such as *Bear* and *American Bear* were coming out, saying, "Hey, wait a minute, here we are!"

RON: "We're here, we're Bear, get used to it."

RICK: Yes. I remember one incident in particular that helped. I went to high school and college with a gay friend. We didn't come out to each other until we were about 20 years old, but he liked Bears, and he offered comfort to me in saying, "This type of man is what I like, and this is what a Bear does for me." And because my first contact with a gay friend (and we were just friends) happened that way, when he told me that he liked Bears, I have carried that into my adult gay life. Because of his affirmation, it was easier for me to feel OK as a Bear.

RON: That was helpful to you in terms of accepting your body just the way that it is?

RICK: Yes! In terms of accepting myself and being comfortable with who I am. Coming out as being gay is one process, I believe; then if you further refine your identity—whether you're a drag queen or into leather or a Bear—that's definitely another coming-out process. Some people are stuck between the two. And those who have taken both steps are the happier.

RON: If you have any sort of image-based identity in our culture, other than as a Waspish guy with a boy-next-door look, there's definitely a process you have to do to accept yourself as looking and being other than that.

RICK: Even with Bear lovers. They are also included in that process too of people coming out in steps, as opposed to just once. People who like Bears are special too because of their willingness to say: "Screw all that, I know what I want, and I'm going to act on it!" As opposed to: "Oh, man, I really want that but I better go for this young blond over here that's going to be more attractive to gay culture and society as a whole." I don't want to say "society at large" [*pats his stomach to emphasize his pun, laughs*]: society as a whole.

RON: Well, you wouldn't want to make too *broad* a generalization, would you? [*Both laugh*] Do you feel that body image plays a significant role in the way that people perceive you as a politician? I'm referring to your public body image.

RICK: That's a very good question. People in politics ask themselves all the time, "What's the formula that works for me so I can come across best to the public?" I'm very comfortable with both one-on-one situations as well as with addressing large crowds. The more people see me— not how much they see of me physically, but see me personally—the better off I am. And many people who've worked with me in campaigns said to me, "The voters have to see you, you have to meet them, that's your strong point," and I agree with that.

RON: Does your own body image matter significantly to your constituents, or do people really vote for candidates solely based on their platform and qualifications?

RICK: Well, the rule in politics is: Don't wear a beard because no one will vote for you. All the PR people tell you: Don't have a beard. When was the last bearded president we elected? In the 1800s, if I'm not mistaken.

RON: Benjamin Harrison, I believe. But I'm curious to know how your Bearness might affect your work as a politician.

RICK: I think it has influenced my political life without even my declaring anything about Bear subculture. One day a while back, a woman on my senior staff said to me, "You're nothing but a big ol' teddy bear!" You know, Bearness has two sides to it. One is the nice cuddly bear everyone wants to touch and get to know—trustworthy, honest— qualities a politician needs to have. If people are willing to look at you, that quality of cheerfulness, that cuddliness, really jumps out at them, which is terribly helpful. I think when people say, "Aw, I'm just going to have fun, I'm just going to be myself," that works.

RON: But there's not just the tenderness but also the strong aspect of your personality.

RICK: It's that grizzly bear, the fierce and aggressive aspect, yes. That strength is something that appeals to folks too. It's as if people feel, "OK, we're going to go into battle, we're going to fight the Republicans on this, and the big guy's going to lead!" There are times when you have to use that that sort of grizzly bear side. For example when I say to a colleague, "I want this bill. This bill is very important to me. You understand that?" And they'll say, "Whoa! This is different." And then they worry.

RON: Do you find time to attend any Bear functions elsewhere in New England?

RICK: I just have way too many commitments at this time. Every time I have to travel it is politically centered and takes away from the law office. Quite frankly, I'm not a workaholic but I do feel very guilty when I'm not in the office. I do marital law and I have a very, very busy law practice. When I'm over at the State House three days a week and over here in the law office for only two days, it makes it very hard to travel to Bear events. I do manage to take two weeks off to go to Provincetown each year.

RON: With your boyfriend.

RICK: Right.

RON: Do you have other friends who are Bears?

RICK: [*Hesitates*] Yes. I socialize with all types of people. It's generally people who are politically oriented because it's tough not to get a dose of politics being around me. Politics is just my thing, you know—election night is like my Christmas Eve. Every four years we elect a president and we have the first primary up here in New Hampshire. And since that's been gearing up, I've been working for Al Gore and supporting him.

RON: One of your local newspapers made quite a point about the number of times Al Gore has called you.

RICK: [*Chuckles modestly*] Yes, I know the vice president. I feel very strongly that he's the only candidate who will continue the gay agenda. I'm as partisan Democratic as they come in as Republican a state as they come. I'm convinced that Al Gore understands gay issues and is not doing it merely for political reasons. He sincerely believes in civil rights. And he's a great guy.

RON: So, if he were to offer you a position in the new administration...

RICK: I wouldn't say no. [*Laughs*]

RON: Do you think that having a Bear-type body stigmatizes you in any way?

RICK: Not at all. People are attracted to a rollicking, fun-loving guy. And when I go to political events I like to laugh. A lot. Not only that, but also people are drawn to the security of my size, too. I've found that people like to hug me, and I think that's because of being a Bear, I do. They're much more willing to go with that intimate contact, they're not so threatened, and they liked to be hugged.

RON: This might be a silly question, but do you think we'll ever see a political Bear in Washington?

RICK: Could I win a national campaign based on being a Bear?

RON: Well, not *based* on your Bearness, but—would it hurt you?

RICK: No, it wouldn't hurt me. But then again, I think that's due to my strong sense of being comfortable with myself. Not everyone looks like JFK. But if you put someone who looks like JFK one-on-one in a room with a happy Bear—I think the Bear will win! Because he's got that connection with regular folks.

CHAPTER 11
SURVIVING AS A FAT NAKED FAG
~ AN INTERVIEW WITH RICH HATCH ~

RICH HATCH is the celebrated million-dollar winner of summer 2000's smash TV hit *Survivor*, the Robinson Crusoe reality game show in which he successfully managed to "outwit, outplay, and outlast" his 15 island competitors. Since then the single, 39-year-old corporate trainer and father (he has an adopted 10-year-old son, Chris) has made numerous TV and radio appearances and was featured on the cover of *The Advocate*. He has also authored a book, *101 Survival Secrets: How To Make $1,000,000, Lose 100 Pounds, and Just Plain Live Happy*, in which he writes candidly about growing up being big and gay, discusses the evolution of his life philosophy, and offers advice and "rules for a better life."

Although Rich does not particularly identify as a Bear, the body issues that he has dealt with successfully are common to many gay men with Bear bodies. Rich has risen above his early experiences of sexual abuse, shame and guilt for being gay, and poor self-esteem for being fat, to become a successful, happy, very self-assured man.

I interviewed Rich at his lovely home near Newport, Rhode Island, where we talked about nudity and body image, Bears and sexuality, self-esteem and surviving life on and off the island, among other topics.

RON: Rich, when did you actually realize you were gay?
RICH: I was always attracted to boys and then men, but when did I

know for sure? I'm not certain. I thought that I was just like everybody else, that I'd grow up and get married and have kids, but that everybody else must have these feelings too. I thought that other boys must find that guy cute, and that guy hot, and they must all think that way but just date women and then maybe get turned on by them later. This idea was going on in my head and I believed it, and so all through high school I dated girls. I certainly wasn't sexual with them. I had absolutely no sexual attraction to women.

RON: But you played the game.

RICH: I played the game. Yet there were all kinds of interactions from as early as I can remember with boys, such as masturbating in the woods with this one neighborhood guy. These other neighborhood kids and I had this club where you had to take your pants off to come in, and silly things like that, which were very...

RON: Homoerotic, but not necessarily with homo sex.

RICH: Yes.

RON: It sounds as if you assumed that being gay was a normal affectional situation for yourself rather than looking at yourself as being a pervert or degenerate.

RICH: I never thought of myself as perverted. I thought that I couldn't be what they were talking about. Queer? Fag? With those negative connotations, that hateful demeanor that they used when they said it? That couldn't be me. So gosh, everybody must have these feelings, to a certain extent. When I somehow realized that what they were referring to was me, just because I was attracted to men, it must have been hurtful on some level. But it certainly was relatively fast that I came to see their ignorance. How stupid they are to be so hateful and disparaging of something they know nothing about! And so what? Who are they, to anybody who is anyone, to decide who anyone else should be attracted to—and why would it matter? It's not as if my attraction to somebody else affects other people in any hurtful way.

Religion didn't play a huge role in my life, ever, either. Certainly, I was raised Catholic and explored all kinds of religion—Mormon, Methodist, Judaism, and so on—but none of it made any kind of logical sense. It seemed to be the blanket, if you will, covering up an excuse for hate and conflict and war, so it never made sense to me.

It didn't take me long to conclude that people are simply stupid. Most people aren't open-minded enough, introspective enough, self-aware enough, bright enough, to examine reality. They get too caught up, I found, in a particular paradigm and stay with it to keep from feeling unsettled.

RON: That attitude displays remarkable self-esteem. Is this something that you feel you had innately, or something you developed over time?

RICH: It grew, it certainly wasn't innate. I remember being the kind of bright kid, somewhat ostracized, an outsider, feeling fat and ugly, and just feeling bad for many, many years. It's hard for me to get back in touch with that right now because it seems so foreign to me. I really have somehow lost that, thankfully, mostly due to a good friend of mine, an amazing man who has just challenged the living hell out of me for the past 17 or so years. But I still can remember those incredibly negative, confused feelings.

RON: You've written about your early experiences of sexual abuse, instances where it would have been easy for you to take onto yourself a sense of guilt or wrongfulness or shame.

RICH: I never got the guilt, but I did feel shame at some point, probably even somewhat for being gay.

RON: How did you begin to heal those experiences?

RICH: It was a long process of self-analysis and introspection, constantly asking myself, *What's real? What's honest? OK, here's what I'm feeling, and here's what I'm hearing, here's what someone is saying to me. Now, what's the reality of this situation?* Through one example after another, I came to a place of self-confidence, a place of understanding that my perspective, because I was focused on it more than most people were, was accurate more often.

A big part was an outdoor adventure I did when I was a kid— Horizon Bound—that was a very powerful experience. It went defunct about 14 years ago, and I've now incorporated under the same name. We're going to take two groups of kids in the woods by this summer.

At that age—14 to 19, which is the age group we'll be taking out— you think you know so much more than adults can recognize, and so you're often battling against everyone and expressing yourself in all sorts of negative ways. It's a great time to just get real, get in the woods, and not worry about any of the social crap. You find out if you can lean over the back of a cliff and rapel, how long you can hike, and how much you can carry. Are you helping somebody out, or are you a hindrance? Those kinds of things are just incredibly meaningful.

RON: I wish you all the best with that. It's a great project.

In your book, you said very candidly that as a kid you worried about the size of your dick. How did you go from that inhibited state of mind to being an avid nudist appearing naked on national TV?

RICH: Again, getting a perspective on what reality is, what dick sizes are, and why does it matter? I was always kind of embarrassed about my body and about nudity in general. I don't know why I felt so ashamed of my body or of my dick in particular. My parents would never be undressed around me, so that's probably where it started.

RON: But that's true of most Americans.

RICH: Well, the New England kind of cover-up: nudity equals sexuality.

RON: Ah, the neo-Puritan ethic. But virtually everybody has some body issues. If you have a body, generally, you have body issues.

RICH: Yes, and when I came to realize that everybody has some kind of a body issue, I explored the reasons why, and it just seemed asinine that we have these issues. It's not anything that anybody has any control over: We're all born nude, and we all put clothes on and take them off. Whoopee. At some point I just realized it's stupid to stress out about being naked just because I had a roll of fat, or because I hadn't lost enough weight, or because I might not know whether my dick's too big or too small or whatever. It was just asinine, and somehow I just stopped, luckily, caring. For many years it has been a meaningless issue to me; so meaningless that it just didn't matter on the island.

RON: So on the island it was totally natural for you to be naked, besides the fact it was so hot.

RICH: 110 degrees, humid as hell, on a deserted island in the middle of the South China Sea. Where else would it be more appropriate?

RON: Yes, but with cameras, though.

RICH: True, the cameras were there, but they just weren't a consideration. I wasn't naked because they were there, and I wouldn't have not been naked if they hadn't been there. It wasn't a consideration. Certainly, I knew they were filming all the time, but I figured, *Well, how much of that are they going to use? Oh, well, whatever they want to use they can.* I don't really care who sees me naked. It just doesn't matter to me: "Oh, damn—you saw me naked! Oh, my God! Now what am I going to do?" I just don't get it.

RON: An acquaintance that you and I have in common told me that when he asked you if you consider yourself a Bear, you replied, "Of course I'm a Bear." Now, what makes you feel you're a Bear, and why?

RICH: My understanding of "Bear" is a kind of big, hirsute or hairy guy, usually with a beard or some facial hair being a big plus. I don't know if there is more to it. I've heard the term "cub," but then I've seen guys who are considered Bears—one was the papa and one was the cub, and the cub was just as burly and bearded as the papa Bear. So "cub" originally in my mind was a smoother, smaller guy. I have no idea what's accurate about those definitions, so I'm not sure I would have said something like, "Of course I'm a Bear." But I think I'm probably Bearish. I'm hairy-chested—not hairy-backed—I'm not *that* hairy, but hairy enough, sure. I play with my beard whenever I feel like it. At any given time, I might have a beard or a goatee or a mustache or whatever. I've never lived in one permanent facial-hair routine for any period of years. I've always flopped around.

RON: Also, self-identified Bears are gay or bisexual men.

RICH: Yes, I forgot the gay part! [*Both laugh*]

RON: Up until the time when you left the island, how long had you worn your beard?

RICH: I might have had it six or eight months or so. I was in a beard phase. I might have had a goatee before that, and I might have been smooth-shaven for eight months before that, and I might have had a beard for a year and a half before *that*. I've never been attached to any particular look. Particularly when I was huge, 360 pounds, for many years, and had a beard, I looked a lot older than I wanted to look.

RON: The "fat naked fag" moniker that [*Survivor* competitor] Sean invented on the island—and which you audaciously used as a chapter title in your book—is a term of identification that many Bears would probably feel is derisive.

RICH: Sean didn't coin that phrase. Actually, my friend Tom made it up. I told Sean the story behind that expression and he picked it up from there. My friends Tom and Valerie and I went camping in Maine and Canada two summers ago. We drove up there, and I was naked within five minutes after we arrived, and stayed that way. They weren't... They're not comfortable that way. So, there we were hiking for miles, and I was naked the whole time. We got to a beach, and they climbed down to the beach. I climbed down after them and Tom turned around and looked up and got a perspective that he'd rather not have had. So Tom started laughing and pointing, "Oh, God, look at this fat naked fag!" We just about pissed in our pants, so to speak, just because it sounded so funny. And then we thought of a business concept—a calendar called "Fat Naked Fag Goes Rock Climbing" or "Fat Naked Fag Barbecues" or "Fat Naked Fag Goes Spear Fishing."

RON: Like the Naked Coed or Bear Whizz merchandise you find at truck stops.

RICH: Right. So for the rest of our camping trip, we were coming up with various shots for the calendar, and then the T-shirts—we just went with the concept.

RON: Followed by a whole line of clothing? For Fat Naked Fag fans.

RICH: Absolutely. I still think it would be a great, humorous idea. And at the time I would have been a perfect model: 300-plus pounds (not that I cared), always naked, and kind of goofy looking.

RON: So rather than being a term of derision, it was a concept or image that you embraced.

RICH: I *was* a fat naked fag. I'm still a big naked fag, most of the time. I'm not fat per se, but I'm nowhere near skinny.

RON: In any case, now that you've lost 100 pounds—

RICH: 130-something pounds.

RON: Yes. Now that you've lost all that weight and shaved and are dressing nicely, do you feel you're accepted more by mainstream America?

RICH: Oh, I don't know. Was I accepted before, when I was fat and hairy and naked? Am I accepted now? I'm still a big hairy gay man. I have no idea of the level of acceptance or if any of this plays into it. Maybe the weight coming off makes me more appealing to more people. Certainly, nowadays I have a more "marketable" image to mainstream America than I would as a fat man. That's just the way it is.

RON: My understanding is that you're not currently partnered.

RICH: I am not! And I'm on the prowl. It's my most important goal.

RON: What attributes do you look for in a companion?

RICH: Intelligence, first. With that come all kinds of things, such as wit and self-awareness. A kind of introspective journey will have to be a big part of the life of whoever will be my partner. A clear, comfortable, confident sense of who they are—I find that extraordinarily sexy. I believe that I'm about to be featured in *Hero* magazine as their bachelor of the month.

RON: Do you have a particular type, such as Bearish men?

RICH: Yeah.

RON: Yeah?

RICH: Gotta have a penis. I just love men with penises!

RON: A minimum requirement. Well, are there any *other* attributes that attract you?

RICH: I wish there were. It might be easier to narrow things down, but I don't have any other prerequisites. He's got to be attractive. What does that mean? I don't know. I can go through lists of people in my head that I find attractive, and they could be 6-foot-4 to 5-foot-9, dark-haired and hairy-chested to blond and smooth swimmer type—they're across the board. I have a vivid imagination and a wildly wide spectrum. I just really, really love men. Men who are men. I'm not particularly attracted to men in women's clothing or men who are seriously effeminate. That's not to say I don't enjoy being with men who camp it up. That's fun, and certainly a part of my life. But if I were attracted to femininity, I'd be with a woman. So I'm not attracted to femininity itself, particularly sexually.

RON: What are you doing to pursue this foremost goal of yours?

RICH: Talking about it with everybody I can.

RON: Do you get many love letters from fans?

RICH: Yes, most of which are very sad. Naked guys in bizarre scenarios and positions, or desperate-sounding pleas from uneducated guys who live with their moms, saying, "You're the man for me. I know we could be friends. Can't we be friends? Why haven't you written?" It's a really, really, really odd place to be in, as I am, to see firsthand the mental state of America. I think people are far less mentally healthy than we as a society pretend we are.

RON: I suspect you're correct. But do you not get any diamonds among the coal?

RICH: I have yet to meet that gem. I have yet to figure out who it is will click. I got an interesting call from a guy in New Jersey, and we were chatting, and I said, "Well, why don't you hang up, drive up here, and find out if we've got something going?" Then he became so nervous, saying he wished he could, but, uh, he was going to be in Rhode Island for business sometime later, and maybe the two of us could connect then. I tried to explain to him that one characteristic of a guy that would interest me and would make me respect him and draw me to him is risk-taking. I'm not particularly attracted to this kind of overcautious person.

That's a good example of why I'm single. I'm very challenging, very honest, and very direct. I'm also very open-minded and willing to listen, but I want to get at what's real, so if I think that something's going on under the surface, I'm going to challenge you and talk with you about it. And if you haven't done that work already, it's going to cause you to be defensive.

RON: You're looking for someone with a comparable level of self-awareness, someone who's also on a path of self-discovery.

RICH: This is a time in my life that I'd much rather be sharing with somebody. I'm travelling all over the world, staying in gorgeous places—not that that means everything in a relationship—but I really want to share that with someone, as well as to cuddle and have sex and massage and play with somebody special. That's not part of it quite yet.

RON: What other desires and ambitions do you have in your life? What do you see ahead of you?

RICH: What don't I have ahead of me? There are some very exciting things on the horizon that I can't talk about for various reasons. Until contracts are signed and papers are passed, I can't even talk about the negotiations. Fun things that will keep on surprising people. Talk about the 15 minutes of fame that should have been over a long time ago—even if 10 percent of what's on the table comes to fruition, I will be doing something in this business for quite a while.

RON: As well as continuing your regular consulting?

RICH: Right. My career as a speaker and corporate trainer just keeps growing as well.

RON: What was the greatest lesson that you learned on the island?

RICH: A lot of people have asked that. It wasn't for me a particular learning experience. By that I mean that my whole life is a learning experience. I'm constantly introspective. I didn't so much learn anything new on the island as I learned more about how and why I should trust my own perceptions, which is an ongoing lesson that I've kept learning.

RON: So the island experience reinforced what you already knew?

RICH: It was a physically challenging environment, more so than you could ever tell by just watching the television show. It was difficult, but it was much more of a social game, much more a mental challenge, how to interact, how to live to be the last one standing. But all the skills that I used are ones that I've always applied in my life. So there wasn't any major lesson from winning "Survivor."

RON: Would that also apply to your life since the last episode aired? Have you learned anything new since the world first learned of your victory?

RICH: Truly, I haven't. I think this would be a most amazing time for most people, an explosive learning environment, but for me, it's been a lot of superficial crap. And that has been nice, that's the best possible way, that all of this whatever-it-is is external; it's all crap.

RON: So you feel detached from your celebrity?

RICH: Oh, yeah, quite a bit. I was really well grounded, thankfully, before I left for the island. It took a long time and a lot of work to get to the place where I really love me, and I'm very, very comfortable with who I am. Celebrity status is very, very superficial and utterly meaningless and inconsequential to me, unlike some of the other contestants, who have talked about when they walked out the door and found the *Enquirer* going through their garbage as being the best day in their lives. I don't get it. I've never had that desire or interest.

RON: You don't feel that your celebrity is a mark of your success?

RICH: In my book, I talk about how happiness is success, and success is happiness. They're the same thing. It took me a long time to get to that understanding, and I don't think that many people recognize that when they're happy, that *is* success. When they're successful, that means by definition that they're happy.

I was happy and successful long before the island, and so, coming back and being in the public eye, facing myriad opportunities that probably would be overwhelming to many people, they're just questions for me to evaluate: Will this make me happy? Will I continue to be happy doing this? Would doing that be something I would enjoy? And I like having the opportunity to do that, but I feel as if I've created it. Otherwise I'd be involved in evaluating other options based on other risks that I'd be taking, to see what else I could learn and explore. That's what my life is about, and that's what makes me happy. So, although it doesn't look like it to everybody else, it's par for the course for me. It's just how I live.

RON: Last question: If you were to be stranded on a real deserted island with one other person, whom would it be?

RICH: It would be my partner. And we would be buck naked!

RON: [*Laughs*] Well, that's a good abstract answer, but can you think of any specific person?

RICH: Well, there are a number of different guys, for different reasons. I find Ed Norton incredibly sexy. Or Kevin Spacey—he works for
me. [*Long pause*] I could walk down the street and pick someone out. I
could even picture you there. I have a vivid imagination, but my true fantasy would be the guy with who I am intensely, sexually attracted to as
my compatible mate. I don't know who that is, but that's who I'd want
to be stranded on the deserted island with.

CHAPTER 12
PORTRAIT OF THE CARTOONIST AS A MIDDLE-AGED BEAR
~ AN INTERVIEW WITH TIM BARELA ~

TIM BARELA (yes, pronounced "Bear-ella") is the celebrated Bear artist and creator of the popular *Leonard & Larry* comic strip. The strip, which ran first in *Gay Comix* in 1984 and then in *The Advocate*, is currently featured in the national edition of *Frontiers* magazine and on the Web at www.frontiersweb.com. Tim has always demonstrated his fondness for Bear-type men in his artwork; he even penned a one-shot *Grizzly & Ted* cartoon for *Bear* issue no. 4. Tim is author of three collections of *Leonard & Larry* strips: *Domesticity Isn't Pretty*, *Kurt Cobain and Mozart Are Both Dead* (a finalist for the Lambda Literary Award in humor), and *Excerpts from the Ring Cycle in Royal Albert Hall*, which was released more than a year after this telephone interview was conducted. Tim has enjoyed and nurtured his relationship with the Bear community over time, offering his talent and artwork for various Bear causes and, every so often, especially as Larry has grown balder over the years, drawing a Bear cap on his character's head.

While visiting southern California in October 1999, I stopped in sunny Temecula to meet Tim. When he arrived in town to pick me up, we walked toward each other with bemused grins on our faces. Tim remarked, "You're a lot smaller than I thought you'd be!" To which I shot back, "Well, you're a lot bigger than I thought *you'd* be!" At which point we laughed and embraced.

Tim was gracious enough to spend the afternoon and evening with me on rather short notice. He showed me all around his colorful and historic hometown, and we had dinner at a charming bistro. Then we went back to Tim's house and he showed me his etchings—honest! When he showed me the inked-in boards for the upcoming three installments of *Leonard & Larry*, I felt like I was getting insider information.

The part of the evening I most treasure in my memory came next, when Tim disclosed that he'd written a children's book but had never shown it to another writer. I was delighted to hear of this project and insisted that he read me part of it. We sat down in his kitchen and Tim began to read to me the story of Mozart's mouse, who...

Well, I won't give away the whole marvelous story here, but before I knew it, Tim finished reading the last page and set down the manuscript. I thanked Tim for so abundantly sharing his day and talent with me, and we exchanged a warm bear hug, just as my ride arrived to pick me up.

RON: The title of your new collection of *Leonard & Larry* strips is *Excerpts from the Ring Cycle in Royal Albert Hall*—

TIM: Which is a line from one of the comic strips. I usually like to choose a punchline from the strip that's amorphous and ambiguous, that really has no direct meaning to anything, so that the reader has to go into the book and find out what I'm talking about.

RON: How else do you enjoy making your readers work?

TIM: I will not automatically show visual humor. I've always felt that something is funnier if you don't show the pratfalls and all the action sequences. I like to leave a lot up to the reader's imagination.

RON: Did you develop this approach over time? Originally, *Leonard & Larry* was more of a gag strip: Each strip would end with a punchline. Now, of course, the content is richer and more continuous.

TIM: Well, originally the strip appeared in *The Advocate* just once a month. So, the punch lines had to be much more decisive than they are now. *The Advocate*'s editorial staff told me that they did not want continuing story lines. All that changed when I went to *Frontiers* [in 1990] because I was doing the strip every other week and, as far as my editor there was concerned, I could do any kind of story line I wanted. Eventually it evolved into what my old editor referred to as a "soap opera"—it goes on and on and on!

By now everybody has gotten to know the characters and their situations so that I really don't have to spell things out. People already know how the characters are going to react in certain situations, and all I have to do is suggest something and it's immediately funny to established longtime readers. It's a wonderful position to be in because I can be more creative with my writing.

RON: So having a sitcom-oriented strip was what you had in mind all along?

TIM: Oh, yeah, that's my writing style. I'm a child of the late '60s and the '70s. I grew up with television and my greatest influences were the sitcoms on TV. That's why *Leonard & Larry* is such a sitcom-type comic strip. When Theatre Rhinoceros launched a stage production of *Leonard & Larry* in 1994, the playwright asked me, "How should Leonard react to Larry?" and I said to him, "Think Alice Cramden from *The Honeymooners*!"

RON: And he got it then?

TIM: Yeah! That is exactly how Leonard reacts to Larry: dry, deadpan. Larry flies off the handle, he's emotional, he overreacts, he does stupid things, and Leonard just stands back and watches it all. He reacts in a very calm, evenhanded—but sarcastic—manner most of the time. So I naturally relate to old TV sitcoms.

RON: How do you create your stories? Do you work from an outline that covers a period of time, or just see how the story unfolds as you go along, or is the process something else?

TIM: All of the above. [*Laughs*] I did have a recent story that is going into the new book: The story line involves Larry's gay son and his partner and their lesbian roommate all getting together to have a child. Now, on top of of this, I had already done this thing before about Larry becoming a grandfather—twice—and so I thought, *Oh, how boring. What can I do?* So I fixed up one of the characters who's straight and single with Larry's ex-wife, and he got her pregnant. So Natalie, the lesbian roommate, and Larry's 45-year-old ex, Sharon, were pregnant at the same time! That meant I had roughly a nine-month time window. Then once I got toward the end of the nine months, I got terrible writer's block, and it just went on and on! I had to add layers and layers—it got so complex and so convoluted. I couldn't believe I'd written something so incredibly ridiculous—but I did. These things just organically evolve sometimes, even though you have a time frame to work with. But that story line finally did get finished, thank God. I was really glad to move on to something else. I'd been drawing Larry wearing the same shirt for about three months.

RON: It must have been getting kind of skanky.

TIM: I hope not. It was a nice shirt.

RON: Which brings up something else about your personal life that has made its way into the strip: your fascination for western wear?

TIM: Oh, my cowboy fetish! It's just part of my midlife crisis, yet something I've always, shall we say, appreciated. I've always, in all of my comic strips, had one character or another who has dressed like a cowboy. It has always appealed to me but, being a rather large, long-haired biker type myself, I never thought that I could get away with dressing like that. Lo and behold! My midlife crisis took over, and I thought, *What the hell! I'm going to do this anyway.* And it's been downhill ever since. [*Laughs*]

RON: How do events in your life influence what happens in the strip? Can readers see in the strip some reflection of your life?

TIM: Insofar as we were just talking about someone going through a midlife crisis, I guess I was anticipating that in a way because Leonard and Larry are just a couple of years older than me. God knows, I have no idea what it's actually like to become a grandfather. I'm just using my imagination.

RON: Is there any conscious effort on your part to try to incorporate current events or political topics into the strip?

TIM: I like to do that, but it's difficult because I like to give myself a certain degree of lead time. I once read how Garry Trudeau actually reads the *Congressional Record,* and he keeps right on top of current events. He only draws his comic strip something like two weeks ahead of the time it goes to press. I don't have that luxury, or at least I wouldn't want to be that way because I like to give myself much more lead time than that. If I tried to do something topical it wouldn't be topical any more.

RON: You wouldn't want the pressure, nor would you want to be that topical?

TIM: Yes. It's really not a political strip. It's more about the relationships and the interactions of the characters. Yes, the politics and events in the world, insofar as it affects them, but it's not directly about politics. Besides, if I were going to be that topical and have that short a deadline, my editors and the art department at *Frontiers* would be tearing their hair out waiting for my next strip, wondering if it's going to be on time for the next deadline.

RON: Aside from political content, in an ensemble strip like yours or Alison Bechdel's *Dykes to Watch Out For* or Eric Orner's *Ethan Green*, there's an underlying feeling of the continuity and strength of gay community that comes across. Is this sense of community—a very Bearish one, at that—among your characters something you intended to achieve?

TIM: I've seen that a great deal in real people that I know, especially ones that do not have good relationships with their families, their parents. Their group of friends becomes their family and community. Although Leonard and Larry and everybody else in the strip enjoy really good relations with their parents and family, I do want to reflect this reality in the greater gay reality: how we come to depend on our friends as extended family, as community.

RON: One of the great things about Leonard and Larry is that they actually age in real time. In the new book you have a fresh surge of child-bearing that occurs within a nine-month period. More or less.

TIM: Well, I tried.

RON: Is this abundance of new births significant?

TIM: It's significant to me in that I've gotten tired over the years of constantly hearing from the religious right that they're the only ones with family values, that they're the only ones who know what raising children is all about. I guess that reflects my idea of extended family within a group of friends and the good relationships that my characters have with their families. This is a comic strip of family values. It just happens to be a strip about a lot of gay people, but we know about the importance of having families, having children, and raising them right. It's about standing up to all that bullshit from the religious right.

Besides, when I first started doing the comic strip, I knew I had to have this situation in play because, after I first came out of the closet and started meeting people, I got to know so many people who had been married, who had children and families of their own, and I wanted to reflect that in the comic strip. Just about everybody else out there who was doing a gay comic strip out there was doing stuff like coming-out stories and a lot of sexual innuendo type stuff, a lot of tricking and bar scenes and stuff like that. I wanted to have a completely different focus in my work.

RON: You're rather modest in your depictions, not only graphically but also in terms of the kind of scenes you choose to include in the strip.

TIM: I don't want to be known for doing a sex strip. I do not want to be known as a cartoonist who does X-rated material. That will follow you around for the rest of your life. I'm very proud to say that I do a PG-rated comic strip. Occasionally something might be a soft R but never an X! Besides, I've always contended that, as in comedy, comics work better if you leave things up to the reader's imagination. I think that some things I've done in the past are sexier and more exciting because I don't show everything. I have gotten comments from readers saying that they also feel that way. So I don't intend to change. You're not going to see full frontal nudity on any of the characters or any sexual scenes. Definitely no penetration!

RON: Do you receive any responses or pressure from readers to spice things up?

TIM: Not really. Every once in a while somebody will ask, "Have you ever drawn them...naked?" And no, I haven't.

I'll never forget doing a book signing with some other cartoonists who were in *Gay Comix*, up in West Hollywood's A Different Light bookstore. One of the other cartoonists did really explicit stuff. A friend of mine who had come to see me at the book signing gravitated over to this other guy along with all these other people who were crowded around him, looking at samples of his stuff, because it was very sexually explicit. And everybody was sort of ignoring me, including my friend! So I know that people expect to see that, they want to see that, but I want to do something different; I don't want to do the same thing as everybody else.

RON: This sensibility is also reflected in the kinds of situations your characters get into. Or don't get into, as the case may be.

TIM: Yeah, they're a boring bunch. They're generally monogamous, they don't trick around. Like I said before, everyone else has tackled the open relationships and the tricking in bars and the one-night stands and lots of explicit sex—and I just want to tackle something else. These are boring, middle-aged guys who've settled into their boring, middle-aged monogamous existence, and they're happy and confident about who they are and what they are. So my feeling is let's move on from there and find the comedy in some other aspect of their existence.

RON: Regarding your readers: Do you get much fan mail?

TIM: Actually, no. I receive a piece of fan mail every once in a long while, and it's very gratifying whenever I do. I have struck up friendships and gotten to meet some people that way. Not that I write back and become pen pals with everybody who writes me, but there have been some folks who write fan mail, and I realize we have something in common, and I write them back, and it turns out to be an interesting correspondence, and we become friends. I've met some very good friends that way.

I have a very dear friend in Pennsylvania who was a reader of my old motorcycle stuff. He's a biker—just like I used to be. He used to read my cartoons in the motorcycle magazines. Later on—just when he was coming to grips with his own sexuality, coming out of the closet, and starting to make gay friends—he saw some of my *Leonard & Larry* cartoons somewhere. He couldn't believe it. He realized, *Hey, this was the same guy who used to draw those cartoons in those straight biker rags from years back that he used to read!* So, he just had to write me. We've become great friends.

I've also struck up this wonderful correspondence with a reader in Oslo, Norway. He's not a biker but a photographer, like Leonard, strangely. One of these days I hope to actually talk to him on the phone and maybe even meet him. I don't know when that might happen but he writes me all these wonderful letters about the fan base I have in Norway! It's really amazing and gratifying to find out I've got readers in other countries.

RON: Not surprising, however, considering that the strip is now carried on the Internet on *Frontiers*' Web site.

TIM: True. The friend of mine in Oslo, though, found a copy of my first book, *Domesticity Isn't Pretty*, in a bookstore in Stockholm. He stumbled on to one of my books—in Europe—and came to the Internet afterward. It's shocking to know how my stuff gets around.

RON: Do you yourself identify more with Larry or Leonard, or some other character, or none of the above?

TIM: I used to tell people that I identified more with Larry, but as his character and personality have evolved, he really has gone beyond me, beyond reflecting my own personality. I'm much more identified with Jim, believe it or not! He sort of looks like me. We both have long hair, salt-and-pepper beards. Jim used to be the loneliest guy in town...until he met his cowboy! Until he met the Marlboro Man of his dreams. Which still has not happened for me, but, you know, I can't live vicariously through the strip completely. I gotta give somebody like Jim a happy ending sooner or later. He was getting to be kinda pathetic before Merle came along and I decided to put them together.

RON: Your strip is well known for its abundance of bearded characters.

TIM: I draw what I like. Other people who draw other comic strips can draw what they like, but I draw for myself and I know what kind of audience I have. All the people who've felt that they and their tastes have been neglected in the world of gay comic strips all these years have sort of rallied around my stuff.

RON: It seems to me that the effort involved in drawing beards and body hair—with the level of detail that you use—must be somewhat a labor of love. Alison Bechdel commented to me, "No one renders facial hair like Tim Barela, I always say. He does the most fabulous beards—he seems to draw each individual strand of hair."

TIM: It's a lot of work. But I can't imagine not drawing men who are worth looking at and worth spending time with every couple of weeks when the comic comes out. I can't imagine drawing men any other way. It's the type of men I like to draw, and the type I like to see, and that my readers like to see. My readers expect nothing less, and I'm not going to give them anything less!

RON: As a friend of mine says, "You find a fetish that works for you, and you stick with it."

TIM: Of course, yes! Bearded men and leather and cowboys—it all works for me.

RON: And these are some of the features that have made your strip so popular with the Bear community around the world. How have you related with this particular group of readers?

TIM: The Bears are a very large percentage of my readership. I'm well known in the Bear community. They're the type of people I relate to significantly and the type that most of my friends are. I don't have anything against other types, but I'm a Bear myself—what can I say? That's where I'm coming from.

RON: What was your initial reaction to learning about the Bear phenomenon in the mid '80s? Considering that the whole thing began around the same time as *Leonard & Larry*—you even did a one-time guest cartoon for *Bear* issue no. 4—did what was happening with the Bears influence what you were doing in your strip?

TIM: After *Leonard & Larry* became a regular gig, I never did *Grizzly & Ted* [in *Bear* magazine] again. Besides, as I mentioned before, I never really wanted to do a "sex strip" and *Bear* magazine was shaping up to be a very sex-oriented magazine, which is fine—I have nothing against that. I just didn't want to do a sex strip. The type of strip that I wanted to make of *Grizzly & Ted* was more like what I do in *Leonard & Larry*. I didn't think that that type of more conservative strip would have fit into the format. But I love that magazine and *American Bear*— don't get me wrong. I definitely love the way the whole thing has evolved.

RON: What's your take on the whole Bear subculture? Like me, you've watched the whole thing blossom since before—

TIM: Watched it evolve since before the moniker "Bear" was a common expression, way, way back. It's just wonderful to know that there's a reactionary movement to the mainstream gay press, who think we all look like the pretty models on the covers of some of the more mainstream gay magazines...

RON: Like *Frontiers*?

TIM: [*Laughs*] I don't want to criticize my art director! Don't make me do that!

No, but there is this mindset that we all want to see are these pretty, blond, bald-faced, bald-chested individuals. They may be very pretty, but they don't do a thing for me. It's nice to see that there's been a reaction to that, this collective cry of "No! We don't want that, we're not going to take it, we're going to have things the way we like it."

RON: So perhaps it follows that the success of *Leonard & Larry* is yet more evidence of the interest of other Bear-minded and -bodied folks.

TIM: Yes, I agree!

RON: Personally, Tim, what does it mean to you to age along with your characters? You've mentioned your earlier midlife crisis. We've also seen Larry—

TIM: Larry's gone through midlife crises of one sort or another, Leonard has grown grayer and grayer over the years, and Jim is growing grayer and balder—fortunately, losing hair is not a problem I have.

I don't think I could do the strip any other way. I really couldn't do one of those comic strips where nobody grows older and the kids never grow up, and things don't change. But it's not only about the strip reflecting real life; I think that if I drew one of those strips which stays the same year after year, I'd grow bored to death of doing it. I don't know how I could come up with funny things to say. So many of the comic strips in the newspaper—where nothing ever changes, and nobody gets any older, and the children never grow up—they end up recycling the same stale humor over and over again, year after year after year. I couldn't handle that. I couldn't stand writing stuff like that.

Someone once asked me at a public appearance how I manage to keep my stuff fresh. I don't know! I do it because I just couldn't imagine doing it or writing it any other way. I have to keep it fresh to keep myself from becoming bored with it, and in turn to keep the readers from becoming bored. I guess I've achieved a certain degree of freshness every time the strip comes out. That's what I want.

RON: Is that the hardest part for you about creating the strip? Keeping it fresh?

TIM: Sometimes it is, because even I fall back on old gags and old situations. I think, *Well, I've gotten humor out of this situation before, maybe I can squeeze some more humor out of it again.* Like Larry becoming a grandfather for the third time: to use a hackneyed old gag like that but to make it fresh can be really difficult. That's probably part of the reason why I ended up in the midst of last year's writer's block.

RON: What part of creating *Leonard & Larry* gives you the most pleasure?

TIM: Drawing bearded men with hairy chests! [*Laughs*] The thing that gives me the most pleasure is knowing that my little cartoon brings so much pleasure to the lives of regular readers of the strip. I once got the most wonderful compliment from someone. This was years ago when the AIDS crisis was raging. He told me that one of the nicest things about my strip is that I make people laugh and at the time that it was important for the community to laugh. I appreciate it when I hear things like that or hear from other people that they had always aspired to having a "normal" life as a gay person, to being monogamous, to being settled. When they say they wanted to be happy with themselves but didn't see that around them, yet were able to see that in the characters in my strip, and that my strip was a positive influence on their lives, on their coming to terms with their own sexuality—that gives me a tremendous amount of pleasure.

Chapter 13
Hoping for Something Bigger
~ An Interview With Bruce Vilanch ~

BRUCE VILANCH, blond Bear and self-described "big queen," has written for every conceivable televised awards show, including the Oscars, Emmys, Tonys, and Grammys. In fact, he's almost more well-endowed with Emmys won from writing these shows than his—well, let's just say he's got more than a hairy handful.

He's also written the Daytime Emmys, People's Choice, American Comedy Awards, Comic Relief telethons, and countless other such entertainment award shows. He's put hilarity in the mouths of Bette Midler, Whoopi Goldberg, Robin Williams, Lily Tomlin, Shirley MacLaine, Diana Ross, George Carlin, Ann Margret, Nathan Lane, Eddie Murphy, Joel Grey, Angela Lansbury, Cher, Joan Rivers, and (gasp) Donny and Marie, to name but a few fortunate souls.

Last year Hollywood showed its appreciation in an adoring Miramax documentary, *Get Bruce!* which tells of his life growing up in Paterson, New Jersey; as the class clown, disarming bullies with humor and appearing in high school plays; as feature writer for the *Chicago Tribune*; as writer and friend to the stars; and as contributor to benefits for AIDS-related and gay and lesbian causes.

Bruce is head writer and regular guest on *The New Hollywood Squares*. He's also respected as an actor, lyricist, and sitdown comic. In fact, he received rave reviews for his one-man comic extravaganza, "Almost Famous," at the Westbeth Theatre Center in New York City during May and June 2000.

Although I had been aware of Bruce's work for years, it was in Bruce's monthly *Advocate* column, "Notes From a Blond," that I first noticed he might have some affinity to Bears. After much polite, persistent pestering, Bruce took time out from his incredibly busy pre-Oscar schedule in early February 2000 for a phone interview.

During the run of *Almost Famous* I E-mailed Bruce beforehand to let him know I was planning to come to the show, and he included almost 10 minutes of hilarious Bear-related material for everyone's benefit. Bruce and I finally met, albeit briefly, in person after the show. He showed me a gag mock-up of the cover of *American Bear* magazine, in which someone had cut and pasted a photo of Bruce's head onto the body of the near-naked coverman. Once again, as he had done regularly during the following interview, Bruce made me laugh out loud.

BRUCE: Proctology...

RON: [*Laughs*] Is the doctor in?

BRUCE: Hang on, I'll just get my rubber glove... [*Both laugh*] and I'll be ready for you. Or anyone else who calls.

RON: Oh, very good. Bruce, it's a real pleasure to speak with you.

BRUCE: Thank you! We'll have a good time.

RON: In your "Notes from a Blond" column last year [*The Advocate*, February 16, 1999], you seemed to indicate that the Haworth Press catalogue listing of *The Bear Book* was the first place that you heard about Bears. Is that correct?

BRUCE: Yes, it was.

RON: Did you actually get to read *The Bear Book*?

BRUCE: Yes, I did. I looked through the book after I got all this E-mail from the *Roseanne Show*. I decided to write another column about it for *The Advocate* [which appeared March 14, 2000], so I started reading up on Bear culture to make sure I wasn't on a completely wrong track.

RON: So, it was on the *Roseanne Show* that you came out nationally as a Bear.

BRUCE: I guess I have, if the *Roseanne Show* can be considered national—it's more like public access with a house band.

RON: [*Laughs*] It only plays in something like four or five markets, right?

BRUCE: It's more like theater, I thought—about as many people watch it as a play on Broadway. About a thousand people around the country watch it.

RON: Really? No! But you certainly got some response from that.

BRUCE: Oy, I got plenty! I got more than I ever thought I'd get. I got more responses than I thought were people watching.

RON: What kind of response did you receive?

BRUCE: Well, all the response I got was hostile. People said things like, "Why are you putting down Bears? Why are you putting down people who like men your size?" and all that kind of thing. So what I said in the column was that no one wants to be objectified. I don't want to be objectified. The women's movement has been saying for years that it's no fun to be objectified. It makes you feel interchangeable.

RON: What do you mean by "interchangeable"?

BRUCE: I mean that if somebody wants to love me because I'm big and hairy and they perceive that because of that I would be some kind of cuddle-bunny, that's nice, those are all admirable qualities, but that's not who *I* am. My look is not who I am. I don't want to be loved just because of that. Just suppose I shave and lose 30 pounds? Then I don't mean anything anymore to someone who objectifies me in that way. I think it's like going from one kind of clone to another. I think there's more to life than that. I don't blame anybody for doing it; I think that if it works for you, great. On a highly personal level, though, it's nothing that I really want. I don't want to be worshipped and adored by somebody because I wear a 52-inch waist or because I have hair down to my shoulders.

RON: Or on your chin and cheeks.

BRUCE: Exactly! On my chin and cheeks. It just strikes me as being wildly superficial. And the idea of building a whole culture around that seems to me wildly superficial as well. Of course, I feel like, to each his own, whatever makes people happy, but it's just not for me. But I find myself, because I'm on TV every night, being at the center of this kind of attention. I find that bizarre, because it's not attention that I really court, that's not why I look like this, to find people who are turned on to this look. Does that make any sense?

RON: Yes, it certainly does, although I think some folks feel that it's not being objectified that bothers them, it's the fact that some bodies are objectified and glorified, while others are shunned and ridiculed. They view the "feminist critique" you speak of as faulty in that it's unrealistic to expect people to not objectify others' bodies; the problem in this culture in that some bodies are considered acceptable to objectify while others are not. How do you respond?

BRUCE: Actually, I think that that argument is faulty. The people who objectify my body are way past wondering whether or not it's socially acceptable to objectify a fat guy—they're into it! I think anybody with any self-esteem will have the sort of reaction I had, and that includes gorgeous guys I talk to who get objectified all the time. It's fun and flattering for a minute, but then it's a drag because it's not about you anymore, it's all about your archetype.

[*Bruce is interrupted by a phone call*]

I get the impression that you feel that your looks in a sense are also comedic.

BRUCE: Sure. It makes it much easier to get a job when you walk in a room as a comedy writer, and you look like this, and they think, *Well, he must be funny—just look at him!*

RON: "He's a funny-looking guy."

BRUCE: Right. On the other hand, there's a lot of other comedy writers who don't look like this and have no trouble getting work.

RON: No doubt.

BRUCE: You wouldn't point at Neil Simon as he walks through an airport and start laughing, saying, "Look at that guy!" I get a lot of that. I've always gotten that. Now it's different, now I get recognized. It's shifted to, "Oh, he's on TV!" Before it used to be, "Who's that?" They would think I was a wrestler, or in rock 'n' roll. Another Jerry Garcia.

RON: Garcia with a dye job.

BRUCE: That's right. Now it's back to Shelley Winters. If she shaves, I'm in real trouble!

RON: [*Laughing*] Let me ask you: Were you big as a kid too?

BRUCE: Yeah, always.

RON: How long have you worn your beard?

BRUCE: Thirty years. I grew it for a movie. Actually it was for a picture in 1971, and I had to have a fixed three-day growth of beard.

RON: Which movie was that?

BRUCE: It was an Italian picture, which was called *Excuse Me, My Name Is Rocco Papaleo* [released in 1971 as *Permettete? Rocco Papaleo*]. It was the only Marcello Mastroianni movie to flop in Italy. Marcello and Lauren Hutton are the stars. That's when Lauren was a big model. They shot it in Chicago when I was writing for the *Chicago*

Tribune, and I got cast. For six weeks I had to have a three-day growth of beard, and every day I came in, they would cut it back to yesterday's growth.

RON: Perpetually nubby.

BRUCE: At its itchiest and most awful point in beard-growing, and I vowed when the show was over, "As God as my witness, I will never shave again!" And I haven't. Of course I would, if somebody came along with a fabulous part. But so far they haven't.

RON: You'd be a beard slut?

BRUCE: I am a beard slut. Whatever they pay me. Of course, any slut that's waited 30 years has grown cobwebs.

RON: Well, that's longer than some young cubs have been even a sparkle in their mamma bear's eyes. Now, your own personal looks aside, you don't particularly prefer Bear-types, correct?

BRUCE: No.

RON: What is your type of man?

BRUCE: I don't have a type, truthfully.

RON: What do you look for, then, in a guy, in companionship?

BRUCE: [*Pause*] I guess it's a cliché, but I like somebody with a sense of humor. I'll be with somebody, and we'll just connect. There's something special...probably their body language does it. They can have any kind of body, but it's the body language that I think that's key in general in human relationships. People often ask, "What is it about Bette Midler that's so wonderful?" and I say, "It's her body language." There's something about the way she moves and her whole attitude that's inherently comic, and I think it's what makes funny people funny. And I think it's what makes sexy people sexy. I don't know that it can be broken down into component parts, but I know in my case, it's the way somebody comports himself that attracts me. And of course, they have to be very, very well hung! [*Both laugh*] I mean, they can be big and dumb and it's just a sign. We all get turned on by different things. But I've never been attracted to one particular type. It's not like, "Oh, it's black guys for me."

RON: Right.

BRUCE: A friend and I went to a circuit party a couple of years ago, and we were on the dance floor at 4 in the morning. He was wearing sunglasses, and this little blond kid came up to him and said, "Why are you wearing sunglasses at four o'clock in the morning?" And my friend said,

"It makes kids like you look Latin." He's Miss South of the Border.

RON: He was looking at the world through Latino-colored glasses.

BRUCE: Right, he was. But I don't have that "thing." Of course, I'm a size queen, like everybody else. Nobody will ever admit that they are, but everybody is.

RON: But speaking of circuit boyz, as you were a moment ago...

BRUCE: Me? A circuit boy?

RON: You mentioned on the *Roseanne Show* that you'd gone to a Bearclub meeting. Was that one of the L.A. Bearclubs?

BRUCE: No, I went to a Bear bar. I was taken to the Faultline for Bear night.

RON: You were taken by another similarly bodied person?

BRUCE: No, this was a Bear lover. Actually, is he a Bear lover? No, he's not. He's a white-collar guy and he loves anybody who isn't. That's his type. And he said, "They'll love you at this place," because I had been saying, "Oh, well, I'm not seeing anybody, it's so hard, everybody I meet is interested in fame and just wants to get into show business," and all that kind of stuff. So he said, "I'll take you to some place where they'll just love you for you"—but of course what he meant was they would love me for my look.

RON: Right.

BRUCE: And yeah, I did meet lots of guys, none of whom interested me. They were all so tiny! So when I said this on *Roseanne* that they were like "ticks on a rhino," a lot of people got upset. So I apologized for that one. That was an unfortunate simile.

RON: Perhaps a poor choice of metaphor.

BRUCE: In any case, there were all these huge guys walking around, and they had all these little guys hanging off of them, and I just wasn't interested in any of these little guys who were there! They were all, like, completely struck by my look, worshipping the look, and I suppose I would be singing a happy tune if any one of them had appealed to me, but they didn't, so, here I am, old Johnny One-note.

RON: So it sounds like you weren't able to strike a happy medium between the really big guys and the Bear lovers.

BRUCE: Yeah. Am I the happy medium?

RON: You might have been. Or the happy XL between the Ls and the XXXLs.

BRUCE: I see. Well, yes, maybe I'm just a big ol' Bear.

RON: But it didn't work for you.

BRUCE: It didn't, for the reasons I said. It was a weird sensation because I've never been pursued for that. I've been actively rejected for the way I look. And so I thought at first, "Well, it would be nice to be pursued," but after a little bit of the pursuing, it didn't appeal to me at all. Although I've gotten well known—I mean, I'm pursued in public by people—I still haven't come across anybody I'm interested in.

RON: That brings up an interesting question. Do you feel that among entertainment people in Los Angeles—or anywhere else, actually—that you're stigmatized for your looks? I mean, straight or gay?

BRUCE: Among entertainment people?

RON: Yeah, your cohorts. You were saying that you felt you were stigmatized in some way, or rejected.

BRUCE: Oh. Well, that was sexually, romantically.

RON: I see.

BRUCE: In conventional business, of course, it's a different story. Who looks like this in conventional business? Show business is the only place you can look like this and have a career. Or a garage mechanic. Even the Bears—most of the guys in that bar, if they work in a bank, they probably dress up in suits. They're not in those lumberjack outfits all the time.

RON: Except when they're having sex.

BRUCE: Yes, but not if they have straight jobs in the real world. If they run Bear bookstores, I suppose they can look like that all the time. I can look like this all the time because of the career I've chosen.

RON: Same here.

BRUCE: And I've been lucky enough to make some money with my looks as well. But a lot of people have to conform in order to make a living. So they can be heavy and bearded, but they have to be heavy and bearded in an Armani suit.

RON: Right, but maybe that's just the kind of Bears you met in Los Angeles. Rural Bears may actually look that way all the time. It's true, though, that many of these men probably aspire to working-class looks when in actuality they're just, as I sometimes like to call them, "furry technoqueers." It's very different from the "Bear look" you find in Detroit, or Denver.

BRUCE: Technoqueers?

RON: Furry technoqueers.

BRUCE: Oh, sort of like role playing by computer geeks. You're probably right.

RON: Obviously this is a generalization.

BRUCE: I haven't been around it that much to make that observation, but it makes sense to me.

RON: Now, have you investigated any of the Bear magazines, like *Bear* or *American Bear*—any of the Bear smut rags?

BRUCE: No, not really. I've seen it. I've run across some Bear porn.

RON: Did you know that last year *Saturday Night Live* was parodying specialty magazines and actually flashed a copy of *Bear* magazine?

BRUCE: Really? Interesting.

RON: I'm curious to know if you had any impressions about that form of erotica.

BRUCE: I haven't really looked at it. I think I've seen the magazines, and looked at a few photos, which struck me as hilarious. But that's because I don't find it erotic. I think it's hysterical. I think people's reactions to most things that are meant to be erotic but don't strike them as erotic make them laugh. So I laughed.

RON: Is that perhaps you have perhaps a more comedic than erotic sensibility? Or that your erotic sensibility is innately comedic?

BRUCE: That could be, yeah.

RON: Are there other persons in the entertainment industry that you are aware of that are Bears, or might be considered Bear-types?

BRUCE: Not that I'm aware of. Guys who look like me, I suppose. I guess they qualify, but I don't know anybody who's into it.

RON: Right.

BRUCE: Like I've never run into Grizzly Adams somewhere. Never got an E-mail from Sam Walker saying, "Hey! Let's go to the Faultline."

RON: Do you know the Bearish-looking Richard Karn, formerly of *Home Improvement*?

BRUCE: No, I don't, oddly enough. I think I've maybe met him, just for a minute, on an awards show. I've never worked with him or had any real contact with him.

RON: He's considered by a lot of gay male Bears as kind of a straight Bear icon. He's even been offered honorary Bearclub memberships.

BRUCE: He could be a Bearclub president!

RON: Sure! For a lot of Bears he seems to be the ideal sort of Bear, masculine, handsome, just a bit chubby, the flannel shirts, the beard, kind of shy... He almost embodies a kind of Bear archetype. However, Karn apparently is very embarrassed by the fact that he has a lot of gay male fans.

BRUCE: I see. And he's embarrassed by this? Well, you know, there's a certain element—a large element—of the straight world that views our antics as incomprehensible. Literally, incredible. They can't believe that people go to these lengths. Of course, they also don't believe that people in the straight community go to the lengths they go to, because they're not part of that party, either. These are not people who are into swinger ads. I suspect the majority of straight people who lead straight lives and who maybe have a kink once in their lives, or are in deep denial about whatever kinks they may have in their lives, find it astonishing that there is a culture. I'm gay, and I find it astonishing that there's such a culture.

RON: It is peculiar, if you stop to think about it, but part of its value is that it gives people pause.

BRUCE: One of the things that I said in *The Advocate* article is that, maybe, because we're celebrating diversity, all these various elements of our culture are emerging and growing because it's a revolt against the gymbots. People are looking for other clone models to attach themselves to.

I don't know what the factors are, but whatever it is, it's more out in the open now than it ever was before. And I think a lot of people can even hardly believe that it exists in the first place. So an actor like Richard Karn, for example, who is straight and married with children, goes on television. Then all of a sudden discovers that he's got a gay following he never counted on, or even knew existed, his reaction is obviously just to close his eyes and think, *Maybe this will all go away.*

RON: Wishful thinking on his part. They call that, I think, denial. I'm curious, Bruce, what sort of backlash or response did you receive from *The Advocate* piece you wrote about your Bear experience?

BRUCE: None that I know of—but *The Advocate* doesn't send me letters. [*Bruce is interrupted by another phone call*]

So, where were we, in this fascinating world of overweight, hairy men and their admirers?

RON: Let's talk about your contacts with Girth & Mirth.

BRUCE: Girth & Mirth. That's something else. A precursor. In the column I also said that I think I'm a bit older than the Bear culture—I go all the way back to Girth & Mirth.

RON: Were you aware of Girth & Mirth early on?

BRUCE: Oh, yeah. They wanted me as their poster boy! Years ago, when I first appeared on TV. I showed up on their radar and they said, "Oh, boy! He's a fat one—we like him!"

RON: Who contacted you from their group and what was your response to them?

BRUCE: L.A. Girth & Mirth, who I guess at the time had a lot of chubby chasers. My response was exactly the same as it is now, which is: "Thank you, but I'm not interested in someone who's only interested in me because I'm fat."

It strikes me that this is a rant that women have, all these women who have breast implants so they can attract men who want women with big tits. What happens if, God forbid, they have to have them taken out? If they have to have mastectomies or anything like that, what happens with this man who loved you for your big tits? You have to hope that there's something deeper, that there's something bigger than that. Or not—or you move on to the next guy who wants you for your big tits.

So it's all wildly superficial. I don't want to be loved because I'm fat. I want to be loved because of who I am. [*Affecting a sad voice*] That's not too much to ask in this world!

RON: No, of course it's not.

BRUCE: At times, I'm struck by the irony that I get all these offers from all these men but for all the wrong reasons. But that's not the first time that's happened. When you become public and then famous, a lot of people attracted to you for that reason. And that's a wrong reason as well.

RON: Certainly.

BRUCE: And so this issue of my looks is one on the list of wrong reasons that people are attracted to me for, and I just have to live with it. Why is no one attracted to me for my big dick? That's what I can't quite figure out.

RON: That's a good question. Thank you for your time, Bruce. It has been a pleasure.

BRUCE: You're welcome. Now, back to the salt mines....

Part Four

Bear Sex and Styles

CHAPTER 14
WEIGHT AND FAT AS MASCULINE DRAG
~ A DISCUSSION WITH DR. LAWRENCE MASS ~

LARRY MASS, MD, is a cofounder of Gay Men's Health Crisis and the first journalist to write about AIDS in any press. He is the author of a memoir, *Confessions of a Jewish Wagnerite: Being Gay and Jewish in America*, and is author and editor of three collections: *Homosexuality and Sexuality: Dialogues of the Sexual Revolution, Volume I*; *Homosexuality as Behavior and Identity: Dialogues of the Sexual Revolution, Volume II*; and *We Must Love One Another or Die: The Life and Legacies of Larry Kramer*. Dr. Mass is a unit director of addiction treatment programs at Beth Israel Medical Center and Greenwich House, Inc., in New York City, where he lives with his life partner, Arnie Kantrowitz (interviewed in chapter 18).

One weekend at the upstate New York cabin of some Bear friends, I met Larry Mass, with whom I'd corresponded previously. While the group of us relaxed and enjoyed the country life, Larry brought forth a draft copy of his contribution to *The Bear Book II*. His ambitious essay on "Bears and Health" adroitly covered many aspects of the health problems that Bears face, ranging from sleep apnea to pediculosis. I encouraged him to consider serializing discrete sections of the piece. Publisher Tim Martin readily agreed to carry Larry's column in *American Bear* magazine, and Larry continues to use his forum there to speak out on Bear health issues.

As a relatively trim Bear myself, I've not ever had to deal with a weight problem personally (although my approaching middle age seems to be changing that). I have, however, supported many of my Bearish friends in their struggles to contain or lose excess weight and have witnessed the inner psychological tumult they endure, as well as the near-constant barrage of negative societal messages that demoralize big people's psyches.

I was excited at the prospect of examining this issue with Larry, whose medical knowledge, cultural insight, and experience with the Bear community combine to make this online conversation both enjoyable and informative.

RON: Larry, is there a medical definition of being overweight for men?

LARRY: There's no absolute definition, although there are tables and suggested ideal weights, and there's a figure called Body Mass Index (BMI) that requires some mathematics to determine. There are many different charts with normal ranges for body weight based on height, which you see at the gym, in medical offices, at clinics. They come from various medical and public health institutions and studies and are all within a few pounds of each other in recommending ideal weights.

RON: As of 1998, National Institute of Diabetes & Digestive & Kidney Diseases statistics indicate that more than half of American adult males are overweight; less than 20 percent of American adult males are obese. [See the References and Resources section for more information.] How serious is being overweight compared to smoking or drinking?

LARRY: As for the seriousness of being overweight in terms of health consequences, the best analogy is to cigarettes and alcohol. In fact, being overweight can have some of the same health consequences that smoking and drinking have, such as high blood pressure and hardening of the arteries. And the analogies don't stop there. Indeed, eating disorders are widely regarded as phenomena of compulsivity and addiction, just like drugs and cigarettes and alcohol and gambling.

RON: I was surprised to discover recently that men don't store fat in the same way as women: Whereas women store their fat around their hips, men store their fat around the abdomen, which, because it surrounds the vital organs, is potentially dangerous to health.

LARRY: Of course, there are people who are large yet look healthy and happy and wonderful, and those of us who are turned on to big men certainly think they are just that. In reality, though, many or even most of these folks have health problems. Happens to me all the time! I meet some big Bear who I think is just the hottest, only to then discover all these health problems he has—including some of the same ones I have.

RON: Is that a turn-off?

LARRY: No. So powerful is the attraction to bigness in men for me and many other Bears that we don't care—or act as if we don't. As a physician and writer whose highest value is truth, however, I can't pretend the truth is something it isn't. In other words, just because I'm turned on to big men doesn't mean bigness is healthy. Another example of this truth problem is the dichotomy we see between our affirmation of sex and questions of sexual compulsivity. Just because many of us are still acting out sexually and are sexually compulsive doesn't mean that [author and AIDS activist] Larry Kramer's critique of us doesn't have to be taken seriously.

RON: What do you mean by "Larry Kramer's critique of us"?

LARRY: Well, Larry Kramer believes that as a community, gay men have always been and remain sex-obsessed or besotted. He's generalizing, of course, and it can seem easy to dismiss Larry as older and embittered and erotophobic. Actually, Larry never used the paradigm of sexual compulsivity or addiction—he's much too straight-talking for that—but that, I believe, is the phenomenon he saw and has tried to critique.

RON: Can you be more specific about how compulsive eating and being overweight contribute to physical health problems for gay men?

LARRY: As you know, some of these topics I've covered in my health column for *American Bear* and my chapter for Les Wright's *The Bear Book II*.

There's a slew of specific health consequences to being overweight. The biggest are diabetes, hypertension, ASCVD [arteriosclerotic cardiovascular disease], ASPVD [arteriosclerotic peripheral cardiovascular disease], heart attack, stroke, sleep apnea, arthritis, as well as various gastrointestinal disturbances. Not everyone who's overweight gets these, of course, just as not everyone who smokes gets lung cancer or COPD [chronic obstructive pulmonary disease].

RON: That's a good thing, considering that so many North Americans are considered clinically overweight.

LARRY: Yes, it's a problem of the whole country, as a recent entire issue of *JAMA* [*Journal of the American Medical Association*] was devoted to pointing out.

RON: What are the implications, then, for big men?

LARRY: At the obvious level, the *JAMA* issue is saying that many of us are too overweight; that in the best interests of preventive medicine, we need to be more conscientious about diet and exercise.

RON: What's the best way to do that?

LARRY: While there is no surefire regimen for weight reduction, two recommendations are crucial to all programs: greatly reduce the intake of fat and sugar, and exercise regularly. Another common suggestion is to avoid being famished and to reduce the bulk volume of food intake by eating smaller meals at shorter intervals (six small meals instead of three big ones). Finally, issues of self-esteem may play critical roles in compulsivity, and are often best addressed in group-therapeutic programs (such as Weight Watchers and Overeaters Anonymous).

RON: Aside from the standard "listen to your hunger pangs" adage, that sounds like solid prevention advice. Let's get back to the idea of the changing standard of obesity in men.

LARRY: Between the lines, I think what the *JAMA* issue is saying is that the notion that "fat is good" is causing trouble. It's one thing for us to learn to be more inclusive and not express overt prejudice toward the overweight and fat, but it's another to say that all of that is now normal and healthy.

RON: True. In the Bear world, there's a whole different level of acceptance of size. I think Bears are probably guilty of participating in that blind acceptance, but perhaps not more than other Americans.

LARRY: Precisely. I wonder to what extent the sanctioning of being overweight is a result of images of celebrities such as John Goodman— images which have been positive because they've broken a lot of stereotypes. I've had fantasies about Tom Arnold, especially in uniform. And what about the hottest of them all—Chris Penn?

RON: John is one of the sexiest big men I've seen. Certainly the popularity of men like him, Tom Arnold, Drew Carey, and other big guys have influenced American culture. They've helped to make fat phat. Nevertheless, bigness carries an overweening stigma throughout our culture, which is odd, considering how commonplace it is. In any case, let's look at the masculine appeal of fatness.

LARRY: For many gay men, bigness has always been a feature of masculinity. Why and where that comes from I'm not sure, but women view bigness similarly. One archetype of masculinity is bigness—for example, football players, construction workers, weightlifters. On the other hand, plenty of gay men are most attracted to pretty boys, mainly because they see them as masculine. And what about Asian countries where bigness is rare?

RON: I guess that's true, but even there, there are exceptions, such as sumo wrestlers.

LARRY: All of which goes to show how socially constructed so much of this is, how arbitrary. By Bear standards, many Asian and native peoples would be considered effeminate. It's ridiculous.

RON: Western culture has largely, it seems, associated fat with women and femininity, and muscle with men and masculinity. An ironic feature of hypermasculinity is that it seems to compel men to want to emasculate others.

LARRY: I believe that the fetishization, as we might call it, of "masculinity" is a reality in the Bear world. Where it really comes out is in the use of epithets like "twinkie" or "pretty boy" or "Chelsea boy."

RON: As they say, you can understand much about a society or culture by looking at the people it excludes and shuns. But that works both for and against Bears.

LARRY: Yes, it's interesting to see how the massively obese are accepted in the Bear world that is centered more around being big than being seriously obese.

RON: Would you characterize Bear culture as being primarily about overindulgence?

LARRY: I don't want to say that the subculture can't have positive spiritual energies and values. I feel that in its current state, however, ultimately the Bear world is overwhelmingly about sex. When all is said and done, it's another circuit-party subculture like the gay leather or gym-body world, and like the proliferation of Plato's Retreat–type places for swingers that were a hallmark of what we used to call "the sexual revolution." In that sense, it's more like than unlike the world of the big White and Black and Blue and Morning parties in Palm Springs, Montreal, Miami, Fire Island, and elsewhere.

RON: Could you say more about this equation, Bear culture = sex culture, with a view toward Bear health risks?

LARRY: Bear culture is organized around big social events wherein the main thing going on is sexual connecting. "Bear busts" [beer-soda fund-raising socials], and Bear organizations are primarily social and sexual, although they, like the big party dance events, also raise money for charities. Take away the sex from Bear culture and what do you have? Some very scattered and disparate notions of masculinity and preference for body types, tribal bonding based on similar or complementary sexual preferences.

Let me say this about Bear sensibility: the same criticism I'm leveling has been leveled against gay sensibility—that there is no such thing. Well, there is and there isn't. The Bear subculture is this real thing that we're all involved in, and yet it's constructed of nothing real, enduring, nothing absolute—it's made up of bits and pieces of things that are part of bigger trends. Ultimately, there is no singular, circumscribable entity— the Bears—any more than anything you can define as gay sensibility, the gay community, leatherfolk, or the sexual revolution.

RON: Forming community through sexual-preference similarities may not be the most enduring of values—but it is not nothing.

LARRY: Right. No matter how mutable it is, it's what's happening to us, and we're not discounting its power or importance, whatever it is or isn't. Personally, it has had a huge presence in my life. Once, Arnie asked me: Why are you so involved with Bears? What's that really all about? My answer was clear and immediate: "Because I love them," I said. I should have said *us*. They/we are my people. How? Why? I don't know.

RON: Perhaps that's part of the attraction: that those intense feelings are both familiar and unknown.

LARRY: At the most primitive level, it's because I just feel instinctively that these are my people.

RON: Perhaps exactly because Bears are so indefinable, they are so easy to love as a sort of archetypal man-loving man.

LARRY: Yes. I went on to say to Arnie that my love of Bears is like his (and my) love of gay people. Ultimately, how rational is it?

RON: Primal urges like hunger and sex are not particularly rational processes. I'd like to examine Bears' mental health and behavior problems further, and in particular, self-esteem issues. How does being big affect gay men's early sense of self? Is it possible to say how being big and gay might relate?

LARRY: Well, I'm not a psychologist or psychiatrist, but being big and having issues around that are by no means limited to being gay. As far as being gay and big is concerned, it's just a double load of social non-conformity to deal with. In some ways they come together, in others they are separate issues; that is, some people have eating disorders, which is a problem of addiction and compulsivity not necessarily related to being gay, but it helps to deal with the two together.

RON: So it's not uncommon that self-esteem issues of big men are compounded by coming out or just being gay or vice versa?

LARRY: In many instances, sure. A lot of gay men and lesbians have to deal with secondary minority and other identity issues and concerns—being Jewish, being overweight, being Black, being an alcoholic, being big, and the like. The varieties and permutations of how all that can come out are infinite.

RON: Fat perhaps can be seen as a body-based mechanism developed to shield the self from insult or injury instead of mental or psychic armor. When groups like Bearclubs or G&M [Girth & Mirth] celebrate the essential fatness of big gay men, does it help to diffuse the stigma that fat people usually experience?

LARRY: Oh, yes, and that aspect of it is wonderful, but as I've stated, it's troubled at the level of saying that fat is good, normal, healthy. I agree with my fellow Bears that big and even fat are beautiful, but as a physician, I can't say it's healthy.

RON: Getting back to the topic of compulsive overeating: I understand you're not a shrink, but I want to ask your take on the psychological dynamic of encouragers and gainers—which to me seems a very codependent type of relationship. What does it mean when someone who's overweight wants to gain even more weight and is encouraged to do so in a sexual partnership?

LARRY: This is a frontier of gay subcultural behavior and of psychology—something very much of our time and culture. Encouragers and gainers publish a newsletter and I have some issues, but there are no formal studies on this, as far as I know. Nor has there been any public discussion, though there has been some art (Nayland Blake's video of an encourager-gainer encounter between himself and former MetroBears president John Outcault). So anything I have to say is shooting from the hip.

RON: Forewarned is forearmed.

LARRY: OK, here goes. I'm attracted to big and even fat men myself, so I know what it is to fetishize weight and body parts like bellies (for me, big butts have the most power). I think the phenomenon of encouragers and gainers is mostly about eroticization and fetishization of eating, of weight-gaining, and sometimes of body functions. For example, for some folks, observing, rubbing, and listening to the gurgles of a big belly as they watch their partner eat is highly erotic.

RON: Right, there's a great word for those digestive sounds: borborygmy. But please, go on.

LARRY: Anyways, these actions have erotic appeal to the extent of fetishization, just as certain other people are into feet, shoes, lingerie, other cross-dressing during sex, SM, and toilet activities. Now, when the activity becomes more important than the individual, it's called paraphilia (the newer psychiatric term for perversion)—but that doesn't mean that people can't spice up their erotic lives with this stuff. Many of us get into this and that to some degree. It's when an activity becomes exclusive and takes over your sexuality to the extent of determining your erotic life entirely at the expense of other considerations that there may be something to look at critically.

On the other hand, encouragers and gainers are people who have felt very isolated and abnormal with their preferences, like leatherfolk, Bears, G&M, and others; they now have a subculture they can connect with that makes them feel less alone, less abnormal and wherein they can find like-minded partners.

RON: When someone encourages another person to gain weight, isn't one partner actually causing harm to the other? Doesn't that add to the other person's likelihood of unhealth and disease?

LARRY: Yes, but so does licking dirty ass, getting whipped to the point of bleeding, getting fucked bareback, or getting fist-fucked, all stuff people make legitimate choices to do. (I left out drinking piss because there's really no health risk there!)

RON: Is it just that one method is overt and the other subtle?

LARRY: No, I see no difference between encouragers and gainers and shit eaters and shit feeders or tit torturers and tit torturees—as long it's consensual and both are doing what they want.

RON: Perhaps, then, there's not a difference.

LARRY: I have no more interest than you or even Pat Califia in telling people what they should or shouldn't do, what's "right" or "wrong," but when it comes to what's healthy or what are the health risks of certain behaviors, that's another matter. If you want to fist-fuck, fine, but you should know that there are some health hazards. As you put it earlier, and as I tried to put it once in an article on fist-fucking from which this final concluding remark got censored: "If you're going to be forearmed, be forewarned."

RON: So encouragers and gainers consciously and mutually consent to this situation? I always thought it was more underhanded and unspoken.

LARRY: Of course! Do you think encouragers and gainers aren't consensual?

RON: I suppose they are. I'm sure this reflects my own bias, but I couldn't imagine agreeing to do that in a relationship.

LARRY: Well, that's because you're not an encourager or gainer. On the other hand, it is underhanded in the same way S&M is: The top seduces the bottom into doing something self-punishing or "destructive," but the reality is that it takes two to tango. It's not sexual sadism (as opposed to sadomasochism) or Strasbourg geese—the ones that are force-fed in order to make foie gras—where stuff is being rammed down throats nonconsensually.

RON: An apt metaphor. Let's now examine some of the symbolism of fat and weight. First, there's the aspect of fat that represents abundance, richness, fecundity, fertility.

LARRY: There is a vast literature and legacy of art and history to attest to that. With artists, you see countless examples—Rubens, Renoir, and Botero, to name just a few. Michelangelo's stereotypically beefy men—often middle-aged or older—also could easily be classified as Bear art or even Bear porn.

Notwithstanding the *Vogue*-Twiggy look, fat is often seen as an ideal of beauty with implications of richness, fertility, and fecundity. Think of all those pink and alabaster fleshy nudes by the great painters! A famous statue by Maillol, front and center outside the Louvre, depicts a plump and fecund nude woman. Looking directly at her, the Louvre behind her appears as the fruit of her womb.

RON: Fat as fertility also seems to represent a very earth-motherly way of being that relates to the rural-pastoral ideal of Bears.

LARRY: Yes, I think some of these qualities are part of the spiritual atmosphere and energies of Bear culture. As if we are being drawn and revitalized by great spiritual forces and energies we can't fully glean or appreciate or articulate. I think scholars will someday be able to look at us, scrutinize us for patterns that can be found in other subcultures and times.

RON: Again there appears something significant yet intangible in our collective unconscious that draws us together.

LARRY: There was an exhibit of Egyptian art at the Met that featured a large statue of a fat magistrate. Who made this statue? Why's the fat so lovingly rendered? I wonder what Botero could tell us about Bears. What would he say if we took our porn pictures and mags to him? Or one step further: what would Jung have thought about us?

RON: It would be interesting to see a real critical study of the large male body across history and cultures, and especially how it has been reflected in art.

LARRY: But it's not just these deep energies that art taps into that may be shaping our attraction to girth. Some time back, Pat Califia interviewed Ed White for *Poz* magazine ["The Symphony Plays On," November 1997, pp. 62–65]. There she wondered if Bear culture weren't some kind of response to AIDS—wherein being trim and thin took on the aura of illness. Intriguing, but I think that's too narrow. What do you think?

RON: Bear culture, or even the simple attraction to big men, is far richer and more complex than that.

LARRY: I agree. In fact, I think Bear culture would have emerged even in the absence of AIDS.

RON: Yes, but AIDS images, and the realities of AIDS all around us, certainly fed it. One wonders, though: if Bears were a genuine response to AIDS, then why are big men and Bears still absent from the images presented in HIV/AIDS magazine advertising?

LARRY: Yes, but the same absence of Bear images pervades the mainstream gay media. It's had no impact there. We're still not in *Out* or *The Advocate*. There's a baths here in New York City called the West Side Club that caters exclusively to the Chelsea-boy and gymbot-boy types. They find us just as (sexually) repellent as we find them. Middle-aged Bear types are unwanted there, and vice versa.

RON: American mass media is just now warming to the concept of showing diversified images, which include bigger and hairier bodies. To the extent that gay culture reflects the mainstream media, we're seeing more of those images in the gay media.

LARRY: Yes, that is finally beginning to happen.

RON: Yet in many other cultures, weight and age are respected and honored.

LARRY: In America, it's still something new. Remember when James Stewart and Ronald Reagan were ideals of male beauty? Remember how nobody in those old films ever had chest hair? But times are finally changing. When Arnie and I celebrated his 59th birthday, we went to see *Kiss Me Kate*. Incredibly, the choreography included fat, hairy, and stocky people—not just as chorus members, but as leads and stars.

RON: Beautiful!

LARRY: It was incredibly exhilarating and a key ingredient, I'm convinced, in the phenomenal success of this production. Yes, this is a new trend in modern dance—to include unconventional body types. It's thrilling! Fat people dancing is fabulous! Why not? What closed off, circumscribed worlds we've led!

RON: If elephants could do it in *Fantasia*, fat people can certainly do it in *Kiss Me Kate*. But let me redirect here. I want to know if you feel there might be some correlation between some men's sense of their own Bearness and their size? You know—the beefier, the Bearier.

LARRY: I think I know what you're getting at here. There is prejudice against bigness and fatness, of course, but what the mainstream doesn't realize is how well bigness and fatness fit into their own subculture and are considered attractive. In Terrence McNally's *The Ritz*—a play that was made into a movie—all of which takes place in a gay bathhouse, one angle of the plot is this chub being pursued by a chaser. What's remarkable is the intensity of the attraction. The chaser is absolutely obsessed with getting the chub and is in ecstasy whenever he does. So we who are fatter and bigger have this experience more than is generally realized: Instead of feeling bad about ourselves, we feel wonderful! We see our size and fat as attractive and we get plenty of proof of the pudding, if you will.

RON: Not merely as attractive, but also worthy of celebration.

LARRY: Absolutely. I think the celebration comes from that feeling that, rather than being unappealing, we are in fact quite desirable, although admittedly not to everybody.

Speaking of celebrating our differences, there has been an interesting development here in New York City. The current chair of one of the Bearclubs, the MetroBears, is also an erstwhile drag queen involved with the local Imperial Court [gay and drag queen organization]. The

MetroBears' 1999 Bear Bust was co-hosted by the Imperial Court, and nobody complained, just as nobody complains when drag queens or extremely obese people show up at other Bear or leather events. There can be an amazing level of tolerance and diversity. That's why it's ultimately impossible to pin Bear culture down to anything more than "those are my people." Didn't we say the same about the leather world before the advent of Bears? About the gay community per se? In real measure, I think we did, and just as those communities turned out to be not exactly perfect or the right fit for us, so it is with Bear culture. It really speaks to us, maybe more than the others, but who knows what or when the next one will be?

RON: I agree that there's a feeling of belonging that's hard to describe—like when you're sitting out on the patio at the Lone Star and you feel like, *This is home.*

LARRY: Yes! I've shared that exact same feeling, though perhaps a little less so as I get older.

RON: There seems to be a special significance of fat gay men as drag queens: I'm thinking of people like Divine and Sylvia Sydney, who were like deranged polymorphous goddesses. The archetype of Drag Queen Bitch.

LARRY: The point here is that there is overlap: some big Bears are indeed also drag queens, and their Bear drag is of a piece, if you will, with their femme drag, a change of costumes.

I once went to the Imperial Court's annual drag ball as the escort of my agent, Norman Laurila (owner of A Different Light Books). I went as an Arab sheikh (now, there's simultaneous male and female drag). The desire to cross-dress for me is dead. I don't know whether I killed it or it died a natural death, but I can no longer get in touch with it.

RON: Maybe you just haven't met the right clothes designer!

LARRY: Well, never say never!

RON: I wonder how Imperial Court events compare with Bear events and leather events, especially the competitive aspect.

LARRY: Drag queens are also interlaced in leather events and those people are often one and the same.

RON: Maybe their presence serves as a reminder for us not to take the contests so seriously.

LARRY: Indeed. Remember Divine in *Hairspray*? S/he plays both a big drag mamma and a very Bearish macho character too. What this all says is that we shouldn't take the gender thing and ourselves so seriously. I think we get into more trouble with the "I'm more masculine than thou" stuff than we do with allowing more fluidity and humor. So I think that drag queens at Bear events is a good thing and very healthy.

RON: It certainly serves to keep things from getting too homogenous. Drag shows us that outer appearances are innately deceptive.

LARRY: I think the "country club for only genuine, real men" stuff is quite troubled. The whole gay movement was initiated by these heroes/heroines; we Bears can continue to learn much from them. Talk about real courage! Do you know any Bear who has had to face the stuff drag queens have? They're the real men!

RON: It's easy enough to hide behind a facade of manliness or masculinity when you're a biological male.

LARRY: Precisely. I had it easy. I was never teased for being a sissy because I always fit in with the guys. I got in fights for being Jewish, but never for being queer.

RON: Were you bigger when young?

LARRY: No, bigness gradually developed as I got older, though I always had this little pot belly, which was a sex object and has attracted people since I was 11 years old. One fetishist recently suggested I should have it cast!

RON: Revered as a Buddha belly?

LARRY: That's an idea! Truly speaking, though: Fat is one of the few things left that people still feel free to moralize and insult people about. People will no longer say things about your being queer or Jewish or black or a drag queen. If you are fat, however, they feel very free to tell you about diets and health, and offer unsolicited advice up the wazoo! It's hideous. It's one thing to let people know about health issues and hazards, and another to lecture them from a moral standpoint. I mean, I'm writing this column on "Bears and Health" for those who might be interested, but the idea of holding someone hostage to your ideals, or even to sound advice, is repellent to me. My mother got in the habit of lecturing Arnie about his dieting—he's overweight and has diabetes. She needed to understand how inappropriate this was and we told her.

RON: Holding someone hostage to one's ideals is just a different example of Strasbourg geese. I think many people are totally unconscious about how their perspective sounds.

LARRY: Yes, because they mean well. What's the saying about good intentions?

RON: The road to hell is paved with the suckers. Well, fat's an easy target. Still, fat definitely affirms some men's selfhood. Bear subculture in part seems to be about that affirmation.

LARRY: Yes, in part, definitely, but as we've also observed and agreed, it's made up of many and diverse elements. You are a Bear and you are not fat. What do you say about that?

RON: Well, I have been told that I'm not a Bear because I'm not big.

LARRY: Obviously, in light of all we've said, that's ridiculous.

RON: It demonstrates that many people, including Bears, want someone else to exclude, someone else to dump on.

LARRY: Yes, the exclusionary thing is very troubling. That's why the mixing of drag queens with Bears is a wonderful thing.

RON: Do you think we'll see more of it?

LARRY: I hope so, to the extent that any exclusivity of the kind we're discussing gets cut out. A former chairman of Metrobears, John Outcalt, was black, an encourager and gainer, and really big on this issue of diversity and inclusion. I really admired and identified with him.

The inclusion of so much diversity is a real turnoff for some Bears—one of whom both you and I know, for example. He's withdrawn from the Bear scene, along with plenty of others. He longs for the good old days when the Bears were real men—I mean [*Clears throat, deeper register*]—"real men."

RON: Hypermasculine, heteronormative bullcrap, if you ask me.

LARRY: Exactly. It's what Dan Harris picks up on when he observes in his book, *The Rise and Fall of Gay Culture*, that Bears are just older, fatter, furrier, fey gay men with new forms of (masculine) drag.

RON: Well, I fear that may be an oversimplification, Larry. Final comment?

LARRY: I feel that it's wrong for us to try to hold on to who or what we think we were. The healthy thing is to embrace change. Bears cannot continue to be the little macho outlaw group it originally fancied itself. There's no going back. We can still value and cherish our masculinities, but not at the expense of others. If we expect to survive and thrive, we will have to go with the flow, embrace change, and evolve.

CHAPTER 15
BEAR BEAUTY AND THE AFFIRMATION OF BEAR CONTESTS
~ A DISCUSSION WITH CRAIG BYRNES,
GENE LANDRY, AND MICHAEL PATTERSON ~

CRAIG BYRNES was born in 1957 in Brunswick, Georgia. His hobbies include photography, singing, playing guitar, bowling, and skating. Craig started his involvement with Bears as a founding member of the Chesapeake Bay Bears in 1993. Craig was featured in *American Bear* no. 3 and no. 28, and *American Grizzly* no. 3. In 1996 Craig cocreated the International Bear Brotherhood Flag, and has since started Bear Manufacturing, which creates, markets, and licenses products with the Bear flag design elements. He's held several titles, including: Mr. Baltimore Bear Cub 1993, Mr. Teddy Bear Leather of Virginia 1994, and Mr. DC Bear 1998. Finally, Craig hit the big time when he captured the title of International Mr. Bear 1999. Somewhat unlike his predecessors, Craig decided to use his title to travel around to Bearclubs around the country in the interest of spreading brotherhood among his fellow Bears.

GENE LANDRY is a native of Houston, Texas, where he lived for 31 years before moving to New York City early in 2000. He is an accomplished musician, actor, and director who works as an executive assistant at a prominent accounting firm. Gene joined the Bear community in 1996 after being invited to a Christmas party hosted by the Houston Area Bears. Since then he has been an active member of the Bear community on both local and national levels. Gene has been awarded three titles: Mr. Grin 'N' Bear It 1999 (Houston), Mr. Texas Bear Round-up

1999, and Mr. D.C. Bear 2000. He also competed in the contest at the 1999 International Bear Rendezvous, where he was a finalist.

MICHAEL PATTERSON comes from a very small town in Texas and has lived most of his life in the Southwest. He married his high school sweetheart at 17, divorced at 19 (all the while working out at the gym and playing with the men in the saunas). He then moved to the central coast of California, where he received a performance degree in dance from the local college and performed with several dance companies from San Luis Obispo to Santa Barbara. He met his husbear of 20 years in San Luis Obispo. They now own a home in Antioch, an outer suburb of the San Francisco Bay area. After joining the Sacramento Valley Bears, he was coaxed into running for the local title, which he won. He then represented Sacramento at International Bear Rendezvous in 1999, where he was bestowed the title of Mr. International Grizzly Bear 1999.

Bear contests owe their genesis to leather contests, such as the long-standing International Mr. Leather and Mr. Drummer annual competitions, which draw contestants from smaller regional contests around the globe. "Bear beauty pageants," as they are sometimes called, seem to originally have been intended as parody of these gay leathermen's contests, as well as mainstream beauty contests.

But like so much else about Bear subculture, the contests have developed their own unique slant. There is no highly structured regional run-off system in place, for example, although several regions do send representatives who have won locally every year to compete in the International Mr. Bear contest at International Bear Rendezvous.

I was able to experience firsthand the dynamics of the contest when I served as judge for the contest at IBR 2000. Judging was hard work, and a lot of fun—as is participating as a contestant. As the panel of judges interviewed each contestant, one by one, it became much clearer what motivates these Bear men—many of who appeared incredibly shy—to get up on stage before a crowd of over 1,000 men in order to be objectified.

My overriding sense is that, although there may be political or ego-driven sexual motives that compel a contestant to the stage, the basic drive is one that seeks to affirm the Bear's own self-esteem as well as strengthen his connection with the Bear community (regardless of how he defines community).

In this discussion, I met with three men whose lives have been deeply transformed by their experiences in the contests. We might have delved more into the relative value of Bear contests for the larger community, but examining the lives of these men seems the right focus.

Grateful acknowledgment is due John Caldera, the first International Mr. Bear. John was scheduled to participate in this online discussion but due to technical problems was unable to join us.

RON: Let's start with some background info. Gene, since you're the youngun among us, why don't you start? How long have you identified as a Bear or with the Bear phenomenon?

GENE: I'm probably the youngest in that respect, too. I just discovered the Bear movement about three years ago, after my hubby dumped me. He was a twinkie and I thought that was what being gay was about. I was miserable. I found the Houston Area Bears at a party and it changed me profoundly. I guess I'm really lucky that so much of the movement is based on physicality and I'm the type. I think there's a lot more to the movement, though, than just physicality.

RON: What was your first impression like?

GENE: It was great! You can imagine what it was like being in a room of guys who, for once, wanted me rather than shunned me.

RON: I think perhaps that we've all had that remarkable first experience. Michael, how did you get started on the path to Beardom?

MICHAEL: It was much different for me. I had been married to the same man for 16 years, and we had stayed away from the gay scene due to the pervasive twink-clone look, which we never fit. When we stumbled into the Lone Star just by chance, all of a sudden it was like walking in the front door of your home, with a WELCOME sign up. The legendary Lone Star: wall-to-wall hairy men and those that appreciate them. Wow!

We then met the Sacto [Sacramento] Bears, and got heavily involved with them, or at least enough so that I entered their contest, reluctantly, and won. All of a sudden I was representing a subculture of a gay community. It was quite intense for me.

RON: When was that first trip to the Lone Star?

MICHAEL: It was about four years ago.

RON: Not so long ago either, like Gene. And Craig, what was your genesis as a Bear?

CRAIG: I was attending a church consecration ceremony in D.C. as music coordinator of MCC [Metropolitan Community Church] from Charlottesville. A friend took me to a "Bear's dessert" at the Chesapeake Bay Bears' first club function in 1993—30 hairy men and lots of sugar! I became a founding member of CBB [Chesapeake Bay Bears] that night, seven years ago. Because of my home location, I'd travel 178 miles to do things with the club.

RON: What was your initial reaction to being in that environment?

CRAIG: I felt comfortable, and I got a lot of attention. I was not used to that. I think I was a cub for about six months.

RON: And then you were graduated?

CRAIG: I won a cub contest in 1993 and, after that, people started to call me a Bear.

RON: Why did you first want to enter the contest? Let's talk about what sort of self-image you had beforehand.

MICHAEL: I had to prove to myself that I could take my shirt off and be in public. Hairy is not the best picture people address, and I had always been hairy, since 14 or 15 years old.

GENE: I have a picture from my high school days of me on the beach in which you can clearly see all the fur on my back. My adolescence was hell.

CRAIG: At school, very early also, I got made fun of for being so hairy.

GENE: I still get laughed at when I go out in a tank. I let it roll off me, but inside it hurts.

MICHAEL: I struggle day to day with the fact that I don't look like the actors you see on screen. When I look at myself, I see a heavy-set man, hairy, and on top of all that, gay. It all boils down to building that wall inside.

RON: Gene, do you compare your self-image to those in the media, too?

GENE: Not just on screen, but print, TV—everywhere. Society really emphasizes the ideal male body type as being slim and smooth.

CRAIG: I wasn't heavy at first. It came later. But, when I grew my first beard in the sixth grade, the boys called me Wolfy.

RON: How does participating in a contest affirm your looks and your being?

MICHAEL: As I entered the contests, and then especially when I won the International title, I began to realize that the contest had brought out in me items that would have remained hidden.

RON: What do you mean by "items"? What inner qualities did being in the contest show you that you have?

MICHAEL: I discovered qualities such as being proud of myself for being big, gay, and hairy. I found I was capable of being in public with my shirt off and woofing at hairy men. I realized that everything that my husband of 20 years had seen was actually there.

RON: Did you feel that the contest validated something deep inside of you?

CRAIG: It did initially, yes. I entered contests later for different reasons, not so much to take something, but to give something back.

MICHAEL: Validation is important to all of us.

GENE: I think contests are more about camaraderie.

CRAIG: I agree, Gene. You, Michael, and I have become loving friends because of contests.

MICHAEL: The contest made me realize that even though I didn't fit the media mold, I was still an attractive person to the proper culture. It made me find myself within my relationship with my lover.

GENE: It's all about finding your target audience! One of the things I like about acting is that you get to put aside the "you" and have fun. I think contests are a great opportunity do just that. However, I am the person you see in the contest.

CRAIG: I've met both these men and spent time with them. What's inside them is pretty significant.

RON: Craig, what else did that process bring out in you? What does it take to put it all out there in front of a crowd of horny men?

CRAIG: I overcame self-doubt doing contests. It helped me to evolve from being someone who needed validation to someone who in later contests wanted to give validation to others. Creativity, honesty, and presentation are everything. Different contests, though, have different criteria. Some are more physically oriented. The International Mr. Bear contest wasn't about physicality so much as it was about character.

MICHAEL: Entering the contests takes pride in yourself and in your Bear community. It's amazing how many men can't do that.

CRAIG: I think anyone who enters a Bear contest has courage, but some contests are based on looks only. I never won a looks-only contest.

GENE: Yes, people don't understand that. Different contests have different focuses. I think that's fine. I've done both and had a great time.

MICHAEL: My observation is that there will always be a political side, looks side, and quality side to the contests.

GENE: I agree, Mike. I think we need to have all those sides in order to attain diversity.

RON: Some folks would say that putting certain men on a pedestal based on their attractiveness is the same old looksism that Bears were originally trying to get away from. Agree, disagree, and why?

CRAIG: I have never asked someone to put me on a pedestal based on my looks. I always encourage someone to investigate my heart. Yet I agree with that statement.

RON: What constitutes Bear beauty?

CRAIG: Bear beauty is not theoretical in Beardom: it does exist.

MICHAEL: Bear beauty is nothing but straightforward honesty. Be who you are.

RON: So Bear beauty is not merely fur deep?

CRAIG: I think Bear beauty is deep, but that depends on the person looking at you.

GENE: Bear beauty is very deep, but I don't think there's anything wrong with us celebrating who we are.

RON: In context of that celebration of our Bearness and our masculinity, the contests seem a perfect vehicle to display—and view—Bear bodies, which previously were so deprecated in the common gay culture.

MICHAEL: Bear beauty is also what I experience when I walk into the Ramada in San Francisco at International Bear Rendezvous and among 300 Bears, immediately I see 30 that I know and want to hug all at once.

GENE: Exactly! It's great!

CRAIG: Or when someone you have met keeps in contact with you because they love the real you.

GENE: I'm amazed, repeatedly, at the friendships that I've forged over the course of a weekend. Most of my best friends have come from my contacts in the community.

MICHAEL: I attend events now to see the wonderful Bear brethren that I have made friends with.

CRAIG: Me too. Friendships that are very different from the ones I made before being introduced to the gay community.

MICHAEL: Yes, don't we know that.

GENE: Fellowship is a big part of the experience.

CRAIG: I came to Bear culture because my needs were fulfilled by fellow Bears who allow me to be myself.

MICHAEL: I very much feel the same. As much as we may want to be part of the larger gay culture, we also want to be able to fulfill our personal needs of tactileness, tenderness, and friendship—which you just can't find in most gay subcultures.

RON: I think we're tapping into some of the essence of what makes Bear subculture great, but I'd like us to look at how being in the contests affected your lives and your relationships specifically. Michael, you mentioned that your primary relationship underwent a lot of transformation.

MICHAEL: I was a shy, introverted man. If we went into a bar, Earl would have to go in first. When I won the Sacto contest, I had to measure crotches to sell the raffle tickets. [This refers to the traditional Bear contestant "waist or inseam" method of doling out raffle tickets for charity: for a fixed price, the raffle-ticket buyer can get either his waist or his inseam "measured—usually requiring plenty of body contact— with a string of raffle tickets.] This meant I had to watch my husbear watch me touch other men's crotches. We had been completely monogamous this whole period. When I went to IBR, I met hundreds of people. I learned that I needed to have a life outside of my relationship. The contest forced me to be by myself most of the weekend (that is, not with my husband). I learned I could function as an individual without my husbear. I became a man of my own, in a sense.

RON: Do you mean you became surer of yourself and less dependent on your partner?

MICHAEL: Yes, and on my friends. I learned that I can function as a single unit, hairy, big, likeable, and huggable. The Bear community's contests give you that option to explore those arenas, which can be quite significant for a man.

CRAIG: I'm so proud of you, Michael.

RON: Craig, how did winning a title (or two) affect your primary relationship or that with your close friends?

CRAIG: I had won several contests, and then lost several. I even competed in the International Mr. Bear contest in 1995. But this recent title just seemed to express the nurturing person that I was becoming. I had a firm sense of self, and I wanted to give something back to the community with this title. So, I did. The title didn't affect my relationship with other people. My friends never treated me differently.

RON: Did you feel perhaps that they accorded you more respect?

CRAIG: I never felt that, no. Being International Mr. Bear proved to be a humbling experience for me. I'm always careful of ego getting too big. But it's important to realize that each person's experience is different.

RON: True. It seems that being a titleholder could easily inflate one's sense of self. Gene, how have your relationships been affected?

GENE: That's a very interesting question. It really hasn't affected my relationships, as I haven't had a successful one since I've become a Bear.

RON: Well, perhaps not with a significant other, but with close friends?

GENE: My close friends are still as close as ever. In that sense, I've been really blessed. I have an amazing group of friends that are very supportive of my endeavors in the community. But as far as a partner—no luck. Sometimes I think that's OK, though. Not all of us can find someone as wonderful as Mike has. A lot of Bear relationships go south because of jealousy and possessiveness.

RON: Jealousy jeopardizes many non-Bear relationships as well.

GENE: Many guys are intimidated by the status of the titles and are afraid to approach me.

MICHAEL: The Jack Radcliffe syndrome.

RON: I assume you mean that, although Jack is quite an amiable guy, most guys are too awestruck or starstruck to approach him in person. Have you guys had the same experience?

MICHAEL: I received a lot of attention in San Francisco due to the title, but I'm a local boy and was able to make appearances at local functions, so I was a little more visible.

RON: Craig, have you found that people are intimidated by your being a titleholder?

CRAIG: I go out of my way to make people comfortable about "titleholders." Some people are intimidated, but for the most part, I was not made a "Bear Idol."

GENE: An important part of being a titleholder is to be accessible to the guys who supported you in the contest. Too many times, you see guys that are unapproachable, and that's a shame.

CRAIG: I agree. I want people to know that I'm a human being, not someone on a pedestal.

MICHAEL: I must admit that when I walk into the Lone Star and a certain bartender screams, "Hey Mr. Grizzly!" it gives me good memories.

RON: What did it feel like for you that moment when you were announced as a top titleholder? Gene, what was the first thing that went through your mind?

GENE: It's amazing! The rush of achieving a goal is always great, but when it's something that innately personal, it's magic. I thought another guy was going to win. In the DC contest, there were only three guys, so after they announced runner-up, there was a first and then a last. I couldn't tell which one I was. My first thought this time was, "I can't believe this is happening!" I was completely shocked.

CRAIG: Well, don't laugh; I cried.

MICHAEL: Yeah, he sure did, all right!

GENE: Like Nancy Kerrigan!

CRAIG: It was self-doubt melting away. I never cried like that for a crowd. Some people later scoffed at me for crying, like it was an act, but I know it was real. I experienced it.

RON: A tremendous release?

CRAIG: Yes, it was cathartic. I was very thankful, and it humbled me. I only got one nasty comment from another contestant that year, but I have incredible friends from it—friends I wouldn't trade for anything.

RON: Michael, what was your reaction?

MICHAEL: All I could feel was pride, like being at a baseball game and winning the game. I remember the Sacto Bears screaming—I was their first titleholder ever. I remember my husbear coming up on stage. Then I realized the amount of work I had ahead of me. I was the local boy to the San Francisco Bay area. Craig travels everywhere, but for little events, it was going to be me. To this day, I hold the International Mr. Grizzly Bear title as my greatest achievement. I feel I made a mark in my gay culture.

CRAIG: The interview day, all 23 contestants sat around. That was the magic day we all got real with one another. We showed ourselves one by one. I remember waiting with Michael, since we were last on the block. I spent only a short time with Michael, but it was so powerful. It changed us as two men, as we relate. I'll never forget that.

MICHAEL: That's true—a rich connection was made, and was made with many contestants, as it does every year. That's more what the contest is about for contestants, it's the soulful connection, the spiritual phase you go through and release with each other.

CRAIG: The same thing happened with Gene and me at later events. I just connect with people because of the contests. I feel very loved by these two men and I love them.

RON: Such relationships should be considered the true prize contest won. Well, gentlebears, thanks so very much. I'm very honored to have been in such handsome and loving company.

CHAPTER 16
BEAROTICA AND THE SELLING OF BEARSEX
~ A DISCUSSION WITH RICHARD LABONTÉ
AND TIM MARTIN ~

TIM MARTIN was born in Louisville, Kentucky, in 1952. He received his Master's in Theology from St. Mary's University School of Theology, Baltimore, in 1978. After a serious burnout in ministry in 1994, Tim wanted to do something in and for the gay community. (Though he was not out in the ministry, he was very involved in typical gay social activities—bars, clubs, events, and the like.) Tim had become familiar with the Bear movement a few years before his leaving the ministry and felt a kinship with it. Dissatisfied with *Bear* magazine, he decided the market was ripe for a more professional Bear publication with a non–West Coast point of view. Having had some experience in computers and graphic design, Tim collected his life's savings and plunged head-first into publishing. In June 1994 the first issue of *American Bear* was published, followed in January 1998 by the first issue of *American Grizzly*.

RICHARD LABONTÉ is a 51-year-old former bookseller who helped found A Different Light (ADL) in Los Angeles in 1979; he retired in July 2000 as general manager of its stores in San Francisco, New York City, and Los Angeles. Before bookselling, he worked for a decade for a daily newspaper in Ottawa, Canada. After bookselling, he is spending a year or two of low-key life in rural Ontario on a 200-acre farm he has owned communally since 1976. He reads a lot but luckily lives with a man who reads hardly at all (and a dog that never does), so the word-count karma in his home is well balanced. He continues to dabble in writing, mostly book news and reviews for PlanetOut (www.planetout.com), and columns and bookselling commentary for Contentville (www.contentville.com). For 10 years he contributed a volunteer column on gay male books for the trade magazine *Feminist Bookstore News*, has written reviews for *Q San Francisco*, and continues to edit the *Best Gay Erotica* series for Cleis Press. Reach out to him at tattyhill@hotmail.com.

The Bear phenomenon, despite its ineptitude at self-definition, fiercely displays itself as a sexual way of being, although not solely as such. The evidence of Bearsex is scrawled everywhere across the surface of the subculture like urban graffiti. The magazines are virtually free of thoughtful editorial content and the little of that one can find among its pages is crammed among the graphics as an afterthought. Surfing the Internet for nongraphic or nonsexual content is hardly more fruitful. Most Web searches on "gay Bears" yield scores of raw pornographic material with an occasional Bearclub or personal home page.

Despite being preoccupied with the outer trappings of masculinity, something seems deeper, tenderer, and more communal about Bearsex than most of the rest of gay life. In Bear terms, sex is often expressed through affectionate actions such as hugging, cuddling, and group gropes. But is that quality about Bearsex depicted in its popular representations in the media?

In their essay for *Opposite Sex: Gay Men on Lesbians, Lesbians on Gay Men*, "In Goldilocks's Footsteps," Beth Kelly and Kate Kane collected a group of Bear-themed magazines and analyzed their content. Their reactions were heavily influenced by the "ick factor" (gay and lesbian repulsion for the opposite sex's genitalia), a general lack of understanding about gay men's bodies and representations, and (in my opinion) too small a sampling of material. However, their initial response—as well as some of their more considered responses—rings dead-on: "a far cry from the glossy technoporn with the cold, hard edges, huge erect dicks, and unattainable models...that we associate with gay male iconography."

Although basically accurate, I felt that it was important to delve deeper into the subject of Bearotica and, in order to hit that spot, I knew I needed to enlist the help of men who know a significant amount about gay erotica, the gay community, and Bears. This led me to coordinate this discussion with Richard and Tim, both of whom have years of experience in the field. Representatives from Brush Creek Media, which publishes *Bear* magazine, declined to participate in this online discussion.

RON: Greetings, gentlemen! Thanks for joining our "Bearsex" chat. Richard, you don't particularly identify as a Bear, correct?

RICHARD: I'm perceived as being a Bear, and certainly my presence at the sales counter during a Bear weekend in San Francisco, or during the Folsom Street Fair, generates a certain comfort level among conference attendees. The cruising level too is elevated, though I'm more chubby than Bearish.

I've had a substantial beard since 1966—my beard is older than some men I've slept with—and quite hairy wrists and forearms—but that's pretty much the extent of my hirsuteness. I've had a hefty body over those years, too, though more rotund in the past few years.

I've only been to the Lone Star once (but to bars in San Francisco maybe half a dozen times total during my 12 years in San Francisco). Bears, however they might be defined, are just one part of my sexual radar. I self-identify more as a sexual man whose world takes in short men and tall ones, hairy and smooth, my age and younger and older. Right now I live with a man, seven years so far, who at first was afraid of me because of my size. Love sorted it out.

RON: That last part is very sweet, Richard; perhaps it will inspire smaller men who are intimidated by bigger guys. Tim, please tell us something about how you relate to being a Bear.

TIM: The proverbial question, hey? I just know I like the company of Bear types—hairy, masculine, beefier men who aren't too concerned with fitting into the stereotypical gay male pattern. I never saw myself fitting that stereotype, and so before the Bear phenomenon began, I guess I felt I didn't belong anywhere. Since then, though, I've certainly grown to accept my self and my body as it is.

RON: When did you first become aware of Bears as a gay phenomenon?

TIM: When I saw one of the first issues of *Bear* magazine—and then bought every back issue and subscribed! Up to that point, I bought *Honcho* and *Mandate*—any of the mags with hairy, beefier, more masculine types. The last I saw any of those magazines, though, they changed. But those magazines never did seem to really portray what I was looking for—and at that time, I didn't really know what it was that

I wanted.

RON: Richard, when did you first become aware of Bears?

RICHARD: Probably in the mid-to-late '80s, and most notably when I was asked several times as a bookseller if there were any especially "hairy, beefy" guys in any of a new month's porn magazines—*Honcho* being the likely one back then, and occasionally *Drummer*. There were customers who commented they were buying an issue for just one photo.

RON: Richard, did you ever encounter Richard Bulger, the first publisher of *Bear* magazine?

RICHARD: Yes, we chatted some about the potential for the magazine, and I remember I was quite reassuring about its prospects.

RON: Did you believe there was a significant market for that kind of man?

RICHARD: I had no real sense of how big the market was, but I did know that enough people over the years had expressed an interest in Bear-type images. I also knew that since there was interest in me as a sexual partner, there was every reason to assume that the twinkie was not necessarily everyone's piece of cake.

RON: A reasonable assumption, I'd say. Tim, why did you decide to start publishing *American Bear*?

TIM: When I left the priesthood after 15 years of ministry, I needed a job! I always wanted to do something in the gay community. At that time, *Bear* magazine was in bad shape—issues were late, sometimes very late, sometimes not showing up at all—and subscribers like me were very unhappy. I wanted a magazine with a little more class. I never related to that "homo smut" thing *Bear* was about. So, I decided to take a leap and start my own.

RON: What do you mean when you say you didn't relate to the homo smut thing?

TIM: *Bear* always had a kind of sleazy attitude. Now, I didn't come from a sleazy gay sexual background—I never did bathrooms, the woods, dark alleys, and the rest. I really wanted to do a magazine that informed and helped people as well as aroused them. That's why, in the very first issue, I did a spread with a couple, one of whom is HIV positive, and we noted that clearly.

Another initial consideration was that I felt the market was big enough for another magazine.

RICHARD: I agree. And my experience is that, when *American Bear* joined *Bear*, most customers bought both.

TIM: Yes, we were very different—and are different even now, I think, and that's what people like. My focus, too, was the Midwest and East Coast, since we are here in Louisville. That brought a different flavor and focus as well.

RON: Many folks' first impression when they saw their first issue of *Bear* magazine was that that sleazy attitude and sort of good ol' boy drawl—were all rather affected. Later, as they developed that countrified rhetoric, one friend of mine speculated that they intended to appear backward and down-home-like as an excuse for the countless typos and the poor production quality.

TIM: Yes, and that's what I meant by doing something more classy— better paper and photographic reproduction and graphics, and so on. A lot of Bears are white-collar guys!

RON: Before we go any further, though, let's look at our definitions. What is Bearsex, exactly? What distinguishes it in idea or reality from other types of man-to-man sex—leather sex, sex by gay men of color, and mainstream gay sex, for example—and, if so, how? Is it softer and cuddlier? Or is just as hard, but thicker and hairier? Richard, how would you define Bearsex?

RICHARD: Sex is sex in all its infinite varieties—but Bearsex is a component of the initial turn-on, the excitement generated either by a particular stimulus, be it a photo, some writing, or the look of a man. It involves an element of finding what most turns you on, physically at first, then emotionally.

TIM: I'm not sure there's a big difference from the others you mentioned, Ron. Bears encompass all kinds of guys with every sexual proclivity imaginable. But I think that because the word "bear" is used it tends to portray something more soft and cuddly. I think the only real difference is that the persons involved are turned on physically by Bear types. I mean, I couldn't get it up for a twinkie if I tried!

RON: Would either of you say that the Bear thing is just part of the general rise of homomasculine erotica that began in the early '80s? Or is there more to it than that?

TIM: Yes, I think there is more to it. Homomasculine erotica has been around a long time, but it wasn't until the '80s that we finally saw the stereotype begin to change. We began to see that we are many different kinds of gay men with many different tastes. And I think the rise of both

Bears and Girth & Mirth helped that to happen. It has brought a lot of men out of their preference closets. *So* many guys tell me that they were ashamed to admit they liked bigger, hairy men.

RON: Richard, how do you feel about the emergence of this market? What has been your experience as a bookseller to a primarily gay customer base?

RICHARD: I'd say that there's less to it, actually, than being part of the rise of the culture. The act was certainly extant before it became publicly eroticized, primarily through magazines, which since the physique mags of the '30s and '40s have always been most gay men's introduction to lust. I'd suggest that Bearsex wasn't the result of a general acceptance of homomasculine erotica but rather its cause. As Tim says, though, there was a tipping point when it became OK to come out as an admirer.

RON: So your point is that since Bear-type men had already always been having Bearsex, that was the source of Bearotica. Yet it would seem that part of the process of publicizing a Bearness, if you will, was completely tied into its commercialization.

RICHARD: The market was always there. It had a great appetite, but for a long time, all it got were table scraps. I've seen happen with the Bear movement what happened even earlier in the bookstore with literature on SM; when we opened A Different Light in 1979, there were a handful of titles, and now there are a couple of hundred. A more recent example would be the parenting section, where concurrent with the real-life adoption and parenting community, more writing appeared. It's a chicken-or-egg thing, so to speak, where a real need, once perceived, led to material being created, which in turn increased its visibility.

TIM: What I find so interesting now, and I wrote about it in an editorial for *American Bear*, is that now everyone seems to be using the word "Bear" to sell their wares, whether it's really Bearish at all. At least *Bear* and *American Bear* and others involved are really about Bears, whereas some of the Web sites I check out that talk about Bears haven't a clue—just hairy men.

RON: Yes, Tim, I think I understand your point about the confusion. But isn't that odd that confusion about Bears' sexual identity should exist both outside and inside the community? The "What is a Bear?" debate still gets tons of attention on the Bears Mailing List.

RICHARD: Tim, this gets into the matter of community, and in that sense, I see a lot of similarities in the Radical Faerie community. Many men who define themselves as Faeries are committed to a philosophy of free-spirited sexual and cultural play—and yet there are also a bunch of people who don't really care about the community, but like to sleep in tents with other guys.

TIM: Yes, that confusion does exist on both sides. I guess what I mean is that in many cases the men portrayed as Bears would not consider themselves being ones. It's a label put on them merely based on how they look as opposed to how they perceive themselves.

RICHARD: That gets back to the point I made earlier about myself. I'm perceived and cruised as being a Bear, and I don't really identify myself as one, but I'm aware of a vibrant, self-supporting, and stereotype-shattering community. And I certainly enjoy being cruised by Bear lovers and by men who identify as Bears.

RON: Would you consider the Bear community to be solely a sex culture? Or is there more to it?

TIM: Sex is certainly a large part of it, but from my experience traveling to so many events, I sense a very fraternal sort of thing: men bonding in friendship with others like themselves without sex having to be part of it.

RICHARD: I think there's more to it. Sex is the mortar between Bear men, but I think there's a shared mindset that can exist among certain types of men. We often adapt to the expectations placed on us by how we act, what we look like, what our interests are, so it's no leap of faith to understand that Bears like Bears for reasons other than having to do with sex.

TIM: I agree. I sense we have something in common, but what it is isn't so easy to describe. Some things just exist deeply within our unconscious.

RICHARD: As Tim says, that something is intangible; the triumph of the Bears, like the Faeries, is to sense that intangible and build both a sense of self and a sense of community around it.

TIM: Richard, thanks for saying that. I agree that it is not sex. Sex is very fleeting. There has to be more to create and bond and perpetuate a group.

RON: The marvelous book *The Sacred Paw* discusses the significance of the four-legged bear in history, culture, and literature. I think that intangible something has to do with the archetypes we've received from the animal Bears.

RICHARD: I remember stocking it, either after getting a customer request, or reading about it somewhere.

RON: Very good. I'd like to ask how you think the cottage industry of Bear-themed erotica has grown over the past 15 or so years. Obviously, it has expanded, but how else might it have changed?

RICHARD: There has been steady growth and sales of the magazines and certainly also videos. Hardly any erotic prose of quality (know anyone who can write a good Bearsex story for the for the *Best Gay Erotica* series I edit every year?) and virtually no Bear depictions in general gay fiction; not much in nonfiction, either. Now, this could be because Bears are a minority within a minority; on the other hand, so are gay men as parents, and there's been a boom in fiction, memoirs, how-to, and social issues around that topic.

TIM: We've seen some publications come and go already, but I think the Internet is where it has really expanded. There are so many pay-per-view Bear sites ripping off those of us who are in the print media by scanning our photography. I would have to hire a full-time person to stop it and keep it in check. Talking to other publishers, they all confirm it. We all feel the Internet's pinch. A Web presence is almost crucial in this market.

RICHARD: I don't cruise the Internet much, so I'd forgotten that component. I've caught several sites selling CDs of Bear pics—which include a slew from *Bear* and *American Bear*.

RON: Internet piracy is a major concern for any publisher these days. How, if at all, has the impressive growth of the Bear-themed smut market—in all components—over the past 10 years influenced the way mainstream gay erotica is presented?

RICHARD: I can't say that it has. There's more smut than before, and it's a larger percentage of the books published, but I don't think there are any implications there for Bears.

TIM: I can't say I've seen any influence except for an occasional article or reference in the mainstream publications.

RON: So that would definitely exclude Bear smut having any sort of influence on the mainstream (straight) erotica industry?

RICHARD: Yes.

TIM: Yes.

RON: Have any Bear-themed videos earned AVN [Adult Video News] awards, for example?

RICHARD: Sorry, no idea. I'm just addicted to that print on the page. As I said, Bears are now much more visible but still a minority among a minority.

RON: Is it simply that it's a minuscule market? Tim, any idea?

TIM: I think it is. And most of the people in those fields are not Bear types.

RON: Oh, I'm sure that true, Tim. It's just that I can't help but think there's some effect, no matter how minor. When I see the Bear and big men magazines in the male-to-male section of this local suburban sex shop, it always makes me think about those men who see a big, furry guy on the cover and think, "There are guys out there who are into guys who look like me!" And that helps such straight guys come out of the closet. Ten years ago this might never have happened.

In any case, let's look more closely at written Bearotica. What distinguishes Bear-themed "friction" from other sorts? Is there a formula or format that you look for in publishing or writing Bear smut?

TIM: Well, we look for something literate! Really, the only difference is the description of the men involved in the fiction, so as a person is reading they have a Bear-type in their mind. And of course, the description of the sex involves rubbing fur, bellies, and so on. I guess it's really about the adjectives.

RON: What do you mean, "about the adjectives"?

TIM: Well, you wouldn't use words like *smooth, hairless, thin*.

RON: You're looking for the right descriptors, correct? *Furry, hairy, thick*, and so on.

RICHARD: You use whatever images, words, and adjectives invent for the reader the man he's attracted to.

TIM: Exactly. You create an image in one's mind or leave it open enough for them to round out their own fantasy from what you have fed them.

RON: Right. Richard, you mentioned that you don't get much Bear-themed erotica for the *Best Gay Erotica* series. Why do you suppose that's the case?

RICHARD: Out of more than 200 or so stories submitted last year, only two or three were written by/for/about Bears, and they weren't good enough to pass on to the judge, since my aim is to attain a hard-to-define literary quality. Mostly, though, it was a case of really inept use of the English language—but I'll always look at work that a magazine editor submits too. It could be that Bear smut writers don't see themselves as part of a broader writing community.

RON: Do you review all Bear-themed erotica publications?

RICHARD: Not as much as I should, but I glance at most issues and squirrel away anything with potential; I know I miss work, though, which is why I invite editors to bring work to my attention.

RON: Sexpert Susie Bright says that, in a porn story, you know that X will meet Y and thus Z will result. Or XXX meets YYY and thus ZZZ. She said that she looks for something more, some special quality that makes her sit up and take notice.

RICHARD: Exactly.

RON: Tim, what sort of Bear smut writing grabs you by the balls?

TIM: Actually I've never been into erotic fiction. That's why I have someone else do the editing on that. Curiously, for a time I had a woman edit our fiction. I thought it would bring some objectivity to it. And she could be turned on by the thought of men having sex together.

RON: Does homo smut turn on straight women?

RICHARD: It does, though not in great numbers. This is a very subjective analysis, but I'd say far more women buy *Bulk Male* for themselves than buy *American Bear*.

TIM: That I don't know. I do know we have a few female subscribers and that every once in a while a wife will make a purchase for her husband or son! I'll never forget one letter I got from a woman who was upset because a print error cut off the final paragraph of a story. She wanted to know how it ended.

RICHARD: Of course, if they're straight, they have to be pretty determined to come into a gay bookstore in the first place. They really know what they want.

TIM: My former secretary was female and she loved to look at the photos we published. She liked Bearish men.

RON: Must have been heaven for her!

TIM: Yes, she always had some choice remarks for those who were particularly well endowed. Which by the way, is one element of the bear community that does not seem to be particularly important. And in our publications, big cocks are not the be-all and end-all of a model.

RON: Yes, Tim, excellent point. Two lesbian academics [Kelly and Kane] who analyzed the content of a group of Bear-type magazines for an essay in a book were amazed that many images portrayed men with smaller, flaccid cocks.

RICHARD: Which is the way real life is, of course.

TIM: I get many letters from guys who actually prefer the models semi-clothed.

RON: To me, those qualities—de-emphasis on cock size, flaccidity, and partial clothing—really distinguish Bear erotic images in the magazines. Do these images reflect a true representation of the natural man, or are they as affected as any other porn?

TIM: Often, men I've approached to be a model respond that their dick isn't big enough. I say, it's a Bear magazine, not *Inches*.

RICHARD: I think there's a willingness to accept the more natural look as erotic.

TIM: I do, too. Most of our spreads begin with the man clothed and work their way to naked. There's something for everyone, and it's more real, I think, not just page after page of hard-ons, which leave nothing to the imagination.

RON: Why is this more natural look considered erotic?

RICHARD: Accepting that your own sexiness is not the norm allows one to accept an eroticism that needs not be fixated on the genitals; in this way, big tits, hairy backs, and everything else all come together to make the man.

RON: Tim, what do you look for in a model?

TIM: Everyone asks that. First, we like to really know what kind of person he is. I've met many too many magazine models who were assholes. I want our men to be likeable when others meet them. They're ambassadors for our publications. As far as physical traits, we look for a variety of body types that reflects the Bear community. Finally, we want someone who actually considers himself to be a Bear.

RON: Well, I'm glad I asked the obvious question. I want to get back to the idea of the "selling" of Bearsex. Some critics of Bear subculture denounce the way Bear images have become commodified. As Tim said, some Web sites seem to think "Bear" means just about anything. There's also the issue of the increasingly market-driven commercialism of Beardom in general.

RICHARD: Well, that's inevitable. Everything gets commodified eventually—just look at how the gay movement has been morphed into the gay market, with advertisers targeting queers and airlines underwriting political conferences.

TIM: Richard's right: It can't be avoided. We do live in the world's most capitalistic society. But what really upsets me about it is that gay people are screwing other gay people in the market. When a gay Web site uses my copyrighted images, that really galls me.

RICHARD: As it should.

TIM: I guess I'm a little Pollyanna about thinking that gay people would look out for other gay people. Not!

RON: Does the erotica industry in general, perhaps, attract a less responsible sort of businessperson?

RICHARD: Possibly. Greed preys on the needs of other people.

TIM: I've not worked in the stock market, insurance, or the like, but it's probably no worse. I think it's just a little more overt.

RON: Hard to say, perhaps, although the industry doesn't have a great reputation. Finally, I want to ask: Can you project ahead for the future of Bear-themed erotica? How is it likely to change, along with the rest of gay and straight erotica?

RICHARD: There's a ready market for it, and I see no reason why it shouldn't continue as an element of the overall gay male community. I do see Bear themes (not necessarily erotic) in gay studies as likely to increase. Also, some better-written work, with that zip which Susie Bright and I look for, might emerge as writers hone their skills on stories that just a few years ago wouldn't have found any place to be published. Overall, however, the past is present and the present, future.

TIM: I don't think I can make a projection about that. I would agree with Richard's remarks. I do think the Web will become more significant for those who really want to make a lot of money. Right now, though, I do not see any major trends that illuminate what the future might be.

CHAPTER 17
CIRCUIT BEARS AND THE BEAR CIRCUS
~ A DISCUSSION WITH LOU DATTILO, FRANK PERRICONE,
ADAM STEG, AND DANNY WILLIAMS ~

LOU DATTILO first became aware of Bears via American Online, where he networks with Bear buddies from all over the world. He is 52 years old, and a fourth-generation native Texan. His interests include the natural environment, gardening, writing, art, cultural anthropology, world music, and comparative religion. His second and third languages are Italian and Spanish. Currently and proudly a member of Austin's Heart of Texas Bears, Lou enjoys outdoor activities with his good buddies. Lou is a leatherbear by nature, so he attends Bear and leather events with equal enthusiasm. He works as an insurance examiner and lives in Austin, Texas, with his life partner of 20 years.

FRANK PERRICONE was born and raised in New York. Living in Florida after college, he discovered the Bear scene at a bar in Orlando. He got heavily into the whole Bear movement, and began attending numerous Bear events. In 1994 he started a Bearclub in Southwest Florida. They hosted an event each year in Key West called Bears in the Keys®. It is still an extremely popular event that he and his partner (whom he met in 1997 at the event) host every year. They now share their lives together with homes in Alabama, California, and Florida. The couple still attends Bear events, although not as many as in the past. "The scent of freshly ironed flannel in the morning can be a bit overpowering at times," says Frank. "We travel a lot, and if we happen to run into a few Bears, even better!"

ADAM STEG still can't seem to leave New Orleans, no matter how hard he tries. His job for more than 20 years, working with media professionals and teachers, takes him away from home two weeks out of every month to many places around the country where he's joined Bearclubs (as many as 10 clubs in one year). Adam has participated in all sorts of runs and functions and has actually planned his work schedule to coincide with them. When he returns home, there are often some great out-of-town Bears to entertain. As Adam made the transition over the years from "cute preppie boy in tight cutoffs" to "cigar-smoking daddy in uniform and boots," he's found the Bear community very welcoming to his evolutionary development.

DANNY WILLIAMS has been performing as a comic since 1982, starting at the legendary Valencia Rose in San Francisco, and has won many awards and great reviews over the years. More importantly, he has met countless amazing members of the GLBT community. He has been the host of RSVP, a gay and lesbian cruise line, since 1989. He has performed and served as the emcee at many Bear events throughout the U.S. and is four-time honorary Mr. Lone Star. He loves being a Bear!

Bearclubs sometimes resemble, as David Bergman put it (chapter 3), "Elks clubs for homosexuals." This is perhaps most apparent at Bear events, or "runs," as they are sometimes called. Bear events are the bastard cub of motorcycle club runs and gay circuit-boy parties, and virtually every weekend of the year there is a Bearclub–sponsored weekend happening somewhere in the U.S. or Canada—and they're becoming increasingly popular elsewhere in the world as well.

For an enlightening discussion of individual Bear runs, consult Kampf's *The Bear Handbook*. For this online panel discussion, I felt it was important to look at these events through the eyes of Bears who've been to their share (some would say "more than their share") of Bear weekends and who could provide varied perspectives on these events.

RON: Gentlemen, thanks for joining in. Adam, when did you first become aware of Bears?

ADAM: I probably heard the term "Bears" around 1987—although I had a thing as early as the '60s for proto-Bear men such as Dan Haggerty [star of the Grizzly Adams movies]. After I realized that I liked Bearish men myself and that I enjoyed the camaraderie as much as the hunt, I began to hang out at Jewel's Tavern in New Orleans in the early '80s where we a group of us congregated every Sunday. We started to go for drink, drugs, and dick initially, but later we just enjoyed the companionship and became an extended family.

RON: Danny, when and how did you first become aware of Bears?

DANNY: I've always been attracted to "natural" men. The whole pretty-boy buffed look never did anything for me. I never hung out in a bar that was the hot bar at the time. One day a bar opened here in San Francisco called the Lone Star—I heard that it attracted many of the guys who used to hang out at the bars I liked. I went one night to do a benefit. It was very tiny and narrow and the stage was the stairs to the storage room. It was "Hot Ash" night—cigars—and I thought I'd pass out from the smoke. Then the '89 earthquake happened and the Lone Star was wiped out.

RON: You're speaking about the old location?

DANNY: Yes. When the new location opened, somehow, almost magically, Bears showed up. It didn't seem like a planned thing. Most people thought it would be more of a leather bar, because it was so near the Eagle. Well, the Lone Star was heaven to me and, to this day, I hang out there and another bar with a lot of the same crowd, The Edge. I always feel completely comfortable at any Bear bar or event.

RON: Lou, how long have you identified as a Bear?

LOU: I have AOL to thank for finding out about Bears, initially. When I went to BearBust in Dallas, which was only about five years ago, I felt so at home and appreciated! I was in my element again. Until then I was virtually a non-person in Austin, which is incredibly body fascist in its outlook.

RON: For the first time anywhere, you found you were attractive in the Bear crowd?

LOU: Yes. I used to live in San Antonio and everybody who I knew there died. So then about 18 years ago my partner and I moved to Austin, and I volunteered as an AIDS volunteer, trying to re-establish some sense of community, but I was always invisible—not badly treated, just not acknowledged or ever invited to anything at all.

RON: I think we all know that feeling. And, last but not least, Frank! Please tell us a little bit about your life as a Bear.

FRANK: In many ways, I feel that I relate well to the Bear community, but in some ways I feel that I am far from the Bear ideal. Physically, I think I fit right in: big, hairy, the whole nine yards. But being in a monogamous relationship seems to me to be a minority in the Bear community.

This is something I have observed from the many events that my partner and I attend. I don't really have anything against the whole open relationship thing; it's just not for me. I don't like to share. It is amazing how many circuit Bears classify you as a snob when you don't want to jump in bed with them!

RON: But otherwise you enjoy Bear runs, right?

FRANK: Oh, yes! My last job description was "homophobe on acid," so I was always looking for an excuse to go to an event! Being gay and a deputy sheriff in the South was very tense!

ADAM: Can we have a private chat about being a cop sometime *EG*?

RON: How many events have you attended, Frank?

FRANK: Well, I would guess about 20 to 25 in the last eight years.

RON: What's your attendance record, Dan?

DANNY: Around 15, plus tons of Bear events at bars, and about 12 regular circuit party events.

RON: Lou, how many Bear runs have you attended?

LOU: Ten, in all, and specifically Southern Decadence three times. Not that many, actually.

RON: Was that BearBust in Dallas your first?

LOU: Yes, I've been to all four or five of those. Maybe four—I'll have to count the run T-shirts! *LOL*

RON: Adam, how about you?

ADAM: For me, around 20 events over the past 10-plus years. I also go to Southern Decadence annually, as a host, during Mardi Gras.

RON: What does it take to make one a circuit Bear?

ADAM: It's when the other Bears cry out as you arrive: "Oh, it's you again!" that you're a circuit Bear officially.

DANNY: I don't really hear people call themselves circuit Bears in the way that people are called circuit queens.

LOU: I've also heard the term used, but it's a loose association between the two kinds of events.

RON: I doubt that circuit boyz call themselves circuit queens—but the resemblance between young gay men's circuit events and the yearlong string of Bear events is undeniable.

DANNY: Many Bears think of these events as a way to meet old friends and make new ones. As far as circuit party queens are concerned, however, the event itself is the point of going.

LOU: Agreed. That's a prime difference, Ron. Bear events are much chummier and more camaraderie oriented.

RON: There's definitely a community of men that you see, over and again at the same Bear events?

DANNY: Absolutely, just as I see the same people at benefits, at political dinners, and such. The majority of the passengers on RSVP cruises are return passengers. It seems like when people find something they enjoy, they become very loyal to it.

FRANK: For me, it's nice not being the biggest guy at the bar for a change!

RON: Adam, as the veteran circuit Bear here, how do you feel about the comradeship at Bear events?

ADAM: You can plop yourself down on a couch with guys you've never met and there's no discomfort. You just share a knowing glance and start sharing thoughts.

LOU: For me, it's a way of meeting guys, whom I've met online beforehand, in person in a comfortable setting. In general, my comfort level depends on how the events are spaced. Three in one year is enough to burn out on.

RON: Adam, do you ever feel burned out on these events?

ADAM: Well, I have a rather idealistic hopefulness. If I'm looking for something specific to happen ("I'm going to bed so-and-so"), it never works out that way. It's truly best to just go with an open mind and relaxed expectations.

RON: Just as in the rest of life. Well, what makes a Bear happening successful? More than simply everyone getting laid, I would hope.

DANNY: The most important feature of a good Bear event is having a place where everyone can hang out, talk, meet, drink, laugh, and relax. The only Bear events I've been to that didn't work had no central spot. A Bear event ultimately is about creating community on a very personal level, which is, again, the same goal that we work for on the cruises. A circuit party creates community on a group level: the people on the dance floor are the community, not as individuals but as a single entity.

I think the other thing that is important is to have some structured events. If you only have a lot of loose meet-and-greets, the shyer guys end up getting left out. And of course, if at all possible, have a big hot tub. *VEG*

RON: Frank, how do you structure Bears in the Keys in order to foster community among the participants?

FRANK: We try to structure the event loosely, but there is definitely structure. After all, this is Key West—the most relaxed place to be gay! The most popular event is the after-hours pool parties.

RON: What structured activities do you include in the event?

FRANK: We have group dinners, a moped bike run, and a few bar parties. We try not to do everything in or around a bar. We have different entertainment as well; this year we have a singer from Boston, Ernie David Lijoi. We haven't snagged Danny yet, but you never know! We also take over the entire resort, which sits right on the Atlantic Ocean. Plus it is clothing optional. It is fantastic!

RON: But you limit attendance, correct?

FRANK: Yes! The event isn't sponsored by any club. The only downside is that we keep attendance at 135, and no more than that. We like the more intimate feel of the smaller events: you actually get to meet everyone.

RON: That's a downside?

FRANK: Unfortunately, the event sold out very early this year, so I'm sure that I'll have some upset Bears on my hands when they try to register. That is the downside.

DANNY: We have the same downside with the cruises. When things sell out it's hard for new people to be able to attend.

RON: Lou, how do you manage to go to multiple Bear runs while maintaining your jobs?

LOU: Bear events are often in conjunction with national holidays, so I take off a day here and there, and it works out OK. I think it's deliberate that they fall on holiday weekends. The nature of my work doesn't permit vacations longer than one week anyway.

RON: The major Bear events, certainly. Adam, how do you manage?

ADAM: I'm lucky that my job allows me to schedule business where and when I want, so I always manage to be in Orlando during October [for Bear Bust], in San Francisco during February [for the International Bear Rendezvous], in Chicago during late May [for Bear Pride], and so on.

RON: How convenient!

ADAM: It's one of the few perks of my job. Now, if I could just figure how to get on an RSVP cruise or to Bears in the Keys for business, I'd be ecstatic!

RON: My sense is that for some men, Bear events are their only vacations all year long.

DANNY: Yes, and for a lot of guys, it represents spending a large percentage of their money. They scrimp and save to attend. Many people aren't aware of how hard some guys have to work in order to attend, and how much they have to sacrifice during the year.

ADAM: Bear events are family reunions!

LOU: Expensive family reunions—it requires money, big time!

DANNY: I'd like to say something about the contests at the events, which really amaze me. The year that I emceed International Mr Leather [IML] in Chicago, I was given a script, told that I shouldn't kid the contestants—all very serious.

Then another year, I emceed the Bear contest in Chicago, which takes place at the same time as IML. At Bear Pride, the contestants are the first 20 to sign up. And the contest is just me kidding and playing with the 20 contestants. Most Bears are so comfortable with who they are that they are able to not take themselves so seriously. The contests are just silly and fun, and no one expects the winner to go out and change the world with their title.

RON: There certainly seems no lack of silliness at Bear events.

LOU: The funniest thing that comes to mind is when the host hotel got their elevators wrecked.

RON: What was that about?

LOU: Well, the elevators have a weight limit—and Bear events are very hard on them! At Roundup one year, the elevator froze between floors. Eventually the Bears managed to pry the doors just slightly open, and one by one the Bears squeezed through. As they emerged, it called to mind a kind of primordial Bear Mother giving birth.

ADAM: And of course, at Chicago '98, a Bear got stuck in the elevator with a Jewish tenor. He started stroking the guy's beard before he realized the guy was straight!

RON: Let's examine Bears' behavior during some of these events. I think we've all heard of the years in Chicago that Bears were behaving badly: accosting straight men in the lobby and the elevators, having sex in the hotel pool, and so on. Men were apparently acting so irresponsibly that the hotel refused to host the Bear group again.

DANNY: Being a Bear doesn't equal being a slut or going down on someone in the lobby. I was there that year and most Bears were very angry with the guys who were doing that stuff. When it was happening, guys came up to those doing it and asked them to knock it off.

LOU: Hotels need to be careful who they book us with. Why, Oh, why, do they insist on these bizarre cobookings with Bears, like Jewish cantors, Brownie scouts, Avon Reps, and those kid talent-beauty pageants?

RON: I hardly think you can blame the hotel for those Bears' immaturity and recklessness.

FRANK: That's one reason why we take the entire resort in Key West—but granted, it is a small event!

LOU: Good idea. Mostly the guys are very nice and behaved. I don't see that sort of bad behavior happening much at all.

DANNY: Being in a monogamous relationship, I don't think that not doing people next to the check-in desk means I'm no longer a Bear.

RON: Do you feel that men have since realized that they have be more responsible to the rest of the group?

DANNY: Exactly. Last year in Chicago there was no trouble.

ADAM: The regulars know what to do. One of the challenges faced by Bears and other gay men is the popularity of barebacking (unprotected sex), which has found its way into the sexual side of many Bear events. It's important for the circuit Bear to remain aware of the potential consequences of the circuit lifestyle, from shallowness, to substance abuse, to AIDS.

RON: Good points. It's interesting to consider that Bear events—even simply Bearclub nights at the local bars—seem to allow or encourage some guys to think they can participate in behavior they wouldn't ever consider doing elsewhere.

LOU: As a man in an open monogamous relationship, I'm so grateful my lover lets me let my hair down occasionally.

FRANK: "Open" and "monogamous" in the same sentence? You lost me there!

ADAM: That's how many relationships stay together, Lou.

LOU: My partner and I are just fine, thank you. I have lots of buddies, and that's how we relate. It's not love. I'm not morally deficient for doing that, either.

FRANK: I guess it must be me. I hate to share! ;-)

ADAM: I think it's very important to share specific experiences of what goes on in a circuit Bear's life, rather than to generalize about loose morals or superficial relationships. I find that my primal hunting male mindset comes out during circuit events, and it's very amusing and satisfying to join the other Bears in rutting around the hallways of strange hotels trying to satisfy our hormonal urges! It's the hunt!

RON: Danny, how do you manage going to events along with your partner? How do you maintain a significant relationship while attending these events?

DANNY: My partner and I live in San Francisco, which is like being at a big Bear event year 'round. If we don't fool around here, why would we at an event?

LOU: I'd like to share an observation. Bear events are, of course, by their nature, inclusive of a variety of guys, and this means including young, smooth guys who apparently like Bears. There are some older guys who also attend these weekends just to meet these Bear hunters and who have little or no interest in the Bear movement, other Bears, or Bear pride.

Ironically, the younger guys get lots of attention from these Bears, which in turn causes lots of grumbling and resentment in the very men to whom Bear events are intended to provide affirmation. Bears have such painful experiences being rejected or ignored in a society where if you're young, smooth, buffed, and pretty, you have it all.

RON: I think we'd all agree that that affirmation is important, but what's the solution?

LOU: I'm not sure. While I certainly don't espouse excluding anybody (not that that would be possible anyway), I have mixed feelings. I'm sympathetic to the misgivings of Bears who feel upstaged at their own party!

RON: It's definitely a conflict not easily resolved. Finally, guys, what's your favorite part of Bear events?

LOU: I'd say that Bear events are a chance to relate on many levels with guys whom I'd never get to see otherwise. The pool parties are the best—give me a pool anytime.

FRANK: It is always enjoyable spending time with guys that we see every year. Some are friends, and some are acquaintances.

ADAM: Bear events give me a chance to step back and look at my life in relation to my buddies. It's kind of a retreat from the rigid rules of straight or even some parts of gay society. I can listen to my friends' problems, hopes, successes, and it helps me figure out my own life a bit better. I meet new friends—and sometimes get laid! I love the pool events, too.

DANNY: At a typical bar or a circuit event, people see me as a short, balding guy with a belly and a pronounced limp, using a cane. When I'm at a Bear event or a Bear bar people see me as a man who is happy and secure with himself. My lover accepts me for who I am—no, more than that, he *celebrates* who I am, just as I do him. At a Bear event or Bear bar, I feel that sense of acceptance from people who don't know me.

RON: Very nicely put. To me, Bear events are a celebration of all things Bear. Bear runs, like the first gay pride march I attended, have affirmed my being in a way I never felt before or feel anywhere else.

PART FIVE

BEAR AGES AND STAGES

CHAPTER 18
BEAR MATURITY, BEAR MASCULINITY
~ A DISCUSSION WITH ARNIE KANTROWITZ
AND MARK THOMPSON ~

ARNIE KANTROWITZ is a professor and chair of the Department of English, Speech, and World Literature at the College of Staten Island, City University of New York, where he has taught Gay Male Literature, Film and Minorities, and Walt Whitman, among other courses. He was vice president of Gay Activists Alliance (GAA New York) in 1971 and a founding member of the Gay & Lesbian Alliance Against Defamation (GLAAD) in 1985. He is the author of the groundbreaking autobiography *Under the Rainbow: Growing Up Gay*. His writing has appeared in *The New York Times, Village Voice, Harvard Gay & Lesbian Review, Lambda Book Report, The Advocate, Outweek*, and other periodicals; and in many books, including: *Poets for Life, Hometowns, Leatherfolk, Sissies and Tomboys, Walt Whitman: An Encyclopedia*, and *Gay Histories and Cultures*. His personal, political, and literary papers have been collected for the Gay and Lesbian Archive of the Fifth Avenue branch of the New York Public Library. He lives in New York City with his lover, Lawrence Mass (interviewed in chapter 14).

MARK THOMPSON served at *The Advocate* for two decades beginning in 1975, working as a feature writer, photographer, and senior editor. He's best known, however, for his influential trilogy of books exploring gay spirituality. The first, *Gay Spirit: Myth and Meaning*, is a widely acclaimed anthology and was recently on *Lambda Book Report*'s list of "100 Lesbian and Gay Books That Changed Our Lives." *Gay Soul: Finding the Heart of Gay Spirit and Nature*, a collection of in-depth conversations and photographs with 16 prominent writers, teachers, and visionaries, was nominated for a Lambda Literary Award. The trilogy was completed with *Gay Body: A Journey Through Shadow to Self*, an autobiographical memoir combining elements of Jungian archetypes, gay history and mythology, and New Age spirituality. His other work includes the anthologies *Leatherfolk: Radical Sex, People, Politics, and Practice* and *Long Road to Freedom: The Advocate History of the Gay and Lesbian Movement*, as well as numerous essays in other collections. Thompson holds a master's degree in clinical psychology and works part-time as a psychotherapist with gay and lesbian youth. He lives in Los Angeles with his longtime life partner, Episcopal priest and author Malcolm Boyd.

This telephone conversation, conducted in February 2000, was the first time Arnie and Mark had made contact since—well, in many years. They met more than 20 years ago, as Arnie described it, "when I was visiting San Francisco in December '79 and January of 1980. And I remember distinctly visiting Mark's apartment and discovering the music of Vangelis...and we became friends, and it was very nice."

One theme that ripples through the following conversation is that of respect, and I think that respect, or esteem, is perhaps what best describes my feelings toward Arnie and Mark. Although I've not met either of these two men, through their work and other writerly associations I came to know of them years ago. Both men have written groundbreaking books that have changed my life as a gay man.

As I put this book together, I decided that one theme I definitely wanted to explore was that of the mature aspect of Bears. Bears clearly have origins among middle-aged men—the men who, like myself, were kids or already young adults at the time of Stonewall. I hoped to explore what it meant to come to middle age during the past decade and a half during the advent of the Bear subculture, and what it means to be an older gay man now, looking back at the Bears as one of many gay subcultures.

One of the unexpected delights of this conversation was when Arnie started to speak about Walt Whitman, and I found myself chiming in, with Mark, asking Arnie to tell us stories of the "good gray poet." In that moment I felt like a kid sitting at the feet of an uncle, listening with rapt attention while he told us a tale of one of our gay ancestors. Rereading the conversation, I still feel a magical rightness about that moment shared with love and respect.

RON: My understanding is that neither of you particularly identifies as a Bear. Both of you, however, as well as each of your partners, could reasonably be described as Bearish, at least on the outward physical level.

ARNIE: I've got a hairy chest, and a beard, and a belly if that counts for anything. And I have had all of them for quite some time now. Back in the early '70s, when I was trying very hard to fit the norm, I lost a great deal of weight. My motive in those days was, of course, cruising. In recent years, though, I've become a little more distant from sexuality—which does not mean unhappy or bitter. I'm very busy in the world, very active, but the accent has changed.

Generally speaking, I find Bears attractive physically. There's a certain feeling that I have of being liberated from gay liberation. In the '70s clone era, there was a kind of male posturing that went on. It didn't even need to extend to leather—flannel shirts were sufficient. I think that still exists in the Bear community. It's a reclaiming of masculinity, but I often feel that it's a masculinity one dons for the occasion. I sometimes think that all masculinity, in terms of mannerism, is wearable that way.

Once, when I was arrested politically, I saw the young rookie cops in the police station squaring their shoulders and trying to look more butch before they appeared in front of their superiors. When I saw that, I realized that all men put on their masculinity.

I do think Bears are a step either forward or aside from the uniformity of the ideal look. I think that's a common thought. However, it creates a new uniformity of its own. When you're a Bear or trying to be part of the Bear community, there are certain requirements of how one dresses, how one acts, including even the familial friendliness that I certainly see in the Bear community. It's not all a bad thing.

RON: To what extent, Arnie, do you find yourself participating in this "Bear patterning"?

ARNIE: Well, as I said, when one is sexually hunting, one is willing to do anything. [Laughs] I mostly dress the way I please these days. It's not important for me to wear a flannel shirt. I feel free to wear sandals rather than boots. It's just me. It's not masculine. It's not feminine. It's just comfortable. I feel a little uncomfortable around people who have the kind of identity that somehow suggests a rigidity to me.

RON: Very good. Mark, have you participated at all in Bear activities?

MARK: I never really have been much of a joiner or a card-carrying member of anything. I certainly have participated in a lot of clans and circles and all of that, but I never have pinned down my identity as a man. I came out in my early twenties in San Francisco during the 1970s when the modern gay world was rapidly forming itself. We were all in a state of self-invention, wildly experimenting with many different postures and guises. So these points about masculinity and all men sort of carrying the butch veil are well taken.

RON: Are you particularly attracted to Bearish men, Mark?

MARK: No more than any other gay type. As a matter of fact, I didn't even know I was a Bear until you called and suggested it.

RON: [*Laughs*] I wasn't only speaking of your own physical description. I thought there might have been a connection with you in terms of the inner nature of Bears, or the Bear community.

MARK: From my point of view, as a gay man in his late forties— there's the outer wrapping, and then there's the inner trappings, which to me gets down to what is real masculinity or masculine authenticity in a man. The outward adaptation of roles and affectations is just another form of drag.

Life unfolds in a series of developmental stages. And it's how we are able to successfully navigate each stage that marks our success in life and in our ability to move on to the next stage. Unfortunately, we gay men seem to have an expiration date tattooed somewhere on our foreheads or asses. By the time we're 30 or 35, most of us become unseen or discarded by those younger than us.

RON: A kind of freshness dating: "Best if used before..."

MARK: Right, until that particular time. And then you are out of it [the gay scene]. Those were kind of the role models that were prevalent in the past, and still are to a large degree. You were young and then—all of a sudden—you don't exist anymore.

ARNIE: I think that leather became one of the first ways in which older gay men could remain sexual. Older gay men were finding alternative routes to being male and connecting with other men.

MARK: Very much so, Arnie, and that's what certainly attracted me to those elements of gay male culture in the past. Certainly at that time [the 1970s], there was life after Castro Street elsewhere. I found a lot of men full of worldly wisdom and experience and...

ARNIE: Wrinkles. [*All laugh*]

MARK: Well, yeah. But that never bothered me. These were the men who'd really been through life and been tempered by it. They had a sense of humor and intelligence that in all circumstances they were willing to share. And I found that very attractive. What I like about the Bear sub-culture is that it represents a maturing vision of gay men.

RON: I think that with the emergence of gay men's leather sex came the daddy archetype. My own attraction to older men was always very consciously tied into a desire to be around and to absorb the worldly wisdom that mature men embody—a very different dynamic from a daddy fixation, which seems more about sexual role-playing.

MARK: Right. But what we're talking about here is something beyond just sex or outward posturing. It's really an attitude—how we think about ourselves. I think that's very important. There is life for gay men after 40—a brighter life. We didn't all know that back then.

ARNIE: Part of the issue here is the aging, the maturing, of a whole generation. Another part is the gaining of wisdom.

MARK: And weight! [*All laugh*]

ARNIE: This was the '70s generation, which had just en masse emerged from the closet and politicized itself. Its underpinning was the '60s attitude of self-respect and respect for your differences from the mainstream. Being a freak, for example, was admired rather than despised. It was a badge of honor, in fact. And one of the slogans of those days was, "Do your own thing," which not only meant, "Follow your own star"; it also meant, "Be more of what you are." So we found, for example, tall women being willing to wear high heels. And people of whatever sort being willing to accentuate what they were and make a virtue out of what had seemed to be their limitation in the past. And masculinity in gay men emerged from much of that.

MARK: Right. In other words, the power to define oneself didn't remain codified with the state or other entrenched institutions—power resided within the individual. That sounds simplistic now, but you have to think historically just how important that was. People were coming to power in all kinds of ways. I don't want to do an East Coast versus West Coast comparison here, but there were certainly different cultural elements at work in each area, which have all blended over time by now.

In terms of coming into one's personal power or authenticity, the image of a Bear as a gay male archetype is genuinely profound. It's a potent image, and images are more powerful than words, I believe. Connecting with the Bear image has enabled a lot of men to really get in touch with certain places inside themselves that were previously denied. It's a way of stating: "I'm OK the way I am. I'm not going to let myself be discarded either by the majority culture or by gay culture."

ARNIE: But Bears didn't exist as a subgroup in the community until later. What happened first was self-respect as gays and the realization that one could be a man by one's own definition rather than society's. But then there came the chubbies, who were perhaps the first manifestation of alternative body type. I understand that Girth & Mirth, for example, was one of the progenitors of the Bears. Which also means that all of the people who founded the image or predated the image of Bears weren't necessarily, for example, hairy-chested. Sometimes they were just bulky.

RON: Right. Girth & Mirth gave dignity and sexual affirmation to chubbies in the same way the Bears did a decade or more later.

I'd like to delve into this area of respect for oneself and others that seemed to arise back in the '70s. As a high school student, I went to GLF [Gay Liberation Front] meetings in Detroit, and I was very aware of the power of the words my elders in GLF were using. It was the first time I'd ever heard of the concept of human liberation. I understood the importance of the work that they were doing, paving the way ahead of me. For the most part, though, my peers didn't really express any kind of respect for our gay elders. And I think this kind of disrespect has been pervasive and persistent in American gay culture for a long, long time.

ARNIE: In American culture in general. It's good to remember each generation has fought its predecessors in order to redefine itself. The gay generation was reacting to the homophile generation. The gays felt that the homophiles were too timid and seeking only tolerance. The gays sought political equality and openness about themselves. And following them came the queer generation, which found the values of gayness to be too much about identity politics and too parochial and limiting. And now we are talking postgay. And post-postgay.

I think it's a necessary part of evolution in a community to move in a different direction from your predecessors and, in some sense, the Bears, at least sexually and culturally, if not politically, are doing that too.

RON: In the same way, perhaps, as the general example you gave, the Bear generation descended from Girth & Mirth and the leather generation.

MARK: It's definitely living against type, too, that I find so powerful and interesting. I'm fairly in shape for my age, yet I can walk down the streets of West Hollywood and feel almost completely invisible. Admittedly, on some days, that's a really nice feeling. But I'm of a different generation from many men on the streets there and I have, in some ways, a different sensibility. I find Bear culture, which is in some ways against type, so refreshing in that aspect.

Another historic element here that we should consider is the '70s back-to-nature movement. People were getting out of the big urban ghettos and arenas and forming rural communities.

RON: Such as cooperatives and intentional communities?

MARK: Intentional communities, yes. There was so much of that going on, at least on the West Coast. It was a reassertion of connection with nature and all of the values that went with that kind of living. The Bears are situated very urbanly, but I think that rural life was also an element of it. It typifies a rejection of the hype—the urbane, the superficial, and the slickness that certainly feels like a greasy patina covering all of our culture these days.

ARNIE: The Bears who talk about naturalness, being natural men, and even the image of wild animal—the bear—are really romanticizing the concept. They're urban people creating a romance of naturalness. I would imagine some of them must go camping and do outdoorsy stuff, but a good portion of them stay in the city.

RON: The rural-romantic component of Bears has, in my mind, always associated them with the Radical Faeries. To some degree, both seem less concerned with conforming to the polished urban hard bodies of the gay male youth ghetto.

MARK: There certainly are a lot of Bear-type men at the Faerie gatherings, not just sylph-like men in their twenties, dressed in chiffon, as many outsiders from that scene might imagine. There is acceptance of everyone. We're learning to get past body type and other superficial expectations and fantasies. There are many types in the gay world. Certainly, the ever-youthful *puer aeternis*, or Peter Pan type, has always been very popular and desired. But at Faerie gatherings and other similar situations, there has been acceptance of people just as they are.

ARNIE: I found uniformity even in the liberated Radical Faeries when I went to the 1987 Washington March. The Radical Faeries all showed up all wearing skirts made out of camouflage material so that though they may have been expressing something unique about themselves, to look at them, one was looking at a form of paramilitary force. It was like, "We are the Radical Faeries, but we are organized and we are angry and we have a look." It's almost inescapable that when a group of people defies the norm they develop their own norm.

Another example was when the hippies, who felt that they were very liberated from the people in suits and ties, began to develop a typical look.

Another time was when gays liberated themselves into the clone look, whether it was on Castro Street or Christopher Street. It became so rigid that it had to be the right brand of dungarees, the right brand of leather jacket, and the handkerchief code, which was so famous. Everything was codified to the point where individuality got lost again. And Bears are also prone to valuing a particular body type, even though that seems to be rebellion against the cultural ideal of the Chelsea boy or whatever the West Coast term is.

MARK: Yes, that was certainly true, but don't you think there's always a little bit of that in any group one is going to belong to?

ARNIE: I think so. That's the nature of groups.

RON: Especially in rampantly superficial American popular culture.

ARNIE: There are a few more points about identity that I'd like to make. Back in the '50s I was attracted to men with beards. Not necessarily big men, although burly was certainly a plus. Maybe a lumberjack type, rather than a heavy man. But even a man in a suit with a pipe and a beard was fine with me. The beard, back in those days, represented a kind of rebellion against the culture, and it frequently signified intellect, not just masculinity. It signified also the willingness to go one's own way, and I found that very appealing back then. So on a personal level, if there's some underpinning to my attraction to Bearish guys (who are not the only guys I'm attracted to, but who certainly have a lot of the things that I like), it may have been for other reasons to start with.

Once I came out into the gay community, I had the experience again and again of seeing subgroups within the community come together and practically weep with joy and relief at finding each other and feeling a part of the same thing. When I myself found the gay world, I had been actually quite isolated, and so to belong to that meant something to me. Then I watched within it—for example, I went to early meetings of the gay synagogue in New York City and saw gay Jews thrilled to find a Jewish community within the gay world, or a gay world within the Jewish community, whichever it was. But I saw the same sense of celebration in the early meetings of GMSMA [Gay Male S&M Association], as leathermen shed their shame and started to talk to each other in lighted rooms. And I found that in group after group.

So when I went to a couple of Bear events—I've been to Bearsex parties, of course—

RON: Of course.

ARNIE: —and when I went to a Bear panel discussion at the Gay Community Services Center, I had that same sense. There were younger men as well as older men, and there were men of varying body types, all of whom wished to identify as Bears. But it was that sense of a community within a community that was so exciting.

MARK: But what is the connection point? Within the leather subculture or the arena of political activism, we can find some easily identified common interest or theme. What is it about the Bear culture that people would have that same sort of experience—almost a rapturous coming into an identity? What in them is being so profoundly moved?

RON: I think Bears' sense of community contrasts with the community of leathermen partly because whereas leather is a look you must don and wear, Bear is one that many Bear men feel that they are intrinsically—it's their naked form. It's seems more a way of being than a way of acting, although there's certainly performance in Bearness.

ARNIE: Bearness seems to be a place or a community where one can be valued, after being isolated in a world that's full of conformist people busy shaving their body hair and modifying their bodies. I think body modification is a very powerful issue in a lot of cultures, from tattooing to discs in lips and rings around necks. What may seem alien or exotic or bizarre is no more bizarre than all the plastic surgery in our culture, the liposuction, and so on. Why do gay men go to gyms for endless hours to perfect their physical bodies, and remove their body hair, as well as get the fashionable tattoos of this generation, and the piercings? It's very clearly, "I'm going to transform myself into something, and we are going to be a community of self-made, transformed people." Bears, in a sense, reject that. They say, "I do not wish to alter myself, because I'm coming from a different tradition where I value what I am."

RON: That's a very good point, although tats and piercings are not uncommon among Bears, either.

MARK: There's a class issue here that I think needs to be discussed as well. I don't want to overromanticize the Bear phenomenon, but there's almost a Whitmanesque democracy to it—the sort of democracy of gay life that reminds me of when we were all coming out in the early days. Just through intense relating or through the sexuality one could experience in the bars and bathhouses, there was a kind of erasure of class distinctions and the discovery of a commonality that extended beyond arbitrary lines.

ARNIE: But there was an open romanticization of working-class people—middle-class and professional gay men dressing like blue-collar workers.

MARK: Yes, definitely. Although personally I grew up in basically semirural areas near central California towns. My dad was a contractor, a plumber by trade, and did construction work.

ARNIE: Oh, do you have any of his old clothes?

MARK: I have his old sailor hat! [*All laugh*] I grew up in Carmel Valley, and for a while we lived out by Salinas. We had horses, and did things like go to rodeos. There were real cowboys working up the road, and the atmosphere was just fun. I never thought twice about it.

RON: Were you particularly attracted to men who evoked the cowboy–Marlboro Man archetype, which was seemingly so foundational to American gay male images?

MARK: Truthfully, I never really noticed it in any particular way, because that was the world I grew up in. I myself didn't feel myself being more or less masculine because of it—but I did have a pair of cowboy boots. I went out and shoveled manure from the horse pasture, built fences, and all that kind of stuff. So those were the kind of men that I grew up with, and there's a kind of man I see naturally directed to that way of life. I don't want to say that they were any more real than any other kind of man but, in terms of style, there's a strong degree of being an authentic self that I related to. Even today, I'm attracted to the type of man who has that kind of lack of affectation. I see a lot of put-upon affectation here in Los Angeles, which is the body-image capital of the world. A decade ago or a generation ago, all the gay publications were filled with ads for poppers and lube and all of that kind of stuff; today, they're all filled with ads for hair removal, liposuction, and laser surgery.

ARNIE: It is a particularly American thing to reinvent yourself and reshape yourself, and we have a long, long history of doing so. I remember my father used to wear Adler elevator shoes to make himself a little taller, for example. He was maybe an inch shorter than my mother, so he used to wear these shoes that had lifts in them.

MARK: I believe that the working-class ethos that seems to be so popularized or exemplified in the Bear subculture must be satisfying some other needs. Certainly it speaks to the needs of being a man in today's culture, where so many men are separated from what I would call real work, the kind of physical work that I saw and grew up with. Today, men are increasingly white-collar or pink-collar workers, doing their work on computers. It's all very ephemeral, and often results in a lack of meaningful connection with the physical world. People, particularly men, have been socialized to see themselves via the work they do. What does it mean when you're part of a vast corporate enterprise and you're not quite sure what it is exactly that your contribution is? It's all very removed from the daily reality known by our fathers.

RON: Are Bears trying to reconnect with that part of themselves, with the blue-collar images handed down from their fathers? Is it a way to avoid becoming alienated with the all-pervasive technology of the postmodern soul? What purpose does it serve to relate one's sexuality, the more animalistic part of themselves, to this image of the bear?

MARK: I wouldn't say *animalistic*—I would use the word *totemic*; but certainly finding connection to the world of physicality and some sort of substance and meaning in a world that is continually being compartmentalized and fractionalized. A lot of men are having a crisis around this issue: What does it mean to be a man?

ARNIE: Bear identity is another compartment, is what I'm suggesting.

MARK: Right.

ARNIE: It may be more comfortable and it may be a way of ameliorating that problem, but back in the '70s when gay men started donning these blue-collar looks, they were imitating not country people necessarily but urban industrial workers. These blue-collar workers themselves were alienated from society because their jobs kept them on assembly lines, where they were working doing just one repetitive task, and in other places they felt they had lost their connection with the whole, with one another, and with the larger community.

RON: I think that the gay Bear image is infused with the blood of ethnic migrants who came to America and became the middle class in mid-20th-century America. Growing up in Detroit, my coming of age was filled with images of these older immigrant men who worked on factory assembly lines.

ARNIE: And remained quiet about their feelings about it.

RON: Certainly.

MARK: And your father?

ARNIE: The strong, silent type.

RON: Right. That's him.

MARK: There's something else that we're beginning to touch upon as we talk about the world of our fathers, and their fathers. There's sort of a nostalgia or sentimentality being revealed—what some psychologists would call father hunger.

ARNIE: Yes.

MARK: All men in our culture have this longing, especially gay men, because so many of us were divorced from the world of our fathers while growing up because of homophobia. And so I see the Bear culture meeting the need for good fathering from male figures that bring with them some heft, authority, and sense of responsibility.

ARNIE: The comfort of bulk.

MARK: Yes, Bear culture provides both the comfort and the needed male nurturing.

ARNIE: I think that's very true.

RON: By reaching out to other masculine men in community, Bears may be soothing their own rejection from their fathers, as well as healing others' (their brothers') wounds of rejection.

ARNIE: I want to ask what happens to this community when you get a group of men who find some kind of a common bond, in one sense because they are rejecting the rejection of them by the mainstream icon-makers, then create their own alternative icon. That's a strong bond: a community of the disaffiliated, in a sense.

RON: Yes, a loving circle of gay men who are told they don't even count as gay men because of their maturity and masculinity.

ARNIE: Another thing that bonds them together is what Mark was just talking about: that father hunger, which they find in each other or act for each other. I've always found in the gay community, and the Bear community within it, this lovely way of men sensing each other's needs and providing them. I don't want to use the word "theatrical," but knowing what was needed and offering it, even if it wasn't one's own natural self, was still something one could still give. And that's a very loving thing to do.

RON: Excellent point, Arnie. Performance, like playing daddy for the evening.

ARNIE: What happens when we transcend those deep kinds of connections and move away from the sexual and even the social arena, and start talking about who we are out in the world? Within the Bear community, there are some guys who connect in the other parts of their lives as well, but many might find that solace and comfort with one another physically, and find the nurture that they're really desperately seeking. If these men start talking about their politics, or their religion, or some other aspect of their lives, they may find that their ideas are totally out of sync. It's hard to hold a community together based on physical appearances, even when it's a small group that has reinvented itself and then made an alternative, or even though it meets certain very deep-seated needs. It's hard to stay together in the way that the Gay Activists Alliance that I was part of was hard to keep together. Even though, in those days, the idea was "let's be gay together," then the subdivisions began to paralyze the group.

MARK: You've brought up a really important point here, because what we're trying to do is to place this subculture, or identity system, in a timeline of modern gay life. What we're talking about is not an end but a means to something else. In other words, we've been talking about a gay male identity and how it has been internally shaped, as well as how it has adapted to the external circumstances of AIDS while claiming civil rights and justice. Perhaps this thing we're now calling the Bear culture is going to transform yet again into something else.

ARNIE: I totally agree with that.

RON: What it means to be a Bear and to be part of this community has very definitely evolved into something greater. And in an oddly postmodern irony, something lesser as well: People already are speaking about being in a postbear phase.

ARNIE: I knew it, I knew it! [*Mark and Arnie laugh*] It's become a question of who's going to be first to declare that whatever we're doing is dead. They're the cutting-edge people. When too many people take the train, people say, "Well, that trend is over. We're all walking. We're post-train!"

MARK: I keep hoping this conversation will go back to Walt Whitman, and all of those other wonderful late–19th century icons like Edward Carpenter, which is how I first began to become aware of my gay identity and its historical continuity. There was a lot of wonderful, deep-rooted gay male history in the local San Francisco Bay culture too. All the gold-miners coming out West in the 1850s helped create a very homoerotic milieu.

RON: That's where the hanky code originated. It was originally intended to indicate, in the all-male dances they held, which men would lead (left) and which would follow (right). Eventually it became translated to top and bottom, or dominant and submissive.

MARK: The roots of so-called Bear culture are actually very deep. What we're dealing with here goes back to the meaning of self-respect, feeling OK with ourselves. If we're big and have a belly or balding and 50, we can still be loved and adored and find our place in the world as gay men. It's a solution, you might say, to a dilemma, or a pitfall. That's what I find interesting about it.

ARNIE: As you may know, I teach a course in Walt Whitman and I've written about him and really done a lot of research on him. There is a kind of quality about Whitman—the natural man, the earthy man. The thing you have to remember about Walt Whitman is exactly what I have been saying about the Bears. And that is, he was a posturer. His honesty was itself a posture. And his masculinity was a posture. I'm not saying he was a very effeminate man. I think he wasn't. But he was a softer man, and a more poetic man, than he presented himself as in his own poetry. There's a contradiction that's implicit in his work. Here he is, writing poetry that most of the people it's theoretically addressed to couldn't even begin to deal with or comprehend. His manner was the manner of an older gay man who was trying to endear himself to younger gay men whom he finds sexually attractive. So he would sit and talk with bus drivers and ferrymen and so on, which is how he met Peter Doyle, who was a streetcar attendant. And he had a series of relationships. He kept getting older, and the guys kept staying the same age, because he had a preference for men around 20. I'm sure he was "daddy" to them in a lot of ways. No one's ever been able to ascertain exactly what went on physically. I've really studied this as much as one can [*Ron laughs*]. There was love going on, certainly, and there was a connection that we can't define. What they did with their bodies I'm not totally sure.

MARK: Well, Arnie, isn't there that famous story about Carpenter going to bed with Whitman?

RON: Seeing that we're discussing gay generations, Arnie, would you mind recounting the story, please?

ARNIE: Yes. I know the story well. This is told in a book called *Circle of Sex* by Gavin Arthur, who was the grandson of President Chester Alan Arthur, and it extends past Arthur all the way to Allen Ginsburg, who tells it himself in some documentary film.

RON: Right—Ginsburg popularized the story in our day.

ARNIE: The story goes that Gavin Arthur, as a young man, met Edward Carpenter when he was an old man. And Carpenter had visited with Whitman a couple of times and actually written a book called *Days with Walt Whitman*. So when Gavin Arthur went to bed with Edward Carpenter, the young and the old, he asked Carpenter about Whitman's sexuality. Now, Carpenter originally said that they went to bed together and they didn't have exactly sex but they stroked each other until his "whole body had a cosmic orgasm," as opposed to having a physical orgasm.

RON: They were doing frottage?

ARNIE: I guess that was popular then. The "Princeton rub," they called it. [*All laugh*] But Carpenter's assessment was that Whitman was bisexual and also liked women. Years later, at a public dinner, Carpenter gave a speech in which he said he felt Whitman was a lover of men, that he wasn't really as bisexual as people had said before. But that's not in Gavin Arthur's book. And then supposedly Allen Ginsberg encountered Gavin Arthur and had a connection with him. And the elegant image is that Whitman's sexual touch gets passed from generation to generation and we have a member in each of these generations who inherits that. I actually wrote a fiction (which is unpublished but it's on file in the library with my papers), in which there's a scene where my character tries to seduce Allen Ginsberg so that he can inherit that Whitman touch for another generation.

RON: [*Laughs*] I'm familiar with the legend of this lineage. Now, once when I was in college, I met Allen Ginsberg and he pinched my butt. Does that count?

ARNIE: Well, it'll do. As long as you're aware of the situation. And be sure to pass it along.

RON: Which do you mean, pass on the story, or the physical contact? [*All laugh*] Of course I will. I mean, I have.

ARNIE: Walt Whitman was, in a sense, the granddaddy of us all, the way that Mark is saying, though it was the image that was the issue. Maybe not the Bearish body, but his sense of what it was to be a man, and he really invented in a sense the latter–20th century gay man. In the meantime we had Oscar Wilde and the paradigm of the urban effete.

RON: The gay archetype of the Dandy.

ARNIE: The dandy, right. That was the model for the first half of the twentieth century. But then it came back to Whitman in the latter half. Do you know the story about Wilde and Whitman meeting? It's a very sweet and touching story.

RON: Please tell us the story, Arnie.

ARNIE: The story basically is that Wilde made a kind of pilgrimage when he came to America. He made a point of coming down to Camden, New Jersey, to meet Whitman, and they got on famously, though they were obviously two extremely different types. Whitman considered his mind very slow and calm while Wilde, as you know, had a very razor-sharp wit and was very urbane. Apparently they sat and talked, hand on knee, as usual, very close. After Wilde left, his companion said to him, "It must have been awfully hard for you to drink that homemade elder-berry wine that he offered you, considering your exquisite tastes in wine!" And Wilde said something like, "I would have drunk poison if that man gave it to me, I thought so highly of him."

RON: That is very sweet.

ARNIE: Yes, they are the two reigning queens!

MARK: The mom and dad of us all! Although each man is a bit of both.

ARNIE: The bear and the bull! [*All laugh*]

RON: Today's gay men are spawns of both characters and have, to a greater or lesser degree, aspects of both personalities.

MARK: I was just thinking about gay men getting in touch with whatever we're calling masculinity. To define it is so suspect these days and so up for grabs. But for the sake of our conversation, I will say that I do see some gay men getting in touch with their masculinity—as grown-up men, not as boys. We're meeting those intense male needs for bonding with other men, but in atypical ways. I detect a real sweetness of romance and respect for one another in Bear culture that I think are hard to find in other situations between men in mainstream society.

ARNIE: I think part of the evolution of that, in a sense, is that gays have compartmentalized themselves by body type and recognizable stereotypes—though the stereotype has now changed from the angora sweater sissy with the pinky ring into the buffed, shaved-chested, at least exterior masculine person. And then the Bears deviate from that. It's good to deviate from deviation, I suppose. In a sense, if you're deviating from deviation, therefore you're in a sense normalizing, you're returning to the mainstream, albeit with a new sense of dignity and self and—

MARK: Security.

ARNIE: And security. You've made yourself. You have your own rules. You've declared that you're OK. Society is beginning to accept the obvious gay men—that is, the ones they can recognize by their stereo-typical tags—at least in part. Yet I think there's a different kind of accept-ance possible for the Bears, who have returned in a sense to looking, as we were saying, like their fathers, or like middle-aged heterosexual men tend to look.

RON: Or does it seem that just as mainstream America starts to become familiar and comfortable with that stereotype of gay men, here comes along a different paradigm of how gay men can be that further challenges their concepts?

MARK: On the surface, at least, it certainly seems just a little less neu-rotic than previous stereotypes.

RON: Is this one of the keys to Bears' formulation of masculinity, to the emotional or psychological makeup of Bears? It's not just a matter of finding acceptance from others, although that's obviously an important thing. It's centrally a matter of finding self-acceptance.

ARNIE: Exactly. Which leads in turn to acceptance, not only by the gay community but also by the larger straight community.

RON: Yes, ideally. So this may be the Bear agenda.

MARK: A major aspect of gay liberation is about resolving the wounds of growing up in a homophobic culture. That is a very impor-tant healing stage to go through, and sometimes we have to isolate our-selves to accomplish that. But the whole argument I've made about being gay is that our ultimate place is in the wider world, simply being our fab-ulous selves! It's all about the individuation process. One of the ways I see the Bear culture being a healthy advancement is that it helps gay men find themselves as more fully realized individuals.

ARNIE: Gay liberation and identity politics, as it came to be called afterward, is a very self-conscious undertaking. You are re-creating yourself, you are defining yourself, you are proclaiming yourself, you are very aware of your self, your image, your place in the world. Bears, in a certain way, are a progression from that. Yet in another way, Bear culture is still self-conscious, and I think what we're talking about—finding your individual place in the world with your various identities intact—goes beyond that self-consciousness. You don't have to walk a certain way; you don't have to dress a certain way. You can be who you are, and it tends to transcend the identities of which you are composed, but you're not denying those identities.

RON: Do you feel that what will evolve from the Bear subculture is a far greater level of acceptance and awareness with unself-consciousness?

ARNIE: Yes, and that's pretty much why this is a stage and a necessary stage.

MARK: Yes. I can see it as a stage—I would put as "the graying of the modern gay man."

RON: Graying—moving from the colorful vigor of our naive youth to the white hairs of mature experience and wisdom. As we learn to embrace the eldest and youngest members of our community, we more fully exemplify the spectrum of its constituency. Bears have typically always taken pride in their age diversity—the Bear brotherhood flag includes white as symbolic of the older "polar Bear," for example.

MARK: There is one thing I like about all these kinds of identifications, the Bears and the Faeries and all of that. Underneath, there is a very deep sense of humor. You've got to have a sense of humor to say, "Yeah, I'm a Bear!" or "I'm a Faerie!" or "I'm a queen!" [*All laugh*] A good sense of humor is definitely one of the most important things a man or anybody can have in life.

RON: Laughter certainly helps us get some perspective on who we think were are.

ARNIE: Yes, we shouldn't take ourselves too seriously.

RON: Do either of you have any final thoughts you'd like to add?

ARNIE: I wish the Bear community all good luck, wherever it is heading. We can dissect it and deconstruct it and all of that, but it's very important that during this stage of their, or our, evolution, to have a damn good time.

MARK: When I mentioned to a friend that we were going to be doing this interview, he said, "Oh, well, you're a Bear now." I'll accept that.

RON: It's never too late to be initiated.

MARK: I think it's a fundamentally authentic place for a lot of gay men to be coming from at this particular point in our collective story. It speaks very well for gay men and our capacities to survive and to take good care of each other.

RON: The invention of Bears demonstrates the incredible creative power of masculine queerness—even as we face massive assimilation by the straight world.

ARNIE: It just occurs to me that Bears are at the same time in America another way of being a consumer. Is someone soon going to be marketing hairshirts?

MARK: What kind of hairshirts did you have in mind, Arnie?

ARNIE: Hmm, something soft 'n' fuzzy.

A Chicago native, MANNY LIM is the oldest child of Filipino immigrants. Before his current job as a faculty assistant at Harvard Law School, he worked as an award-winning newspaper copy editor and page designer, college chaplain, bookstore events director, and church music director. Manny is active in Boston's GLBT community, having served as chair of the Pride Interfaith Coalition and on the board of the Queer Asian Pacific Alliance. He is a member of the Boston Gay Men's Chorus, where he serves as bass section leader and chairs the Membership Services Committee. A "good Catholic boy," Manny has been a liturgical musician for more than 15 years, most recently with the Paulist Center and Dignity/Boston. His other interests include singing cabaret, folk dancing, cooking, and reading. And cuddling. He resides with his partner in Cambridge, Massachusetts.

KIRK READ grew up in Lexington, Virginia, and attended the University of Virginia. His writing has appeared in *Q San Francisco*, *Christopher Street*, *Genre*, and the anthologies *A Day for a Lay: A Century of Gay Poetry* and *Best Gay Erotica 1999*. He is the former editor of *Our Own Community Press* in Virginia, and his columns have appeared in over 75 LGBT publications worldwide. His writing can be seen at www.kirkread.com. His first book, a memoir about being openly gay in high school, will be published in 2001 by Hill Street Press. As an organizer, he has served on the planning collective for the Gay Men's

Sex Summit in Pittsburgh and two Gay Men's Health Summits in Boulder, Colorado. He spends volunteer time with San Francisco City Clinic's free health clinic for sex workers, where he facilitates a support group for men. Kirk lives in San Francisco.

What happens when a man who lacks the outward markers of Bearness—the fur, the beard, the belly, maybe even the wardrobe—is primarily attracted to Bear-type men? Ever since gay men began to call themselves chubbies, there have been men who love them called chubby chasers. When the same dynamic is applied in the context of Bear men, the pursuers are called Bear hunters, or Bear chasers, or Bear lovers.

Bear lovers are confronted with some intense difficulties in their interactions with Bears. The contrast between Bear lovers' looks and those of the objects of their affection may complicate or even completely foil the lovers' attempts to connect one-on-one with Bears, especially in Bear spaces, where a certain "herd mentality" reinforces a peculiar like-seeking-like dictum and discourages expressing interpersonal diversity. And so, the Bear lover may find himself—not unlike those men who may identify as Bears yet not fit the full description of a Bear—excluded and at odds with the larger community of Bears around him.

I met Manny in 1998 at a Boston-area GLBT gender role–free folk dancing group, which not surprisingly attracts a significant proportion of Bearish men. When I mentioned to Eric Rofes that I was looking for another Bear lover for this project, he put me in touch with Kirk, whom I connected with Manny for this online conversation, which turned out to be not only edifying but also incredibly fun.

RON: Welcome to both of you.

KIRK: Are we supposed to shake paws or hock loogies or do something appropriately Bearish? Ron, you must act as our guide here.

RON: For the moment a big bear hug will do. *squeezing all together*

MANNY: (''') BEAR HUGS (''') [cyber punctuation meant to suggest bear paws]. OK, enough of the mushy stuff.

RON: Let's begin by finding out how long each of you has been aware of Bears and Bear subculture. Kirk, please begin.

KIRK: I've been attracted to Bear-type men since I can remember. I think the first time I heard of Bears was when I was in college. I saw these big chubby cuties woofing at each other and realized that this was a sub-culture. I asked them, and they told me about Bears. They amazed me with their array of Bear merchandise. Hats, T-shirts, hankies, shorthand terms, and nicknames. This, I quickly discovered, was a franchise. Much to my chagrin, my lack of a pelt meant that I wasn't even a cub. I would have to settle, alas, either for otter or Bear-chaser. Otters, I figured, are cute. Chasers, I figured, are aggressive. A good combo.

RON: I'd say so: cute and aggressive. How long ago was that encounter?

KIRK: It was in 1992 that I first heard of Bears. My first Bearish idol was Jim Palmer. When I was 11 years old, I used to jerk off with his underwear ads. I'd hide the ads in a huge box of seashells, next to cigars I'd stolen from the coat pockets of my father's friends.

RON: Jim Palmer ads and cigars: now *there's* a fetish in the making. Manny, how did your attraction for Bears form?

MANNY: I really didn't have any knowledge or awareness of Bears as a subculture until about a year or so ago. Of course, I've always been attracted to hairy and bearded men, but I'd chalk that up more to an "opposites attract" dynamic than anything else.

RON: Do any Bearish icons of your youth stand out?

MANNY: I have to laugh at this question. My answer is almost embarrassing. When I was asked to think about the whole Bear question and my first recollection of Bears, the first person I thought of was the character in that animated feature of *Santa Claus Is Coming to Town*— you know, the one that tells how Kris Kringle became Santa Claus. As a young adult, Kris Kringle was this strapping redhead—with Mickey Rooney's voice, I believe. Anyway, at the end, Kris needs to hide from the authorities, so he grows a bushy red beard. That was enough to hook me on redbears forever.

RON: So redheaded Bears, or redbears, is a particular favorite of yours, Manny?

MANNY: I grew up in a predominantly Irish neighborhood in Chicago, so everyone around me was Irish, and perhaps down deep I wanted to be Irish, too. I did watch a lot of basketball as a kid, and to be honest, the only bearded athlete who stands out in my mind was Bill Walton of the Celtics. Red beard, Irish, all that.

KIRK: One of the ways that I bonded with one of my brothers was to attempt to keep up with professional sports through bubble-gum cards.

It was nearly fruitless for me, since football and baseball and basketball all struck me as particularly barbaric. I was a soccer and Judy Blume kind of child. However, it did give me early access to Bears. Even when I was eight, I had daydreams about Mike Ditka as my daddy.

MANNY: I can see how you would, bushy 'stache and cigar and all, though I can't say that I found Mike Ditka particularly attractive. My attraction to Bears appears to be on a case-by-case basis.

RON: Bearness is almost certainly in the eye of the beholder. To what extent have you participated in Bear cultural life, such as Bearclubs, the Bears Mailing List, magazines, or other Bear-laden social activities?

KIRK: I see most of the Bear periodicals at the San Francisco gay bookstore A Different Light—and I love Bear video porn. I haven't worked up the nerve to go to a Bear gathering quite yet, but I expect that will change next month [referring to International Bear Rendezvous 2000, which Kirk did attend].

MANNY: I'm not really one for porn in the first place, but I did buy a mag about a month ago, and it was my first copy of *Bear* magazine.

RON: Manny, how much of a Bear bar hag are you?

MANNY: Not much, really. I know where Bears meet, where to go if I want to be around them, but as far as being in clubs or Bear-specific activities, that's a tricky question. I don't envision myself joining a Bearclub, if only because I know that a lot of Bears frown upon their dens being invaded, as it were, by nonbears. But I do like to hang out in Bear bars and just be around Bears.

I also sing with the Boston Gay Men's Chorus, which has quite a few Bears and Bearish men. There are lots of singing and dancing Bears out there. I'll say, though, that it's hard to focus during rehearsal when you'd rather be groping and nuzzling.

KIRK: I love going to the Lone Star, the premier Bear bar in San Francisco, though I stick out like a sore paw.

MANNY: In Boston, if I really need a Bear-sighting fix, I'll head to the Ramrod or, better yet, 119 Merrimac. I made my first visit to New York last October, and spent all weekend at the Dugout. The Sunday beer blast was incredible.

KIRK: I love those beer busts, either at the Lone Star or the Eagle here in San Francisco. They're very frat party–suburban barbecue. Bear bars are hilarious. It takes three times as long to get from one end of the bar to the other because you have to squeeze past everyone and their bellies.

In other bars, people cop feels on butts. But in Bear bars, it's all about feeling bellies.

RON: How does it feel to be in that situation, surrounded by so many guys that look so different from you?

MANNY: I have to admit that I often feel like a fish out of water in a Bear bar. I'm not hairy, chubby, or very Bearish at all. I'm not what most Bears are looking for, so it becomes a one-way attraction.

KIRK: Well, I've never been a Bear and never will be, barring some sort of medical breakthrough in full-body hair transplant surgery. So I've had to get over apologizing for not being a Bear. But one should never apologize for finding someone else attractive.

MANNY: I agree, Kirk. I'm not apologizing, but it does add an extra level of frustration to the already frustrating bar experience.

KIRK: Sometimes Bears huff and puff at me, call me a "twinkie" under their breath, what have you. But I'm there to pay homage to my sweet, meaty brothers. They should take it as a compliment.

RON: Does it ever feel as if you're invisible in those spaces?

KIRK: Yes, but I don't mind being invisible in a Bear space because I adore seeing Bears together. I have a photograph on my wall of two Bears. One is kissing the other's forehead. It heals me to see two masculine bodies being tender toward each other.

RON: Beautifully put, Kirk. Manny, do you find that you disappear in a Bear den?

MANNY: Sometimes. I'm attracted to Bears, but most Bears aren't attracted to me. It can feel like searching for a needle in a hairstack.

RON: Very funny! But seriously, do you ever encounter hostility in these spaces?

KIRK: There are times when bartenders give me that "Don't you know what kind of bar this is?" look. And some Bears ignore me altogether. I figure that's part of the environment. These bars are about reclaiming space to celebrate Bear bodies. I'm not there to have my body affirmed. So invisibility, for someone who looks like me, seems a part of the subculture.

MANNY: I agree. Invisibility exists in all bar situations, unfortunately.

RON: The whole Bear phenomenon, some would say, seems to be about rejecting the dominant gay archetype of the smooth, thin, young, pretty ephebe and embracing that of the bearded, hairy, big, mature gay man.

KIRK: Let's face it. Many Bears are attracted to other Bears. They want someone to raid the fridge with. But every now and again I'll find either a Bear who's versatile in terms of type, or a Bear who's flattered that a twink is attracted to him. So we go home, have midnight snacks, and cuddle up a storm.

RON: But doesn't that rejection based solely on your looks alone seem like unfair reverse discrimination to you?

KIRK: There are more than enough spaces where young pretty gay boys are valued. I go to a Bear bar precisely because the beauty standards are different. It's refreshing, actually, because in Bear bars I tend to have better conversations. The focus is not on my body, because the space is about Bears. I'm a tourist, an admirer. It's nice to be an admirer and not just an object.

RON: It must be a refreshing change of pace for you, particularly in San Francisco, which can seem at times to be one enormous cruising runway.

KIRK: I think it's healthy for people who are culturally overserved to experience being in the minority. For instance, a straight guy in a group of gay men. A man in a group of women. A white person in a contingent of people of color. A cute gay boy in a Bear bar. It's a humbling, eye-opening experience. We need to get all of West Hollywood into a Bear bar. Then we'll see some things shift!

MANNY: Perhaps. On the one hand, we like whom we like. There's no discrimination in that. On the other hand, it still amazes me that we still discriminate within our own community. That is, the gay and lesbian community. You know the sort of discrimination: too hairy, not hairy enough, too dark, too light—and in the Bear community, sometimes a man isn't heavy enough. Who would have predicted that?

KIRK: A Bear friend once complained to me that a cub had told him he'd look much better if he gained 10 pounds. My friend had been struggling with his weight for years and was finally losing some of the weight he wanted to lose, and then here comes this chubby-chasing cub!

RON: So, perhaps there's a downside to Bears turning upside-down the standards of gay beauty. Manny, I'm curious to ask your perspective as an Asian-American: considering that the vast majority of Bears are white, do you perceive any sort of racial discrimination in Bear environments?

MANNY: Not overtly, but I think that that's because of how Asians and Asian-Americans are genetically built: smooth, limited facial hair. Bears sometimes exhibit a kind of subtle, though not necessarily racial, discrimination. What's worse is that I find some Bears view me with a suspicious eye or have already decided what kind of gay man I am and what it is I'm looking for in bed.

RON: How do these men type you?

MANNY: The stereotype of Asians and Asian-Americans as quiet, shy, unassuming, and submissive signifies to some that (1) I'm looking for a daddy (which I'm not), and (2) I'm a bottom (which I'm not).

KIRK: People assume I'm submissive until I open my mouth. They assume I'm a bottom until they realize how thoroughly filthy and versatile I am. And many assume I'm looking for a daddy, which is something I can live with. Daddies are like undershirts. One can never have too many.

MANNY: *LOL*

RON: Kirk, any comment on the invisibility of Bears of color?

KIRK: I notice that a lot of Bears are attracted to Asian and Latino guys, especially Asian guys. The men of color who have it toughest, I think, are African-American guys. I hardly ever see African-American men in the Bear bars. It's not that different from broader queer culture, in that it's a very white subculture.

RON: Manny, would you agree?

MANNY: Definitely. Sometimes it strikes me as odd—though I guess it shouldn't—to see a big, Bearish, African-American guy in a Bear bar. But I think that's only because, as Kirk says, you don't see that a lot.

KIRK: My Asian Bear-loving friends complain that often, even when they are deemed attractive in Bear spaces, they feel like fetish objects. They're attractive to guys who are into Asian guys as opposed to just being attractive. It's a very complex issue.

MANNY: You have a point there, Kirk. I can't say I've ever met or seen an Asian Bear, but that may be a locational thing. But this is a difficult issue for me to come to grips with. Is it any worse for me, an Asian-American, nonbearish Bear lover, to be into Bears than it is for Bears to be into Asians? I don't know.

KIRK: There are definitely Asian Bears here in San Francisco, but there's a little bit of everything in this fishy little sleeping village [meaning San Francisco, a play on "sleepy little fishing village," meaning Provincetown].

RON: True, a lot of water goes under the Golden Gate Bridge. I know of a handful of Asian-American Bears, scattered around the country. And of course, there's a Bearclub in Japan.

MANNY: I guess my position on the attractiveness issue has evolved, or at least changed. When it comes down to it, you like whom you like.

KIRK: That's what Bear culture is all about—people gathering around a sexual desire and building communities based on what makes us tingle.

RON: Have either of you developed social mechanisms for cruising or making yourself noticed in Bear-centric situations?

KIRK: I definitely let Bears approach me. Perhaps it was all of my mother's childhood warnings about killer grizzlies. In a Bear bar, I try to walk gently. It's their space. More of them are going to be attracted to Bear bodies than not. I approach cruising in a Bear space with a degree of caution and respect. I'm also more likely to meet people in Bear spaces who turn into nonsexual friends. Then again, if I'm at the urinal and a Bear reaches over, all bets are off.

RON: Fair enough. Manny, what's your M.O. in Bear spaces?

MANNY: I think that I already get noticed just for not being a Bear! Beyond that, though, I have to agree with Kirk. More often than not, a Bear will approach me before I'll approach him—it's his/their space. Strangely enough, if I dress the part—flannel, jeans, boots—that adds a completely different ingredient to the mix, as far as some Bears are concerned. It's like a big buffalo plaid flag just went up. It's amazing what you have to do at times just to get some cuddling.

KIRK: I wear leather, Levi's, and often, an uncharacteristic flannel button-down. I've never attempted facial hair. It would be unwise and would take years.

RON: Somehow dressing the part to fit in with the Bear crowd strikes me as a way of trying to pass as Bear by using the accouterments. Not that that's a bad thing.

MANNY: I didn't say that I like having to stoop to that. But as they say, you dress like the kind of guy you're trying to attract, Bear or otherwise.

RON: Is generational peer pressure another layer you have to reach across in trying to relate to and cruise Bears?

KIRK: I think being in my twenties complicates the situation even more. By and large, Bear spaces cater to hairy, ample men in their forties. I don't think my age helps me out with men who resent twinkies.

MANNY: I've never worried about the generational aspect. Since I've come out, I've found that I just naturally gravitate toward men older than me. It's not a daddy thing; I just haven't met a lot of mature guys my age.

KIRK: I've always gone for guys in their forties and fifties, so Bear bars are a candy store for me. But there are drawbacks. So you snag a 240-pound boyfriend—then you have to worry about his cholesterol levels and all that. But that's off-subject.

For me, it sometimes is a daddy thing. But a daddy is a very different thing than a father figure. I wasn't sexually attracted to my father. *Daddy* is a specifically gay archetype that, in my mind, means nurturing and solidness. Someone you can cry in front of. Someone who cuddles well. Someone who has self-confidence. It's not necessarily a father replacement. For me, many daddies have been strong male influences in my life. They've helped me develop as a man, and, specifically, as a gay man. Bear bodies are often great daddy bodies.

MANNY: All of this, I think, is an outgrowth of the nonconformity issue. Many Bears have been pushed to the fringe of an already fringe community, often based solely on their non-smooth, non-gym-chiseled physiques.

KIRK: Amen. Another thing I love about Bears is that they often do fabulous white trash things like bowling and two-stepping and roller coasters. They're not as obsessed with pushing heavy objects around at the gym.

RON: What else do you like about Bears?

KIRK: Something I find endlessly amusing is a propensity among Bears to use terms like "pal" and "buddy" and even (gasp) "dude." My friend Eric Rofes, an intellectual teddy Bear, always calls me "pal," and I tease him relentlessly for it. I think many Bears are reclaiming these words and letting go of feminine terminology like "girl" and "sweetheart" and "Mary."

MANNY: And thank goodness, Bears do what they want, when they want, and without apology. They're just as likely to call each other "buddy" as "Mary," watch football as twirl a baton, work out at the gym as not.

KIRK: People talk and network in Bear bars like nowhere else. They exchange cake recipes, plan camping trips, and all those things that Bears do. It's such a refreshing change from bars where the music is too loud to hear anyone talk. Not only that, the music is better in Bear bars. I would much rather hear Lyle Lovett and Bob Seger than some British DJ's 12-minute remix of a 1978 disco hit.

MANNY: My experience is that Bears, by and large, care much less than most of us about what the gay community and society as a whole think. I guess that's where my real attraction to Bears lies: their redefinition of what it means to be a man and what it means to be a gay man. I have a lot of elder Bears in my life, and they've really helped me in my transition from boy to man. They've given me a variety of role models.

RON: Both of you have a lot of positive regard for Bears. What aspects of Beardom are you critical of?

MANNY: The view of many Bears that to gain admission into The Club, you have to meet certain physical standards: white, furry, large— that's when it appears that the Bear subculture has started to become larger than itself. It's no longer about a look, it's about a philosophy.

RON: Kirk, how about you, pal? What aspects of Bears turn you off?

KIRK: I think Bear culture has inherited many of the existing limitations of queer culture. As Bear culture matures, we're going to see people grappling with complex issues: How do people of color fit in? What about women who have Bear bodies or identify as Bears? What roles do young people play in Bear culture and how can Bears cultivate future Bears? What political and social identities go along with being a Bear? When will Bears, once and for all, stop calling one another "pal"?

MANNY: *LMAO*

RON: *Ditto, wipes tears from eyes* All excellent questions.

MANNY: *Hands Ron a plaid flannel hanky*

KIRK: As specifically Bear spaces emerge and flourish, Bears will deal more with the assimilation of Bear ideas and bodies into mainstream queer culture. It's time we saw Bears on the cover of *The Advocate* and *Genre*, for goodness sake. But it would need to be a straight but gay-friendly Bear for that to happen. Then Bears will really start asserting themselves into gay-beauty quotients.

RON: What do you mean?

KIRK: Bears have a cosmic role in queer life, I think, and that is to remind all of us that most gay men do not look like Falcon porn stars. Bear porn reminds us that our dicks aren't always hard during sex, and that nine inches is not the norm. Bears help us celebrate our authentic, uncommodified bodies.

MANNY: Exactly.

KIRK: It's not enough for gay men to lust after Colt models instead of pretty, hairless porno boys. Culturally, we need to get comfortable with fat boys poking each other. That will help us accept each other. That will help us accept ourselves.

RON: Perhaps that's another version of what Eric Rofes calls the Ick Factor, which relates to how gay men and lesbians view each others' bodies. Further complicating this is the view that most Americans—even those who might be overweight themselves—imagine sex between chubbies as repugnant because our culture has shamed us into hating our bodies: the larger the body, the more shame we should have.

KIRK: Yes. But I think that every gay man needs to get over his fear of vaginas if we're going to stop being so sexist. I think it's essential that the definition of Bear be broadened to include the skinny, the smooth, and the clean-shaven.

RON: Maybe even the non-penile, like women and [pre-op] transmen as Bears. What would you do to introduce more integration between the Bear body-type community and that of other types, particularly Bears of color?

MANNY: I'm not sure that there's one way to do that, Ron. There are a lot of other elements involved. Even something like geography can affect how open the Bear community will be to Bears of color, or even other gay men in general. The primarily white Bears in the American heartland may never get used to or accept the idea that a Bear can be Asian or African-American. But the more it happens, in my opinion, the more our idea of what it means to be a Bear will shift.

RON: Well, Manny, you're 100% correct, I think, about how it will take a lot of influences to change people's perceptions, even supposedly progressive ones like those of queers. Ten years ago hardly anyone in the heartland had ever even heard of Bear culture. But look what a decade has done—now they have Bearclubs in Topeka, Kansas, and Omaha, Nebraska!

KIRK: A successful Bear invasion could occur from following the following trajectory, some of which is already happening: Bears develop their own subculture with gatherings, publications, porn, and Web presence. Next, Bears start showing up in a proud way in popular media. Beardom will help queer culture to accept fat bodies as erotic and healthy. Next, Bears deliver their lesson for the rest of us, which is, as I understand it, that there are valid alternatives to accepted notions of what is beautiful. This will happen in magazines and books and movies. It's a similar liberation trajectory for any minority group.

MANNY: But just as the gay community had its origins as a subculture and then evolved, the Bear subculture will continue to evolve, change, and ultimately influence society as a whole. Just try to imagine what Bears will be like in another 10 years!

RON: It could be something great, but I must admit that at times I'm dubious as to whether it will be evolution or mutation. It would seem largely to depend to what extent the Bears subculture becomes assimilated into larger gay male culture and to the extent that queer culture in general become assimilated.

MANNY: But again, this is an uphill battle...

RON: Exactly. And *your* inclusion in Bear subculture is part of what helps to keep it alive and evolving. Don't let Bears get stagnant ever, please.

MANNY: But who's including us? I think that more than inclusion, we've inserted ourselves into a subculture that could take or leave us.

RON: You're including yourselves, I would say. Wouldn't contemporary identity politics dictate that if you call yourself a Bear, you're a Bear?

KIRK: I think Bear lovers have a definite role here. Every time we say out loud that "I like Bears" or big guys or daddies or older men, some of the stigma of being attracted to these men is removed.

RON: Yes. Even if it's only because you include yourself in the Bear community, you're still in. Manny, do you feel Bear lovers are part of the community of Bears?

MANNY: Can we truly say that Bear lovers are really part of the Bear community? I wouldn't necessarily say that men who love Asian men are part of the Asian community.

RON: Part of the Asian gay community? I'd say that an Asian man's lover (partner) is part of the Asian community. Yet that's a different kind of kinship tie from someone who considers himself a lover of Asian men.

KIRK: I'm not a Bear. I'm a Bear lover. I don't have any aspirations of being a Bear, either. I'm happy to cheer you guys on. I'm a Bear troll. ;-)

RON: Kirk, you're a Bear doll. And that's a good thing.

MANNY: I like to think of myself as Bearish in philosophy if not in physique. But only because another Bear once identified me as such. I'm still on the fence about that.

KIRK: This fence-sitting for nonbears is kind of like being non-Mormon in a family of Mormons. You can go to church, you can go to potlucks, you can even say "Oh, my heck." But full Mormon membership has its privileges, which means if you're not a member you can't go inside the temple. As a Bear lover, there are aspects of the subculture I simply can't access. I'm OK with that.

MANNY: Oh, I'm OK with it, too. I just don't necessarily consider myself part of the community. Not in its current form, anyway.

RON: So, as to whether nonbears are inside the community or out-side...the jury's still out on this one, it seems. Final comments?

KIRK: Hmm...advice I would give to aspiring Bear lovers: Stock your fridge well and get fans for the bedrooms. Those big boys can get over-heated and faint on you.

Sometimes Bear hugs are problematic. I'm all for good squeezes, but you Bears must keep in mind that I'm half your size. Don't crush me if you want me to be useful later.

MANNY: Somehow, I don't feel like we've even really scratched the surface of what it is about Bears that we appreciate so much. Perhaps it's the relative newness of the subculture, or perhaps it's plugging into per-sonal issues (body image, self-esteem, presence of a father figure). Who knows?

KIRK: A beard feels awfully good on your butt. That, I think, is the secret essence of Bear subculture.

RON: Well, there's a lot to like about Bears. I don't know about you guys, but my cock looks best when framed by furry lips. It's most flat-tering.

MANNY: Don't they all? ;-) Bears are going to conquer the world.

KIRK: I'm going to conquer the world, pals, but I'll appoint Bears to my cabinet.

RON: Thanks to you both.

Chapter 20
Ethnic Bears and Bears of Color
~ A Discussion With David Gerard, Ali Lopez, and George Varas ~

DAVE GERARD was born in the Bronx during the blizzard of '61, the second youngest of seven siblings, and has an older brother who is gay. He has been involved professionally in the advertising field ever since he graduated from the School of Visual Arts in New York City in the early '80s, and currently works in the PR department of an ad agency in Boston. Artistically, he has performed professionally as a poet, musician, writer (music journalism), part-time DJ, composer, photographer, and painter, including concert performances, gallery exhibits, and feature readings. He has an encyclopedic knowledge of various types of music, as well as eclectic musical tastes, and has been a contributor to the *Boston Globe* and the *Boston Phoenix*. He is blessed with his friends, ocean-view studio, hobbies, and job.

ALI LOPEZ grew up in the small coastal town of Dorado, Puerto Rico, where he began to draw in his early teens by looking at comic books. At age 17, he joined the U.S. Army and was stationed at Fort Riley, Kansas, where he became a staff sergeant. After six and a half years in the military, he moved to the DC/Baltimore area, where he became involved with the Bear and leather communities. His artwork has been featured in *Daddybear*, *In Uniform*, *Bear*, *German Bear*, and *Bulk Male*, and he has created comic serials for *American Grizzly* and *Bulk Male*. His graphics work has been included in the "Bear Icons" art exhibition. Ali is also a contributor to *The Bear Book II*.

GEORGE VARAS was born in 1969 in New York City of West Indian and Greek heritage. He came out in 1984 and has since been involved in various gay activist groups (ACT UP, Men of All Colors, GLYNY, and MetroBears). Bear-identified since 1987, he was introduced to Beardom when some older Bears brought the concept over from San Francisco to New York City. He runs many Bear-oriented E-mail mailing lists and works in Web and graphic design and audiovisual engineering. He was formerly married to David Michael Merk, a red-bearded engineer, and currently partnered with Keef Robert, a burly Canadian Bear musician and audio-technician. His online presence is at www.ursinedesign.com.

The International Bear Brotherhood Flag was supposedly designed "with inclusivity in mind and represents the fur colors and nationalities of Bears throughout the world." Its design parallels the Rainbow Pride Flag and the Leather Brotherhood Flag, with stripes descending through seven tones—brown, tan, gold, the sand color formerly known as flesh tone, white, gray, and black.

If the stripe colors are to represent the fur colors of the world's four-legged bears, however, why is there a stripe of white human flesh tone, a color that no bear bears on his fur? And if the colors were to represent the diversity of human Bears, it would indicate that a majority of the world's Bears were other than white. (Besides which, where are the red-bears?) In any case, although there may be great diversity among the four-legged creatures, Bear men are by far predominantly white.

The issues of diversity and inclusion facing ethnic Bears and Bears of color are complex and deep. Eric Rofes (chapter 1) addresses some of these issues from an academic and activist's perspective, but as a community we truly need to hear what men from this segment of Bear subculture have to say for themselves. It was not easy to find men willing to let their voices be heard, however; time and again I encountered Bears of color who would only speak off the record—a problem which itself speaks volumes about the repression of minority voices in gay culture.

Finally, Dave, Ali, and George came bravely forward to speak out about their opinions and experiences. It was difficult to maintain the discussion's focus on ethnicity and race as it specifically relates to and manifests in the Bear subculture. We seemed to either veer toward the personal or the universal aspects of racism. I hope that we found a happy medium, or at least made glancing blows at the bull's-eye in our careening around the topic.

Less than four months after this conversation, Brush Creek Media—publisher of *Bear* magazine—ceased publication of four of its erotic magazines, including the specialty-marketed *Hombres Latinos* and *GBM* (Gay Black Male), because "they were not self-supporting."

RON: First, I'd like each of you to please comment briefly on how you personally relate (or don't relate) to being a Bear. George, how long have you known about or identified as a Bear or with the Bear phenomenon? To what extent have you participated or do you now participate in Bear events or Bearclub functions?

GEORGE: I'll tackle the first question first: I personally relate as a Bear by simply being a hairy, thick-bearded, burly young man with a friendly disposition. That was how I was introduced to the Bear concept initially so many years ago. I've been a self-identified Bear since 1987. I've been involved in Bear activities and groups, off and on, the last 10 or so years—although as of late I'm not involved in any Bear groups on any active level, apart from just being a member.

RON: Dave, you don't quite consider yourself a Bear, correct?

DAVE: As definitions are purely subjective, let me say I consider myself to be a cub—partly because I define a Bear as having a certain percentage of hair, body composition, and size. Also, as I have been involved with and have a sexual interest in men who fit the daddy-bear mold; there is that father/son dynamic that easily translates into Bear/cub. As for the Bear scene, I have been around the Bears and their various organizations for the past decade-plus, from my days in New York to my time here in New England. I have gone to IBR [International Bear Rendezvous], routinely attend NEB [New England Bears] meetings, am a current member, and last year officiated as judge in the New England Mr. Bear contest, and helped to picked the winners who went to IBR this past February.

RON: Ali, please tell us about your first contacts with Bears.

ALI: Well, I've been involved with Bears since 1991, when I was living in Baltimore and became involved with the Chesapeake Bay Bears. It wasn't an easy transition since the president at the time didn't like black men. He asked me to leave more than once. *LOL.*

GEORGE: What a dick he was!

RON: What reason did he give for asking you to leave?

ALI: Because there was no such thing as a "Blackbear." So, I had to prove them all wrong.

RON: How did you do that?

ALI: I became one of their most visible members in the community, entering contests, serving as the cook for events, and welcoming new members.

GEORGE: *LOL* Boy, did I laugh when somebody first insinuated that to me—"Uh, you're a Bear? But you're, uh..."

DAVE: That raises one of the major issues for men of color, the having to "prove ourselves" factor.

RON: Does proving yourselves mean having to change people's concepts or to overcompensate? Or both?

DAVE: I think that often there is a tendency to overcompensate to dispel the prejudices of others. It's not fair, but either you try to change some minds, or you just become angry.

ALI: I agree with you, but I feel that we also have to educate the rest of the Bear community that we are as much a part of it as they are. The only way that I saw that possible was to let them know me for who I am, and not let them think of me as what they want me to be: an outsider.

DAVE: Actually, the agenda needs to be raised in the entire gay community!

GEORGE: Damned right.

RON: Agreed. Is educating others and proving yourselves to Bears an ongoing process for all of you?

ALI: It is for me.

GEORGE: Not for me, really, although earlier on it was. It's funny— I think it may be a New York City thing, but I didn't have that much of a "color" problem among Bears, apart from people new to the scene who seemed to judge what a Bear was solely by who appeared in *Bear* magazine or *American Bear*. By the time it became an issue, I was already an identified Bear. Besides, we have many Bears of color here. Until recently, a blackbear headed MetroBears. But it's like what a member of my Backhair [E-mail] list commented on—he thought it was funny that he didn't see more Bears of color. Growing up here in New York City, I saw so many burly bearded men over the years—black, Arabic, Latino, Polynesian, Asian, and Mediterranean. They were all varying degrees of burly, or bearded, or hairy—and quite a few of them made the rounds!

Now who is to say those guys aren't Bears just because they may not be as light-skinned or hirsute? The whole question made no sense—so the argument was made embarrassingly moot here. Ali is right, however, that we have to stay visible. I do realize that not everywhere is like New York City.

RON: Certainly. Bearness seems entirely subjective in many ways, especially how it's formed in different regions. Dave, how has that process been for you with the Boston community?

DAVE: First, let me say that my experience in New York in the '80s was substantially different from George's. New York is so full of denial when it comes to racial discord that I don't even know where to begin.

GEORGE: It still is in many ways, yes.

DAVE: Being in Boston, I've found the racism to be a lot less frequent, and a lot more challenged than in New York. Just look at what Danny Glover's been through! [referring to black actor Danny Glover's discrimination complaint, saying five New York City taxi drivers refused to pick him up]. As for the Bear scene here, there is prejudice and ignorance, yet probably no more than in the community or the society at large. I do not, however, crusade to change minds any longer. I live my life as an example, and those who have not yet gotten it can be enlightened by my interactions with them, or not. Honestly, I have more problems in the gay community with racism than in the so-called straight world.

RON: Many gays and lesbians of color, especially if they're of mixed backgrounds, find they need or want to rank their identities for political reasons. I'd like to ask you if, and how, you prioritize your identities—and where does Bear fit in?

ALI: I see myself as a Black Puerto Rican Bear. I am very proud of my heritage. In the past, I was not comfortable with the idea but I have found my identity after years of denial.

DAVE: Me: Multicultural, bisexual, Bear cub.

GEORGE: All-American Bear mutt. To me, being American has always meant being multicultural, in spite of naysayers to the contrary.

RON: Personally, I would have to echo your self-definition, George. Although others would probably construct me as a white ethnic.

ALI: I used to be afraid and felt out of place in this community. After a lot of self-examination, I have concluded that I can only be who I am, and nothing else.

GEORGE: So when I get that schism-bait question—"Are you a black type, or a Latin type, or a Bear type," I say, "Yes, all of the above—and more!"

ALI: Me too.

GEORGE: Because it's da truth, bebeh.

RON: In many ways there's no difference between the way Americans perceive race and ethnicity—although one would think that gay folks would understand the difference.

GEORGE: Very true—people tend to forget (gay people too, which is a crime!) that we build on communities by our diversities as well as our similarities.

ALI: Some welcome it, and some fear it.

RON: Perhaps, though, it's most significant that your Bear identities are the least prioritized. I'd like to talk about ethnic culture influences on your sense of masculinity. To what extent might have Latino machismo or urban black toughening up culture affected your ideas or performance of masculinity?

DAVE: What do you mean?

RON: In these particular cultures, there are certain cultural stigmas around the masculine way of being. There are powerful cultural rules about what it means to be a man, and how that's acted out. And I want to know if any of you have been influenced strongly by those cultural ideas.

DAVE: That influence certainly is present in the black community, especially with the force of religion behind it. Personally, however, it didn't really influence my masculine identity. I have an older gay brother who's a little on the effeminate side, and until I knew better, I thought if I liked men, that was how I had to act.

ALI: My culture has greatly influenced my sexual identity. Growing up in Puerto Rico, I had no examples of masculine gay men, and my image of a gay man was that of the limp-wristed sissy. And that's not me. So I denied my sexuality for a long time. My Catholic upbringing also had a lot to do with my denial of my sexuality.

DAVE: Yet with Latin culture, there is a certain rule that says men who are not passively receiving sex from a man are not queer.

ALI: Also, while I was in the military, the cloaking of my true self went even deeper. I was afraid of being seen as a queen.

GEORGE: It's interesting, as I had sort of odd experiences in my youth regarding that. In African-American culture, the idea was always "proving" your manliness in a variety of ways. It was as if you always had to show that you were manly, or that you could actually score. Once when I was young, I was cornered and told, "We never see you with anybody—are you a punk or what?" I had to lay this chick just to prove to them that I was just as much a "man" as they were. (Never mind that this girl was my pal who turned out to be a lesbian—that's another story!)

On the Latin side, it was weirder: it seemed that you were accepted, in an odd sort of way, if you were effeminate or not very butch. It was almost expected that there would be men who were *maricones*, if you will. If you happened to be a regular butch guy who actually only liked guys, though, they didn't like that at all. That was almost as if you were infiltrating them, or perhaps shaking their foundations of what manliness was supposed to be.

RON: Ali, was that your experience as well?

ALI: As a child we played many games, and many of us would grab our dicks in defiance—kind of like a power stance—but I never advanced more than that for fear of retribution from a strict cultural view. My family was and still is not gay positive, and therefore I've chosen not to divulge to them my gay identity.

RON: Dave, do you have a personal experience of this particular issue?

DAVE: Here's one: In high school, I had a Latino buddy who was the big jock on campus. He must have perceived me as gay because he was always taunting me with his dick, offering me a chance to feel it up in our history class. He even asked me if I wanted to suck him. I think in his eyes, it didn't matter, as long as it was he getting the blow job.

ALI: That would make him gay in my eyes.

GEORGE: He is gay. It's a popularly held conception that if you aren't on the receiving end—the so-called female end—then you are not gay. But if you get your dick hard for a guy in any capacity, then you are gay, or bisexual.

DAVE: Exactly, but religion does play a part in a lot of people's denial of sexual appetites.

GEORGE: It's akin to the gay for pay phenom in hustler circles or in porn. Whether these men want to admit it or not, sex with a man and sex with a woman are two very different things. Religion just adds fuel to the fire—the guilty pleasure syndrome—doing something that is perceived to be wrong, or less than male, in this case. I think that may have been a factor in what attracted many men to Beardom initially, as it did for me.

RON: Performing in typecast gender or sex roles is reinforced by all aspects of our upbringing: ethnicity, faith, and more. But do you feel that Bearness offered you an alternative to that binary way of being?

GEORGE: I've always held the idea that you can do whatever you wanted—be receiving, giving, whatever—but you are still a man (as if that should ever be in doubt anyway!). Or at least, if you believe the slogan: "Masculinity without the trappings"?

RON: Actually, I find it hard to believe that slogan promotes anything but a very narrow masculinity. Look at the models *Bear* promotes heavily! Those men are chosen not because they're the most sexually dynamic men available but because those icons reflect the desires of the largely homogenous group of middle-aged, middle-class white men whom *Bear*'s marketing targets.

DAVE: Ron, I have to ask you: The other day we were discussing a certain well-known Bear, and when I asked you about his ethnicity, you said you didn't know, even though you had interviewed him fairly extensively. Is it possible that only those who are perceived as being "ethnic" are asked about their backgrounds?

RON: Good question. Hard to say...

ALI: Hmm!

GEORGE: Oh, I would say so!

ALI: I agree!

RON: I did ask about his background—his family, where he grew up—but he didn't disclose any particular ethnic identity. Very likely you're right, Dave—most people are not WASPs—although you need to verify your claim that the Bear in question is indeed from an "ethnic" background.

DAVE: I think it likely, too. The Bear in question may or may not be a Bear of color, but that misses the larger point I'm making. As for me, I have no problem asking anybody I meet about his background. I am always fascinated by that, not as a divisive thing, but because it is a part of every human being's makeup.

RON: Well, I get awfully tired of being asked my background. Most times, it feels like the person asking just wants to plug me into an ethnic stereotype.

GEORGE: I always get that—Are you Puerto Rican? Italian? West Indian? Arab? Samoan? Cuban? French? Turk? Dominican?

RON: Same here! Italian? Jewish? Arab? Greek? Native American?

GEORGE: I always answer, "Sure." *LOL*

RON: Right—yet that evasive response infuriates some people. I was born with a Hispanic surname, and have Native American blood as well. Years ago I legally changed my surname to a Sanskrit Indian name—I revel in the fact that nobody can figure it out.

GEORGE: Stereotyping doesn't bother me now to the extent I used to be. If I can show them that I'm not merely what they thought I was but more than that, then by example I'm opening up their heads a little. But Dave is right: if you are less than pink-skinned, the question always seems to be posed.

DAVE: I just got the U.S. Census form, and put in "other," just so I could include all my cultural backgrounds. And yes, I wrote them all down.

RON: In a certain way, copping to a singular ethnic or racial identity is as narrow-minded as calling yourself a Bear—

DAVE: There you go!

RON: Simply because you can't find a more complex way to express yourself and your sexual tastes.

DAVE: The Bear movement is hugely hypocritical in that Bears expect inclusion in the gay community, but the Bear movement itself discriminates. It was initially a response to the so-called factioning of groups like gym types, preppies, and the like, where hirsute guys felt left out. Now the Bear community has so insulated themselves that they don't even see they're practicing the same thing they were rebelling against!

RON: Not just hirsute guys, but big and older men felt excluded, too. I think a lot of guys see the discrimination, but are unmoved to do or say anything about it.

DAVE: Exactly. They always say, "I'm 250 pounds, and looking for someone bigger and hairier than me"—you know the drill.

GEORGE: Unfortunately, this is what happens when all groups hit a certain level of acceptance: They jockey for a space in the spotlight, as opposed to sharing it. Ultimately, it's easier to typecast someone by what they don't fit into as to what they do fit into.

DAVE: Actually, it's more about narcissism than anything else, if you really get down to it.

GEORGE: We mustn't forget that this factioning is also fueled by so many other influences as well—commercialism, sexual tastes, the ethic of "me, me, me," and what sells.

RON: Good points. But how do Bears offer you men a better fit than, say, those "gym-bunny Waspish-type" groups?

GEORGE: Well, I've always liked furry-faced men, so I'm not sure I know how to answer that. Beards, and men who look like they enjoy life on their own terms, not what's popular, have always been a turn-on for me. I think that I really became comfortable with my "Beardom" when I decided that I could define myself as so many things: not only as a Bear, but also a Greek, a West Indian, a chunky guy, a libertine, an activist, a patriot, an American. When people see that you are not ashamed, that you're proud, then you have to be reckoned with, whether you are accepted or not.

RON: Ali, we haven't heard from you in a bit.

ALI: I've always felt that, for a community that wants to be recognized as part of the mainstream, Bears seem rather unwilling to welcome those who are different, or who don't fit the image that the big men mags have etched in our mind over the past 10 or so years. It took 58 issues of *Bear* to have a blackbear in the cover.

RON: Exactly. Although I'd like to point out that they did have black and Latino men pictured in very early issues, even before they went glossy.

DAVE: What really pisses me off is the notion that to like or admire someone who isn't white is almost marketed as being a fetish.

RON: Not "almost," Dave. It is marketed precisely that way. If you look at Brush Creek's portfolio of magazines, you see that black and Latino men are specialty marketed exactly like Bears, cowboys, rubber, BDSM, foreskins, and other "exotica."

DAVE: Daddies, top-men... I personally know what turns me on, and while Bears are at the top of the list, they are not the entire list by any means! I have nothing against those magazines that just cater to a specific ethnicity, if that floats your boat, but the publishers of these magazines take a lot for granted.

ALI: Thank you for saying that. The publishers don't realize that we are humans and Bears and are part of that special market. I would love to see a magazine with the balls to show a biracial or multi-ethnic couple or group getting busy, but so far only *Bulk Male* has.

DAVE: In the '70s there was a lot more intermixing, not only in magazines, but in gay culture as well. This intercultural dynamic tells me that the pendulum of bias is swinging back to the '50s.

RON: Why do you think so, Dave?

DAVE: In the respect that in the '50s, people didn't seem up to challenging the current thinking.

RON: Good point, Dave, about folks not engaging in challenging thought or politics. So, Bears' lack of political sense or motivation is not different from the rest of this society.

DAVE: That seems to be where we're headed. I feel a visceral numbing in society at large.

ALI: How so?

DAVE: People seem exhausted by the dynamics of what it means for us to envision ourselves as a larger community in the new millennium. It's like the movie *Pleasantville*—we are desperately trying to hold on to an era that has outlived its usefulness.

RON: That's a valid observation, I believe, but let's return to the dynamics of mixed Bear couples. Ali pointed out that there are virtually no mixed couples portrayed in the magazines.

GEORGE: There was a couple in *Bulk Male* and in the old *BearFax*, but not sure if you want to count that.

RON: That counts, yes, and it relates directly to Dave's point that many gay men view the idea of loving Bears, or men of color, or perhaps especially Bears of color, as a fetish.

DAVE: So why is there less interracial mixing taking place now in the gay and Bear worlds?

RON: Yes, particularly as it is represented in Bear smut.

DAVE: I think there are two reasons. First, the editors and publishers look at the bottom line, or should I say, bottom dollar. But second, I believe they sell us purveyors of smut short.

ALI: So far, there haven't really been any mixed couples in the Bear magazines or videos. The only interracial images are usually found in small-format magazines. Many magazines see it, as Dave pointed out, as a bottom-dollar issue. They don't believe it would sell.

RON: Certainly, this interest is a narrow portion of an already marginal population.

DAVE: Let's not forget the narcissism factor, which is an unspoken truth in the gay community.

RON: You mean the "looking for same or similar" syndrome?

DAVE: Certain Caucasian Bears (who buy a lot of this material) cannot envision themselves with someone, anyone, from a vastly different culture, because that person doesn't mirror their ideas of beauty or sensuality. From my personal dating experience, however, I find that the truly secure man doesn't need a clone in bed, whether it's gym bunny, preppy, or Bear.

ALI: As an artist, I've found a lot of resistance to my producing art featuring any other type of Bear.

RON: Can you give an example, Ali?

ALI: Until recently I have never been able to feature any art with Bears of different races, or mixed couples. I have been lucky to be able to control my art for *American Grizzly*, where I have a lot of latitude in the subject matter. In many cases, magazines will turn down art of black or ethnic Bears engaging in sex, because they don't see it as what the buyer wants. I try to bring a balance in my imagery, but most of the work that I use is that of white Bears.

RON: George, any comment on images in Bear print and video media?

GEORGE: I'm glad that a Bear of color finally made it to the cover of *Bear* recently. I don't know if it never happened before because the magazine had no one of color to pose for it, which I might like to believe. I'm not sure. Or is it that they're getting some sort of feedback or demographics done for them that says it would be better not to present those images, or to keep it sporadic?

ALI: I would have to agree with your latter idea, especially since I did pose for that magazine a few years ago.

RON: It's hard to say, perhaps, but I believe there was an editor's note explaining that there was a considerable lack of blackbear models.

GEORGE: Personally, I don't buy that excuse. I do see quite a lot of couples of mixed races here, but that's just the way it is here in New York City. These magazines may be catering to a perceived majority, but the feedback I've always heard from Bears here is that they wanted more variety in print—which almost always meant men who were something other than white, even when it wasn't said straight out.

DAVE: I think a lot of it is just plain lip service.

RON: You go, Dave!

GEORGE: It also may be some weird idea of some sort of perceived crossover. Brush Creek has magazines that spotlight Latin or black models exclusively, so perhaps they believe that selling this kind of image as an ethnic type is more profitable. The whole proposition is silly anyway, as I notice they throw in a Bear of color in those magazines more than once!

DAVE: A real question is who needs the educating: their editorial staff, their readership, or maybe both? It's obvious to me the focus has become way too narrow, which is why in addition to *Bear*, we have *Daddybear, American Grizzly*, and the rest.

GEORGE: Perhaps both groups need educating in varying degrees. I know that a substantial number of men really wants to see more variety in the racial and cultural strata of Bears. Then again, it's the stereotyping syndrome—rather than enjoy different types for what it's worth at face value, they have to pigeonhole it for the sake of convenience or sales.

RON: Stereotyping is not about valuing diversity. But if it were just a matter of fulfilling a niche, why isn't there a *Blackbear* magazine? Or *Oso* magazine?

ALI: Funding?

GEORGE: A very good question. There are E-mail mailing lists for those special-interest groups.

RON: It would be interesting if an ethnic Bears mailing list would actually talk about some of the issues we're discussing now. Do any of you know what sorts of discussions go on within those lists?

GEORGE: It's usually just sexually oriented, really.

DAVE: To be honest, I don't know if the talent pool of men-loving Blackbears could sustain that kind of specialty magazine.

ALI: I would love to see one issue of any of the magazines to be dedicated to ethnic Bears.

DAVE: Now, that would be a step in the right direction!

ALI: That would be a start. It would be a low-risk proposal that they can write off if it doesn't work.

GEORGE: I would like to see an issue dedicated to ethnic Bears, too, but there may be a downside to that. Ideally, I would want to see all sorts of Bears all the time, not just perhaps once a year, or once in a while.

RON: Right. It saddens me to think that the media are incapable of including a genuinely representative spectrum of images without making a gargantuan special effort, and then promoting up the wazoo as "Our

Multiethnic, Multiracial Issue."

DAVE: Ron, do you think the problem is that there aren't enough gay Bears of color being more vocal about their discontent?

RON: I'd like George or Ali to respond first, if you don't mind.

ALI: I believe so. I have been involved for the sake of representation in every major Bear event that I could attend. We need to be seen in order to be recognized as part of this community, and many men indeed now understand that. I have tried, not for personal glory, but due to my early rejection in this community, to educate others by getting in their face!

GEORGE: Being vocal about discontent really isn't enough. The answer has already been given by both Ali and Dave: Be proud and visible, make yourself known as what you are—as a Bear, a person of color, and anything else you wish to define yourself by. Show yourself by being your own best example. It's not the fastest way, but it's the best way to help expand their horizons.

RON: And my answer, Dave, to your question is yes, and no. Part of the problem is, as all of you say, about Bears of color being more vocal. But as long as white Bears keep their traps shut and reinforce the status quo, I think, Bears of color will remain largely unseen.

When I asked an Asian-American Bear lover in another chat if he ever felt invisible at Bear events, he said he felt just the opposite—he felt he stuck out "like a sore paw" because of the apparent racial difference. Now, do you ever feel invisible at Bear events?

DAVE: Sometimes I feel not so much invisible, but more like a mascot. A mascot is there as a cheerleader, comedian, entertainer, but not truly part of the team. Too many of my Bear buds, although they care for me deeply, would never think of me in "that way"—and sometimes color has something to do with it.

RON: It seems regretful that you would feel anything other than a fully accepted participant. Ali, you seem able to address any invisibility issues head on.

ALI: In the beginning, I did feel invisible, seeing all these Bears around the room, and me by myself in a corner. Not good. So I changed the rules of the game. I became Bear Central. I began to approach people in a nice, friendly way to break the ice, to show them that I'm not as scary as they think I am.

RON: "Bear Central"—I love that! But how awful that you had to work so hard for acceptance.

ALI: In complete darkness we are all the same. Only our wisdom and knowledge separate us. Don't let the darkness deceive you!

RON: Beautifully put, Ali. George?

GEORGE: It's odd that, initially, I found myself the center of attention. It was like being in a sea of Anglo faces, and I was this new piece of candy to sampled: "Oh, he's black—or Latin, I think—they've always got big dicks and are good in bed." But it had a very insidious side to it.

RON: What was the downside to all the attention?

GEORGE: I felt like an exotic novelty. These men felt it was OK to sleep with me, but that was all there was. Afterward, the attitude was sort of like, "been there, done him." They had no desire to be friends or hang out with me because they couldn't see past my skin color or dick. I was good enough for an overnight of passion—but not to bring home to mother!

RON: I'm not sure if the "been there, done him" thing is particular to Bears of color. In fact, there was a column by that name in *American Bear* magazine.

GEORGE: It's true that that sensibility is endemic to gay culture in general, really, but the idea was that I was a must-do because I was merely different in color to them (and not much else) sort of confused me for a while. As I got older, however, that attitude changed quite a bit. People began to see past my skin and crotch and understand that I was worth a workout on the bedsprings *and* a movie and coffee afterwards.

My current husband is head over heels for me, which I'm so happy for, but he was surprised when I suggested that it might be because I'm not white. His reply was that he loves me for me, which is how it should be. But then again, he is literally colorblind!

RON: Gentlebears, we could undoubtedly talk about this topic for many more hours, but we need to wrap up here. I hope we made a significant dent in the topic.

Chapter 21
From Boomer Bears to Gen-X Bears to Bear Youth
~ A Discussion With Terry Jamro,
Brian Kearns, and Heath McKay ~

TERRY JAMRO was born in St. Louis, Missouri, in February 1977, and grew up in Cherry Hill, N.J., and Wilbraham, Massachusetts (a small town in the western part of the state). In 1998, he transferred to Northeastern University, where he now studies Computer Engineering. Terry was the Chapter Coordinator for Gen-X Bears Boston from 1997 through March 2000, which grew to more than 120 members. He also coordinated the Gen-X Bears Fourth Annual East Coast Gathering in April 1999, attended by more than 100 Bears from around the Northeast. As the current Chapter Development Director for Gen-X Bears International, he helps forming chapters worldwide and serves as a resource for other chapter coordinators. Some of his hobbies are football, amateur wrestling, and camping. Terry likes big guys with goatees ("You must be at least 200 pounds to board this ride!") As of this writing, he's single!

BRIAN KEARNS was born in January 1980 in an industrial city east of Toronto and raised nearby. He chose to stay close to the area after high school and is currently studying interior design at a local design college located (surprise!) right in the middle of the gay district. His involvement with the community itself has been mostly limited to the Internet: in 1997, Brian started BearYouth.com, a Web site for teens and young men who are looking for support and a safe social outlet. So far, so good:

BearYouth.com has been up and running for three years now.

HEATH McKAY was born in June 1974 and grew up in Millis, Mass., a small town southwest of Boston. His sexuality revealed itself to him at 18, he came out to all his friends at 19, and told his befuddled parents at 20. He attended college at the University of Maine at Orono, where he threw himself into activism and into "token queer" stature. He also became involved with Wilde-Stein, the gay group on campus—as well as about 20 other campus clubs and activities. In 1999 he won the Mr. Grizzly New England title. He went on to compete at International Bear Rendezvous 2000 and was awarded International Mr. Bear 2000, the youngest man to hold that title. Heath lives and works as a graphic designer in the Boston area. He has a wonderful boyfriend.

In *Much Ado About Nothing*, William Shakespeare observed, "He that hath a beard is more than a youth, and he that hath no beard is less than a man." But the distinctions that define manhood, or even manliness, have drastically changed since the days of the Bard (who himself sported a scant beard).

Secondary male growth attributes—such as beards, body hair, extra fat tissue, and even graying or male pattern baldness—have typically characterized the mature Bear man. Indeed, one aspect that has distinguished Bears from clones is the maturity of the man—undeniably, something more than "clothes make the man," in this case.

But what do we make of the Bear-identified man who may have only a few of these characteristics due to the simple fact that their bodies have not yet caught up with their desires? What place is there in the Bear community for young men who have just come out and aren't ready for the Bear bar or Bearclub scene?

Gen-X Bears International was formed in 1995 to provide "a positive social meeting agenda for Bears [in the] 18–35 years old range." Of course, in 2001, that age group is now 23–40. These shifting sands of time are part of the reason that the popular Web site BearYouth.com was initiated: to meet the needs of even younger Bears and Bear lovers who are just now coming of legal age.

Gen-X Bears and BearYouth have each been the subject of an article in *The Bear Book II*. However, these two age groups have much in common that deserves to be explored together. I've long felt that Bears are one of the least age-segregated communities in North America. In the future, I would love to see Bears from all generations, including senior Bears, interacting within a similar panel discussion framework as our online discussion here. Such interaction would foster, I hope, the sense of intergenerational brotherhood among all Bears.

RON: First, how long have you identified as a Bear or with the Bear phenomenon? Heath, let's start with you.

HEATH: I heard the word "Bear" when I was 18. At first, I thought it was an insult to guys of my stature. I didn't accept it until I was like 21. Finally, I learned to love myself for it over a year ago—and love myself I do. :)

RON: How did you first hear about Bears?

HEATH: Well, when Quest (a Boston club-kid bar) closed, I had no life. I started going to the [Boston bar] Ramrod. Got into the leather scene and the butch thing. I met Bears there, including one friend who helped me to meet others. So, leaving that earlier social climate was really liberating. I was able to see myself the way I am, and not the way I thought I should be at the time—or at least the way I was made to feel I should want to be.

BRIAN: I first found out about Bears searching on the Net for adult stuff, and it just so happened that it was Bears that I was looking for. Then I found out more from there, from people's home pages and such.

RON: So, Brian, it was a while before you connected with Bears in person?

BRIAN: You might say that, although I ended up seeing a guy who you could say was Bearish. And I did manage to make my way to a Gen-X Bears meeting when I was 18, I believe, but I didn't go regularly to any Bear functions.

RON: Why was that?

BRIAN: I definitely knew I liked Bears, but soon noticed the large age gap. I was 17 and all the Bears seemed to be 30- 40- 50-something and wanted nothing to do with me. I knew that younger, good-looking guys did exist, but it was just finding them that was difficult.

RON: That must have been frustrating. I'd like to get back to the age gap problem in a moment, but I do want to ask Terry first about his first involvement with Bears and the Bear subculture.

TERRY: I first found out about Bears on the Internet in 1994, when I was 17. From what I saw, I said to myself, "Big hairy gay guys—I'll have to check this out!" When I was 18, I went to my first Bear event, which was the New England Bears bar night at the Ramrod in Boston.

RON: How was that first encounter, Terry?

TERRY: It was definitely overwhelming: my first time at a leather gay bar, and my first time seeing all of these big hairy men, who are all gay. Before that moment, all I'd ever seen were those skinny little hairless gay men on TV.

RON: How did most of the guys react to meeting you and finding out you were so (relatively) young?

TERRY: From some of the people, I definitely got the vibe that I was too young. Most people were cordial. I don't think I remember anyone's name, though! :) When I told people my age, a lot of them said, "I could be your father." I heard that a lot. I felt that some of them didn't want me there because I was underage, but there wasn't anything else out there for younger Bears, so it was my only choice.

RON: Heath, did you have a similar experience meeting Bears for the first time?

HEATH: My first meeting with a self-proclaimed Bear was kind of interesting. I was hanging out with my best friend who lives in New Hampshire, and this big, bulky, hairy guy comes up to me and handed me a flyer. He was trying to start a Bearclub and the flyer said, "Are you big? Are you hairy? Are you butch?"

RON: No kidding. Really? It said, "Are you butch?"

HEATH: Yep, and that's when I decided to read him the riot act. At that time in my life (I was 22; I'm pushing 26 now) I was a little bit on the bitchy side. I was still a little tender about my weight and inability to stop growing all this damn hair. I felt that I could be kind of cute, as long as I could wear masking clothes. So to have this guy come up to me, include me on two points and dismiss me on the third, was rough. You see, that's the problem: often we aren't accepted unconditionally, and I see that fault with older Bears. They have a tendency to clone at NEB [New England Bears], and I always got shit for not meeting the full description—as in, I'm not butch enough, I'm not hairy enough, I'm not large enough, or worse—I'm too young. My most recent melodrama has been my age. Let me interject that this is 100% not the case with Gen-X Bears.

RON: Brian, Terry, have you also felt this way?

TERRY: The most I hear is that I'm too young. The process of discovering myself as a Bear was very difficult for me. At the time, I was still living at home in western Massachusetts, so Boston was about two hours away. The Northeast Ursamen in Connecticut were close, so I started going to their Bear events. There was one other guy that was two years older than I was; then the next youngest was 27 or so.

RON: Did the Ursamen give you attitude about your age?

TERRY: I was definitely considered young, fresh meat.

RON: Brian, did you ever feel like "young, fresh meat" at a GXB meeting?

BRIAN: Well, I could say I did. It's one reason why I've been hesitant to get too involved with Bear groups. But I brought a boyfriend with me the last time I went, so no real comments were made.

RON: But still, you've felt this gap between yourself and most Bears?

TERRY: I really didn't relate to most of them. Sometimes, I was in chatting circles and people would talk about their vacation to Key West or their second house, and I was thinking, "Wow, I'm sure glad I had twenty bucks for gas tonight."

HEATH: I felt like a pauper because I had to stay at the San Francisco YMCA rather than the host hotel during IBR [International Bear Rendezvous], when I won the International Mr. Bear title.

RON: Terry, you've brought up a great point about there being a huge income difference between most gay men and younger guys who are likely in school without a job.

TERRY: There is some difference of white-collar and blue-collar, but most Bears seem to intermingle well.

RON: Do you feel that GXB and the BearYouth.com Web site were formed in reaction to these feelings?

BRIAN: I started the BearYouth Web site because I didn't feel there was anyplace—on the Web or elsewhere—that younger people could identify with Bears. Gen-X Bears came close, but I found it still missed teens and those youths who were still coming out to themselves.

RON: Has it gotten difficult to maintain the site now that it's blossomed so much?

BRIAN: It is difficult, and I do make mistakes and fall behind in some updates.

RON: Terry, you're familiar with the BearYouth Web site?

TERRY: Yes. My picture's in their gallery. I think BearYouth is a great site. I've referred a bunch of guys to BearYouth, and they said it helped them a lot. I think it's difficult for many guys just to find out who they are. First, they have to decide that they are gay or bi. Next, they have to figure out that they are Bears. Furthermore, if you're in high school, or even still living at home, it is very difficult to physically meet other people like yourself, especially if you're young and from a small town. That's why I think BearYouth is an excellent site.

RON: That's a good point, Terry, that many Bears say that they've had to come out twice: once as a gay or bi man and then again as a Bear.

TERRY: Before I knew what a Bear was, I knew I always liked the bigger, hairy linemen on my football team. Then the whole Bear concept encompassed what I liked, and I found a place where I fit in. So I agree, it was like a second coming out.

RON: Brian, I was really moved by the BearYouth site's section on accepting your looks. Did you write that?

BRIAN: Yes, I did. I want to write some more on the topic, too, but I think more needs to come from guys who have faced the issue firsthand. Being fat and hairy isn't something that I've dealt with, after all.

RON: Where did you find the inspiration to talk about self-acceptance so heartfelt?

BRIAN: I knew what kind of guys that I found attractive, and I really wanted those men to be able to accept themselves, too. My now-former boyfriend told me that he never thought that his hair was attractive or that he thought anyone would like him because he was a bit overweight. I proved him wrong.

HEATH: I totally know how he felt. Most of the guys who dug me did so because I was big and hairy, and that bothered me for a long time. I couldn't understand how anyone could like me and fixate positively on my size and fur factor.

RON: Did you feel that your admirers must have been really kind of fucked-up to like someone with those attributes?

HEATH: Yes, because I felt so unsexy. I thought they were sick, and I was projecting my self-loathing onto them.

TERRY: I never had a good self-image of myself, either.

BRIAN: I can't blame anyone for thinking that way about himself because it seems that it was even difficult just admitting that I could be attracted to someone who didn't fit into the stereotypical role of what is beautiful.

RON: I'd like to point out that you guys have reached a level of self-acceptance that some gay men of my generation (and older) are still struggling with. I'm a spunky, mature 41, by the way. :)

HEATH: Nothing wrong with that!

RON: Now, regarding older men, I want to clarify something that has become something of a stereotype about Bears from outside the Bear community. It's not that you're particularly *into* older guys, right? Are any of you looking for a daddy-son relationship?

TERRY: No. For me I like big guys, whether they are 20 or 40, it all depends on the guy.

HEATH: I'm just into guys, they take on all forms nowadays. :)

RON: Brian, are you attracted to older men or to men your own age—or does it matter?

BRIAN: I've always found older guys attractive, but at the same time I'm a bit uncomfortable dating anyone old enough to be my father. For me, being able to accept I was gay was difficult, but I knew I wouldn't be happy unless I was with someone I found attractive. On the same note, I also had to accept that what I found attractive wasn't what I saw in the mirror, but I still knew I was good-looking and I hoped that the guys I was interested in knew that too.

TERRY: I don't really understand the whole daddy-son thing. Nor do I understand the entire leather scene either. I find them both strange.

HEATH: It's just another subculture. No better nor worse than any other.

RON: Terry, I want to ask you about the GXB organization. It's highly structured in a way that many Bears object to. These men seem to feel that Bearness is about not having rules and bylaws and structure and politics.

TERRY: I think the Gen-X Bears structure is beneficial. The Bear movement started in the bars, and Gen-X Bears does not have events in bars. This is a new concept for many Bears to grasp—it takes a while for people to change their mindset of only going to the bar. The bylaws allow a group to be flexible, but are strict enough to be sure that the chapters follow why we exist: to be a social group for Bears in a comfortable environment. I never thought of Bears being nonstructured. My sense is that being a Bear is accepting yourself for who you are. On the other hand, any Bear group has got to be at least structured enough to coordinate having events in bars.

RON: But why hang the "Gen X" label on it—especially since you allow folks from all age groups? Doesn't that actually turn some older—and younger—guys away?

HEATH: True, but that all depends on whom you ask. The Bear movement seems to be taking on the characteristics of any other gay subculture and it kind of frightens me because I don't want that. I want it to remain about loving yourself and accepting others.

TERRY: I think that Gen X gets a younger crowd because I feel a lot of young guys have a bitter taste in their mouth from other Bear groups. We primarily have younger Bears, but in Boston, for example, guys in their forties come to events... Putting the Gen X label on the group lets people know that there are younger Bears out there. A lot of people who are not in the Bear community have this vision of all Bears being 40 or older.

HEATH: Except we are running into a problem there, aren't we, Terry?

TERRY: What is that?

HEATH: The title Gen X and the fact we are aging. Not too long from now, either the mission or the name will have to change.

BRIAN: I think it will be interesting to see what kind of change does happen because the whole gay movement is going through a lot of changes and that's having a wide range of effects. Gay youth are more open and more people are coming out because of previous generations pushing for equality. Nowadays, with more rights and freedom and acceptance, things are much different from even 10 years ago.

TERRY: I think being gay is more accepted, and it seems like everyone my age and younger deals with it just fine. My experience working at a large insurance company in Springfield was that if the topic of gayness came up, the older people seemed uncomfortable talking about it, but the younger people didn't have a problem.

HEATH: At least the Boomers get reminded of their imminent retirement when they see us.

RON: Before we launch into a tirade of boomer-bashing, I'd like to remind you that many of the liberties we all enjoy today are due to the efforts of our elders. One 25-year-old Bear I know complains that older Bears don't reach out in any kind of mentoring, but then he turns around and denies that Stonewall was any kind of milestone for gay men and lesbians.

BRIAN: I still know gay people who still feel like they can't come out and are ashamed of being gay and think they need to live a straight life. Sometimes you still have to step back and see that there's still a long way to go.

RON: Let's try to relate the coming-out experience nowadays back to Bears. I can imagine that gay-straight alliances in high schools today might even know about Bears and thus support Bearish or Bear-loving youths in the coming-out process.

HEATH: Sure. The gay-straight alliance thing is awesome. I was so proud to find out that my town, the fag-bashing capital of eastern Massachusetts, has one. I couldn't even imagine it when I was in high school, and two years after I graduated, it all changed.

TERRY: When I was in college in Springfield, I went to the gay and lesbian group on campus. I was the only Bear and I felt very out of place.

HEATH: I was in chorus in high school. They had to suspect, but then again, I always had girlfriends. What did they used to call them in the early '60s? Beards?

RON: Right. But that might be different from when you were exploring relationships with girls.

TERRY: In high school I played football and wrestled (and even was captain of the wrestling team) during my senior year. I was too afraid to come out, though. The summer after my graduation is when my high school friends found out, and they were surprised. I was glad to break all the classic stereotypes.

HEATH: Many of us may look butch because of our size and furriness, and a general lumberjack-ness, but inside lurks a big old show-chorus boy or Broadway baby.

RON: Of course, Heath, but some of us actually are butch.

HEATH: Yeah, but it's not a requirement, and it shouldn't be. That's what I love about the Gen-X Bears. We're all different. We accept each other and ourselves for the most part, because of that difference.

RON: Agreed. Briefly, Heath, I want to ask you about the reaction that you received when you won the International Mr. Bear title.

HEATH: It was mostly good, at least to my face. However, the ripples are coming back to me now and it's kind of disturbing.

RON: What do you mean by "ripples"—negative comments?

HEATH: First off, and mainly, my age. People don't seem to think I deserve the title because I'm so young, which I think is ridiculous. I love myself for who I am, and I think I'm a damn fine Bear.

RON: They say you're too young to represent the title?

HEATH: Yes, many thought I should have been Mr. Cub or nothing at all. I think my age is a good thing for the title—it kills some stereotypes. If people feel threatened, then I'll do what I can to help them not feel that way. It might help younger Bears move deeper into the fold.

RON: What do you see ahead for GXB and BearYouth?

TERRY: I think GXB will grow with age, and the ages of its members will primarily be in the Gen X years. I do see a need for a future Bear group to fill in the ever-increasing void between Gen-X Bears and BearYouth.

RON: Brian, are you ready to take the reins of leading the new, younger breed of Bears? Actually you've already done so, in a way.

BRIAN: Bears and the Bear community are one of those vague things. I know that people do like groups, and so I'm sure new ones will always be emerging. What my part may be in that, I'm not certain.

RON: Do you see yourself turning BearYouth over to someone else at some point?

BRIAN: I definitely do want to do that at some point, because I feel that a youth site, like any sort of youth group, should be run by youths.

HEATH: I think with the Gen-X Bears aging so, the Bear movement in general will become less about age and more about how a group identifies with themselves, their bodies, and what they like in others—as originally intended by the Boomers who got the movement rolling in high gear. And to the Boomers, we owe a world of gratitude and debt for making the world safer and more palatable for us to live in as young gay men and Bears.

RON: Heath, thank you for that statement of appreciation, although I can't say we were thinking of that when we were doing all them Bear-type things in San Francisco in the late '80s.

HEATH: I mean it. I wasn't just being cheesy. :)

RON: I want to say in return that I think you're all very brave and wonderful men, doing pioneering work in your own ways.

TERRY: Here is a quick question for our moderator: Were you surprised about Gen-X Bears and BearYouth being formed? When I talk to people about Gen-X Bears, sometimes I get a response from older Bears, "Why would there ever be a need for that?"

RON: I think I was a bit taken aback initially. At first, I felt it was just more divisiveness—but that was before I understood its purpose.

HEATH: Yeah, some think we are ageist and elitist when in reality we are just responding to ageism against us by joining Gen-X Bears.

BRIAN: The fact that so many older Bears have told me that they wished they had had a resource like BearYouth available to them when they were younger certainly tells me that what I'm doing with the site is the right thing.

RON: God, if there had been something around like BearYouth when I was in high school, I might not have tried to commit suicide then.

TERRY: Yes, I agree about BearYouth. Even five years ago when I came out, nothing for Bear youths or Gen-X Bears existed. It could have definitely helped me. That's why I'm so involved in Gen-X Bears—because I know it has helped others.

HEATH: Me too.

RON: Well, guys, we should wrap up. Any last words?

HEATH: Love yourself and others, and then you'll know true happiness. And don't wear white after Labor Day.

Part Six

Bears and Beyond

CHAPTER 22
LESBEARS AND TRANSBEARS: DYKES AND FTMS AS BEARS ~ A DISCUSSION WITH SHARON BERGMAN, DREW CAMPBELL, MICHAEL "MIKE" HERNANDEZ, AND MATT RICE ~

SHARON JILL BEAR BERGMAN is a wild-hearted, genderfucking butchgrrl from Northampton, Mass., where she was expensively overeducated and now lives with her wife, a woman of extraordinary talents and surpassing beauty. Bear (as she's called) is a contributing writer to lesbianation.com and music.com, the owner of doesitquack.com (a queer jaunt in the world of words), and a poet. Also employed as a writer and editor, she revels in taking breaks from wordsmithing at the ocean and being with her wonderful friends. Bergman's uncle is the gay Bear poet David Bergman (see chapter 3), and this is causing her to rethink some of her positions on the influence of genetics.

DREW CAMPBELL was born in New York and educated at Bennington College, the University of Hamburg, and Washington University, St. Louis. He began gender transition from female to male in December 1995, and has since spoken about gender at colleges and social groups across the country. Drew is the pseudonymous author of several bestselling books on erotic dominance and submission, and has published a book on alternative sexual etiquette, *The Bride Wore Black Leather...and He Looked Fabulous: An Etiquette Guide for the Rest of Us*. He is the co-editor, with Pat Califia, of the anthology *Bitch Goddess: The Spiritual Path of the Dominant Woman*. He lives in San Francisco with his wife, Anne, and is currently studying for ordination as a pagan priest.

MICHAEL "MIKE" HERNANDEZ is a rather twisted, gender-variant imp who, at age three, emigrated from Cuba to the United States with his family. Mike is a public speaker on gender, sex, and sexuality. Writing credits include a sex column in the *FTM Newsletter* and at www.koan.com/~Lbear, "The Art of Cruising Men" in *Forge* (May 2000), and contributions in *The Academy: Tales of the Marketplace, Transliberation: Beyond Pink And Blue, Looking Queer, Dagger: On Butch Women,* and *The Second Coming.* He also appears in *Transmen & FTMs: Identities, Bodies, Genders & Sexualities.* Mike has a penchant for Bears (particularly polar Bears) and fishnet stockings, but definitely prefers to keep these separate. He currently resides in the high desert of Southern California with his partner of eight years, Sky Renfro.

MATT RICE is an activist and educator for queer health and transgender issues. Born and raised a girl in rural Ohio, he went to college in West Virginia and lived in Chicago before ending up in San Francisco and transitioning to the guy he is now. He worked on an HIV prevalence study of trans communities for the San Francisco Transgender Community Health Project. He has worked to increase visibility of FTMs from behind the bar at the Lone Star Saloon for five years, and by teaching at Harvey Milk Institute. He has conducted numerous magazine, newspaper, film, and video interviews, including two pieces by the BBC and two by Annette Kennerly shown in queer film festivals. His photograph is in Loren Cameron's book, *Body Alchemy.* His boyfriend is the author, therapist, and activist Pat Califia. Matt created a huge scandal by getting pregnant and then giving birth to Blake in October 1999. Currently Matt lives in San Francisco with Patrick and Blake and their pets and works as a computer geek by trade. He's pagan and a great flirt.

It is said that one can tell everything about a society by examining the persons at its margins. Perhaps the persons most marginalized in the Bear community are queer Bears who are not born male, that is, FTMs (female to male transpersons, or transmen), and lesbians (or "les-bruins," as Ray Kampf puts it).

Where Bears gather, whether informally or organizationally, whether online or in the flesh and fur, the conspicuous absence of women creates an idyllic, naughtily clandestine boys' tree house club—not unlike the cartoon characters Calvin and Hobbes's strictly-for-two GROSS (Get Rid Of Slimy girlS). In the discussion for this book with Michael Bronski and David Bergman (see chapter 3), Bronski characterized the history of this urge for a separate Bear space as "troubled."

While considering the idea of women Bears as a topic for this book—although I knew there had to be some out there somewhere—David Bergman suggested I contact his niece Sharon, to whom David had earlier introduced me briefly at an OutWrite conference. Sharon had further suggestions as to another woman and several transmen who considered themselves Bears. Although the other female Bear never materialized, from there the rest of the panel tumbled into place.

The month after this online panel discussion was conducted, I was asked to judge the Transgender category for the 1999 Lambda Literary Awards. That same month, at a discussion on "Bear Self-esteem" conducted by Craig Byrnes held at International Bear Rendezvous 2000, I found myself sitting next to panelist Mike Hernandez! It was amazing to watch the faces of the men in the group when Mike disclosed his "transness"—eyes agog, jaws agape, one could almost see an invisible line being drawn around Mike as "not one of us." In that moment, I knew this discussion was vital to the book.

RON: Because we have on this panel a whole spectrum of gender identities and body types, it would be helpful to our readers to understand where each of you is coming from. Please state in your own terms just a bit about your gender, body, and sexual status, past and present. Sharon, let's start with you, if you don't mind.

SHARON: OK. Gender: Well, I mostly identify as a butch, lots of boy streaks. Body: all the original girl parts, no hormones, a few tattoos. I'm about 5'9", 265, fairly furry. Sexual status? Can I get a skish of clarification on what that means?

RON: Affectional preference? Whatever you'd like to say about where you like to put your body.

SHARON: *laughing* OK—I'm married to a wild-hearted, genius, pervert femme; when I mess around otherwise, I generally am attracted to boy-dykes, butches, and transguys who are bottoms or interested in bottoming.

DREW: Gender: FTM-transman. Body: large (300 pounds) and furry, tattooed, used to have several piercings. No surgeries at this point. I lived for about 12 years in the dyke world, have had partners of many genders and orientations, now usually refer to myself as "pansexual," for lack of a better term. Gender isn't the first thing I use to determine attraction (or falling in love, for that matter). I'm married to a queer femme GG (genetic girl, though we haven't had her chromosomes checked lately! *G*). We're monogamous at present.

RON: GG—what a great term!

MIKE: Gender: transman. Sex: both/neither. Body: 5-foot-3, 155, very very very furry, tattooed, pierced ears and septum. I have had chest surgery. Sexual orientation: queer. I have small but talented hands that help cross the gender divide. I'm in an open relationship and I guess that eight years counts as long-term these days. That's about it.

MATT: Gender: FTM. Started hormones in 1993, had a bilateral mastectomy in 1996, transitioned while working at the Lone Star. I have always been attracted to men who are now considered Bears, starting when I was about 15. When I was living as a dyke, before transition, I dated women you could consider Bears. Well, they were certainly more butch than many of the boys at the Lone Star. But yeah, I'm a fag who likes Bears, though I'm not skinny and I'm furry, and I look too young to be a Bear, or so I'm told. I don't identify as a cub, but think guys who do are usually pretty cute in their own right. I do lots of things I'm not supposed to do, like sleep with girls, and date other younger looking guys as well as Bears, and I'm not deeply in the closet about being an FTM, so that makes getting dates tougher.

RON: Thanks for those great descriptions. Sharon, to what extent do you now consider, or have considered yourself, a Bear?

SHARON: I identify with the Bear community pretty strongly in terms of its physicality and also its ethic. I picked up the nickname "Bear" long before I knew about the Bear community, picked it up repeatedly, in fact, during a very happy sort of confluence sometime around 1992 or '93. I don't really go to Bear events, because none of the Bear communities near me have any interest in your less traditional Bears—but I wish that I could attend them.

RON: Drew, do you also identify as a Bear?

DREW: It's a label I do use pretty frequently within the queer community, mostly as a shorthand way to refer to my body type and take on masculinity. I did use the term before my transition. Actually, it was more applied to me by other leatherdykes, before I even really knew about the male Bear community. I liked the image of being both strong and playful. The other female bears I knew were also freer with their physical affections in the sense that they would roughhouse and give back rubs, and generally touch more than other women. That's something I've found I have in common with guys, too, and I like that aspect of Beardom.

RON: That's considered unusual for leatherdykes?

DREW: It definitely was in the crowd I was hanging with at the time. They have a very "untouchable" style—lots of big boots and studs, that sort of thing.

MIKE: The touching aspect brings up a significant difference between the men's community and the women's community (for lack of better terms). Women have space boundaries.

MATT: Yes, I really noticed that when I transitioned, too.

MIKE: You can't just go up and grab a woman's ass. Men are far freer with touching, particularly in the still-cruising phase.

RON: The male Bear set isn't known for its restraint. In fact, there's a "grope factor" thing as part of the Bear Code that some guys use as shorthand to identify themselves.

MATT: Yeah, my experience was that the more I passed while working at the Lone Star, the more I got groped, and often in ways that made me uncomfortable—especially before my chest surgery. I had lots of funny experiences with guys grabbing here or there and not getting what they expected.

RON: What was that like?

MATT: It was exceptionally difficult until I had chest surgery. Guys were always saying, "Hey, he's got tits," to which I once responded, "Can you tell I'm white too?"

DREW: *snap snap* [cyber for "you go, guy!"]

MATT: So I ended up putting more physical distance around myself until after my chest surgery and that was often read as my being unfriendly.

MIKE: My experience was different from Matt's. I got my chest touched before surgery, and based on the amount of facial hair that I had (full beard), the equation did not compute. Once guys could lay a hand on my chest and not have me flinch, back away, or run off, I was able to socially gain a level of intimacy with the other guys that I hadn't had before. At that point, no one said a word about tits.

DREW: See, there's the difference: I sometimes get appreciative comments on the street about mine. They're not very large to start with, and since I'm so heavy, they fit.

MATT: Guys often reminded me I was FTM while working at the Lone Star. The only time I was ever seriously physically assaulted there (by a patron and not in a nice way) was amid a flurry of "I don't have to listen to you because you're just a woman and no God-damned woman is going to tell me what to do. No amount of testosterone will ever make you a real man..."—that kind of crap.

MIKE: Sharon—what has been your experience?

SHARON: Well, I have a different experience partly because of where I live. I don't really present as a guy to fags or Bear men, so any who are close enough to touch my chest know what they're going to get. The most attention my chest gets is because of the tattoo I have on it—a Zuni-style bear.

MIKE: What about Bear (wo)men?

SHARON: We're sort of short on them out here, unfortunately.

RON: But when you travel?

SHARON: Beargrrl admirers seem pleased. They (meaning Bear (wo)men) like that I'm strong, broad in the shoulders and deep in the chest—tits generally not an issue, except to hang onto. *G*

RON: Is "Beargrrl admirers" a particular type, like chubby chasers? Or Bear lovers?

SHARON: Seems to be. Or, at least I perceive a certain class of attentions that way.

RON: Interesting. I'd like to ask about the Bear archetype, and how you might relate to it. *The Encyclopedia of Archetypal Imagery* comments, "The female bear raises her offspring alone, and she is considered by primal peoples generally to be the ideal mother. Hence she has come to represent the kind of maternity that is both independent and fiercely protective of her young." Do you relate to these aspects of Beardom, Sharon?

SHARON: That's how I originally picked up the nickname "Bear"— from being perceived as being very protective of my loved ones. It started out as Mother Bear and then got shortened. I strongly identify with that image of Bear, and in some ways I have organized my life in that way. I have "sons," boys who are in need of a type of love and care that is neither traditionally feminine, in the "Mom makes it better" way, nor masculine, in the "Father know best" way, but a hearty blend. Currently my brood includes a princess fag, a sturdy little boy dyke, and three big, strapping straight athletes. It's a happy life.

RON: Sounds like a happy family. Matt, let's continue with you here.

MATT: Do I relate to the bear archetype from the female aspect? No. I'm not saying I'm not independent and fiercely protective of my off-spring, but my introduction to Bear stuff was through meeting Steve Stafford [Lone Star Saloon coworker and managing editor of *Bear* magazine] at International Mr Leather in Chicago in the early '90s. He presented Bears to me as a group of guys who were different from other gay men, not puffed-up Calvin Klein model body wannabes. Bears were more accepting of difference and understanding of the fact that men grow older (God willing), and that as we grow older, our bodies change and are still desirable. Steve conveyed to me that as Bears we could be masculine and still queer and that I was pervy in some of the same ways, being a very butch little dyke, and therefore welcome. Moreover, as my identity changed, and I transitioned, I found many guys still accepting of me and willing to make the transition to seeing me as potential bed mate.

MIKE: Steve Stafford—that's a name that I haven't heard in a long time. What an incredibly wonderful and accepting man he was. I was socialized as a guy by Bears, and I think that's a great thing.

MATT: Yeah, he really made me feel great. He was brilliant.

RON: Steve used his incredible creative talent to produce masculine art, and it was fantastic to work with him on projects at the Lone Star. But Drew, how do you relate to the bear archetype?

DREW: Well, in one of the religious traditions that I'm a part of, Druidry, the bear is associated with protectiveness and also with sovereignty (as in King Arthur, whose name derives from a word for *bear*). I don't necessarily see those as gendered concepts per se, but I do identify strongly with them. Sovereignty for me is self-mastery, endurance, making it through the winter, if you will.

RON: HiBearnation?

DREW: Indeed! Knowing when to withdraw and rely on one's resources, and when to come forward and act. I think those are skills needed of all parents, not just mothers—and perhaps all people, on some level.

MIKE: I definitely do not identify with the motherly, maternal, or female bear archetype in the slightest. Independent—absolutely! I think that one of the reasons that my relationship works is that we allow each other the space for exploration, peace of mind, and the like. I can also be overly protective of close friends, but try to keep an open mind and not growl at everyone that I disagree with.

RON: Let's look now at the physical or emotional aspects of male-born Bears. Maybe we can call them (us) "bioBears"?

MIKE: Nontrans Bears.

RON: Sharon, what do you find attractive about Bears? Also, what turns you off?

SHARON: I'm attracted to snuggliness and cuddliness, to bigness which has strength to it, and to the playful but careful sexuality of many Bears. The big turn-offs for me are: A Bear who takes himself and his big studly masculinity way too seriously, and those I meet from time to time who seem to have been poorly socialized and so went and hid behind the Bear community to try and excuse a certain roughness with people's feelings and bodies.

DREW: I'm very attracted to large people of all genders, and body fur is also a turn-on for me. I like to know I can tumble around with someone and not hurt them accidentally. (Now, on purpose is another story! *EG*)

As to turn-offs: I've sometimes seen guys fall into an oddly familiar looks-centeredness. Instead of shaved and buff, it's "the perfect pelt" or "the ultimate gut." I'd much rather see us all just accept our bodies for what they are, no more and no less. And I really appreciate it when I see that kind of acceptance from other Bears.

MATT: I have always been attracted to bigger guys. I had a crush on Grizzly Adams as a kid (I wanted to be his bear—go figure!) I've been fortunate enough to meet several guys, who though they socialize in the Bear scene, don't fall into the 12-year-old, two-dimensional concept of masculinity that many Bears do. I remember when *Bear* magazine used to be about "masculinity without the trappings" instead of nothing but the trappings. I think the shallow "manlier than thou" thing is *très* tired. Still, I've met guys who aren't like that, who can see me as the guy I am, and hold in contrast the rest of me, and who can maintain their queer identity and still let themselves be butch (or not so butch) in ways that make them comfortable. Most of the Bears I've known have been butch-looking but not butch-acting.

MIKE: I've had a thing for facial hair as long as I can remember. There's nothing like rubbing fur, but the biggest turn-on is the eyes. There has to be a twinkle of mischief in them—that and a nice smile will definitely catch my attention. Recently I have discovered this thing for polar Bears. I like some snow on top.

SHARON: Very playful creatures.

MIKE: They'll wear you out if you don't take your vitamins! So, as for turn-ons: fur, tattoos, nice smile, playfulness, impishness, open mind. Turn offs: A-T-T-I-T-U-D-E: check the hat size at the door, buddy.

RON: Regarding this "butch bitch" thing: Why is it, do you suppose, that there's an abundance of pretentious hypermasculinity among Bears?

DREW: I have never understood the desire to look as much as possible like the people who beat you up in high school. I see it primarily in the more mainstream gay world (if there is such a thing), but Bears aren't always immune to it either.

SHARON: Is it done to avoid getting beat up?

MIKE: I view hypermasculinity as a form of overcompensation. Then again, what I might view as hypermasculine will be viewed differently by someone else.

DREW: If people are playing with it, that's one thing: it can be drag, in effect. But when there's no humor—feh.

RON: Some would say that Bears incorporate aspects of traditional maleness with softer, more traditionally feminine aspects. Agree or disagree, and why? How successful do you feel most Bears are at blending genders, sexes, and sexualities?

SHARON: Well, I agree and disagree. The Bears I like and trust are the ones who are more successful at it. They don't try to perform maleness in a way that makes me so crazed and also sad.

RON: Can you describe for us more exactly that manner of performing masculinity?

SHARON: I feel that men, gay or straight, who get locked into a certain portrayal of the masculine, become melancholic about all of the gendered things that they can't show. That is, they grieve, but since their socialization will allow anger as the only acceptable emotion they can demonstrate, the sadness and fear presents as anger and it's very scary. Bears who give themselves permission to be something other than archetypes of masculinity are wonderful—very fun, gentle, and strong.

RON: Very nicely put, Sharon.

SHARON: Perhaps a little theory intensive, but not so bad.

MIKE: Although I'm reluctant to assign behavior to gender, I think the Bears that I've interacted with are fairly successful at it. They have a certain sense of comfort in themselves, the ability to smile in the face of adversity, and this gentleness about them. That's what I mean by a good blend.

DREW: I'd have to second what Mike just said.

MATT: I think some of the Bears I've known at the Lone Star have been able to be sensitive and such, but as years went by, and Rick Redewill died, and the Lone Star changed hands, an understandable change in clientele occurred. I think now, instead of working-class guys, who are flexible in manners of sex, sexuality, gender, body type, and so on, there is a propensity of guys who dress working-class to get tricks, and are just as rigid about their masculinity as any teenage boy. And the guys who are more flexible are harder to find. It's become just another flavor of clone in many ways.

MATT: It used to be that guys who wore flannel were making an anti–queer establishment statement. Now you get ridiculed if you don't show up in exactly the "right" outfit.

DREW: If being a Bear becomes another way to look down on people who don't live up to some grand standard of gay pulchritude, we're missing the point. Which is why I wear penny loafers to leather events! Brown penny loafers, no less! ;-)

MATT: I don't have to wear the uniform, I actually do SM.

[At this point, Drew had to leave the chat.]

MIKE: Nonetheless, I have found greater flexibility and acceptance in the Bear community than in some other places.

MATT: As have I.

RON: Why is that?

MATT: Maybe because I'm attracted to Bears and haven't been chasing anyone else?

MIKE: Perhaps it's having dealt with rejection from the muscle-gym crowd that allows some Bears to keep an open mind. Perhaps Bears do achieve a balance between traditional gender roles and behaviors. Or maybe I've just come across the right Bears.

SHARON: I think that partly you have, Mike, and partly that once a person operates on a certain number of levels of queer—i.e., gay, not traditionally or stereotypically gay, perhaps into BDSM or what have you, that certain pack behaviors get more intensified. If you can prove that your will and the will of the group are not at cross purposes, they'll let you join without much problem, partly because it's a survival mechanism.

RON: A group survival mechanism that ideally benefits the individual. Perhaps it would help if Bears would remember their humble roots, when they were rejected by both straight and gay cultures.

MATT: That too. I've experienced both complete acceptance from Bears and complete rejection.

MIKE: Outlaws of the world, unite!

RON: Is the Trans community the only outlaw group left?

MATT: Nope, they're certainly not immune to the same stuff.

RON: I forgot—there's always pedophiles.

MIKE: Hell, no. It's the trans-fag-leather Bears who are some of the last outlaws. The trans community certainly has its components of xenophobia and conservatism. The "you're only a real trans if (fill in the blank)."

MATT: And I'm like Public Enemy number 1 to them.

MIKE: Yes, Matthew, I understand that there is a bounty out on you. Frankly, I'm waiting for the bucks to go up.

RON: *chuckling* OK, redirect here. I want to ask about the notion of Bears passing, and how you might relate as transpersons or (for Sharon) a butch.

MIKE: What do you mean?

RON: In Jason Cromwell's *Transmen & FTMs*, there's a passage about stigmatization: "Stigma is used to refer to an attribute which is deeply discrediting." Cromwell goes on to identify stigmas such as handicaps, class, education, and race, in addition to sexual and gender identity. It strikes me that Bears' physicality, their hairy, bearded, overweight body selves, are also discredited—certainly not to the same extent as transpeople, but nonetheless quite stigmatized.

In other words, if stigma forces those it stigmatizes into having to pass, to what extent do you think that Bearness might be about gay men passing as straight to avoid such stigmatization and that of being gay?

MATT: To some extent, but it depends: Are they butch, or just butch-looking? Nelly Bears have a harder time.

MIKE: Bears are certainly stigmatized by the mainstream as well as the gay community. Now, as for passing, the mirror arguments have been made regarding lipstick lesbians and the dyke community. I don't see Bears passing as straight at all to avoid being stigmatized.

MATT: Oh, I've seen that. The straight-looking, straight-acting (read: homophobic) types.

RON: "Don't call me gay just because I'm into guys."

MIKE: Then again, I was accused of transitioning in order to make my dating women an acceptable thing, that is, until I started dating men—so I might now be hypersensitive to the "passing" issue. Still, it's one thing to look like you might be straight and quite another to be in the closet.

RON: Mike, care to elaborate?

MIKE: I find that there's a significant difference between being yourself and being perceived as straight by others, and actually creating a fictionalized life in order to pass as straight. The Bears that I have observed are just being themselves. No pretense about masculinity or desire. Now watch you prove me wrong at International Bear Rendezvous.

RON: I might try just for the hell of it. ;-) Sharon, how do you weigh in on the issue of passing?

SHARON: As someone who can almost always choose what attribution I want, if I care to influence it, I see this a little differently, maybe. Obviously I'm not a fan of the straight-acting, straight-appearing fascists either—that business makes me sick. Yet at the same time I have certainly experienced a number of occasions in my life where it was a long mile safer to make sure I got a male attribution than to be viewed as ambiguous, gender-wise. I can see where some men, seeing the safety of not being perceived as a freak, might sort of cling to that, if they can. For me, it just wasn't in my nature—I couldn't become a femme girl (at least not believably), although I have discovered that I can pass for a guy if I need to, and I do—without hesitation. My peers viewed that as being outlaw behavior rather than assimilationist behavior, but that's only because I have a cunt. If I had a cock instead, and I butched it up for safety, it would be perceived as cowardly, I think.

RON: A secondary, not primary, reason that many Bear-type men find refuge in looking Bearish is that it's relatively nonthreatening to straight men who would otherwise find effeminate gay men repugnant. Yet I wonder if Bears seem, in some situations, threatening to queers who despise straight men. How do you feel that Bears and the Bear subculture are viewed by the rest of GLBTQ culture?

SHARON: That's not something I really know about. Not having seen it from the inside, I don't feel qualified to comment.

MIKE: It's hard to tell from the inside looking out. I do know that the Trans community is fairly ignorant about Bear culture, except for those who came from the leather community or who identify as queer in some way, shape, or form.

MATT: I think that Bears have created a space that was, before the late '80s, early '90s, unheard of. It's a space that allows men to partake of a different aesthetic, jointly of masculinity, affection, and class. I mean class in an economic sense; originally, Bears were very accepting of working-class men, as opposed to the more current upwardly mobile dot-comers who want to look working class on the weekends while they talk about their houses and Home Depot accounts. Anyway, I think in many ways, it wasn't OK to be fat, have back hair, eat butter, and be queer until Rick and those guys (may they rest in peace) started up that bar on Howard Street.

MIKE: I agree with Matt about the creation of new space, which was about finding acceptance in just being who you are.

MATT: I watched the changes from behind the bar. It went from a place where guys were basically of the Steve Stafford school of, "Who cares if you're a tranny? You're cute, you do your job, and I like you," to a litany of "If you were a real boy..."

RON: Did Bears' example of self-body acceptance help the trans community in any way?

MIKE: No—the trans community is still very tense about body issues on the whole. There are changes in recent years with more people coming into the Trans community who don't have as many issues about their bodies—or at least if they do have issues, they aren't practicing celibacy.

RON: Younger trans queers?

MIKE: Some are, some aren't.

MATT: Body shame is pervasive.

MIKE: I know that when the transmen started coming from the leather community, things started to get a little more sex-positive. Things are certainly getting a lot more sexual between transmen.

MATT: Thankfully!

SHARON: Partly, perhaps, because the defining characteristic for leatherfolk is behavioral rather than appearance related?

RON: That seems a good assessment of the dynamic, Sharon.

MIKE: And with the conferences that have taken place, folks have opened up about queerness, bisexuality, and pleasure in general. It's been enlightening and has fostered the beginnings of something like what the Bear community was at the outset.

MATT: Some straight FTMs were pretty unhappy that there were queer transpeople at the first San Francisco FTM conference of the Americas in 1995. There were a lot of people griping about there being too many queers. They were real men, you know.

RON: Well, that sort of exclusion sounds awfully familiar. So there seems to be a lot of common ground between the Bear and transmen communities.

MATT: Sure—if not Bears, then gay men who exemplify some of the qualities we admire of Bears. In common I see a bunch of guys who were out as being trans and queer, who just lived their lives, who were honest about what was going on with them, who didn't hide, and who allowed other guys to see what they were doing was an option.

Chapter 23
Technobears and Cybearspace
~ A Discussion With Steve Dyer, Jeff Glover, Mike Ramsey, and Alex Schell ~

STEVE DYER has played a role since the early 1980s in the formation of electronic communities for lesbians and gay men. In 1983, in the
early days of the Internet, he successfully argued for and created the first
Usenet newsgroup for the discussion of gay issues, now known as
soc.motss. In 1988, with Brian Gollum, he started an electronic mail
digest for the then-nascent electronic Bear community known as the
Bears Mailing List, or BML, which was distributed over the Internet and
other electronic mail systems. He handed over responsibility for the
digest in late 1994 and gave an interview about the BML for *The Bear
Book*. Steve has served on the Board of Directors for Boston's *Gay
Community News* and on the steering committee of the New England
Bears. He and his partner, Tony, live in Cambridge, Massachusetts.

JEFF GLOVER grew up in a large Baptist family on a big dairy farm
in a small town in Wisconsin. After high school, he tried college but
hated it and quit before the semester was out. Then in February 1986 at
the Cloud Nine bar in Minneapolis, he met his first partner. In 1987,
after subscribing to *Bear* magazine, Jeff was chatting with other Bears on
the local Internet bulletin board services (BBS). Eventually the group
organized gatherings, becoming the precursor to their local Bearclub,
"The North Country Bears." He and his husbear, Philip, moved in 1998
from Minneapolis, where they had met in 1986, to San Francisco, where

Jeff now works as a Webmaster.

MIKE RAMSEY received his Ph.D. in 1996 from Arizona State University, and worked as a Visiting Professor there from 1996 to 2000. In May 2000 he relocated to the University of Pittsburgh to take a tenure-track Assistant Professor position in the Department of Geology. Having an extensive computer background and online experience for more than 15 years, he has seen the beginning and explosive growth of the online Bear presence. Mike is a founding member of the Phoenix Bears and a member of the Northwest Bears, Burgh Bears, and the Human Rights Campaign. Since 1996, Mike has served as volunteer coordinator for the Resources for Bears (RFB) Web site (www.resources-forbears.com). His essay, "The Bear Clan: North American Totemic Mythology, Belief, and Legend," appeared in *The Bear Book*. Mike has also contributed to *American Bear* magazine and served twice as a judge for the International Mr. Bear contest at International Bear Rendezvous.

ALEX SCHELL grew up in the Pocono Mountains of Pennsylvania, where he attended Pennsylvania State University. He has lived for the past 20 years in New York City, where he works as a caterer and free-lance culinary writer. In October 1998, after one of the moderators stepped down from his duties at the Bears Mailing List, Alex joined as moderator-administrator. When not busy moderating the BML, Alex enjoys music, reading sci-fi, flea markets, and cuddling with his two ferrets, Barnabus and Akira.

In the cybearspace section of Les Wright's essay, "A Concise History of Self-Identifying Bears," as well as in separate pieces on the Bears Mailing List and the Bear Code also published in *The Bear Book*, the connection between Bears and high technology is firmly established. Curious readers may examine a detailed history and analysis of the Bear-tech connection there.

It's hard to imagine how the Bear phenomenon would have evolved sans the happy coincidence of two techno-savvy Bears being at the fore-front of the gay Internet discussion group called soc.motss ("motss" was coded to mean "members of the same sex.") Speculation may be fruitless at this point, but although the phenomenon would surely have continued otherwise, it seems unlikely to have spread across North America and around the world so fast so quickly. And this trend continues to this day: As the final chapter in this book will show, many Bearclubs abroad seem to have sprung up from affinity groups on the Internet.

When GLBTQ historians at the end of the 21st century look back at the Bear subculture, I suspect that they will note its significance as one of the queer subcultures to emerge and spread worldwide (along with AIDS) almost simultaneously with the advent of home computing and the rise of World Wide Web.

One of the aspects of Beardom that some men find particularly cultish is its use of such specialized terms—further codified into a mass of letter-number combinations (e.g., b6 = "very full beard")—which is sometimes hardly more intelligible than techno-babble. It's interesting to note that much of the grammbear, or Bear grammar, if you will, meaning the linguistic innovations incorporating such words as *Bear* and *cub* derived from online use, *cybearspace* and *technobears* being among the first of this vo-cub-ulary that I ever heard.

At present, the fact that Bears have used high-tech tools to further the development of their Bear connections appears obvious. Nonetheless, to explore more of the interpersonal dynamics of Bears' presence online, I enlisted the help of four men at the forefront of cybearspace. Oddly enough, our first attempt to hold this chat online was foiled by telephone-line repair work on one man's home phone hook-up, which was perhaps a humbling reminder to us all that the technology is far from perfect.

RON: Steve, let's start with you. How long have you identified as a Bear or with the Bear phenomenon?

STEVE: I've been Bear-identified for a long time. Even in the early '80s there were U.S. Postal Service mailing lists for guys who called themselves "Bears." I heard about *Bear* magazine shortly after it came out, and then formed the Bears Mailing List in the summer of '88 with BrigG—Brian Gollum (now of Pittsburgh, then from San Francisco).

RON: Much of your genesis into online Beardom is covered in the interview you did for *The Bear Book*. Jeff?

JEFF: Considering that I wasn't genetically predisposed to being a Bear ("Hey, look—I'm furry! These people love me—they really love me!") I'd say I relate more in the spiritual and sexual level. My involvement has been on the same level of just about any community. If you contribute positively and participate, you are generally accepted into that community. I've identified since the late 1980s when I discovered *Bear* magazine. Since then it's been the BBSs, the Bears Mailing List, the Internet, and most recently the San Francisco Bear Scene. It's a community I am proud to be part of.

RON: Have you always favored Bear-type men?

JEFF: Yup. My first partner, whom I met when I was 19, was a furry Bear. Always liked 'em, even before there was a moniker for 'em!

STEVE: Always always always always.

RON: Mike, how about you?

MIKE: I guess I relate to being a Bear in the simplest sense of loving masculine men and facial hair. I enjoy the friendship and, in most cases, the lack of attitude. I started to identify with Bears after I moved to Arizona in 1990 and got online in a serious way. That's when I found the original Bears Mailing List [BML] and soon thereafter, *Bear* magazine. But I really "found" Bears at my first International Bear Rendezvous.

RON: Last but not least, Alex.

ALEX: Well, since the dawning of my sexuality I have been very attracted to what we are calling the "Bear type." It soon became clear that that's where my body type was headed too, so that endowed me with fairly good self-esteem: It can't be bad to look like what you are attracted to, right? I discovered the Bear movement in the early '90s when I became active on the Internet. The Bear scene in New York is not as well organized as I'd like it to be, but I suppose a lot of that has to do with the pace of life here in the Big Apple.

RON: Very good. I'd consider the BML to be the grandpappy of online Beardom. Steve, how has the BML changed over time?

STEVE: There wasn't anything on the Internet when we formed the BML. Of course, there were BBS systems that were Bear-related well before the BML was founded, such as PC Bear's Lair in San Mateo and in the Bay area. I haven't read the BML in several years, so I can't comment too much on its recent incarnation.

RON: Alex, in your opinion, how has the BML evolved, for better and worse? How has it influenced other online Bear activity?

ALEX: I've been a longtime reader of the BML, way before I became moderator. The main change that I've seen is that there seems to be a much more heated exchange of ideas in recent years. Part of that I attribute to the fact that the Internet has been flooded with so many new users in the last five years—what we had taken as standard "Netiquette" [Net etiquette, or courtesy among Internet users while interacting online] has gone by the wayside. The other part of it I attribute to how closely some people have taken the Bear movement to heart.

JEFF: These new users are not as techno-savvy as us old-timers, which I think impacts some of these etiquette issues.

MIKE: Jeff, that still doesn't excuse it. We were all newbies once. As I mentioned earlier, I credit the BML with my discovery of Bears. I read it for many years after that. However, the threads do tend to recycle a lot as new folks join the list. As Resources For Bears started to take up more and more of my time, I left the BML behind and have not been on the list for a few years.

RON: Alex, approximately how many subscribers are there on the BML now?

ALEX: Last time I checked, the number was near 3,000.

RON: That number seems huge to me. How does that compare with other such lists, in or out of gay life?

ALEX: I'm certain that the BML is the largest and one of the oldest lists hosted by queernet.com.

JEFF: Considering that there's a huge turnover on the list, it's actually a very big number.

ALEX: The BML is high volume. Receiving a digest or two every day in their mailbox turns off some people.

JEFF: There are those who have the patience to wade though lots of muck to find the gold, and those who don't have the patience and give up trying.

MIKE: Another factor contributing to the BML's growth is that more Bears internationally are discovering the BML.

ALEX: On the other hand, there's a huge base that has subscribed for years and years.

JEFF: And unlike those newbies who don't understand the medium, these old timers understand the dynamics that drive the BML much better. I agree with Alex, too, in that many Bears see the BML as only a social resource. For many Bears, it serves a specific purpose—to introduce them to their Bear social circles. After that's accomplished, they don't need it as a tool anymore.

RON: See how Bears are with technology? You just use the BML for your own prurient purposes, then toss it aside like so much shaved hair. ;-)

JEFF: There seem to be a *lot* of Bears whose first contact with the community is online. Not too surprising, since the Internet and Bear cultures seem to have evolved around the same time.

RON: Let's move on to the evolution of Bear Web sites. Mike, would you care to say something on the topic?

MIKE: Resources for Bears just celebrated its sixth anniversary—by far the oldest of its type of Web site out there. What has spurred the growth of all these other sites is something we at the Resources For Bears have been discussing for years. Most of these new resource sites fill a very specific need and are quite good. They have forced us to grow and evolve from a site of static links to a fully integrated database-driven site! Competition is good.

JEFF: I see it as really no different from the explosion of just about any topic online. Like most traditional media (TV, magazines), they all reuse and rehash the same stuff, but often evolving (for the better) in the process. So the user really wins.

MIKE: Yep. But I think that the time and energy needed to maintain these other sites will eventually doom a good chunk of them.

JEFF: Agreed. Boredom sets in too quickly.

RON: So, boredom in online Beardom spurs change. Do you see more specialization in the future on the Net?

JEFF: We're already seeing great specialization on the Internet. That's where Internet giants like Yahoo and AOL are feeling the squeeze from the smaller guys now.

ALEX: I think the Net is centrally about specialization; there's room there for everything. Take a look at how specific some newsgroups are!

RON: Anyone care to reminisce about his early cyber sex experiences?

MIKE: Uh-h-h, I can neither confirm nor deny my participation in cyber sex. ;-)

JEFF: Text just doesn't turn me on as much as the real thing.

STEVE: When will kozmo.com offer hustler Bears for one-hour delivery?

RON: Well, speaking of cyber smut, I'd like to turn to the subject of cyber porn piracy. Piracy of Bear porn over the Internet—for personal as well as commercial use—is everywhere and uncontrolled. It's not unique to this particular community, but any thoughts on the controversy of Internet copyright infringement among Bearfolk?

ALEX: Why buy the cow when the milk is free? ;-)

RON: I'm thinking more in terms of personal appropriation, like Bears who've said that they've found other men using their pictures in chatrooms to get dates. For example, if you and I were cyber chatting in the Bear's Den trying to score and you sent me someone else's pic claiming it was you.

MIKE: I was faced with this very issue several years ago when my pics from *American Bear* magazine ended up on several alt.binary [basically, adult-oriented BBS] newsgroups. *American Bear* magazine pursued the issue with one guy, but they don't have the resources to track down all the pirated pics out there.

JEFF: I think that it's just part of Internet life. There's really not much you can do about it. I've found my graphic designs all over the place—including being sold.

STEVE: Comes with the territory. Big porn firms such as Colt use their clout to minimize it, but there's not much the average Joe Bear can do.

JEFF: Colt tries, but it's still impossible to do anything other than wave your hands and yell, "cease and desist."

STEVE: Does that mean I shouldn't use Mike Ramsey's JPEGs [JPEG is a photo image format] to get dates? ;-)

JEFF: Hehehe. That reminds me of a funny story that [former BML moderator] Bobby Thurman told me. At an early in-person cyber-Bear gathering, he thought it would be neat to print the pictures people provided on their nametags. Bad idea. A few people had the same pictures!

MIKE: Honestly, I've never come across that type of weird situation! The closest was someone using my IRC [Internet Relay Chat] nickname and saying it was me.

RON: Is there anything that characterizes the banter in Bear chatrooms from other online chat environments?

JEFF: I would guess it's the same jejune banter you see in most chatrooms.

ALEX: I've found chat in Bear chatrooms to be pretty broad but certainly there is usually a strong sexual tilt. Even looking at the threads that go on in the BML you can see that Bears like to discuss a broad spectrum of issues.

STEVE: In Jurassic days, when I was in chatrooms, I found that the sexual content was a lot milder; it was mostly flirting.

RON: Well, what about the Bear Code? That seems particularly suited for online use.

MIKE: The Bear Code is something that hasn't died (despite many people's efforts) because it does work online!

MIKE: It started purely as a joke and has fathered many other codes and is still used heavily among online Bears.

RON: Bears have further encrypted their characteristics into the Beard Code and Fur Code.

STEVE: There's also the geek code, the Smurf code, and the rest.

JEFF: Perhaps this is not so much the case, now that many people can get a picture scanned and placed online.

MIKE: Personally, I think the code is still far better to describe non-physical aspects of someone (pic or not).

JEFF: Indeed. It certainly helps when there is no pic. Plus you can tell other aspects (like height, demeanor, and so on).

RON: Some folks would decry the Bear Code as limiting one's sexual vocabulary, when we ought to be trying to expand it.

ALEX: The Bear Codes have their place, but things on the Net change so fast that they aren't as important anymore.

RON: I'd like to address the topic of cyber-addiction among Bears. Doesn't obsessive online behavior inhibit real human relationships?

ALEX: Actually, almost all of the important friends in my life, I've met online. It has enhanced my human relationships. Not only that, I meet new and interesting people every day through the Net.

MIKE: The Net does promote cyber relationships, but I do think that it can be tough to get out from behind the screen and meet Bears.

JEFF: On the other hand, there are hundreds of Bears online who have used cyberspace as a jumping-off point for their personal renaissance. For them, it's a chance to discover themselves and move beyond their four walls. Some people make it out, some people don't.

STEVE: Perhaps for some, the Internet can be a substitute for getting out in the world, but I've found that it can foster people getting out to meet each other (and not just for sexual liaisons).

MIKE: It also provided some men with a forum to meet and to express themselves before there were Bearclubs and Bear bars.

JEFF: Indeed. Think of all the married, rural, or shy Bears who never had a voice or a friend to talk to about being gay. For the first time, they have a way to find and express themselves to others in their situation—of which there are many! For some of these men, cyberspace is their only way to get in touch with other Bears.

STEVE: For a while, when I was moderating the Bears Mailing List, there was a flood of married guys joining and sharing their experiences. This is probably still true for the new crowd. Finding their way online to the BML was lifesaving for many of them.

ALEX: Yes, I still hear that on a frequent basis.

RON: That is really heartwarming to hear. Anyway, Gentlebears, we should wrap up. I'd like to thank you so very much for joining in tonight. *group hug*

CHAPTER 24
A SPACE BEYOND BEARDOM: POSTBEARS AND EX-BEARS
~ A DISCUSSION WITH VAN BUCKLEY,
STEVEN EVANS, AND TIM MORRISON ~

VAN BUCKLEY grew up in a small town in Southern Missouri and now lives in Kansas City, Missouri. After receiving a degree in mass communications, he spent five years working as a reporter and editor for newspapers in Missouri and Pennsylvania. For the past 13 years, he has worked in public relations for a university. Van serves on the board of directors and as media coordinator for the National Institute for Gay, Lesbian, Bisexual, and Transgendered Education; he also writes for the Institute's online magazine, www.authenticity.org. In his spare time he enjoys reading (everything from lurid murder mysteries to the latest books on queer theory), herb gardening, fixing up his house, and political activism. His interest in activism stems from his participation in the 1993 March on Washington.

STEVEN EVANS is an artist living in New Jersey who was born in Key West, Florida. He attended Phillips Exeter Academy, Atlanta College of Art, and Nova Scotia College of Art and Design. He has taught a course on "Gender, Representation, and Sexuality" at NSCAD, curated a contemporary art exhibition on the subject, and written for various art magazines as well as *STH* (*Straight to Hell*). Steven's artwork deals with issues of identity, gender, and sexuality. His latest exhibition at the Rupert Goldsworthy Gallery in New York also touched on Evans' self-image during a bout of alopecia areata. In 1994, he and three friends founded New York City's MetroBears, a Bearclub serving the New York metropolitan area. The club has since grown to approximately 200 members. Evans left his position of helping to guide the club in 1996. Evans pays the rent working for a museum in New York, has a lover, Mike, of nine years, and drives a pickup truck for the butch factor.

TIM MORRISON is originally from the St. Louis, Missouri, area. Self-described as a "regular kind of guy with some twists," he divides his time between a career in information technology and his main passions of music, film, spending too much time online, and comic-book collecting, as well as dabbling in writing. Currently single, Tim lives in San Francisco, California.

One winter night in 1996, well into a bottle of Johnnie Walker and a discussion of the emerging postgay identity, my friend Mike and I coined a term, "postbear," in anticipation of Bears who would eventually feel the need to move beyond Beardom.

Why did Mike and I even go there? Did we already feel that the emperor's new bearsuit was indeed a facade of fur and no fiber? We'd both already experienced the cliquishness of the local Bearclub, but it was decidedly not a matter of sour grapes. We were also aware of the increasing commodification or commercialization of Beardom: More and more, being a Bear was about having the right look and buying all the right accoutrements of Bear life, rather than relating to some undefined sense of brotherhood, "naturalness," or even a sexual way of being.

Mike and I identified that, although architects of the term "postgay" seemed to intend it to mean "queer identity beyond the gay ghetto," the central construct centered on where one wished to place one's identity. Did one identify as a gay/lesbian/bi/trans/queer person squarely in the middle of a conglomerate of "lifestyle" choices, or somewhere closer to the periphery or even outside a critical mass of such characteristics?

It's nearly impossible to exist in our consumerist society without being aware of our place in it and how such "lifestyle" choices reflect our consumer behavior. Marketers of every stripe are also aware of these choices and behaviors, and bombard us with advertising messages geared to gain our greenbacks.

So, if "postgay" reflects a desire to reject being labeled and niche-marketed and to return to a idealized gay life where decisions about one's identity are one's own, "postbear" identity similarly symbolizes a desire to escape an increasingly all-consuming consumerism and to rejoin a more primal—hairier and larger, if you will—sense of being gay, or perhaps just being.

Mike's partner, Steve, suggested this topic for the book, and after Van and Tim responded to an appeal on the Bears Mailing List for postbears, I asked them to join us in an online discussion.

RON: Tim, what originally attracted you to Bears, or Bear types, or the Bear movement?

TIM: Well, I've always pretty much considered the whole Bear thing to be based on physical characteristics, and it seemed like the men I was attracted to fit these characteristics. The personality characteristics— how friendly and approachable Bears were—came later for me. But hey, how can a label really quantify a person's actions or demeanor? I think it's silly now.

RON: Van, what about Bears initially turned you on?

VAN: The Bear movement initially attracted me because it seemed more egalitarian. I was big, hairy, and had a beard since high school, all of which was different from the image that existed of gay men. At the same time, getting involved with a group that said you don't have to be buff and hairless was a tremendous boost to my self-esteem. Plus for the first time, I realized that if a guy was attracted to me, it didn't necessarily mean there was something pathological in his interest. In other words, identifying as a Bear freed me to see myself as someone who guys could be attracted to. It put a definition to a phenomenon I hadn't understood or accepted before.

RON: So, all three of you not only were attracted to Bears, but also identified as Bears yourselves, and generally with the "ideology" behind Beardom, so to speak?

VAN: I wasn't so much attracted to Bears as attracted to guys who were attracted to Bears.

STEVE: For me, it was the appearance and the masculinity. I had been harboring that desire for butch Bears ever since I was a teenager and saw that *Honcho* from around 1980 with Mickey Squires and that other bearded guy on the raft. I hid that magazine under my bed for a year until my Mom found it! I didn't identify as a Bear until my late twenties. I also liked the idea of an alternative community.

TIM: I had a very weird and sort of latent gay life, although I came out fairly young, at 19. When I got involved in Beardom, I thought it was great because I felt that basically I could be myself and be accepted no matter what. As I got older, though, I realized that was definitely not true.

RON: Do you mean that Bears were not as accepting as you'd thought at first?

TIM: Exactly. I recall a time when I was taking some Bear-identified friends out on the town. We were going to stop by the Outpost. One wanted to wear a particular outfit and his boyfriend remarked, "Well, that's not a particularly Bearish outfit. You sure you want to go out in that?"

RON: How did that make you feel?

TIM: I felt incredulous that something that was reputed to be an inclusive community would cause a person to say something like that. But then again, I'd found myself doing the same thing to myself.

RON: Right—just as I think we've all probably been guilty of doing at one time or another in our desire to be accepted—or to score! Van and Steve, the two of you are similar in that you both started Bearclubs and then became somewhat alienated from the clubs you founded. Steve, tell us about your experience with MetroBears, please.

STEVE: Well, I founded MetroBears with a couple of friends after visiting Boston a few times. I was really impressed by the New England Bears, and had a really good time as a tourist. I thought, *New York really needs this—something to go against the Chelsea Boy scene.*

RON: At the time, there wasn't a Bearclub in Manhattan, right?

STEVE: There was a Bearclub already, based in Jersey, called the Bergenfield Bears, who did events in Manhattan, but they ran the group like a leather or motorcycle club. You had to pledge, to do favors, and to work for the club, and only then would they tell you if you could be a member.

RON: Sounds more like a college fraternity than a leather club.

STEVE: There were also the rumors that you had to put out for sex. Anyway, it was a real turn-off. MetroBears was founded to be solidly egalitarian, and it was for a while. But it's a great deal of hard work, and as we each became exhausted we had to pass the torch. Later leaders, I felt, made the club less egalitarian and more political—but in the sense of personal power, not activism. So I distanced myself from it. Just lately, I have gone to some events here and there. When it's good, it's great. When it's bad, who needs it?

RON: Van, was your experience founding a Bearclub similar to Steve's?

VAN: When the Kansas City Bearclub held its first organizational meeting, I walked into a group of maybe a dozen other guys. The feeling was genuinely friendly. Those early days of the club were great. Despite the diversity of the members, there was a sense of camaraderie. But over the first year or so, it seemed like a split began to develop. Some members saw the club as a social club, and others expected meetings to end with a group grope. There was real friction between the two groups and eventually the conflict took its toll. Several of the original members ending up dropping out, and the club foundered for a while. I understand it has new leadership now but I haven't been back. I feel like I've grown on my own beyond what the club, or the Bear movement in general can offer me.

RON: That social-group/sex-club rift has been the source of more than a few clubs splitting apart. Tim, what has been your Bearclub experience?

TIM: Interestingly enough, I didn't become a member of a Bearclub until I moved to San Francisco about four years ago. The St. Louis group was, in my opinion, very poorly run and there was way too much infighting and political agendas. When I first joined BOSF [Bears of San Francisco] here, it was fun for a while. There seemed to be a genuine effort made to emphasize social activities, but then somewhere along the line, things changed. The club became a vehicle for its board to use to promote and staff their beer busts and events. I put in many hours working events and going to meetings, and there were very few social activities aside from the beer busts here. Eventually I let my membership lapse. But in all fairness to BOSF, I would have to say my experience in the group was positive overall, and perhaps the new leadership will change things.

RON: Tim, you described earlier what perhaps might be called a "moment of truth"—regarding your friends discussing what was appropriate Bearwear. I want to ask Steve and Van: Was there some sort of decisive moment when you realized that the Bear thing was "up"?

STEVE: It was a few incidents that did it for me. First, a guy I was really hot for told me I was too skinny—at 5'8" and 200 pounds. Then the club introduced *Robert's Rules of Order*. And then I got alopecia areata.

RON: Please describe that medical problem, Steve.

STEVE: It's a condition where your body tells your immune system that your hair is an outside invader, so your antibodies kill your hair at the root. It's disputed as to whether it's caused by stress or an unknown virus. My hair started falling out. I had to shave my head and my beard, or else I would've looked like a dog with mange. I also lost some weight. This lasted for a little less than a year.

RON: It's hard to imagine a medical condition that would more powerfully affect your sense of Bearness.

STEVE: It was devastating, actually, on many levels. I was incredibly self-conscious about my appearance. And the Bears were really shady, except for my close friends. Bears no longer cruised me or wanted even to hang out, and I became attractive to a totally new group of guys, which was very weird. So that really soured me. The illusion of inclusiveness was broken. As a subculture based on physical attributes, I guess I should have expected it, but I didn't.

RON: Van, how about you? Was there some sort of defining moment for you when you realized that you no longer wanted to identify as a Bear or with the Bear community?

VAN: For me, the end came after a meeting when I overheard one of the club members referring to another member as "too Nelly" to be a "real Bear." At the time, I had a very good friend who happened to be very effeminate and occasionally did drag who was dying of AIDS, and I'd seen the prejudice he had dealt with, even within the gay community. Even more ironic was the fact that the guy who was complaining about someone else being too Nelly was flailing his wrists with wild abandon. It really disappointed me that we as a subculture talk about inclusiveness, but when it comes right down to it, we want to divide the world between Bear and not-Bear.

In a way, the Bear community is almost schizophrenic. On the one hand, there is all this talk of being inclusive because we've all felt the pain of being excluded from the larger gay community. But on the other hand, it's human nature to draw a line between *them* and *us*. We can't have it both ways, being inclusive and exclusive at the same time.

STEVE: I've experienced some of that femophobia too in New York. I remember some instances especially early on, but I'm pretty sure that the club got over that bump. Believe me, it ain't all stone cold butches now.

RON: Tim, any comments on Bear exclusivity in San Francisco?

TIM: Strictly in the Bearclub sense or overall?

RON: Well, your perspective is somewhat unique in that you have not only a local scene but also IBR [International Bear Rendezvous], which attracts hundreds of men every year. Plus the throngs of Bears who flock to the Lone Star on pilgrimage.

TIM: Well, as you said, Ron, there are a lot of visitors to San Francisco. Go to the Lone Star any night and that's obvious. I think a lot of people head to the Lone Star thinking that it's a Bear paradise, and then wind up there regardless of whether they're Bear-identified or not to find some fun for the night. But those guys who aren't bearded or who otherwise stand out from the rest of the crowd tend to get ignored. I've seen it happen, and people comment to me about it.

Oh, hell, one of the bartenders is a screaming queen! It's a well-known stereotype that femmy gay men like show tunes. But what's a traditional Bear Pride event? The show tune sing-along at the end of the weekend!

STEVE: I'm concerned MetroBears may become Broadway Bears. Let's face it—Bears are gay guys.

TIM: Exactly. And to rely on Beardom to dictate one's behaviors is asinine.

RON: Well, I'm concerned about your "concern." Didn't anyone expect the Bear phenomenon to expand and change?

TIM: I think we had the idea that Beardom would remain a positive thing; after all, we all got something positive out of it at first. It ended up, though, commodified and merchandised, and so it created an image to live up to, which in turn, made Beardom a sort of island—them and us. It became stifling and suffocating instead of creating a supportive environment. Ultimately, I think it made some men feel more alienated.

STEVE: I've always wanted to be a bit of a renegade or somewhat avant-garde. I guess that's why the commercialization bothers me. A Bear necklace is a real turn-off to me. I try to ignore the ubiquitous Bear-claw tattoos. I guess I'm still buying into the *Firsthand* fantasies of hot man-to-man spontaneous sex.

I still primarily relate to being a Bear in that I continue to find the basic physical type sexually attractive; it's hot. I still enjoy hanging out with guys in that physical way: just having fun, being social, and playing. But where I get off the boat, so to speak, is in the commodification and hierarchy of the whole Bear phenomenon. It's all so boring. We've all heard that being a Bear is another kind of drag, and it just seems the movement is becoming more and more like The Imperial Court [longstanding American and international gay tradition of appointing "royalty"—drag queens and princes—to preside over certain "elite" factions of various gay communities].

RON: Van, how did your expectations of the evolution of Bear subculture differ from what you actually experienced? Would you say that your expectations were realistic?

VAN: Bear identity is in the process of changing, but it's evolving in the same way the entire gay movement has evolved. "Gay" used to be a self-contained definition that was a sort of shorthand for how one acted, thought, voted, shopped for groceries, and so on.

RON: Well, a stereotype, you mean.

STEVE: Hear, hear!

VAN: Now "gay" has become an adjective instead of a noun: like gay mechanics, gay actors, even (God forbid) gay Republicans. I think the Bear movement will become like that too.

RON: And then, Bear Republicans!

VAN: Right now, the Bear movement is trying to define itself. But in the end, I think that it will just have to admit that everyone is his own kind of Bear. Maybe we'll reach a point where Bears will really be egalitarian and inclusive and we decide there are an infinite number of possible permutations of "Bear."

TIM: Have you spent enough time in online chatrooms to notice a certain amount of derision toward Bears?

STEVE: Yeah, but also toward twinks.

VAN: The entire gay movement has become balkanized, it seems. Gays used to have camp—now we just have different camps.

TIM: I've encountered several self-described "hairy men" who won't identify as Bears. If you try to talk to them, they'll cut you off, saying, "not into Bears." This has happened to me online several times, yet a few times when I've approached them using a screen name without the word "Bear" in it, they're not as disinterested. Go figure.

STEVE: In the '80s, Catalina Video types were all the rage; now it's hairy guys. I think that the pendulum is swinging the other way. Bears really are mainstream, gay-wise.

RON: I don't perceive that the gaystream media has shifted significantly in their representations of men's bodies, although there are certainly plenty of gay pay-for-porn Web sites that have misappropriated the term "Bear."

STEVE: The market share of hairy-men magazines is huge now. There used to be nothing.

RON: Maybe you'll find a little stubble on models for International Male catalogs or *Advocate Men*, but not much more. Open any GLBT regional or city weekly newspaper and count the ratio of Bear to typical images.

STEVE: I think the Bear movement is mostly over because Bears have "made it" largely in the gay mainstream. The movement, I feel, is no longer the necessary safe place that it used to be.

RON: Well, it seems that when you speak of market share, you're lumping that phenomenon with the overall assimilation of Bearness into the gaystream.

STEVE: Yes. For example, every U.S. metropolitan area has a Bear bar or at least a Bear night. Tell me that's not recognition of a market.

TIM: But is attendance going up or down or staying relatively the same?

RON: Good question. "Market share" refers to percentage of a total market, and although the "Bear market" is up, and so are the numbers for the gay men's market in general. This gets back to commodification: Gayness is a business. Part of the reason a postgay identity has evolved, I suspect, is because people want to feel that being queer is more than being someone's market share. Would you agree or disagree, and why?

VAN: Definitely agree. I am just so tired of rainbow flags, Bear stickers, and the whole niche-marketing scheme. It becomes a bandwagon one is required to jump on, whether you're talking gay in general or Bear in particular. It reaches a point of saturation where you get bombarded with these items that are marketed specifically to you. In a way, I guess when someone's trying to market to us, it says we have arrived—but being a consumer isn't my only function as a gay man or a Bear.

STEVE: I completely agree. That's what I meant before about a renegade stance. I'm many things, and I don't like being told what to buy based on other's perceptions of me. I like to think I have free will and a discerning intellect. I'm sure that's a market share, too. Damn. *G*

RON: It's hard to escape the tyranny of capitalism, eh, Steve? ;-)

TIM: I agree with Steve on this. I don't go out of my way to buy an item or service from a business just because it's gay-owned or operated, or Bear-owned or operated. The Bear community is almost as bad as Disney is with McDonald's toys!

RON: My guess is that some enterprising folks are already trying to figure out how to niche-market to postgays and postbears.

If "postgay" refers to, simplistically put, an identity where the dichotomy of gay/straight is rendered irrelevant and thus undermined—what do you hope to accomplish idealistically by referring to yourself as "postbear"?

TIM: First of all, I don't feel I have to make a great effort in getting the idea across to people. And it doesn't frustrate me or bother me if other guys refer to me as "Bear."

I don't know that I hope to accomplish anything, really, but I must say that the whole experience has taught me a valuable lesson in that we cannot in any way, shape, or form quantify ourselves on any firm basis, especially one so physically-oriented. It only reinforces the idea that we simultaneously are all the same and we are all different. It's nice to find a group of like-minded people, but to make it the sole focus in our lives closes us off to other possibilities. I think I am more tolerant and respectful of other people as a result of this experience.

VAN: It used to really bother me when some guy would "woof" at me or call me a Bear. I looked like a Bear, but I didn't feel like one. I know I won't change the world by referring to myself as a "postbear," but it does affect my mindset when I apply that name to myself. It's a way of reminding myself that the labels that get stuck on me aren't the only way to define myself. I think the only way to really define myself is to try to live beyond the labels.

STEVE: When I had the alopecia, I got a new online handle, "xbear." Folks are intrigued by the idea of me being an ex-Bear. But I don't feel estranged from the Bear movement all the time. Sometimes, I just want people to know I'm critical of some of it. Sometimes, I want to open up the possibility for myself and for others of moving in, out, and between different worlds or arenas.

TIM: I very much agree with you, Steve.

STEVE: I like flannel but I'm not gonna live in it 24/7. I also like microfibers. I don't want to be confined. That's the overriding desire—

not to be confined. And I don't just mean by clothes! *G*

RON: If you were to go about trying to fix the problems in Bear life that you've identified, how might you do that? Other than complaining about it, that is.

STEVE: I'm not sure it can be fixed. I think it's more about a threshold that has been reached. I just think now it's time for something new and exciting, and I don't mind helping to define it. We'll see what happens.

RON: Oh, fine, help build a subculture and then just dump it when the going gets tough, huh? ;-)

STEVE: You got it. It's strong now. It's not going anywhere for a while.

VAN: I agree with Steve. I'm not sure it can be fixed without fixing human nature so that we don't automatically categorize everything in these dichotomous extremes: masculine/feminine, gay/straight, Bear/twink. Maybe one day we'll be able to just say, "Well, you're one kind of Bear and I'm another," and let it go at that. But that will probably require a bit of genetic engineering to get us over the need to set up strict categories and define ourselves by what groups we're in or out of.

TIM: I don't think that there is any sort of realistic fix overall, but whatever changes are made have to come from within. I need to keep and cherish the positive things that have come with Beardom yet challenge the negativity—to call people on their behaviors when it's noticed, open minds to the possibilities, and make challenges. This is, of course, if Beardom survives. I believe it's in a state of disintegration, or integration, depending on how you look at it.

The [San Francisco–area Bearclub] South Bay Bears, for example, has a lesbian member. I wonder what the group thinks about that.

RON: Another panel I conducted for the book was on, and with, "Dykes and FTMs as Bears" [chapter 22]. Interestingly, they had many of the same criticisms you guys have made.

TIM: It doesn't surprise me.

VAN: Me either.

STEVE: I would like for there to be straight Bears. That would be hardcore.

RON: I've come across some info regarding the formation of a straight Bear identity. A lesbian-identified woman here in Boston contacted me because she loves—lusts after—Bears. She wanted to find

Bears for sex. So I didn't offer to take her to the Bearclub bar night. What I did was to offer to take here to Home Depot to cruise with her and to help her find some online resources.

STEVE: It would have to be more that [comedian] Tim Allen's "Men Are Pigs" type of identity. I wonder if it's possible in the straight community? And of course, now we have the testosterone cream hitting the market. Instant Bear.

RON: It doesn't end there. There are also rumors of musclebears doing speedballs of "T shots"—testosterone injections—and steroids. On a more positive note, however, it does seem that just as Bears are reaching a crest, people are moving beyond it in many positive ways. That the culture is still evolving indicates that there's still juice in it.

TIM: I want to point out here that things are different for men who are in larger cities that are in better touch with the gay community in general. I still see Beardom as a potentially positive thing for someone out in the middle of nowhere who might have a very limited view of what it means to be a gay man. I would hope that he has the fortitude, however, to take what he can from it. To realize the possibilities that exist beyond that identity, and to not let a narrow segment of any community dictate his behaviors, likes, and dislikes.

VAN: I think the Bear movement will be around for a while, but it will continue to be in flux. As more guys, especially young ones, enter the movement, there will also be those like us, for whom it's been something of a transitional experience. While I'm not involved with a local Bear community, I still take an active part in the online Bear community. I think it's going to be in cyberspace where the Bear movement is going to flourish.

STEVE: No doubt about it—there certainly still are positive aspects and a space for something beyond Beardom.

CHAPTER 25
INTERNATIONAL BEAR BROTHERHOOD
~ DISCUSSIONS WITH EDUARDO CHAVEZ (MEXICO), SEUMAS HYSLOP (AUSTRALIA), XAVIER NAVARRO (SPAIN), MARCELO PERALES (ARGENTINA), GLEN PURDON (SOUTH AFRICA), MALI SAHIN (TURKEY), WOODY SHIMKO (U.S./JAPAN), AND JUSTIN SPOONER (WALES, U.K.) ~

EDUARDO "ED" CHAVEZ is a 25-year-old who lives in Mexico City and is openly gay to family and friends. He works as a software developer and client programming manager for an Internet service provider. He has visited the U.S. several times and is especially fond of Orlando and San Francisco. Ed is also a founder of Osos Mexicanos, which is Mexico's first Bearclub, and is currently partnered to a Beary guy.

SEUMAS HYSLOP was born in Gladstone, Australia, and now

resides in the inner western suburbs of Sydney in New South Wales. Seumas is a college student, currently pursuing a Bachelor of Medicine–Bachelor of Surgery at the University of Sydney. As a founder of Harbour City Bears in 1995, he has been heavily involved in the development of the club, and through it, the Bear community in Sydney and Australia, and has also developed Bear Essentials, Australia's premier Bear festival. He is a contributor to *The Bear Book II*, detailing the history of the Australian Bear Community since 1995. Seumas's interests include medical informatics (the use of computers and technology in healthcare). He plans to travel extensively over the next few years. Check out his Web site at www.hyslop.org.

XAVIER (XAVI) NAVARRO was born in 1975. He belongs to the first generation that has lived in full democracy in Spain. He has lived through the explosion of gay life and AIDS in his country in the '90s. Xavi is studying at college for a degree in computer engineering, and works in a bank computing department, and speaks several languages. He came out at 18 with the help of a gay organization. He worked in another gay association for two years, where he first heard news about the U.S. Bear movement. Some time later, through the Internet, he was one of the first members of the IRC [Internet Relay Chat] Bear channel and the Spanish Bears Web page. In 2000 he became one of the founders of Bearcelona, the Barcelona Bearclub.

MARCELO PERALES was born in Buenos Aires, Argentina, in 1967 and has a degree in business administration but now works as a computer instructor and Web page designer. He is currently very happy with his husbear, Cristian, who lives in Chile. Marcelo is a founding member and current President of Osos de Buenos Aires (Buenos Aires Bears), Argentina's first Bearclub. He participated in this panel with the assistance of his former boyfriend, Gabriel.

GLEN PURDON was born in Rhodesia (now Zimbabwe) in 1971, then left for South Africa in 1980. After his family lived four years in Johannesburg, they moved to Port Elizabeth in 1984, where he has since lived. After Glen completed high school, he joined the South African Navy, where he served for seven years as an officer. He has traveled extensively and seen five continents and a hell of a lot of South America as well as Europe and the States. Glen left the navy in 1997 and joined a national company that runs port operations in South Africa. He and his partner Stephen started Ibhayi Bear in their community. He is now employed as a captain of a harbor tug, where he admires the many Bears who work on ships.

MEHMET ALI "MALI" SAHIN was born in 1968 and brought up in Ankara, Turkey. He graduated from Faculty of Arts in their Ceramics and Glass department. In 1994 he turned his computer-aided graphics hobby into a profession and started to work as a graphic designer. Now he works in a multimedia company producing educational CD-ROM titles as graphics and interaction designer and Web master. His hobbies are reading, movies, music, and the Internet. He is founder and president of Bears in Turkey, the country's only Bear group, which he initiated with five other guys in 1998. He contributed an article to *The Bear Book II*, "A Bear Voice from Turkey."

WOODY SHIMKO was born in 1956 in New Jersey with the given name George. His college major was Forestry and his nickname has been Woody ever since. Oddly, rather than pursuing a career as a park ranger, he ended up in New York City in the creative field for almost 15 years. He moved to Cape Cod in 1992 to open an environmental store in Provincetown while maintaining his job as Creative Director at various New York City stores: Bergdorf Goodman, Armani, and then Tiffany. In 1996 Woody accepted an offer to work as creative director for a Japanese department store. He closed his store in December 1999 and nowadays splits his time between Cape Cod, Palm Springs, and Tokyo. He is currently single and prefers that, due to his travels, but always keeps his fingers crossed.

JUSTIN SPOONER is an Internet and E-commerce designer and consultant, and his partner Neal is a music technology specialist. He has traveled to most of the United Kingdom and lived in Hong Kong, and he and Neal have covered most of Europe and been to the U.S. quite a few times. They live in a large house in a town of 50,000 in Wales, U.K. Justin has been active on the Bear scene for several years—not tarting around, however, just chatting, meeting, and online conferencing. Justin and Neal are slowly dragging the local Welsh Bears out from their small caves and into the light.

While in the Bear Store in San Francisco during International Bear Rendezvous 2000, I encountered a deaf Japanese man. He was a short, slight man trying on a pair of double-thick rainbow suspenders with the word "BEAR" emblazoned on them. The image was striking—the suspenders were *so* not in scale to his body. I thought it was so amazing that a deaf Japanese Bear would travel all the way to San Francisco just for four days during IBR.

I sign fluently, and the Japanese man knew some American Sign Language, so we were able to communicate decently. After I interpreted for him with the salesclerk, I helped him figure out the schedule and location of the weekend's events and answered his questions about San Francisco. Throughout the weekend, whenever I saw him, I asked how he was enjoying himself. It was a great experience for me to be able to reach across cultural and language boundaries like that.

Throughout the process of assembling the different voices in this book, I knew it was essential to include a selection of self-identified Bears from around the world. Pulling together the panel discussion of eight men here proved daunting. Again, the Internet proved instrumental in the creation of this panel. I had met only Woody previously, and had contacted Mali when I visited Turkey two years before the panel convened. Through appeals on the Bears Mailing List, BearPress, and Resources for Bears, I sent out E-mail appeals to all non-U.S. Bearclubs and to many individuals. Response was sparse, but perseverance paid off: by the time we first came together online (incidentally, on Canada Day, July 1, 2000, at 8:00 A.M. Eastern Daylight Time), our group included wonderfully diverse, bright, and articulate Bears from seven time zones on almost every continent.

Although technical difficulties beset us, preventing several panelists from joining in with the main group, I managed to connect afterward with the missing parties to conduct individual online interviews, which I've woven into the fabric of the main text here. Ideally, we would have all been online concurrently. Eventually technology will improve to the point where someone will be able to conduct a worldwide "Conference of the Bears," to paraphrase the Sufi folk tale. Given the limitations at hand, however, I'm pleased to present the patchworked transcript of this journalistically historic discussion.

The purpose of this panel was to allow non-American Bears the opportunity to discuss their experiences of and perspectives on the Bear subculture and masculinity in their own regions, as well as in America; and to examine the concept of masculine brotherhood as it might exist in the Bear community.

RON: How did you first hear about Bears, Ed?

ED (Mexico): In 1995, when I first discovered the Internet, I used to surf the Web a lot and came across pictures of hairy gay guys called Bears. I barely understood what "Bear" meant, but then I discovered the Bear Codes and Bear subclassifications and all that, and I identified with that. Although to many purists I'm not a real Bear because I'm not very hairy, I consider Beardom to be more about attitude than looks.

RON: The "hairier than thou" attitude is quite troubled. Glen, please tell us about your genesis as a Bear.

GLEN (South Africa): I have identified myself as Bear ever since I've known about them. I only came out four years back when I met my husbear, who was living in a gay commune house—six large hairy men in one house! That was when I first heard of Bears. Husbear and I started Ibhayi Bears in Port Elizabeth two years back because we love the idea. There are not too many "out" Bears in South Africa, but, as "Bear" is a relatively unknown term here, things are changing slowly.

RON: Terrific—we'll more deeply examine the Bear scene in each location shortly. Justin?

JUSTIN (United Kingdom): About four years ago, I became aware of Bears when I typed "hairy men" into a search engine. At the time, I lived in Manchester, England, which has a large gay community and a thriving Bear movement, as does London. My peers confirmed my Bear status, although I'm not the hairiest man on the planet.

RON: Like who is? No hands raised here, I think.

JUSTIN: I live in Wales now, which has a lot of small isolated communities, so our task here is to get people together in this part of the country. The U.K. Bear scene as a whole, however, is very different to the Bear scene in Wales.

RON: Very good. Go ahead, Mali.

MALI (Turkey): My story is the same as Eduardo and Justin's. I first encountered Bears while looking for hairy gay pictures on the Internet in 1997. At first, the word "Bear" seemed a joke to me. Then I reached the Resources for Bears Web site. I was kinda shocked that day. I spent many hours on those pages. Day by day, I learned more about Bears; I understood that this was what I'd always wanted and had always been. I identified myself as a Bear and decided to become part of the Bear movement. In 1998, we started a little group here with five friends.

RON: Marcelo, was your initial contact with Bears also from the Internet?

MARCELO (Argentina): I have identified with the Bear phenomenon ever since 1995, when I first got Internet access. My initial contact with the Bear movement was from the Internet also. Before that, I knew of certain gay masculine stereotypes, but the word "Bear" was unknown to me.

RON: Can you be more specific about which masculine types you mean?

MARCELO: Well, I consider myself a Bear, both in physical appearance and in attitude. I had a very focused attraction to Bearish guys since I was very little, of course without being aware of any classification whatsoever. Anyway, as far as my teenage sexual desires were concerned, they always were focused on people with beards or mustaches and hairy and stocky men. My first sexual contact was at the age of 12 with a bald, very hairy guy. Everything was consensual, though there was no penetration. It was great for me! You get an idea from where I have a sexual attraction for hairy men! I started dating guys at 21, but I didn't really come out of the closet to my parents until I was 31.

RON: An interesting bit of personal history! Seumas, how did you come to Beardom?

SEUMAS (Australia): My coming out as a Bear was a little different to most. When I was about 18, and getting into the gay subculture, I never did seem to fit in the mainstream gay culture. I ended up spending those young adult years hanging out with a group of lesbians. They noticed my fur and the fact I started growing a beard, and they referred to me as their "little Bear."

RON: How long ago was that?

SEUMAS: My self-identification as a Bear happened about 1994, when I discovered the Bear community out there. Not knowing how to get involved, I went and started up a club, Harbour City Bears, in 1995 with a couple of guys here in Sydney—although I was living in Canberra, the national capital, about 350 kilometers away.

RON: Woody, how do you relate to Bearness and being a Bear?

WOODY (Japan): I'm a Bear in my own way, I guess. I feel that most Bears relate better to hairy men, larger men. I'm not small but not hairy and I think that most Bears shy away from that. I've known about the Bear thing for many years now and have always had an attraction to them even years before that.

RON: I want to take an extra moment here to ask about your experience as an American in Japan. Do you feel accepted by Japanese Bears?

WOODY: I have been in almost every situation in Japan. Where I'm not accepted, it's because of a language barrier. Japanese men are very shy and want to please people. If they cannot communicate with someone, then they cannot please them. So, since we cannot talk, they are quiet and standoffish to me. With the ones who do speak English, and with my limited Japanese, we do very nicely.

RON: As bars in Japan are very specialized, there are specific Bear bars, correct?

WOODY: Yes. There's Snuggle Bear, Bear Tracks, and other Bear bars without the name influence.

RON: Thank you, Woody. Last but not least, Xavi.

XAVI (Spain): When I came out, I joined the gay association of Barcelona. In 1996, in the library of Casal Lambda, where I worked, I found a copy of *Bear* magazine and was shocked. I'd always liked that kind of guy, and I easily fit that description myself. I joined the Internet in 1997 at college, just before the big Spanish gay explosion of 1998–99. The second word I searched for was "Bears" and from then on, I have been a lot on the Net. We founded a Bearclub in the city in January by placing an ad, and 20 people responded.

RON: It's fascinating to note how significant the Internet has been in the formation of many of our panelists' initial Bear identifications, as well as the formation of their local communities. Ed, please tell us about your local Bear community.

ED: It all started when I placed my Web page called Osos Mexicanos, the first Bear information on the Net in Spanish in the world. I started to get tons of mail, and founded a mailing list named LOLA (short for "Latin America Bear mailing list.") Six months later, nine people from that list got together in person, and started the Bearclub for real.

I've never attended a Bear event outside Mexico, except five nights in a row at the Lone Star in San Francisco. But I've learned much about it on the Net and I get a pretty good idea of what's happening elsewhere in the world.

RON: So, the Internet figured centrally in the founding of Osos Mexicanos.

XAVI: It has, Ron.

RON: Continuing further southward—Marcelo, please tell us about the evolution of Bears in Buenos Aires.

MARCELO: In July 1997, my then-boyfriend Gabriel and I had had enough of the twink stereotype here in Argentina. Next, through the Internet, we met Juan, a Bearish guy who had made a Bear page. Juan also had met Jorge, who was also into Bears. We got together and decided to design a Web page in which we could communicate with all Spanish-speaking people about Bears. In July 1997 the first Argentinean Web page for Bears was born. There was no club, of course, no name. We knew that the Internet was a weak way to promote the Bear thing here, so the next step was to call for a meeting.

RON: What happened at the meeting?

MARCELO: Thirty people attended our first meeting in an apartment in Buenos Aires. It was Sunday at 5:00 P.M.—a very unusual hour for Argentine gays to have any kind of meeting. Imagine 30 husky, stocky guys arriving. The old ladies in the building were terrified! *Heh heh* The atmosphere was great. Everyone was so enthusiastic! In that first meeting, Gabriel, Juan, and I talked about the idea of having a place for people like us to gather round and have some activities. So we started having weekly meetings and never stopped!

RON: Can you tell us about Bear activity elsewhere in South America?

MARCELO: In Uruguay the Bearclub had just a few meetings, but then vanished. In Chile, well, my boyfriend is the President of Osos Chilenos, which has about 20 members. As for Colombia, there is a Bear group called Osotes, which has very small meetings.

RON: From South America, let's go to South Africa. Glen, have you been to any Bear events or had contact with Bears outside your country?

GLEN: We haven't been to any Bear events, although my partner Stephen and I plan to attend International Bear Rendezvous 2001. As for contact with other Bears, I have plenty from around the world and a few in South Africa.

RON: Are there other Bearclubs in South Africa?

GLEN: There are at present three Bearclubs. One is in Johannesburg called JoBears, one in Durban called East Coast Bears, and one here in Port Elizabeth called Ibhayi Bears, which Stephen and I founded.

RON: I'm curious if the Bear groups there came together also through Internet contacts.

GLEN: As far as I can tell, the Bear communities in South Africa have formed because of the Internet. Without it, Bears would probably still be in the dark. It is from surfing the Internet that most South African Bears discovered Bear culture. Ibhayi Bearclub was started with Internet contacts and a few phone calls after advertising in a national gay publication.

RON: From here let's skip to Australia and work our way back. Seumas, please briefly catch us up on Bears Down Under.

SEUMAS: Bears in Australia started in 1990, when some people who had seen Bears forming in San Francisco came back to Sydney and thought they'd give it a try. That was OzBears, which was a good club in its time but folded due to internal politics. Shortly after that, other clubs started up, including Brisbears, Wombats (now BearsPerth), OzBears South Australia, Harbour City Bears, and Melbourne Ozbears (now VicBears). Thanks to the efforts of the clubs Australia-wide and some fortunate publicity, Bears are now really booming around the country, and it is a recognized subculture in the gay and lesbian community here.

RON: Great, thank you. Woody, I'd like to get your cultural perspective on the Far East, considering that the Japanese are perhaps most dissimilar from North Americans than any other nationality represented here. How would you characterize Japanese people?

WOODY: Japanese people are very kind, gentle, honest.

RON: How do you relate to Japanese Bears?

WOODY: Most of my life I've been attracted to bigger, older, hairier men. When I moved to Japan, it took me a few years to feel that I'd find anyone there who would attract me. Now I know that there are Japanese men who do fit that description.

RON: That prototypical Western Bear?

WOODY: Yes. Of course, they are different from the Bears at home— no Latin blood there—but in their own way they're quite attractive. The best part is that they are mostly attitude-free, which I find very welcome from a Bear group!

RON: Please describe Japanese Bear men physically.

WOODY: Japanese men for the most part are smaller. Bears are the larger of the Japanese men. Japanese men are also not well-known for their facial hair, but the Bear group does try to grow beards, mustaches, goatees. The big difference between Japanese Bears and U.S. Bears is that the Japanese are more likely to include more sensitive, almost even effeminate men in their group.

RON: Really? What distinguishes these effeminate Bears?

WOODY: Their dress, voices, and mannerisms. We would say

"queens" here, but the Japanese are not so judgmental.

RON: You told me once earlier, Woody, about their pink overalls.

WOODY: Good example. If a Bear type came to the bar in pink overalls, holding a teddy Bear, most Japanese would think it was cute and not be offended to have them in their circle of friends.

RON: It sounds like "Bear" means something much softer and less butchified there.

WOODY: I think it's because there is a definite distinction between Bears and leathermen in Japan. We have a lot of crossover in the U.S.— just look at *Bear* magazine, which has centerfolds with piercings here and there, and leather suspenders.

RON: What was your experience when you attended a Bearclub meeting in Tokyo?

WOODY: The event was very crowded, and again, mostly Japanese. Out of, say, 250 people there, there were five Americans. It was held to organize events for Bears to go out on—swimming, hiking—in a bar that is not a Bear bar but one of the larger places which rents out its space for gay events. Another thing about gay bars in Tokyo, Bear and non-Bear, is that they always advertise other bars—for example, there might be a wall dedicated to posters for other Bear bars, clubs, or baths.

RON: Is that significant?

WOODY: I think so. Bars in the U.S. wouldn't do that for the most part, because that would take business away. In Japan they seem to share more, maybe because the bars are smaller and there are plenty of people to go around. Or maybe it's a culture thing, too: just being nice.

RON: Does this demonstrate the support for other activities in this specific community?

WOODY: I don't think it's a community thing—I think it's a Japanese thing.

RON: Do Bears in Japan organize their social lives any differently from the way other gay men there socialize?

WOODY: From what I have seen, Bears in Tokyo are similar to Bears in the U.S.—we each like what we like. One group might go to a drag show and another certain group might organize a hike. One thing I have noticed, however, even in a Japanese Bear bar, is that a drag performance could happen. Sometimes the bar owner, or "master," will dress up in drag and do a karaoke song to celebrate the bar's anniversary, for example. We would think it's not macho enough, but they do it to entertain—

something that you wouldn't see at the Lone Star.

RON: Well, actually, you might. In any case, they do Western drag or traditional Japanese drag?

WOODY: American-style: big tits and bigger hair, maybe a traditional kimono, but done campy.

RON: What a unique form of Bearness. OK, let's move from the Far East to Eurasia. Mali, would you tell us about the formation of Bears of Turkey?

MALI: The idea of forming a Bear group in Turkey was born when I met "Halfbear," a Turkish guy, on BML in 1997. We spent many hours talking about foreign Bears, their meetings, and the Bear movement. We decided to tell other people we know (mostly on IRC [Internet Relay Chat]) about Bears. We each had a personal Web page in those days, which had a little information about Bears. We targeted men who are Bears but who never heard about Bears before.

RON: When was the initial group meeting?

MALI: When our number reached 10, we decided to meet in person and do a little session. Our first attempt in July 1998 failed, but we managed to meet that September. More than 10 men were invited but only six showed up. Six was a good number for the start. We announced it on the Bears Mailing List and got many supporting responses from all around the world—many of them are still listed on our Web site.

RON: So in Turkey, as elsewhere, the Internet was fundamental in the formation of the group.

MALI: Yes, it was. Our group is still an Internet-based group.

RON: Xavi, please tell us about the development of Bears in Spain.

XAVI: The Internet also bore the embryo of the Spanish Bear movement. Here's a quick timeline: In 1995, the first Spanish Bear page, Osos ibèricos, was created. In 1998, a friend of mine started Gorditos Girth & Mirth club in Madrid, but he hasn't had success in getting people to join. In 1999, El hombre y el oso—the first Spanish self-proclaimed Bear bar—opened in Sevilla. Also, a bar in Costa del Sol created its own Bearclub just for the bar. In 2000, the first Bearclub in Spain, Bearcelona, opened as a legal nonprofit organization. Gay_osos IRC [Internet Relay Chat] channel Web page became Spanish Bears resource page. Plans for more Bearclubs. That's the history.

RON: Finally, we return to Anglo Bears. Justin, what has been your experience of the Bear scene in England?

JUSTIN: There is quite a flourishing Bearclub in Manchester, England, called Paws. They arrange a number of events throughout the year, most notably the Great British Bear Bash. My experiences were in London and Manchester, 1997–99. Mainly Manchester, because that is where I used to live.

RON: How did you participate in the Bearclub activities there?

JUSTIN: I'd say that I attended, rather than participated, in events. I felt very involved in the Bear community but only in the sense of hanging out with all my Bearish mates when I went out on the town. I could always find someone to talk to when I visited the local bars and clubs, just because I was a Bear.

RON: How did that make you feel?

JUSTIN: I felt valued and accepted, and recognized as a Bear by other facets of the GLB community too, though perhaps not involved in their scene.

RON: Has your contact with Bears helped you with your own self-image issues?

JUSTIN: Yes, I've become a lot more comfortable with my appearance. I even used to dance with my shirt off in the clubs. I'd never have done that before.

RON: Were the British Bearclubs more social or sexual?

JUSTIN: They were quite sexual, in fact sometimes too sexual, considering I was in a monogamous relationship. It was kind of off-putting sometimes.

RON: How so?

JUSTIN: Well, one extreme would be Bear saunas—there are a few bathhouses that have regular Bear nights. I think you'd be putting a target on your ass if you went to one of those. *LOL* Clearly, some of those events weren't for married Bears. Most other events were similarly geared to sex, such as dark-room parties. There were some other non-sexual events though, mainly involving music and beer.

RON: Did you feel the Bearclubs there you experienced were limited in scope?

JUSTIN: I do think partnered Bears felt excluded a little. I'd like to have had more events that involved socializing rather than screwing.

RON: Do you and your partner now hang out with other Welsh Bears?

JUSTIN: I used to regularly attend Bear events in the U.K., then I moved too far away from any clubs and events. :(So all that is left is to start something ourselves.

RON: Xavi, would you care to do a quick Europe Bear roundup?

XAVI: I only know Italian, French, and Portuguese Bear scenes well. The things for other countries are second hand, but we have a lot of tourists here who inform me.

Culturally, we have a lot of affinity with Italians and Portuguese. The Italian Bear scene is quite similar to Spain, but more organized. Portugal is building things, but it's largely an effort of two guys. The Portuguese Bear scene is small. They've had a lot of problems setting up anything there, since it's a very conservative country.

France is relatively new to the Bear scene, despite the large number of Bears. I think the French resist Bearclubs because the people are too individualistic. Paris boasts the best Bear bar in Europe.

Now, Holland is a great example. Their Bearclubs work hard and get along with all the gay associations in everything. Belgium has relatively little Bear stuff, although Europe's biggest Bear event is organized by Girth & Mirth of Belgium.

As far as Eastern Europe—well, they have to do like Spain: first normalize all liberties, then work at attaining gay rights, and then see what happens with Bears. In a country such as Morocco, well, being gay is a crime, but in their culture, as long as you aren't effeminate, you aren't gay.

RON: That brings me to my next general question: To what extent has traditional male or macho ideas in your culture affected your ideas of masculinity? How does that fit in with your view of Bear culture and of yourself as a Bear?

ED: There's a saying here: "The man and the bear, the uglier the better," but the Bears have adapted it: "The man and the Bear, the hairier the better."

XAVI: Eduardo and I belong to the most macho Western culture!

RON: Rather macho of you to assert that so proudly, Xavi. ;-)

MALI: Same culture here. :)

XAVI: *Macho* is a Spanish word! Machos hit their wives, spit on the floor, insult a lot, and are rude.

SEUMAS: And what's positive about that?

XAVI: What's positive? That depends. I've grown up with a very progressive education and was always told I didn't have to act like a macho to be masculine. I mean, as a man, I don't have to spit, swear, fart, and so on. It's a big revolution in Spain.

RON: So, traditional Spanish masculinity is changing, it sounds like.

MALI: Do macho men there fuck men to prove that they're more man than others?

XAVI: Nope, Mali. Here they say, *"Maricún o maricona, es tan gay el que da como el que toma"*—"Queer or fag, the one who gives is as gay as the one who receives."

MALI: Here that's not the case. In our culture, the word "gay" means "a bottom homosexual." A man who is a top does not count himself as gay here.

XAVI: So too in Spain, but traditionally there has been an image of mustachioed gay that was not effeminate. That's the ancestor of Bears in our culture. Nowadays, the image of gays here is that of a very effeminate TV showman named Boris Izaguirre who works with the yellow press in all her glamour.

SEUMAS: Australian culture has always coped with gender fluidity a little better than most, and Sydney particularly. This city has a strong drag and transsexual culture, and it's not just in the gay & lesbian community. For years in Kings Cross [district] there was a cabaret club called Les Girls, where straight men, football teams, and similar types would go and watch drag and transsexual performers on stage, and they loved it. Remember, this was the country that spawned the film, *The Adventures of Priscilla, Queen of the Desert.*

RON: Mali, Turkish culture holds some relatively long-standing homomasculine traditions, correct?

MALI: In order to get to the root of our cultural sense of masculinity, I have to tell about Ottoman Empire days, I think. Ottomans ruled between 1299 and 1923, until the foundation of the Turkish Republic. There was a special division in the Ottoman army called *oglan ocagi*, meaning "boy school." This school educated young boys to service soldiers when the army was away from home. Thus, in their Army, the government actually sanctioned same-sex relations. The reputation of *hamams* (baths) in Turkey also comes from the Ottomans. The hamam *tellaks* were young boys who not only helped men bathe; they also served as male prostitutes.

At the end of 19th century, the Ottomans decided to send some intellectuals to France to learn their culture. When they returned to help rebuild their homeland, the customs brought from France affected the empire in many ways, one of which was about this *oglan ocagi* and gay life in Ottoman land. The *oglan ocagi* was closed, and man-to-man sex in hamams was banned too. After that, to many people, "gay" denoted a bottom man, and those who were considered tops did not count as gay. Later this gay image became a generalized stereotype of feminine bottoms.

RON: Thank you, Mali. It's important, I feel, to understand the cultural influences behind the construction of our sense of masculinity.

ED: On Bears and machismo: When we started the Osos Mexicanos, I was still scared of being gay, so I stated that a Bear is a man who thinks like a man, who looks like a man, and who likes men. Now I realize that Bears are just gay guys with beards and fur, entitled to be whatever they like to be. Masculinity sure helps differentiate between the common gay and Bears because we look more butch, meaner, and masculine, but we all know Bears can be bitches too.

A lot of people hide undercover in an exaggerated masculinity to not be considered effeminate. I know lots of Bears that don't like effeminate people, especially femmy Bears. I think that's why Bears are so welcome in society, and why lots of people want to be considered Bears—because they stay within the society's guidelines of machoness, yet they are gay.

RON: So being a Bear, to these people, means being able to deny their own feminine aspects and to piss on women otherwise? And that's what makes them socially acceptable?

ED: I guess machoism got to us all, and that's why we make Bears overmasculine—to set us apart from the rest of gay culture so that we'll feel that we fit in. Let us remember that machismo dictates that "Men fuck and are always top, and gays are effeminate and are always bottom." Lots of Bears will only top, so they don't feel they're contradicting their manliness or something like that. Pretty twisted stuff.

XAVI: And in Mexico, you don't say that about *"tanto es el que da como el que toma"* "the one who gives is as gay as the one who receives"? It is quite an old phrase.

ED: No. Here, it is more rejected to be a bottom than to be a top. If you fuck, you're a man; if you get fucked, well, you're fucked!

JUSTIN: In the U.K., there's no difference between top and bottom in the manliness stakes—most Bears here are seen as equal. To the rest of the gay community, Bears are seen as the more masculine end of the spectrum.

RON: Seumas, what about the concept of "mateship" in your culture?

SEUMAS: Australia is traditionally an egalitarian society, and that tends to hold true in Bear culture. It doesn't seem to matter who you are or what you do—when you turn up to a club night or a major Bear event in Australia, there will be people who will walk up to you and say hello. Everyone's equal: we're all mates.

RON: Glen, what are some of the traditional views of masculinity in your culture there? Are they mostly aligned with European ideas?

GLEN: I would think they would come down from our forefathers— either from the U.K., Germany, or the Netherlands. We also tend to see a lot of American and British TV, which reinforces those ideas.

RON: Marcelo, to what extent have traditional male or macho ideas in your culture affected your sense of masculinity?

MARCELO: My ideas of masculinity are mainly drawn from TV series (U.S., by the way) and football players. Sure, traditional values must have affected my ideas. I have always lived in Buenos Aires and here the macho ideas are not as strong as in many other areas. I'm not trying to be the ultimate macho man!

RON: Mali, can you tell us about the Kirkpinar episode? It's significant because it made international news. I should explain here that Kirkpinar is the annual Turkish wrestling competition, which is done by muscular men in leather pants with their bodies oiled.

MALI: Well, it all started out when we decided to organize a tour to Kirkpinar to just to go and watch the event. Four days after we put the program on our Web site, it appeared in national Turkish magazines. The next day, the governor of Edirne (where the wrestling event is held) banned gay people from the event and [international news wire service] Reuters spread the news around the world. Then the madness really began. Our Web site was featured on almost every national newspaper and on national TV news, yet only two reporters contacted us for interviews, and the rest wrote what they wanted.

JUSTIN: What excellent advertising!

MALI: Exactly—it was excellent advertising for the *event*. The wrestlers and organizers used gay people for their own self-promotion. Later, the media started a hunt for Bears of Turkey and they openly said that there'd be a gay-Bear hunt in Kirkpinar this year. They'll be the hunters, of course.

RON: And they weren't looking for dates with you guys, for sure!

ED: Hunting for pics and interviews or hunting for nasty purposes?

MALI: Both. We decided to cancel our tour and not go there.

RON: This story made not only gay newspapers around the world but also Salon.com and other international mainstream news.

MALI: Can you believe that the local media added a picture of transsexuals in the news story that they wrote about Bears of Turkey? Our site still appears on TV news, and they still ask if we are there or not. They didn't believe what we put on our Web site about canceling the tour. I'm sure that next year this thing will be repeated, as it was an excellent and completely free advertisement for Kirkpinar.

JUSTIN: That's what annoys me about the press; they think that all gay people are effeminate, transvestite child molesters.

RON: Yes, Bears get lumped together with other, dissimilar queers. Which leads into my next set of questions for the group: How are Bears viewed by gay men and lesbians in your country or region? Are the Bear groups well known and respected? Do you do anything in particular to promote Bear visibility among gays in your region?

WOODY: I can't really answer that—I do know that things are kind of underground there. There are a lot of gay bars in Tokyo but no one talks about being gay. If someone is, it might be OK—it's just not discussed. And other gays whom I know never talk about Bears, per se—it is just that they are noticed to be big and *higé* (bearded).

RON: Do Bears there do anything in particular to promote Bear visibility to other gay men and lesbians? It sounds like they wouldn't be so forward.

WOODY: I think it's all in the look, similar to the U.S.: bigger, bearded, overalls, baseball caps with a Bear logo. That's about all—they don't scream there.

MALI: Our Bear group is very well known here. We did nothing special for this but a tour to Kirkpinar. We're well known but not accepted, not respected, even by most of the gay population here. Sometimes I feel like we're completely rejected: by gay people, because we don't fit their image; by gay organizations, because we are too anarchistic; by Turkish people, because we are gay.

JUSTIN: Bear groups are mostly known about in the GLBT community here. I don't think the straight community in general is aware of Bears, although the whole thing fascinates many of my straight friends.

There is a small divide between the general gay community and Bears, as Mali said; we don't really fit their image. But we are accepted as another part of the community.

RON: I think the general perception among GLBTQ people here is that Bears are just another splinter group. Although Bears are generally well tolerated on the outside social level, they're apparently not well understood by other gay men and lesbians—they just don't get what Bears are about. On a deeper level, I think the larger cultural emphasis on youth in gay culture puts Bears in a situation where, as hairy/bearded/bigger/older people, we're ignored.

JUSTIN: We have as many old Bears as young ones here.

MALI: Do you mean "old, hairy, fat, ugly faggots," Ron?

RON: Exactly my point, Mali. That's how the rest of gay culture characterizes Bears.

XAVI: Ron, that's because of your [American] culture, not gay culture by itself. There has always been variety in this world and it's up to each person to accept or not accept it. In the end, Anglos are very intolerant, in my opinion. In Latino cultures, people think, "it's ultimately up to him." We can gossip, we can criticize, but in the end, it's all up to you. Of course some queens say, "Aaaarghhh, a Bear! Shave that back," but we just reply, "Shut up, bitch," and we all keep on dancing and having fun. That's the one-on-one stuff. Organizationally, the Bearclub here is federated with all the rest of gay organizations of Catalonia. On our Pride Day, we do everything together. The Spanish gay press also gives us a lot of support because there's a feeling of "all together, we'll be stronger." It's quite cool.

SEUMAS: I have a friend who went to a particular bar and was greeted by a young twink that said loudly, "Why don't these Bears fuck off back to another hotel where they belong and leave us alone?" The guy decked the twink.

JUSTIN: The twink must have felt threatened.

SEUMAS: Bears stand up for things when they get pissed off about what they believe in.

MALI: That happens here sometimes too. Not just by twinks but by the owners of the places too. We've been refused admittance when we wanted to go to a gay disco or have been made to pay a higher entrance fee than others.

RON: That kind of blatant discrimination is terrible.

MALI: That old, outmoded gay image is what we (gays of Turkey) are trying to change. But I think we (Bears of Turkey) are the only group who has effectively and significantly changed this image.

RON: How can you be sure that you've changed the mainstream image of gay men?

MALI: Bears of Turkey and this wrestling tour event was listed at number 14 in a national article of "100 Most Popular Topics in Media." Nine of the first 13 subjects are about soccer, one is about the earthquake, and the others are about politicians.

RON: What does the article say about the wrestling event?

MALI: I'll translate: "The international group of gay men who call themselves 'Bears' rocked the news agenda of Turkey. Some said, 'It's an insult to our traditions,' while others replied, 'They're human and have rights, too.' When at last we learned that the *Ayilar* are as burly as the wrestlers, a profound silence followed."

RON: Meaning that they all had to shut up because you weren't the little fag boys they expected you to be.

MALI: Essentially, yes. The great thing is that is has opened up a whole new dialogue about gay and lesbian rights in Turkey.

RON: Bravo! Justin, are Bears respected by other segments of the GLBT community in the UK?

JUSTIN: They're recognized rather than accepted, although I think that lesbians respect Bears more. That's just my personal opinion.

RON: Have you experienced discrimination as a Bear by other gays?

JUSTIN: Yes, some people just think we're fat old men. It's bizarre how someone can think you're old just because you're a Bear!

RON: Has being in a group helped you to deal with that sort of encounter?

JUSTIN: Sure, as soon as I heard of the Bear movement, I was able to deal with a lot more in life. It was good to know that there were others in the world who felt like me. Once when I was in a club, an extremely thin guy came up to me (one could describe him as a twink). I talked to him for a while, and at the end of the conversation, he thanked me for talking to him. He said that all the other Bears ignored him. He said he liked Bears but hated getting shunned by them because of his appearance. It was sad, really.

RON: That sort of reverse discrimination by Bears is also very disappointing.

XAVI: In Barcelona, we're just beginning our specialization.

RON: Ed, why don't you tell us about your recent Pride Day event?

ED: This year was the first time ever that a Bear organization attended gay pride. To many Mexicans the gay pride event is like a gay costume parade, so we were typecast by some as "gays in Bear costumes," yet to the gay community at large we were really a shock.

As the parade started, everybody wanted to be next to the Bears when we were moved from position number 9 to position number 3. One of the gay parade deputies approached us just to tell us that we were dignifying the gay community. Families with children standing on the sidewalks were cheering us, giving us thumbs up, and just plain supporting us. We made it in the newspaper and TV for our 15 seconds of fame. We sang a gay hymn (translated from German into Spanish) and people sang along, and even had a group of Deaf gay guys "singing" along in sign language.

The most amazing part was when lots of gay and straight people approached us because we look like regular guys and they couldn't believe gay people are like that. We were a real eye-opener for some folks. I must say all of this success is the result of hard-working Bears such as Armando, Eduardo, and Pedro (current president, public relations, and secretary), who actually came up with the idea of building a nine-foot-tall teddy bear to carry on a pickup truck. Those guys really got us into the gay scene with style.

JUSTIN: Cool, Ed! :)

XAVI: The Mex Bears are really cool!

SEUMAS: Bears were really on the fringe in this country until 1997. There had been Bearclubs here since 1990, but in terms of visibility in the mainstream GLBT community, it wasn't until two events happened.

The first event, Bear Essentials, hosted by Harbour City Bears, included an entry in the Sydney Gay & Lesbian Mardi Gras parade—somewhat similar to the Osos Mexicanos. We carried a series of 20 polystyrene bears on poles, dressed in flannelette, leather, and the like. They were like holy icons, and the crowd loved them. It put the Bears on the map! We've developed our exposure from television broadcasts of the following years' parades, where up to 350 Bears have marched.

The second major event was the development of the Mr. Australian Bear and Cub Competition in 1997, which was a focus for the Bear community in Melbourne, and which received incredible media coverage within the community (including live radio coverage of the event). These were the big two events that made people in the broader GLBT community sit up and take notice.

To a lesser extent, it's also had to do with several of us being small-time Bear activists. I for example led a campaign against Sydney Gay & Lesbian Mardi Gras Party Ltd. over its handling of Bears recently—most Bears got behind it, too. And as a bit of light relief with a tinge of activism, I run NAPBIS (the National Association for the Promotion of Beards in Society), where I just write to prominent politicians and media personalities and suggest that they might want to grow their beards back.

These days, the Bears seem to command a lot of respect from the broader community. There even exists an Internet-based female (dyke) Bears community, known as Grrlbears, which subscribe to the ethos of Bears.

RON: That's awesome—dyke bears are barely a blip on the map here in the U.S. And the idea of having 350 Bears marching together is truly inspiring. Glen, has there been any sort of national South African Bears event?

GLEN: Not yet. I am, however, trying to plan one for May 2001. South Africa is having its first Gay Mardi Gras in Knysna, called the Knysna Pink Lourie Festival. I am hoping that the Bears around the country can put in a float at the parade. Maybe we can borrow the float from Mexico's parade. *LOL*

RON: Good idea! But really out gay social life is still relatively new there, right?

GLEN: That depends on where you live. At present, it's cool to be gay in Cape Town. If you don't have gay friends, then it's a problem. In larger cities like Johannesburg and Durban, it's fine. I've had no problem in Port Elizabeth, and I am open to everyone, even workmates. I think if you live in a small conservative community in the middle on nowhere, it becomes a problem to come out.

RON: It's usually easier for gay men and lesbians to live in urban settings.

GLEN: You must note that South Africa has the most liberal constitution in the world at present. Gays and lesbians are well protected.

RON: Yes, I've read about how South Africa wrote protection for gays into the new constitution. Bravo! Marcelo, are there any plans for a major South American Bear happening?

MARCELO: Next October, our club will participate in PELO: Primer Encuentro Latinoamericano de Osos (First Latin American Bear Meeting), to be held in Rio de Janeiro. We and Ursos do Brasil are organizing the whole thing.

RON: *¡Fantastico!*

MARCELO: Bears from all over the region and beyond are expected. Brazil, Argentina, and Chile will participate—and we hope Mexico, Venezuela, and Costa Rica will too!

RON: Great—I'm sure we all wish we could be there to join you for the event! Now to our final question: Do you believe in a universal Bear brotherhood? If so, what is its creed, or motto, or primary belief? Ed, what do you think?

ED: Sure, it can exist! "Be natural."

RON: Yes, it can exist—but does it?

ED: More or less. I know that if I want to go somewhere and I write a post in the Bears Mailing List, somebody would answer me. I've always seen that, and that's what we do when somebody comes here. I hope it goes for a long time.

RON: That's a good point. So guys can always connect with other Bears, wherever they go, and find comradeship. And sometimes sex!

MARCELO: I really believe there are many things in common, like the brotherhood thing—friendship, fellowship, and sex! Those three words are its motto.

GLEN: I believe that a universal Bear brotherhood could very well exist. As for a creed, I haven't really thought about it, but it kind of makes sense to have something universal for Bears.

SEUMAS: Bears worldwide are dramatically different depending on where you are—there are even differences between the Bear communities in each of the different cities here in Australia. Even within communities, there are all types of Bears and Bear admirers.

I think the most unifying thing is that in having "Bear" as an identity, you know that you can now travel the world and wherever you happen to be, there will be a bunch of guys that share a common bond with you (the identity as a Bear). That in itself is a remarkably empowering thing for me. Yes, we're part of an international community, most of whom we'll never get to meet, but we get a sense of pride just knowing that they're there.

To me, the notion of "Bear" is incredibly empowering. To others, they see the Bear icons and see it as an impossible "standard" from which the next step is that they're not big enough, not hairy enough, and so on—at which point it becomes limiting.

MALI: I do believe in a universal Bear brotherhood. Bears have always been much friendlier, warm, and caring than other gay people I know. I don't know if it is in the nature of Bears or it is really a result of the brotherhood, but I believe that we all are brothers, and I try my best for my brother and expect the same from him.

JUSTIN: I think the International Bear Brotherhood is like the X-Men: in the outset, little was known of them, but as knowledge and acceptance grew, they became more prominent in society. Now we just need to make sure that we remember our humble beginnings, and not fall into the trap of prejudice.

RON: Thank you all very much for joining in this conversation.

Chronology of Interviews and Listing of Excerpts

Articles are listed in the order conducted, each followed by its own publishing chronology.

• Discussion with David Bergman and Michael Bronski (conducted online, May 11, 1998). Excerpted: *American Bear*, December 1998; *Gay Community News*, February 1999; *Art & Understanding*, May 1999; *Lambda Book Report*, January 2002. A complete but slightly different version of this piece was published in *The Bear Book II*: January 2001. Excerpted in three parts: www.resourcesforbears.com, April 1 and 15 and May 1, 2001.

• Interview with Tim Barela (conducted via telephone, January 3, 1999). Excerpted: *American Bear*, April 1999. Reprinted: www.leonardandlarry.com, November 2000. Excerpted in three parts: www.resourcesforbears.com, January 1 and 15 and February 1, 2001.

• Interview with Eric Rofes (conducted in person, April 10, 1999). Excerpted: *American Bear*, August 1999. Excerpted in two parts: www.resourcesforbears.com, July 15 and August 1, 2001.

• Interview with Rick Trombly (conducted in person, July 16, 1999). Excerpted: *American Bear*, December 1999.

• Interview with Dr. Lawrence Mass (conducted online, November 3, 1999). Excerpted: www.gayhealth.com, September 2001.

• Interview with Reed Wilgoren (conducted in person, November 3, 1999). Excerpted: *American Bear*, April 2000. Excerpted in two parts: www.resourcesforbears.com, October 15 and November 1, 2001.

• Discussion with Les Wright (conducted online, December 10, 1999). Excerpted: *American Bear*, August 2001.

• Discussion with Manny Lim and Kirk Read (conducted online, January 24, 2000). Excerpted: *American Bear*, October 2000. Excerpted in two parts: www.resourcesforbears.com, January 15 and February 1, 2002.

• Discussion with Wayne Hoffman, Chris Wittke, and Rex Wockner (conducted online, January 29, 2000). Excerpted: *American Bear*, June 2000. Excerpted in two parts: www.resourcesforbears.com, November 15 and December 1, 2001.

• Discussion with Sharon Jill Bear Bergman, Drew Campbell, Michael "Mike" Hernandez, and Matt Rice (conducted online, January 30, 2000). Excerpted: *Transgender Tapestry,* September 2001; *Diversity Idaho,* September 2001. Excerpted in three parts: www.resourcesforbears.com, June 1 and 15 and July 1, 2001.

• Interview with Bruce Vilanch (conducted via telephone, February 8, 2000). Excerpted: *American Bear,* June 2000.

• Discussion with Arnie Kantrowitz and Mark Thompson (conducted via telephone, February 13, 2000).

• Discussion with Pete Vafiades (conducted online, March 15, April 3, and April 10, 2000; concluded via telephone April 19, 2000). Excerpted in three parts: www.resourcesforbears.com, February 15, March 1 and 15, 2002.

• Interview with Jack Radcliffe (conducted via telephone, March 30, 2000).

• Discussion with David Gerard, Ali Lopez, and George Varas (conducted online, April 6, 2000). Excerpted: *American Bear,* December 2000. Excerpted in three parts: www.resourcesforbears.com, December 15, 2001, and January 1, 2002.

• Discussion with Richard Labonté and Tim Martin (conducted online, April 18, 2000). Excerpted: *American Bear,* February 2002; *White Crane Journal,* Spring 2002.

• Discussion with Van Buckley, Steven Evans, and Tim Morrison (conducted online, April 23, 2000). Excerpted: *American Bear,* April 2002.

• Discussion with Steve Dyer, Jeff Glover, Mike Ramsey, and Alex Schell (conducted online, April 26, 2000). Excerpted in three parts: www.resourcesforbears.com, February 15 and March 1 and 15, 2001.

• Discussion with Lou Dattilo, Frank Perricone, Adam Steg, and Danny Williams (conducted online, April 30, 2000). Excerpted: *American Bear,* June 2001.

• Discussion with Al Cotton, D. Alex Damman, and Jim Mitulski (conducted online, May 16, 2000).

• Discussion with Craig Byrnes, Gene Landry, and Michael Patterson (conducted online, May 17, 2000). Excerpted: *American Bear,* October 2001.

• Discussion with Terry Jamro, Brian Kearns, and Heath McKay (conducted online, May 18, 2000). Excerpted: *American Bear,* February 2001.

- Interview with Jack Fritscher (conducted via telephone, May 27, 2000).

- Discussion with Eduardo Chavez, Seumas Hyslop, Xavier Navarro, Marcelo Perales, Glen Purdon, Mali Sahin, Woody Shimko, and Justin Spooner (conducted online, July 1–10, 2000). Excerpted in eight parts: www.eurobear.com, October 2001 through May 2002.

- Interview with Rich Hatch (conducted in person, December 9, 2000). Excerpted: *American Bear*, April 2001; www.resourcesfor-bears.com, October 1, 2001; www.alyson.com, November 2001; *Diversity Idaho*, November 2001.

Glossary

BD	BONDAGE AND DISCIPLINE
BML	BEARS MAILING LIST, OR BEARS DIGEST
EG	EVIL GRIN
G	GRINNING
GLBT(Q)	GAY LESBIAN BISEXUAL TRANSGENDERED (QUEER)
IBR	INTERNATIONAL BEAR RENDEZVOUS
IML	INTERNATIONAL MR LEATHER
LGBT(Q)	SEE GLBT(Q)
LMAO	LAUGHING MY ASS OFF
LOL	LAUGHING OUT LOUD
SM (OR S&M)	SADOMASOCHISM
VEG	VERY EVIL GRIN
;-)	WINKING
:)	SMILING OR HAPPY
:(	FROWNING OR SAD

Selected Bibliography, References, and Resources

Barela, Tim. *Domesticity Isn't Pretty: A Leonard & Larry Collection.* Minneapolis: Palliard Press, 1993.

Barela, Tim. *Kurt Cobain and Mozart Are Both Dead: Leonard & Larry 2.* Minneapolis: Palliard Press, 1996.

Barela, Tim. *Excerpts from the Ring Cycle in Royal Albert Hall: The Third Leonard & Larry Collection.* Minneapolis: Palliard Press, 2000.

Bergman, David. *Gaiety Transfigured: Gay Self-Representation in American Literature.* Madison: University of Wisconsin Press, 1991.

Bergman, David. *Heroic Measures.* Columbus: Ohio State Press, 1998.

Bergman, David, editor. *Men on Men* series. New York: Dutton/Plume.

Bronski, Michael. *Culture Clash: The Making of Gay Sensibility.* Boston: South End Press, 1984.

Bronski, Michael. *The Pleasure Principle: Sex, Backlash, and the Struggle for Gay Freedom.* New York: St. Martin's Press, 1998.

Bronski, Michael, editor. *Flashpoint: Gay Male Sexual Writing.* New York: Richard Kasak Books, 1996.

Campbell, Drew. *The Bride Wore Black Leather...and He Looked Fabulous: An Etiquette Guide for the Rest of Us.* Emeryville, Calif.: Greenery Press, 2000.

Cromwell, Jason. *Transmen and FTMs: Identities, Bodies, Genders, and Sexualities.* Urbana: University of Illinois Press, 1999.

Dangerous Bedfellows, Sphen Glenn Colter, Wayne Hoffman, and Eva Pendleton, eds. *Policing Public Sex: Queer Politics and the Future of AIDS Activisim.* Cambridge, Mass.: South End Press, 1996.

Feinberg, Leslie, editor. *Trans Liberation: Beyond Pink and Blue,* Boston: Beacon Press, 1998.

Fritscher, Jack. *Some Dance to Remember.* Stamford, Conn.: Knights Press, 1990.

Fritscher, Jack. *Mapplethorpe: Assault with a Deadly Camera.* Mamaroneck, N.Y.: Hastings House, 1994.

Fritscher, Jack. *Leather Blues: A Novel*. San Francisco: Palm Drive Publishing, 1998.

Harris, Daniel. "A Psychohistory of the Homosexual Body." In his *The Rise and Fall of Gay Culture*. New York: Hyperion, 1997.

Hatch, Rich. *101 Survival Secrets: How to Make $1,000,000, Lose 100 Pounds, and Just Plain Live Happy*. New York: Lyons Press, 2000.

Kampf, Ray. *The Bear Handbook: A Comprehensive Guide for Those Who Are Hairy, Husky, & Homosexual, and Those Who Love 'Em*. New York: Haworth Press, 2000.

Kantrowitz, Arnie. *Under the Rainbow: Growing Up Gay*. New York: William Morrow & Co., 1977; republished with a new afterword by St. Martin's Press, 1996.

Kelly, Elizabeth A., and Kate Kane. "In Goldilock's Footsteps: Exploring the Discursive Construction of Gay Masculinity in Bear Magazines." In Miles and Rofes.

Labonté, Richard, editor. *Best Gay Erotica* series. San Francisco: Cleis Press.

Mains, Geoff. *Urban Aboriginals: A Celebration of Leathersexuality*. San Francisco: Gay Sunshine Press, 1984.

Mains, Geoff. *Gentle Warriors*. Stamford, Conn.: Knights Press, 1989.

Mars-Jones, Adam. "Bears in Mourning." In his *Monopolies of Loss*. New York: Vintage, 1994.

Mass, Lawrence D. *Confessions of a Jewish Wagnerite: Being Gay and Jewish in America*. London: Cassell, 1994.

Mass, Lawrence D., editor. *We Must Love One Another or Die: The Life and Legacies of Larry Kramer*. New York: St. Martin's Press, 1997.

Miller, Neil. *Out in the World: Gay and Lesbian Life From Buenos Aires to Bangkok*. New York: Random House, 1992.

Miles, Sara, and Eric Rofes, editors. *Opposite Sex: Gay Men on Lesbians, Lesbians on Gay Men*. New York: New York University Press, 1998.

Nelson, Chris. *The Bear Cult: Photographs by Chris Nelson*. London: Gay Men's Press, 1991.

Read, Kirk. *How I Learned to Snap*. Athens, Gao: Hill Street Press.

Rofes, Eric. *Reviving the Tribe: Regenerating Gay Men's Sexuality and Culture in the Ongoing Epidemic*. New York: Haworth Press, 1996.

Rofes, Eric. *Dry Bones Breathe: Gay Men Creating Post-AIDS Identities and Cultures*. New York: Haworth Press, 1998.

Rofes, Eric. "Academics as Bears: Thoughts on Middle-Class Eroticization of Workingmen's Bodies." In Wright, 1997.

Shepard, Paul, and Barry Sanders. *The Sacred Paw: The Bear in Nature, Myth, and Literature*. New York: Viking Penguin, 1992.

Suresha, Ron. "Bear Roots." In Wright, 1997.

Suresha, Ron. "Bear Mecca: The Lone Star Saloon Revisited." In Wright, 1997.

Thompson, Keith, editor. *To Be a Man: In Search of the Deep Masculine*. Los Angeles: Jeremy P. Tarcher, 1991.

Thompson, Mark. *Gay Soul: Finding the Heart of Gay Spirit and Nature With Sixteen Writers, Healers, Teachers, and Visionaries*. San Francisco: Harper San Francisco, 1994.

Thompson, Mark. *Gay Body: A Journey Through Shadow to Self*. New York: St. Martin's Press, 1997.

Thompson, Mark, editor. *Gay Spirit: Myth and Meaning*. New York: St. Martin's Press, 1987.

Thompson, Mark, editor. *Leatherfolk: Radical Sex, People, Politics, and Practice*, 1991; *10th Anniversary Edition*, 2001. Los Angeles: Alyson Publications.

Vilanch, Bruce. *Bruce!: My Adventures in the Skin Trade and Other Essays*. New York: Tarcher/Putnam, 2000.

Volcano, Del LaGrace, and Judith "Jack" Halberstam. *The Drag King Book*. London: Serpent's Tail, 1999.

Whitlock, Ralph. *Bulls through the Ages*. Guildford, U.K.: Lutterworth Press, 1977.

Wright, Les K., editor. *The Bear Book: Readings in the History and Evolutions of a Gay Male Subculture*. New York: Haworth Press, 1997.

Wright, Les K., editor. *The Bear Book II: Further Readings in the History and Evolution of a Gay Male Subculture*. New York: Haworth Press, 2000.

Periodicals

American Bear and *American Grizzly*, Amabear Publishing: www.amabear.com

Bear magazine, Brush Creek Media: www.brushcreek.com

Bulk Male: www.afterimage-studios.com
Chiron Rising: www.chiron-rising.com

Online Resources

www.bearcastle.com: Jeff Shaumeyer
www.bearhistory.com: Bear History Project, Les Wright
www.BearYouth.org: Bear Youth
www.chubnet2.com/abc: Affiliated Big Men's Clubs
www.doesitquack.com: Sharon Jill Bear Bergman
www.eurobear.com: EuroBear (Bear clubs, events, resources)
www.gandmny.com: Girth & Mirth New York
www.genxbears.org: Gen-X Bears International
www.hyslop.org: Seumas Hyslop
www.JackFritscher.com; www.palmdrivepublishing.com; www.palm-drivevideo.com: Jack Fritscher, Palm Drive
www.jeffglover.com: Jeff Glover
www.koan.com/~Lbear: Michael Hernandez
www.leonardandlarry.com: Tim Barela, "Leonard & Larry"
www.niddk.nih.gov/health/nutrit/pubs/statobes.htm: Information on weight and obesity from National Institute of Diabetes & Digestive & Kidney Diseases
www.queernet.org/bml: Bears Mailing List (Bears Digest)
www.ronsuresha.com: Ron Suresha
www.resourcesforbears.com: Resources for Bears (Bearclubs, links, events, news, Bear Code)
www.shutterbear.com: Lynn Ludwig, photographer
www.kirkread.com: Kirk Read
www.ursinedesign.com: George Varas
www.mcs.net/~dlhooker/quay.html: Bear Quay (links to bear sites)

ABOUT THE AUTHOR

Ron Suresha grew up in and around Detroit. He began his vocation as editor and writer early in life: He edited his Cub Scout troop newsletter, and 10 years later, edited both his high school newspaper and literary magazine. After studying creative writing and journalism at the University of Michigan, Ann Arbor, he became a vegetarian, edited several alternative periodicals, ran a community switchboard, went to India twice, and lived in yoga meditation ashrams around the country for about 10 years.

He has contributed freelance editorial work to scores of book projects at Shambhala Publications and other book publishers specializing in Eastern studies, philosophy, and psychology. He served for five years as a board director of *The Gay & Lesbian Review* and is a contributing writer for *American Bear* magazine. His writing appears regularly in those two periodicals and has appeared as well in *Art & Understanding, Lambda Book Report, Gay Community News, White Crane Journal, Southern Voice, In Newsweekly, Darshan,* and *Visionary,* and the anthologies *The Bear Book, The Bear Book II, My First Time 2, Quickies 2, Bar Stories,* and *Tales From the Bear Cult.*

In 1998 he self-published a recipe chapbook, *Mugs o' Joy: Delightful Hot Drinkables,* and is actively seeking a trade publisher for a quintuply expanded edition. *Bears on Bears* is his first commercially published book, to be followed shortly by *Bearotica,* an anthology of Bear-themed erotic fiction that Ron edited (also by Alyson Publications). Other projects include a collection of Persian folk tales, and a novel.

Ron has been involved with Bear communities since the late 1980s, when he lived in San Francisco with one of the creators of *Bear* magazine, and created signs, graphics, and promotions for the Lone Star Saloon. Since leaving the San Francisco Bay area in 1994, he has been a member of the Chesapeake Bay Bears, Motor City Bears, New England Bears, and Rhode Island Grizzlies. He acted as a judge for the International Mr. Bear 2000 contest in San Francisco.

Ron is fluent in American Sign Language, enjoys folk dancing, and lives by the verdant Emerald Necklace in Boston.

PHOTO CREDITS

Tim Barela: Illustration by Tim Barela; David Bergman: Jenifer Bishop; Sharon Bergman: Nicole Bergman; Michael Bronski: Joshua Oppenheimer; Van Buckley: Mark Erickson; Craig Byrnes: Collis Kimbrough/GarmanFoto; Drew Campbell: Anne Campbell; Eduardo Chavez: Eduardi Gil/Difracta; Al Cotton: Cindy Sproul; D. Alex Dammon: Billy Toth; Lou Dattilo: Mike Hall, Heart of Texas Bears; Steve Dyer: A. J. Hartman; Steve Evans: Jayne Evans; Jack Fritscher: © Mark Hemry <www.PalmDriveVideo.com>; Dave Gerard: Ray Ackerman; Jeff Glover: courtesy of J. Glover; Rich Hatch: Rudy Bello/WQSX-FM; Michael Hernandez: James Loewen; Wayne Hoffman: Mark Sullivan; Seumas Hyslop: David Hart; Terry Jamro: courtesy of Terry Jamro; Arnie Kantrowitz: Gene Bagnato; Brian Kearns: courtesy of B. Kearns; Richard Labonté: NIQ Sheehan; Gene Landry: Lynn S. Ludwig <www.ludwigphotos.com>; Manny Lim: Lewis Brian Day; Ali Lopez: courtesy of A. Lopez; Tim Martin: courtesy of T. Martin; Dr. Lawrence Mass: courtesy of L. Mass; Heath McKay: Lynn S. Ludwig <www.ludwigphotos.com>; Rev. Jim Mitulski: courtesy of J. Mitulski; Tim Morrison: Lynn S. Ludwig <www.ludwigphotos.com>; Xavier Navarro: J. A. Siverio; Michael Patterson: Kevin Sonnichsen <simonbear1@aol.com>; Marcelo Perales: Gabriel Enriquez; Frank Perricone: Tonnie O.; Glen Purdon: S. N. Robinson; Jack Radcliffe: Lynn S. Ludwig <www.ludwigphotos.com>; Mike Ramsey: Lynn S. Ludwig <www.ludwigphotos.com>; Kirk Read: courtesy of K. Read; Matt Rice: Jeff Spangenberg; Eric Rofes: Steven Underhill; Mali Sahin: QBLI; Alex Schell: Joe Kelemen; Woody Shimko: courtesy of W. Shimko; Justin Spooner: Neal Tomlinson (Welshbear); Adam Steg: courtesy of A. Steg; Mark Thompson: Erin Flynn; Sen. Rick Trombly: Studio One; Pete Vafiades: courtesy of P. Vafiades; George Varas: Alex Schell/UrsineDesign; Bruce Vilanch: Aaron Rappaport; Reed Wilgoren: Ron Suresha; Danny Williams: Savage Photography; Christopher Wittke: Duke Studios; Rex Wockner: Bob Gordon; Les Wright: from the BHP Archive Collection.